The European Peasant Family
and Society

Liverpool Studies in European Population
General Editor DAVID SIDDLE

1. *Urban Population Development in Western Europe from the Late-Eighteenth to the Early-Twentieth Century* edited by RICHARD LAWTON and ROBERT LEE

2. *The Population Dynamics and Development of Western European Port-Cities, c. 1710–1939* edited by RICHARD LAWTON and ROBERT LEE

3. *Improving the Public Health: Essays in Medical History* edited by G. KEARNS et al.

4. *The European Peasant Family and Society: Historical Studies* edited by RICHARD L. RUDOLPH

The European Peasant Family and Society

Historical Studies

edited by
RICHARD L. RUDOLPH
Professor of History, University of Minnesota

LIVERPOOL UNIVERSITY PRESS

Published by
LIVERPOOL UNIVERSITY PRESS
PO Box 147
Liverpool
L69 3BX

British Library Cataloguing-in-Publication Data
A British Library CIP Record is available
ISBN 0 85323 328 4

Typeset by Wilmaset Limited, Birkenhead, Wirral
Printed and bound in Great Britain by Redwood Books,
Trowbridge, Wiltshire

CONTENTS

Contributors   *vii*

Acknowledgements   *ix*

INTRODUCTION

1. Introduction
   RICHARD L. RUDOLPH   1

THE MAJOR ISSUES

2. Major Issues in the Study of the European Peasant
   Family, Economy, and Society
   RICHARD L. RUDOLPH   6

EFFECTS OF THE PHYSICAL ENVIRONMENT ON PEASANT FAMILY STRUCTURE

3. Peasant and Non-Peasant Family Forms in Relation to the
   Physical Environment and the Local Economy
   MICHAEL MITTERAUER   26

4. Late Marriage: Causes and Consequences of the Austrian
   Alpine Marriage Pattern
   NORBERT ORTMAYR   49

EFFECTS OF THE SOCIAL AND CULTURAL ENVIRONMENT ON PEASANT FAMILY STRUCTURE

5. Socio-economic Change, Peasant Household Structure
   and Demographic Behaviour in a French Department
   JAMES R. LEHNING   64

6. The Stem Family, Demography and Inheritance:
   The Social Frontiers of Auto-Regulation
   ANTOINETTE FAUVE-CHAMOUX   86

THE RELATIONSHIP OF THE PEASANT HOUSEHOLD TO THE WIDER ECONOMY AND SOCIETY

A. THEORY

7. The Protoindustrial Household Economy: Toward a
   Formal Analysis
   ULRICH PFISTER   114

B. THE PEASANT AND MARKETS FOR LABOUR AND GOODS

8. Family Labour Strategies in Early Modern Swabia
   MARTHA WHITE PAAS   146

9. Peasants as Consumers of Manufactured Goods in Italy
   around 1600
   DOMENICO SELLA   154

C. DEGREES OF FREEDOM IN PEASANT FAMILY CHOICE

10. Family and Economy in an Early Nineteenth-century
    Baltic Serf Estate
    ANDREJS PLAKANS and CHARLES WETHERELL   165

EFFECTS OF PROTOINDUSTRIALIZATION ON THE PEASANT FAMILY AND SOCIETY

11. From Peasant Society to Class Society: Some Aspects of
    Family and Class in a North-west German Protoindustrial
    Parish, Seventeenth–Nineteenth Centuries
    JÜRGEN SCHLUMBOHM   188

12. Womanhood and Motherhood: The Rouen
    Manufacturing Community, Women Workers, and the
    French Factory Acts
    GAY L. GULLICKSON   206

CONCLUSION

13. Family and Economy: Some Comparative Perspectives
    STANLEY L. ENGERMAN   233

Index   249

CONTRIBUTORS

STANLEY L. ENGERMAN is John H. Munro Professor of Economics and Professor of History at the University of Rochester at New York. He is co-author (with Robert W. Fogel) of *Time on the Cross: The Economics of American Negro Slavery*, Boston, 1974, and has co-edited, with Joseph E. Inikori, *The Atlantic Slave Trade: Effects on Economies, Societies, and Peoples in Africa, the Americas, and Europe*, Durham, 1992.

ANTOINETTE FAUVE-CHAMOUX is Maître de conférences at the École des Hautes Études en Sciences Sociales, Paris, General Secretary of the International Commission of Historical Demography, and editor of the *Revue de la Bibliothèque Nationale*. Her primary research interest is the social and economic history of the family and its reproduction since the seventeenth century. She is working on the city of Rheims in Champagne and on the Pyrenean Baronnies. She has published many articles on family forms, women alone, differential fertility, breastfeeding, malthusianism, and migration. She co-edited, with J. Dupâquier, *Malthus Past and Present*, London and New York, 1983, and *Évolution agraire et croissance démographique*, Liège, 1987.

GAY L. GULLICKSON is Associate Professor of History at the University of Maryland, College Park. She is the author of *Spinners and Weavers of Auffay*, Cambridge, 1986.

JAMES R. LEHNING is Associate Professor of History at the University of Utah. He is the author of *The Peasants of Marlhes: Economic Development and Family Organization in Nineteenth-Century France*, Chapel Hill, 1980.

MICHAEL MITTERAUER is Professor of Social History at the Institute for Economic and Social History at the University of Vienna. He has written numerous books and articles on the history of the family, including, with Richard Sieder, *The European Family*, Chicago, 1972, and *A History of Youth*, Oxford, 1992.

NORBERT ORTMAYR is a Lecturer at the Department of History at the University of Salzburg, and is currently working on comparative family structure in Latin America and the Caribbean.

MARTHA WHITE PAAS is Professor of Economics at Carleton College in Northfield, Minnesota. She holds the PhD from Bryn Mawr College and did graduate work on a DAAD fellowship at the Institute for Social and Economic History at the University of Munich. Her current research interests are in population change and risk-taking in early modern Germany.

ULRICH PFISTER is Privat-Docent for Modern History at the University of Zurich, where he also received his PhD degree. He has published articles and two books on the demographic and economic history of early modern Switzerland as well as the political economy of the Third World during the post-Second World War era.

ANDREJS PLAKANS is Professor of European History at Iowa State University, Ames, Iowa, and associate editor of the *Journal of Family History*. His research interests include the history of family and kinship, population and social change in Eastern Europe and the history of the Baltic area. He is author of *Kinship in the Past: An Anthropology of European Family Life 1500–1900*, New York, 1984, and co-editor (with Tamara Hareven) of *Family History at the Crossroads*, Princeton, 1987.

RICHARD L. RUDOLPH is Professor of History at the University of Minnesota. He has written widely on the social and economic history of Russia, eastern and central Europe. He is the author of *Banking and Industrialization in Austria-Hungary*, Cambridge, 1976, and has co-edited, with David F. Good, *Nationalism and Empire: The Habsburg Empire and the Soviet Union*, New York, 1992.

JÜRGEN SCHLUMBOHM is a fellow at the Max-Planck-Institute for History, Göttingen, Germany. He is co-author of *Industrialization before Industrialization: Rural Industry in the Genesis of Capitalism*, Cambridge, 1981. His books include one on childhood in Germany, *Kinderstuben: Wie Kinder zu Bauern, Bürgern, Aristokraten wurden, 1700–1850*, Munich, 1983 and the micro-history of a rural parish in North-West Germany, *Lebensläufe, Familien, Höfe: Die Bauern und Henerleute des Osnabrückischen Kirchspiels Belm in proto-industrieller Zeit, 1650–1860*, Göttingen, 1994.

DOMENICO SELLA is Professor of History at the University of Wisconsin. He received his training at the Universities of Milan, Venice, Notre Dame, and at the London School of Economics. He is author of four books and numerous articles on the economic and social history of early modern Italy. His books include *Crisis and Continuity: The Economy of Spanish Lombardy in the Seventeenth Century*, Cambridge, Mass., 1979, and *Il ducato di Milano dal 1535 al 1796*, Torino, 1984.

CHARLES WETHERELL is Director of the Laboratory for Historical Research and Associate Professor of History at the University of California Riverside. His research interests include the history of the family and kinship in Europe and the United States. He is completing, with co-author Andrejs Plakans, a community study of an Eastern Euopean peasant estate.

ACKNOWLEDGEMENTS

The Editor wishes to express his appreciation for the encouragement and help of the University of Minnesota's Social History Workshop and especially of Rus Menard, who originally suggested the conference on the European Peasant Family and Economy at which most of the essays in this book were first presented and was instrumental in providing funding for the conference. Andrejs Plakans and Tamara Hareven encouraged the publication of the conference essays, and it was through their invitation that a number of them were published in a special edition of the *Journal of Family History*, which they edit. I am especially grateful to my daughter, Talia, whose delightful presence and constant support helped bring this book to fruition. A key participant in the original conference was to have been my colleague and friend, Franklin Mendels, whose vital ideas are central to much of the discussion in this book and to whose memory it is dedicated.

The following essays have been revised and reprinted with the permission of the authors and publishers. The Editor wishes to acknowledge the following sources:

Chapter 2. An earlier version appeared as Richard L. Rudolph, 'The European Peasant Family: Central Themes and Issues', *Journal of Family History*, **17**, April 1992, pp. 119–38.

Chapter 3. Michael Mitterauer, 'Peasant and Non-Peasant Forms in Relation to the Physical Environment and the Local Economy', *Journal of Family History*, **17**, April 1992, pp. 139–60.

Chapter 5. James R. Lehning, 'Socioeconomic Change, Peasant Household Structure and Demographic Behavior in a French Department', *Journal of Family History*, **17**, April 1992, pp. 161–82.

Chapter 7. Ulrich Pfister, 'The Proto-Industrial Household Economy: Toward a Formal Analysis', *Journal of Family History*, **17**, April 1992, pp. 201–32.

Chapter 8. Martha White Paas, 'Family Labour Strategies in Early Modern Swabia', *Journal of Family History*, **17**, April 1992, pp. 233–40.

Chapter 10. An earlier, and slightly different, version appeared as Andrejs Plakans and Charles Wetherell, 'Family and Economy in an Early Nineteenth-Century Baltic Serf Estate', *Continuity and Change*, **7**, 1992, pp. 199–233.

Chapter 11. Jürgen Schlumbohm, 'From Peasant Society to Class Society: Some Aspects of Family and Class in a Northwest German Proto-industrial Parish, 17th–19th Centuries', *Journal of Family History*, **17**, April 1992, pp. 183–200.

Chapter 13. An earlier version appeared as Stanley L. Engerman, 'Expanding Protoindustrialization', *Journal of Family History*, **17**, April 1992, pp. 241–51.

Chapter 1

INTRODUCTION

RICHARD L. RUDOLPH

The past several centuries have seen an enormous change in human society
with the transformation from predominantly agricultural to industrial and
market-oriented societies, and this transformation has generated many
questions. Why did this change come about? What specifically caused the
economic and demographic revolutions? What were their effects upon human
behaviour, upon family structure, upon political, class, and gender identity
and roles? What constitutes power in society, how is it transmitted, and who
wields it at various levels of polity and community? Such questions are no
longer looked at only on the basis of the study of elites or of aggregative data.
In studying these questions sociologists, historians, demographers, and anthropologists have turned in large numbers to the study of the household. The
hope is that in understanding this basic unit in society, it might prove possible
to understand the key elements in human behaviour on both a personal and a
greater social and political scale.

In the course of the many studies which have followed this line of thought,
particular attention has come to be paid to the structure of peasant families and
households, both to the degree to which they react to their physical, economic
and social environment, and the degree to which they act upon it through their
own agency. In 1988 an international conference on the History of the Peasant
Family and Economy was held at the University of Minnesota, which was
attended by some of the leading historians, economists and demographers in
the field. The themes of the conference are instructive because they provide an
overview of some of the central topics being dealt with in the field of peasant
household studies, and they provide a context within which the present reader
may more readily place the various chapters in this book. The themes were:

1. The effects of the physical environment on peasant family structure.

2. The effects of the political and cultural environment on peasant family
structure.

3. Economic strategies within the peasant household: inheritance patterns;
gender division of labour; free and unfree labour.

4. The relationship of the peasant household to the wider economy and
society.

5. The effects of protoindustrialization on the peasant family: intra-family
relationships.

6. The effects of protoindustrialization on the peasant family: power
relationships.

The following essays are an outgrowth of that conference, and the purpose of the selection here is to exemplify some of the most recent thought on different aspects of the interweaving of economics with other aspects of family life. In these introductory pages I will try to indicate how the various essays fit into some of the larger themes concerning peasant family and society. The first essay, my own, grew out of my feeling that although numerous scholars from many disciplines work on related themes, some of the excellent work is done in isolation. It seemed to me that it might be helpful to explore just what the main issues were and how the various issues and hypotheses might fit together. My essay offers my own reflections on these matters, particularly in the light of the interplay of economic and non-economic processes.

The next essay, by Michael Mitterauer, comes under the heading of the effects of the outside world on the peasant household. He discusses the novel concept of ecotypes, a conglomerate of social and economic circumstances that are seen to shape labour requirements in the household, which in their turn are seen to affect almost every other aspect of family behaviour. A fundamental question raised by the Mitterauer essay is the degree to which the circumstances of physical geography and economy influence some of the major strategies and activities of the household. This is also dealt with in part by Norbert Ortmayr who examines the Alpine regions of Austria, which had the highest marriage age in Europe as well as the highest proportion never married. Ortmayr examines the degree to which the ecotype may have influenced such behaviour and goes on to examine the consequences of this marriage pattern upon family structure, demographic behaviour, and peasant society in general. He also offers an intriguing discussion of the interaction between family structure and various aspects of peasant culture.

This is followed by the study by James Lehning, who examines the relationship between economic and demographic factors within the household. Lehning is one of many demographers who have devoted careful attention to peasant household structure. In essence, Lehning attempts to evaluate the degree to which household demographic strategies are conditioned by exogenous factors as contrasted with decisions flowing from within the family in its own life cycle. Thus Lehning tests various demographic and household economic theories to try to work out effects of the economy and society on family structure and, in turn, the effects of family structure on demographic decisions. (The reader will note that Lehning's village 'social-economic structure' is strikingly similar to Mitterauer's 'ecotypes'.) He uses data from a French department to examine three different types of theory: (1) the socio-economic model, which posits the nature of demographic change as coming from large-scale modernization, industrialization, and urbanization; (2) the newer household economics model that posits the household itself as the basic decision-making unit, operating with a goal of maximizing scarce resources; and (3) a cultural model. Antoinette Fauve-Chamoux, whose chapter follows next, also deals with France, and she too examines a number of questions in the light of various hypotheses developed by demographers. Among other things she examines the history of the stem family in France and takes issue with those who posit the omnipresence of the nuclear family in western Europe. She focuses primarily on inheritance patterns, or more broadly put, patterns of property transmission, which are another central feature in studies of peasant family life. Fauve-Chamoux examines the degree to which the externally imposed rigid non-egalitarian inheritance systems actually controlled the householder's behaviour. She discusses the extent to which people successfully evaded the inheritance laws and goes on to elaborate on the important consequences of this evasion.

As I discuss in my essay in this volume, much of the study of the peasant household and economy has been undertaken in the context of Franklin Mendels' concept of protoindustrialization, the historical phase when peasant cottage handicraft and by-employment becomes the initial stage of manufacture and production for a wide-scale market. The idea of protoindustrialization was part of the breaking down of the paradigm of a rapid 'industrial revolution' and its replacement by the idea that industrialization was a gradual and lengthy process, often beginning in the peasant cottages themselves. The next piece, by Ulrich Pfister, builds upon the model originated by Franklin Mendels and offers a theoretical framework for understanding the decision-making process by which rural households allocate their labour to agricultural and protoindustrial activities. Pfister's model incorporates much of the new work on class, gender, age and family life cycles, as well as the way in which these factors interact. The next two articles are concerned with vital aspects of the interrelationship of the external world with the peasant household; both of them deal with the interaction of peasant households with the markets for goods, services, and labour. The economist Martha White Paas writes about Swabia in early modern Europe. She deals with the interworkings of institutional and market constraints on family labour strategies, and thus underlines the degree to which the outside world impinges on family structure. Domenico Sella, on the other hand, deals with a much neglected and very vital question, the role that the peasant market for goods and services played in the overall regional or national economy. The 'industrial revolution' paradigm often included an emphasis on foreign demand, but tended to neglect domestic markets. More recent studies have stressed the importance of the role in industrialization of the demand for goods and services on the part of the peasants themselves, including even serfs and slaves. In this pioneering article Sella argues that as early as the beginning of the seventeenth century, along with the development of protoindustrial activities in the countryside, peasant demand for goods and services in northern Italy was quite extensive and was a major factor in the development of manufacture.

The article by Andrejs Plakans and Charles Wetherell introduces several other major issues. Plakans and Wetherell deal with the latitude of decision making of the peasant family on a serf estate in Livland, part of the Russian empire. The context of their work is of great significance. First of all, there is a major historical debate about the degree of dynamism in seigniorial dominated societies. For years historians have spoken of a feudal period, and the period of the seventeenth to nineteenth centuries in central and eastern Europe has been seen as a period of crisis for this system. Numerous questions have been raised about the viability of such a system, particularly in areas with unfree labour, and both Marxist and other historians have argued that, while the system existed, any meaningful degree of economic development was precluded. More recently the issue has been joined by those who argue that serf and slave systems not only had a good deal of dynamism and viability, but that these systems themselves played a role in economic development (see the Rudolph and Plakans-Wetherell chapters in this book). A second, and closely related issue, is the degree of freedom of action on the part of peasants who were bound to higher authorities. This has to do not only with the question of decisions affecting family formation, family structure, and the economy, but also with the extent to which peasants were themselves agents of social and political change. Thus if the peasant has economic power, he or she has political power. To cite one example of the newer approach, William Hagen has argued that the Prussian serfs, rather than their masters and the Prussian state, were primary agents in the abolition of the serf system at the beginning of the nineteenth century (Hagen, 1986). Plakans and Wetherell look at the family and the labour decisions available to the peasant householder in the context of rendering labour services to the landlord, and they further examine the demographic and familial consequences of such a system. Of particular interest in their article, and applicable to the major themes of this book as a whole, is their discussion of various approaches to the analysis of peasant family strategies, such as ideas of instrumental, customary, and command behaviour, which delineate the degree to which decisions are autonomous, based on custom, or based on commands from above. In the same vein they discuss peasant-seigniorial relationships in the light of 'moral economy', the idea of a community's internalized sense of what is just.

From this point the book moves on to deal with other aspects of the household and the outside world. Jürgen Schlumbohm, like Plakans and Wetherell, deals with the institutional effects upon strategies within the household, and he also deals with questions of class formation, another major issue in the studies of the effects of nascent industrialization. Gay Gullickson goes further with the effects of industrialization by broaching the question of the manner in which new conceptualizations of both womanhood and childhood flow from the new manufacturing communities. It was in the context of discussions of the morality of women working outside the home, she argues, that images of woman as mother and children as innocents were developed. The final essay is by Stanley Engerman, who was the keynote speaker and general commentator at the conference. Engerman here ties together some of the major themes of the book under the rubric of protoindustrialization; he then goes on to evaluate the concept and expand upon it. While this book can only touch on a sampling of the questions raised concerning the peasant family and society, it is hoped that the innovative topics and approaches presented here will give some indication of the immense possibilities in this rapidly developing field of study.

References

HAGEN, W. (1986), 'The Junker's Faithless Servants: Peasant Insubordination and the Breakdown of Serfdom in Brandenburg-Prussia, 1763–1811', In R. J. Evans and W. R. Lee, *The German Peasantry: Conflict and Community in Rural Society from the Eighteenth to the Twentieth Centuries*, New York, 71–101.

Chapter 2

MAJOR ISSUES IN THE STUDY OF THE EUROPEAN PEASANT FAMILY, ECONOMY, AND SOCIETY

RICHARD L. RUDOLPH

The purpose of this essay is to reflect upon some ways in which the study of the peasant household in Europe has changed over the last decades; how the various studies by economic historians, anthropologists, demographers, sociologists, and women's historians might fit together; and to explore some of my own thoughts on the field of study. The essay could be called an exercise in *hubris*, but in reality it is a modest attempt to stop for a brief time amid the torrential flow of studies in various fields and try to get some general sense of their interconnectedness. It should go without saying that I can only touch the surface here with regard to the studies done in the past several decades, but my hope is that at least a general picture will emerge, and subtlety and nuances must await further work on each of the aspects.[1] The primary focus is on the interrelationship of economic variables with household structure, but it is clear that a number of non-economic variables are closely connected to the economic ones—and in fact frame them, delimit them, and direct them—so that these must be considered as well.

The convergence of scholars from many disciplines on the sanctity of the peasants' most intimate lives began with the questioning by Peter Laslett of old ways of looking at the family and household (Laslett, 1965), Rudolf Braun's examination of the effects of the transition to an industrial society upon all aspects of the lives of peasants and labourers undergoing the transition (Braun, 1960; 1990), and Franklin Mendels' positing of the crucial importance of the economic and demographic strategies of the peasant household in the initiation of industrialization (Mendels, 1972).

It seems to me that the enormous attractiveness of the study of the peasant household on the verge of industrialization has two primary causes. First, the household and family provide the crucial point of linkage between the individual and society as a whole, the point of linkage between the activities of individuals (agency) and the levels of institutional and social structure with which the individual interacts. Operating on a massive aggregative scale, students of social structure from Marx, Weber, and Sombart, through Parsons and Eisenstadt have focused on the ways in which the individual was both

---

1 For a discussion of some of the themes in family studies in general see Hareven, 1991.

influenced by the social structure and how the individual was influential in acting upon the structure, and thereby changing it. In dealing with the various life strategies of the household—demographic, economic, psychological—we have access to the point of this interaction between the individual and the world, what Philip Abrams has called 'structuring' (Abrams, 1982). Indeed, in their initial studies of the history of the family, it was precisely this link of the family with the social structure as a whole which motivated Wilhelm Riehl (1854) and Frederic Le Play (1877). In Le Play's view:

> the elements of social peace were strongly established in private life. Personal interest, ennobled by the sentiment of duty, leads each individual to respect a master: in the household the children submit their will to a father; in the workshop, workers obey their *patron*; in a neighbourhood, the fathers and *patrons* group themselves respectfully around the larger social authority which has the necessary wisdom to balance a union of sentiments and interests. (Le Play, 1877, I, 4–5)

Secondly, the fact that these studies focus on a historical moment of change, the transformation from a peasant to industrial society, permits us to examine the impact of a number of variables upon individual and family behaviour. If the household were not to undergo this change, we could only speculate upon the possible effects of different variables. As it is, by examining change over time in a particular village or household, and by comparing this with similar units elsewhere, we are able to isolate the effects of particular variables. This is a rare possibility, indeed, in historical studies, and probably the closest approximation to scientific isolation of variables that historians can hope to achieve. The main feature of such studies is the assumption that the strategies of individual household and family units do affect and make and remake economic and social structures, which in turn act upon the households and individuals. The individual is thus seen as a core element in a set of relationships (Sabean, 1990, pp. 11–12).

ECONOMIC INFLUENCES ON FAMILY STRUCTURE

The studies of the household are generally of two interrelated types. First, there are the examinations of the influence of economic and institutional factors on household structure (size, household composition, marriage patterns). Secondly, there are examinations of the influence of household structure itself upon demographic, economic and social strategies.[2] (A schematic view of these relationships is presented in Figure 1.) To begin with,

2 Before discussing these categories in more detail, a word must be said on the use of the terms 'household' and 'family'. A minor but annoying problem in household studies has been a confusion between the terms household and family. It is clear that as many identical family functions can be performed by a family living separately as by one within the confines of a single dwelling. For this reason, it seems to me vital to utilize the terms household or family according to the particular functions being examined.

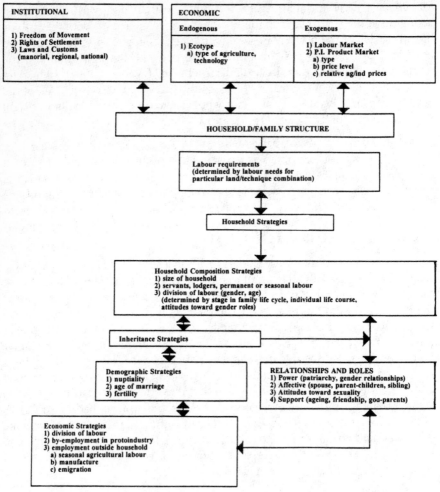

Figure 1: Interrelationship of factors influencing peasant strategies.

let us look at the influence of economic and institutional factors on the household. In the grand Malthusian view, accepted by demographers to a great extent to this day, the period up to the eighteenth century was one in which a homeostatic system existed in which the landed resources established a limit upon population growth, and a primary mechanism for limiting such growth was the age of marriage. For this reason, demographers dealing with the household have focused a great deal on questions of age of marriage, nuptiality and fertility. Franklin Mendels (1972) developed his theory of protoindustrialization with these questions in mind. Mendels' hypotheses are germane for both our categories; protoindustrialization is both an actor upon and a product of the peasant household. For Mendels, a key to the onset of population growth and of industrialization in the seventeenth and eighteenth century lay in the process by which peasant households turned to cottage industry, which not only permitted them to marry earlier and have more children, but also initiated a gradual process of industrialization. Although various aspects of Mendels' hypotheses have been criticized sharply, nevertheless his work has led to numerous studies in economic, demographic and family history, and we shall deal more thoroughly with his theory and its ramifications later.

In my view the most significant recent development in examining a causal relationship between economic factors and the peasant family structure has been the idea of an ecotype. This concept was developed by David Gaunt (1977; 1978) and has been carried further, particularly in the work of Michael Mitterauer and his associates, as well as by others who work with the concept either explicitly or implicitly (Ehmer and Mitterauer, 1986; Kertzer and Hogan, 1989; Mitterauer in this volume). In his study of three different regions in Sweden, Gaunt sought to show 'how differences in the local human-ecological setting—the economic, social and ecological framework for individual and collective action—influence demographic behaviors' (Gaunt, 1978, p. 69). The various components he considered included the natural resources utilized and the manner in which they were used, the intensity and rhythm of the work load over the year, the labour force requirements, and the utilization and recruitment of manpower within the household (Gaunt, 1978, p. 69). Thus every household, or cluster of households in a particular ecological setting, has its own individual combination of these factors, and this blend gives the unique 'ecotype' for that household or region. What is vital is that the ecotype, particularly through its influence on labour requirements, is a vital element in determining household size and structure. Mitterauer, in particular, explores the connection between types of agricultural activity and household composition. He emphasizes even more strongly than Gaunt the key role played by labour requirements. In cattle raising labour power is needed the year round, and there is a correlation between this ecotype and extended families; at the same time, in the small grain growing regions in Alpine Austria, labour requirements are seasonal, so that smaller families are the rule, with either hired seasonal labour or live-in labour during periods in the family life cycle when children are too young to provide labour (Mitterauer, 1986, pp. 190–221; Fél and Hofer, 1969, p. 105). Ecotypes are of many varieties, and include particular ecological structures in which agriculture is combined with by-employment, employment in nearby mining or industry, or with seasonal labour opportunities.

The key element in this concept is that labour requirements are the major element considered as the peasant family works out its household composition strategies, which include inheritance, demographic, and economic strategies. While the notion of ecotypes is extremely useful, it seems to me that its explanatory value is limited unless it is viewed in combination with other factors.[3] Both Malthusian ideas and the ecotype tend to reinforce the idea that for given areas the amount of land is fixed, but in practice there seems to be more of an interaction between a household's landed holdings and its size, rather than a uni-directional causation. In general there appears to be a kind of calculus involved in which there is a necessary balance between the family labour force size and land size, at a given level of agricultural technology. It is remarkable in reading through the literature just how constant the average household size tends to be in given areas over long periods (Segalen, 1986, p. 66). The important thing, then, is either to adjust the household composition to the amount of land or the amount of land to the household size. In some instances, for example in the nineteenth and early twentieth century in Russia and in some regions of south-eastern Poland and Italy, the practice was to change the land holdings to fit the size of the family at given stages in the life cycle. In both Italy and Poland, young male and female peasants would be given small parcels of land by their families; they would then spend their lives accruing more land until the time when their children were of marriageable age, at which point they would give away land and return to holdings comparable in size to those held when they first married (Rudolph, 1991, pp. 368–69; Rudolph, 1992). In Russia as new married couples joined households, the peasant commune assigned more land to the household, so that in this case, too, land was adjusted to the size of the work force, rather than the opposite (Shanin, 1972, pp. 115–21; Rudolph, 1980b, pp. 112–13; Worobec, 1991, pp. 42–62).

In addition, and perhaps most important, a range of institutional factors intervene to influence household composition strategies. In his discussion of the differences in family composition in proximate regions in the Zürich Highlands, Rudolf Braun discusses the ways in which local customs and local laws as to the rights of settlement or the types of houses influenced family patterns (Braun, 1990, pp. 50–51, 119–21). In the same vein, Martha Paas and Jürgen Schlumbohm, in their essays in this volume, both demonstrate the

---

3 See Michael Mitterauer's discussion in this volume of the usefulness and limitations of ecotypes.

effects of the local authorities' decisions on the permissibility of settlement of cottagers or agricultural labourers, as well as laws dealing with their rights to utilize common lands. In these same cases, as in other instances, the nobility could determine rights and ages of marriage as well as inheritance patterns. John Cole and Eric Wolf speak of the way in which in the areas of southern Austria, where areas of mixed German and Italian population changed hands between Italy and Austria, both cultural customs and inheritance laws affected inheritance practices (Cole and Wolf, 1974, pp. 176–80). Thus national, regional and local laws and customs must also be taken into account along with economic factors.

HOUSEHOLD COMPOSITION STRATEGIES

In discussing household composition strategies, we begin with the proposition that the peasant household has two primary goals that it must balance: first, the maintenance and expansion of its property for the family in future generations; secondly, the welfare of the family at given stages in the family life cycle.[4] What is crucial is that a tension emerges between these two goals.[5] The aim of expanding property comes into conflict with immediate economic needs at one stage of the family life cycle, and with traditional inheritance patterns at another stage. Given a balance of some sort worked out within the household, the family needs a given size labour force to achieve its goals. It is at this point that strategies with respect to household composition come into play. By household composition, we mean size of household, the degree to which there is reliance on family labour as opposed to permanent or seasonal hired labour, and division of labour within the family by gender and age.

Household size has probably received more attention than any other aspect of family history in recent years, and a convincing body of research undertaken under the auspices of the Cambridge Group for the History of Population and Social Structure reveals a preponderance of nuclear families (Laslett, 1972; Wall, 1983). Nevertheless, it is vital to remember that household size is not a static, but a dynamic concept. When averages are listed for family household size based on census data, they present a static picture, somewhat like that of a pinned butterfly. In reality, the butterfly in this case is not pinned down, but very active indeed. The members of the household, in the periods not captured in census data, may move away permanently or seasonally, may procreate, may die, or may take in lodgers or relatives. A wide variety of household forms has been described in Europe, at times as stages in family life cycles, and at others, particularly in southern and eastern Europe, in complex types of

4 In the past, particularly in the Balkans, an additional aim was the actual physical security of the household, and this is seen as one of the factors responsible for the development of complex households.

5 For a discussion of the tensions involved in peasant strategies see Cole and Wolf (1974, pp. 176–177) and Rudolph (1991, pp. 365–368).

extended families (Segalen, 1986, pp. 14, 18–19; Wall, 1983; Kertzer and Hogan, 1989, p. 53).

Decisions as to whether to rely on family or hired labour, as well as choices as to division of labour by gender and age, are closely related to particular stages in the life cycle of the family and in the individual life course of particular family members (Hareven, 1978; Pfister, 1989). The increasing attention in the literature devoted to these factors reflects just how important they are; just who carries out particular tasks in the household and outside of it has important ramifications in terms of demographic and economic strategies, gender roles and gender status, and affective and power relationships within the family. Here again, these matters will be touched upon later.

Inheritance Strategies

In determining the specific household composition, the family relies on inheritance, demographic, and economic strategies, which in turn, as we have pointed out, are delimited by institutional, economic and cultural factors. The inheritance patterns are a key element in meeting the goals of the peasant household and are one of the clearest links between the ecotype and family structure. It is through inheritance practices that some of the major aspects of household composition are determined, and conversely the particular household composition may determine the inheritance strategy to be adopted. If there is partible inheritance, the possibility is great that the size of the agricultural holding will be diminished, and this in turn will affect household size and composition, whereas impartible inheritance permits the maintenance of larger households and is most often a concomitant of more extended families. Thus, although there is a great variety of inheritance patterns, there appears to be a strong correlation between the ecotype and either partible or impartible inheritance. The close interrelationship between inheritance patterns and economic factors appears in the case of Poland. From the time that Poland was partitioned in the late eighteenth century to the mid-twentieth century inheritance practices and, until Poland was reunited, laws were different in the Prussian, Russian and Austrian parts of Poland. The Prussian pattern was impartible inheritance, with laws holding that land could not be divided. In the Russian held portions of Poland, partible inheritance was followed, and Russian law permitted division of the holdings, but limited the degree to which this could be done. In the Austrian part, primarily Galicia, where partible inheritance was practised, there was no limitation on the degree to which land could be divided (Rudolph, 1991, pp. 372–77; Kowalski, 1928). In the broadest terms the differences appear to have been reflected in economic strategies: in the Prussian part, large-scale agriculture prevailed; in the Russian part small-scale agriculture was the rule, with some migration and by-employment, while in Austrian Galicia, extreme fragmentation of the holdings was present, with both outmigration of the peasants and extensive development of protoindustrial activities, particularly in textiles (Rudolph,

1991; Kulczykowski, 1976). Thus inheritance factors appear to have a major effect upon household structure and in turn upon economic strategies. At the same time inheritance decisions imply handing over not only wealth but various forms of power, and thus inheritance strategies must be influenced by cultural and psychological factors which lie outside the immediate bounds of ecotypes.

Demographic Strategies

In the literature concerning the economics of the household, demographic strategies have occupied a central role, with primary attention being given to the age of marriage, nuptiality, and fertility. The age of marriage was a key variable for Malthus, for it was early marriage which was seen as a major factor in increasing population (Macfarlane, 1986, pp. 5–22). Demographers have carried this same argument into the present. In his classic article on European marriage patterns, John Hajnal (1965) listed three possibilities for a more prolific population: increased marital fertility, a lower age of marriage, and a rise in the proportion marrying. The importance of increased marital fertility has been fairly well ruled out over the years, but the lower age of marriage and rise in the proportion of the population marrying has been given a primary role in explaining European population growth in the eighteenth and nineteenth centuries (Wrigley and Schofield, 1981; Gutmann, 1988, pp. 15–149; Macfarlane, 1986, pp. 25–28). In the doctoral dissertation which gave rise to his hypotheses concerning protoindustrialization, Franklin Mendels (1981) began with the question of the relationship between prices paid for protoindustrial textile production and nuptiality in Flanders. It was a tenet of Mendels' protoindustrial theory in this and later works that cottage industry permitted land-poor peasants to marry earlier and produce larger families; for him this was a major cause of population growth and also of the spread of cottage industry. The Swiss economic historian Ulrich Pfister, a student of both Mendels and Rudolf Braun, returns to these key themes and elaborates on them in his theoretical work in this volume and elsewhere (Pfister, 1989). David Levine, as well, has demonstrated the degree to which economic opportunity provided the means for earlier marriage, but he stresses the degree to which non-economic factors also influence decisions as to the age of marriage (Levine, 1977; 1983, pp. 9–11). He speaks of the 'moral economy' of the pre-industrial village, with various social sanctions against transgressors (Levine, 1983, pp. 11–12). Indeed it is vital to examine other non-economic variables as well. David Ransel offers a fascinating study of the effects of varying cultural attitudes on demographic variables. Ransel has examined different patterns of infant and child mortality in late-nineteenth-century Russia among Russian orthodox, Jewish, and Tatar Moslem women, often living within the same villages. He demonstrates quite clearly how different cultural practices and attitudes play a great role in determining rates of mortality (Ransel, 1991a; 1991b). What follows from this discussion is that once again, although there are variations, economic variables play a vital role in another building block of household structure, the demographic aspect. Part of our task, which we shall discuss at the conclusion of this essay, is to try to work out a way of dealing with the interaction of economic and non-economic variables.

Economic Strategies

The last and vitally important component in family and household structure has to do with economic decisions made within the household. This is also one of the most difficult topics, because of the complexity of the interrelationship between the economy and the household. On the one hand, the economic strategies of the household at a given time will have crucial ramifications for the various aspects of the household in the future. Thus economic strategies may reverberate upon the household and bring the older structure crumbling down and rebuild it on a new basis; economic decisions made at one point in the family life cycle may affect demographic decisions, household structure, and living standards, as well as affective and power relationships within the family. At the same time, and this is one of the most important features of household economic strategies, there may well be a great effect upon the outside community and economy. In other words, we enter upon the aspects of the household which are not only reactive, but are involved in agency in transforming the economic and social structure within which the household functions.

Perhaps the best way to understand the workings of economic strategies within the peasant household is to start with the theory of protoindustrialization as initially presented by Franklin Mendels. There are those, and I am one among them, who hesitate to use the term largely because it has been so greatly modified and in part discredited over the years. In fact its many transformations have so altered it that it is barely recognizable in the form first given it by Mendels. Nevertheless, the fundamental conceptualization by Mendels seems to me to be very solid, and since much of the research has built upon it, or variations of it, we would do well to begin with its solid core and then add on the emendations which have developed over the years. What we end up with, I think, is not a self-contained theory of protoindustrialization, but a framework, or paradigm, within which we can better envision the causal connections and interrelationships between economic and demographic aspects of the peasant household and its environs.

Mendels began his work with the problem of the interrelationship of economic variables, namely wages and prices, and demographic behaviour, particularly the age of marriage. He was aware of the new body of empirical data ferreted out by demographers showing pockets of sharp growth in population in relatively marginal agricultural areas. His work was also informed by the work of Rudolf Braun and the studies of Joan Thirsk and E. L. Jones on the agricultural origins of industry, i.e. the cottage industrial origins of industry (Braun, 1960; Thirsk, 1961; Jones, 1968). In addition, and very important indeed, was the influence of Marx, whose studies of the role of cottage industry in industrialization were basic to the Marxist view of economic development and social change (Mendels, 1972; 1978; 1980; 1982).

Mendels' theory posited a symbiotic relationship between agricultural regions where land was in short supply and those with productive commercial agriculture. In the poorer areas, peasants turned to by-employment, often involving articles such as textiles or metal products, which were then sold in distant markets. The formerly subsistence peasants now bought their agricultural products from the commercial regions, while the commercial regions now concentrated purely on agriculture. Thus, by the phenomenon known to economists as comparative advantage, the total production of both regions was much greater than it would have been had they not concentrated on what they could best produce. As a result of the increased income through this cottage industry, peasants could marry earlier and provide for more children. The stipulation that markets were distant was made in order to account for the difference between this protoindustrial stage of industry and the traditional practice by which peasant families normally provided their own clothing, linen and tools. Now, with larger and more distant markets, the cottage industry with its contract system was often converted to small-scale manu-factories, virtually repeating the activities done in the home, but now with labourers gathered together in one building, and then there was further evolution of the process through mechanization into full-scale industry. At the same time, production skills were spread to other villages and large numbers of people developed the marketing networks and management skills which provided for the success of full-scale industrialization. What was known as protoindustrialization, then, was the sum total of these processes—the intertwining of cottage industry and commercial agriculture; the expansion of cottage industry and its demographic consequences; the transition from household industry to manufacture and industrialization; and the building of a network of marketing and managerial skills.

A vital corollary of the protoindustrial hypothesis was that the sources of industrialization lay not in the so-called industrial revolution and the inventions and innovations of the late eighteenth century, but rather that industrialization was born through a long and gradual process in the countryside. In time ideas of industrial revolution were replaced in the literature with the paradigm of gradual industrialization. This was typified in the title of Jeffrey Williamson's article, 'Why Was British Growth So Slow During the Industrial Revolution?' (Williamson, 1984). Another key feature of the theory was that by being able to obtain income through protoindustry, more people could marry and they could afford to marry earlier, establishing their own households and replicating the process of cottage industry on a wider scale. And as was discussed earlier, the lower age of marriage and increased nuptiality was seen to have brought about the growth of population so evident in Europe by the late eighteenth century.

In the ensuing years, these hypotheses were enhanced by others, criticized, modified and revised (Coleman, 1983; Houston and Snell, 1984; Gutmann and Leboutte, 1984). By 1982, at the International Economic History Conference in Budapest, some 49 papers were presented on the theme of protoindustrial-ization (Deyon and Mendels, 1982). Several of the modifications are impera-tive for understanding the effects of household economic strategies. Further studies, for example, have demonstrated that it was not only in regions of subsistence agriculture that such by-employment arose, but also in rich commercial agricultural regions, and that a key variable was alternation of the agricultural season with by-employment or cottage industry (Mendels, 1980; Rudolph, 1985, p. 61; Gullickson, 1986, pp. 39–40). Thus cottage industry or by-employment in agriculture could be present and grow anywhere. The key questions then were: Why did it grow in some areas and not in others? Why and to what degree did it become the key phase in industrialization, i.e., in what circumstances did it lead on to further growth instead of dying on the vine? What were the effects of protoindustry upon the household and its inhabitants?

The distinction made that protoindustrialization entails a distant rather than purely local market was intended to differentiate the process which would lead on to the contract (*Verlag* or putting out) systems and onward to manufacture and industry. Yet this distinction was not sufficient to account for the process. Several vital modifications in the theory were necessary. Myron Gutmann and René Leboutte pointed out that in some areas of Belgium, where the arms related cottage industry had developed gradually over several centuries, the impetus for young people to move away from the domestic hearth was weak. They called this 'the novelty factor', and argued that it was not only cottage industry that was important for there to be an impact upon the household, i.e., something which would impel young people to move out and change their ways, but there had to be some new form, wherein the impact upon the household would be great. They also argued that the impact of cottage industry was muffled further by the fact that there was a long training period within the household for the type of industry found in the region, so that young people could not easily move out and set up their own households (Gutmann and Leboutte, 1984, pp. 603–04). These emendations to the theory were elaborated on by others, who pointed out that one must sharply differentiate the different types of cottage industry, because the particularities of different technologies with different skills and different markets had varying impacts upon the peasant or protoindustrial household (Houston and Snell, 1984; Coleman, 1983; Pfister, in this volume). Of particular importance was the question of division of labour within the household. It was Gay Gullickson who first pointed out the degree to which one or another type of cottage industry had more of an opportunity to lead on to greater economic importance according to whether it was seen as women's or men's work (Gullickson, 1981; 1986, pp. 198–99). Judith Pallot has expanded on this idea not only by emphasizing the degree to which some branches of industry were slighted because they were considered women's work, but also by pointing out the degree to which women were often more or less bound to the household according to the tasks they were assigned (Pallot, 1991). Thus by implication, women were limited in their mobility, and thus also limited was the degree to which they could take the initiative of moving the particular craft or industry outside the original household. We see, then, that the gendered character of particular branches of industry takes on a rather high level of significance in the initial stages of protoindustry. It is also argued that industrialization actually reduced the economic importance of women's labour and restricted their labour opportunities, and this topic is the subject of wide debate (Tilly and Scott, 1978; Hamilton, 1978; Middleton, 1985). Pallot has also argued, based on her study of the Russian protoindustrial household, that the size and composition of the household determined the precise nature of the division of labour; she found that smaller households had a more flexible division of labour than did larger ones (Pallot, 1991, p. 167). It follows from this that one should pay close attention to the relation between family forms and the presence or absence of protoindustry.

Of prime importance are questions which relate to economic factors which act upon the possibility of households turning to protoindustrial activity. In her excellent study of the Caux region in France, Gay Gullickson has provided one of the best analyses of what is involved in the protoindustrial process. She holds that the key feature at the basis of protoindustrial activity is not landlessness, but the almost universal nature of seasonality in agriculture and the desire for supplemental income. At the same time, she notes, the need for additional income is greatest among those who suffer landlessness or seasonal unemployment. 'Such landlessness could be caused by a variety of developments, for example, population growth, partible inheritance, the subdivision of leaseholds, or the concentration of land in a few hands to facilitate production. The important factors are seasonal unemployment and landlessness, not their causes' (Gullickson, 1986, pp. 196–97). Gullickson goes on to define the conditions affecting whether or not protoindustry will evolve from these circumstances. She writes, 'given this widespread need for cottage industry, what ultimately determined the location of protoindustries were such nonagricultural factors as the closeness of urban markets, the size of the urban labour force, the ease of transportation between the region and its markets, and the labour demands of urban merchants' (Gullickson, 1986, p. 197).

In our discussion so far of the factors influencing the onset of protoindustry, we have discovered a number of pertinent variables, and in fact as the list grows longer with each new study, the objection is increasingly raised that there are so many factors involved that the whole theory of protoindustrialization should be abandoned. This is the implicit argument in the critique of

Houston and Snell, who are armed with references to a multitude of cases where this or that branch of manufacture differs from another (Houston and Snell, 1984). Nevertheless, there is a basic counter-argument that can be made to their objections, and this counter-argument gets to the heart of the question of the validity of such a theory. What is basic in the variants we have described so far is that they may be divided into two categories: economic and non-economic. As to the economic factors, it is extremely important to note that there is a significant difference in the way in which historians in general describe the economic factors and in which those trained in economic theory do so. This can be seen most clearly by digressing for a moment and looking at a debate which took place some years ago over the comparative strength of industrialization in various European countries. It was argued by some that France was slower in developing than England because of such drawbacks as the lack of coal or the distances between coal and iron producing regions. Similar arguments about the lack of this or that raw material or problems of location were made for other regions as well. Eventually the opponents of this view pointed out that the presence or absence of particular resources was not the question—after all, England with its vast cotton textile industry lacked cotton, but what was important was *relative factor cost*, i.e. the cost of cotton or iron or any other factor of production. Similarly, when we examine the qualities present or absent in relation to the peasant household, and discuss the possibility of their turning to protoindustry, we should be aware that such lists as those compiled by Gay Gullickson, such as proximity of markets, size of urban labour force, ease of transportation or urban labour demand, are really translatable into more simple economic terms. What we are really dealing with is not the proximity of markets, but the proximity as translated into costs of production (transportation), and when we speak of the size of the labour force or the desire by urban merchants for labour, we are really speaking of labour demand as expressed in wages. Thus the economists can help us to see the apparent plethora of factors in the light of really fewer variables. When we speak of the probability of a household crossing over the threshold of protoindustrial activity we are really speaking of the degree to which this alternative is favourable to the household because of the market price for their product as against agricultural products or compared with money obtainable through wages in other fields. This is the great value of the work of such economists as Franklin Mendels, Martha White Paas, and Ulrich Pfister who speak in lucid terms of the relationships of such factors (Mendels, 1978; Paas and Pfister in this volume). As to the non-economic variables, which come under the headings of cultural expectations, such as gender roles as they affect household composition and protoindustrial activity, it may also be argued that we should ever be on the lookout for their presence and their effects on the protoindustrial process, but we should also be aware at the same time that in many cases these work through as economic parameters as well. The answer, then, to the question as to why protoindustry arose in some areas and not in others should be sought primarily, although not entirely, in terms of market factors.

There is another major dimension to the question as to when domestic production will make the transition to industrialization. For many years it was argued that the key to industrialization was the transformation of economic and political power to the bourgeoisie, to a group of entrepreneurs. The essence of the Marxist argument, which was implicitly adopted by many scholars, was that it was merchant capital and merchant capitalists who furnished the initiative and financing for industrialization. With money garnered from trade abroad or from the putting-out system, investment was made in industry. For Marx himself, although the capital came partly from cottage industry, it also came in a greater degree from colonial exploitation and the slave trade, and he could thus write in his famous chapter on primitive accumulation in *Das Kapital* that capitalism entered the world from the womb of feudalism 'dripping blood from every pore'. Thus in the writing of many scholars one sees the ever-recurrent Marxist theme of 'the role of merchant capital'. Without entering into a long discussion of Marxist theory, it should be remarked that the protoindustrial model puts the development of industry in a completely different light. If the roots of industry lie in the peasant household one can see its origins and growth outside the feudal-capitalist paradigm. From the eighteenth century on, in the Habsburg monarchy, particularly in Bohemia, Moravia and parts of Poland, as well as in the vast Russian empire, cottage industry was encouraged and promoted by the nobility, or what the Marxists would call the feudal class, because they preferred to produce as much as possible at home and spend their small liquid assets on luxury goods or goods not locally available (Kula, 1976, pp. 33–55; Kulczykowski, 1969; Rudolph, 1980a; 1980b; 1981; 1983; 1985; Tugan-Baranovskii, 1922). Thus serfs were used in a non-free and non-capitalist system to promote cottage industry and manufacture which was often promulgated by the nobility. The implications of this for the whole idea of the capitalist transformation becomes, once again, a question of avoiding labels and looking at the development of economic and social processes as they unfold on the basis of activities within the peasant household.

The second major question involved in the protoindustrial debate is the degree to which it actually led to industrialization. It has been argued that the protoindustrial theory ignores other paths to industrialization such as urban or state development of industry, or the importation of large-scale industry from other regions or countries. A corollary of this argument is that protoindustry is in many cases a *cul-de-sac*, with real industrialization coming from industrial centres and competing with cottage industry to such an extent that it dies out, a process known variously as 'de-industrialization' or industrial 'involution' (Levine, 1983, pp. 13–14). Indeed cottage industry is clearly not the only path to industrialization, and so far as I know none of the students of proto-industrialization have so argued, but the peasant household in so very many regions was involved in by-employment of such goods that the process is vital to the study of both the economic and social aspects of industrialization.

This is nowhere more clear than when we broach our third question, as to the effects of protoindustry on the household and individual. It is here that some of the most exciting work is being undertaken. The questions raised fall under two broad groupings: class and relationships. With respect to the first, a large-scale literature has grown up examining the relationship of protoindustry to class formation. The major writings in this field—but not all by far—come from German scholars and are associated with what I may call the Göttingen school, and here a strong consciousness of class issues, informed by Marxist theory, underlies works on the role of protoindustry in proletarianization (Medick, 1976; Conze, 1976; Kriedte, 1977; Rosenbaum, 1982). In the same vein David Levine, in his studies of several English regions, has argued that in actuality protoindustrial activities led people to abandon agriculture and rely entirely on manufacturing activities. What this meant, he argues, was that when such protoindustrial activities were swept away by full-scale industrialization, the people engaged in protoindustry did not profit from it, but were turned into the vast and often desolate proletariat (Levine, 1977; 1983).

Relatively recently, the whole question of the effect on the whole array of relationships within the household and community have come to be seen with respect to their interconnections with protoindustry. These involve power relationships, in the sense of examination of the origins and support of patriarchy (Lerner, 1986; Walby, 1990; Worobec, 1991) and gender relations as they may change with the evolution of cottage industry. In this respect a central and unresolved question within the field of women's history is the degree to which the status of women changes or is affected by their economic role. It is clear that the study of gender roles within the household as it evolves from an agricultural to a non-agricultural one may well hold the answer to this question; to what extent, for example, does the gendering of tasks or branches of household industry both flow from and affect attitudes toward women (Hanawalt, 1986; Quataert, 1985)? In her work on family reconstitution in France, Antoinette Fauve-Chamoux has discovered long periods in the family life cycle during which women were heads of households (Fauve-Chamoux, 1986, p. 302; 1990, pp. 225–45). Further, the whole vast area of affective relationships is opened up by study of the household (Medick and Sabean, 1984). These involve parent-child relationships as well as those between men and women and various siblings (see Hawes and Hiner, 1991). The work of Michael Mitterauer, Richard Sieder and Norbert Ortmayr in Austria has opened up intriguing questions in this regard (Mitterauer and Sieder, 1982; Ortmayr, 1986). In particular, their work raises intriguing questions as to the relationship of family structure and inheritance patterns and how these condition affective relationships. In regions of Austria, for example, where there was impartible inheritance, where the eldest son took over the land and the siblings became his servants, and where the eldest son had to wait until his father retired from the land or died to take over the management of the household, there were a multitude of ramifications for intra-family relationships. Although research has not been carried out to any great degree on this topic, one can see that there was room for great annoyance and resentment on the part of the older son against the father, since he could not get married or have power within the household until the father finally retired or died, and the younger siblings from an early age were at the mercy of their elder brother, who would be their virtual master in the future. The younger siblings generally had little opportunity as landless labourers to marry, and consequently the rate of children born out of wedlock reached over eighty per cent in some regions of Austria. The children, for their part, as progeny of agricultural labourers or servants without their own homes, spent a great deal of time being passed from one relative or acquaintance to another. The consequences of this for the physical and mental health of the children could be extensive. Several self-revelatory novels from such children in Austria reveal the effects of such circumstances (Mitgutsch, 1987; Innerhofer, 1974). It is clear that the comparison of extended families, stem families, and nuclear families of various forms with respect to the types of affective relations and especially the attitudes toward children would be extremely rewarding. Further studies are beginning to deal with various periods of the life course in their relationship to the household, such as women's movements in and out of the work force, adolescence and ageing. What the Austrian case suggests is a vital link between family structure and affective relationships, which indeed has ramifications going far beyond the individual household into the surrounding community and into future generations.

What emerges from the foregoing discussion is a sense of the vital importance of economic factors in many aspects of the peasant household. It has also been clear that in many instances non-economic factors are quite influential at critical points in household strategy decisions. To cite two instances, the variety of household forms is indeed striking, as is the effect of cultural attitudes, demonstrated in Ransel's study of mortality rates in Russia. It seems to me that in order to make sense of the variety of phenomena associated with the household as it is affected by and affects economic matters, one should view economic factors not as causal, but as delimiting factors, that is to say elements which act as parameters within which there still remains a large area of play for other variables. It is thus that we see ecotypes at work; economic necessity serves to frame, delimit and direct household activities. Yet even so we see that, given the limits shaped by economic circumstances, the household can still have a wide range of inheritance patterns or household forms. The degree of choice of the latter, in turn, may be further delimited by institutional or cultural factors. It is thus that in a sense by studying the economic possibilities presented to the household in combination with the other, non-economic factors, we have something of a series of boxes within boxes, and within the smallest box, that is within the confines of the limits set by our economic, cultural and institutional factors, we may be able finally to approach, in more proximate fashion, the causal links in household behaviour. The degree to which economic variables are in fact determinate, as opposed to themselves being overwhelmed by cultural or institutional factors, is among the questions which must constantly be kept in mind in research on the household.

It is indeed a great attraction of the multidisciplinary approaches taken to the topic of the peasant household that they so well combine the advantages of theoretical thinking with the constant conscience of the historian, which argues for attention to the uniqueness of circumstance. The development of theories, which are in reality the designation of the logical possibilities inherent in the problem at hand, entails the establishment of initial conditions upon which the theory will be based, and it is up to historians to ensure that the initial conditions are consistent with the nuances of reality. In a sense the field is so new and the concepts are so varied that we can just begin to explore the interrelationships between the different branches of study, something we have tried to do here. The field has come far enough, however, for us clearly to see some of the main links between the economic and non-economic factors acting upon and within the peasant household, and the work that has been done so far also permits us to understand some of the predominant elements in the nexus between life within the family and society at large.

References

ABRAMS, P. (1982), *Historical Sociology*, Ithaca, New York.

BRAUN, R. (1960), *Industrialisierung und Volksleben: die Veranderungen der Lebensformen in einem landlichen Industriegebiet vor 1800 (Züricher Oberland)*, Zurich.

BRAUN, R. (1990), *Industrialisation and Everyday Life*, Cambridge, New York and Paris.

COLE, J. W. and E. R. WOLF (1974), *The Hidden Frontier; Ecology and Ethnicity in an Alpine Valley*, New York and London.

COLEMAN, D. C. (1983), 'Proto-Industrialization: A Concept too Many', *Economic History Review*, **36**,435–48.

CONZE, W. (ed.) (1976), *Die Familie im Übergang von der entfalteten Agrargesellschaft zum Industriesystem*, Stuttgart.

DEYON, P. and F. MENDELS (eds.) (1982), *La Protoindustrialisation: Théorie et Réalité, Rapports*, Lille.

EHMER, J. and M. MITTERAUER (eds.) (1986), *Familienstruktur und Arbeitsorganisation in ländlichen Gesellschaften*, Vienna.

FAUVE-CHAMOUX, A. (1986), 'La femme seule, une réalité urbaine: l'exemple de Reims au début du XIXe siècle', *Mémoires de la société d'agriculture, commerce, sciences et arts du département de la Marne*, **CI**, 295–305.

FAUVE-CHAMOUX, A. (1990), 'Destins de femmes et manufacture textile à Reims avant la révolution industrielle', In *La Donna nell'Economia Secc. XIII–XVIII*, Prato.

FÉL, E. and T. HOFER (eds.) (1969), *Proper Peasants: Traditional Life in a Hungarian Village*, Chicago.

GAUNT, D. (1977), 'Pre-Industrial Economy and Population Structure: The Elements of Variance in Early Modern Sweden', *Scandinavian Journal of History*, **2**, 183–210.

GAUNT, D. (1978), 'Household Typology: Problems, Methods, Results', In S. Akerman, H. C. Johansen and D. Gaunt (eds.), *Social and Economic Studies in Historical Demography in the Baltic Area*, Odense, 69–83.

GULLICKSON, G. L. (1981), 'The Sexual Division of Labor in Cottage Industry and Agriculture in the Pays de Caux: Auffay, 1750–1850', *French Historical Studies*, **12**, 177–99.

GULLICKSON, G. L. (1983), 'Agriculture and Cottage Industry: Redefining the Causes of Proto-Industrialization', *Journal of Economic History*, **43**, 831–50.

GULLICKSON, G. L. (1986), *Spinners and Weavers of Auffay: Rural Industry and the Sexual Division of Labor in a French Village, 1750–1850*, New York.

GUTMANN, M. P. (1988), *Toward the Modern Economy: Early Industry in Europe, 1500–1800*, New York.

GUTMANN, M. P. and R. LEBOUTTE (1984), 'Rethinking Protoindustrialization and the Family', *Journal of Interdisciplinary History*, **14**, 587–608.

HAJNAL, J. (1965), 'European Marriage Patterns in Perspective', In D. V. Glass and D. E. C. Eversley (eds.), *Population in History*, London.

HAMILTON, R. (1978), *The Liberation of Women: A Study of Patriarchy and Capitalism*, London and Boston.

HANAWALT, B. A. (ed.) (1986), *Women and Work in Preindustrial Europe*, Bloomington.

HAREVEN, T. K. (ed.) (1978), *Transitions: The Family and the Life Course in Historical Perspective*, New York.

HAREVEN, T. K. (1991), 'The History of the Family and the Complexity of Social Change', *American Historical Review*, **96**, 95–124.

HAWES, J. M. and N. R. HINER (eds.) (1991), *Children in Historical and Comparative Perspective*, New York.

HOUSTON, R. and K. D. M. SNELL (1984), 'Proto-Industrialization? Cottage Industry, Social Change, and Industrial Revolution', *The Historical Journal*, **27**, 473–92.

INNERHOFER, F. (1974), *Schöne Tage*, Salzburg and Vienna.

JONES, E. L. (1968), 'Agricultural Origins of Industry', *Past and Present*, **11**, 58–71.

KERTZER, D. I. and D. P. HOGAN (1989), *Family, Political Economy, and Demographic Change; The Transformation of Life in Casalecchio, Italy, 1861–1921*, Madison.

KOWALSKI, K. (1928), 'Prawne zwyczaje w zakresie wyposażenia dzieci i dziedziczenia oraz sprawa podzielności malych gospodarstw wiejskich w byłym zaborze austrijackim', in K. Kowalski et al., *Zwyczaje spadkowe włościan w Polsce*, pt. 1, Warsaw, 1–93.

KRIEDTE, P., H. MEDICK and J. SCHLUMBOHM (1977), *Industrialisierung vor der Industrialisierung*, Göttingen.

KULA, W. (1976), *An Economic Theory of the Feudal System*, London.

KULCZYKOWSKI, M. (1969), 'Industrie paysanne et formation du marché national en Pologne au XVIIIe siècle', *Annales, E.S.C.*, **24**, 61–69.

KULCZYKOWSKI, M. (1976), *Chłopskie tkactwo bawelniane w osrodku andrychowskim w XIX wieku*, Wroclaw.

LASLETT, P. (1965), *The World We Have Lost*, New York.

LASLETT, P. (ed.) (1972), *Household and Family in Past Time*, Cambridge.

LE PLAY, F. (1877), *Les ouvriers européens* (2nd ed.), vol. 1, Tours.

LERNER, G. (1986), *The Creation of Patriarchy*, New York and Oxford.

LEVINE, D. (1977), *Family Formation in an Age of Nascent Capitalism*, New York.

LEVINE, D. (1983), 'Proto-Industrialization and Demographic Upheaval', In L. P. Moch and G. D. Stark (eds.), *Essays on the Family and Historical Change*, Arlington, Texas, 9–34.

MACFARLANE, A. (1986), *Marriage and Love in England: Modes of Reproduction, 1300–1840*, Oxford.

MEDICK, H. (1976), 'The Proto-industrial Family Economy: The Structural Function of the

Household and Family During the Transition to Industrial Capitalism', *Social History*, 1, 291–315.

MEDICK, H. and D. W. SABEAN (eds.) (1984), *Interest and Emotion: Essays on the Study of Family and Kinship*, Cambridge.

MENDELS, F. (1972), 'Proto-industrialization: The First Phase of the Industrialization Process', *Journal of Economic History*, 32, 241–61.

MENDELS, F. (1978), 'La composition du ménage paysan en France au XIXe siècle: une analyse économique du mode de production domestique', *Annales, E.S.C.*, 33, 780–802.

MENDELS, F. (1980), 'Seasons and Regions in Agriculture and Industry During the Process of Industrialization', In S. Pollard (ed.), *Region und Industrialisierung*, Göttingen, 177–95.

MENDELS, F. (1981), *Industrialization and Population Pressure in Eighteenth-Century Flanders*, New York.

MENDELS, F. (1982), 'Protoindustrialization: Theory and Reality. General Report', In *Eighth International Economic History Congress, Budapest 1982, 'A' Themes*, Budapest, 69–107.

MIDDLETON, C. (1985), 'Women's Labour and the Transition to Pre-industrial Capitalism', In C. Lindsey and L. Duffin, *Women's Work in Pre-industrial England*, London and Dover, New Hampshire, 181–206.

MITGUTSCH, W. (1987), *Three Daughters*, San Diego.

MITTERAUER, M. (1986), 'Formen ländlicher Familienwirtschaft; Historische Ökotypen und familiale Arbeitsorganisation im österreichischen Raum', In J. Ehmer and M. Mitterauer (eds.), *Familienstruktur und Arbeitsorganisation in ländlichen Gesellschaften*, Vienna, 185–323.

MITTERAUER, M. and R. SIEDER (1982), *The European Family*, Chicago.

ORTMAYR, N. (1986), 'Ländliches Gesinde in Oberösterreich 1918–1938', In J. Ehmer and M. Mitterauer (eds.), *Familienstruktur und Arbeitsorganisation in ländlichen Gesellschaften*, Vienna, 325–416.

PALLOT, J. (1991), 'Women's Domestic Industries in Moscow Province, 1880–1900', In B. E. Clements, B. A. Engel and C. D. Worobec (eds.), *Russia's Women: Accommodation, Resistance, Transformation*, Berkeley, 163–84.

PFISTER, U. (1989), 'Work Roles and Family Structure in Proto-industrial Zurich', *Journal of Interdisciplinary History*, 10, 83–105.

QUATAERT, J. H. (1985), 'The Shaping of Women's Work in Manufacturing Guilds: Households and the State in Central Europe 1648–1870', *American Historical Review*, 90, 1127–48.

RANSEL, D. L. (1991a), 'Infant-Care Cultures in the Russian Empire', In B. E. Clements, B. A. Engel and C. D. Worobec (eds.), *Russia's Women: Accommodation, Resistance, Transformation*, Berkeley, 113–34.

RANSEL, D. L. (1991b), 'Cultural Practices and Infant Mortality among Russians, Jews, and Tatars in Late Tsarist Russia', unpublished manuscript.

RIEHL, W. H. (1862–1869), *Die Naturgeschichte des Volkes als Grundlage einer deutschen Social-Politik*, 4 vols., Stuttgart and Tübingen.

ROSENBAUM, H. (1982), *Formen der Familie: Untersuchungen zum Zusammenhang von Familienverhältnissen, Sozialstruktur und sozialem Wandel in der deutschen Gesellschaft des 19. Jahrhunderts*, Frankfurt am Main.

RUDOLPH, R. L. (1980a), 'Family Structure and Proto-industrialization in Russia', *The Journal of Economic History*, 40, 111–18.

RUDOLPH, R. L. (1980b), 'Social Structure and the Beginning of Austrian Economic Growth', *East Central Europe/L'Europe du Centre-Est*, 7, 207–24.

RUDOLPH, R. L. (1981), 'Light on the Dark Ages in Czech Economic History: The Work of Arnost Klíma', *East Central Europe/L'Europe du Centre-Est*, 9, 39–48.

RUDOLPH, R. L. (1983), 'Economic Revolution in Austria? The Meaning of 1848 in Austrian

Economic History', In John Komlos (ed.), *Essays on the Habsburg Economy*, New York, 165–82.

RUDOLPH, R. L. (1985), 'Agricultural Structure and Proto-Industrialization in Russia: Economic Development with Unfree Labor', *The Journal of Economic History*, **45**, 47–69.

RUDOLPH, R. L. (1991), 'The East European Peasant Household and the Beginnings of Industry: East Galicia, 1786–1914', In I. S. Koropeckyj (ed.), *Ukrainian Economic History: Interpretive Essays*, Cambridge, Mass., 338–82.

RUDOLPH, R. L. (1992), 'Structure de la famille, économie et systèmes d'héritage de la paysannerie polonaise aux XVIe–XVIIIe siècles: un modèle', In C. Kuklo (ed.), *Les modèles familiaux en Europe aux XVIe–XVIIIe siècles*, Bialystok, 41–48.

SABEAN, D. W. (1990), *Property, Production, and Family in Neckarhausen, 1700–1870*, Cambridge.

SEGALEN, M. (1986), *Historical Anthropology of the Family*, Cambridge.

SHANIN, T. (1972), *The Awkward Class: Political Sociology of Peasantry in a Developing Society: Russia 1910–1925*, Oxford.

THIRSK, J. (1961), 'Industry in the Countryside', In F. J. Fisher (ed.), *Essays in the Economic and Social History of Tudor and Stuart England*, Cambridge, 70–88.

TILLY, L. and J. W. SCOTT (1978), *Women, Work, and Family*, New York.

TUGAN-BARANOVSKII, M. I. (1922), *Russkaia fabrika v proshlom i nastoiashchem*, Moscow.

WALBY, S. (1990), *Theorizing Patriarchy*, Oxford and Cambridge.

WALL, R. (ed.) (1983), *Family Forms in Historic Europe*, Cambridge.

WILLIAMSON, J. G. (1984), 'Why Was British Growth So Slow During the Industrial Revolution?', *Journal of Economic History*, **44**, 687–712.

WOROBEC, C. D. (1991), *Peasant Russia: Family and Community in the Post-Emancipation Period*, Princeton.

WRIGLEY, E. A. and R. S. SCHOFIELD (1981), *The Population History of England, 1541–1871*, Cambridge, Mass.

Chapter 3

PEASANT AND NON-PEASANT FAMILY FORMS IN RELATION TO THE PHYSICAL ENVIRONMENT AND THE LOCAL ECONOMY

MICHAEL MITTERAUER

The territory of today's Austria seems well suited for a study of the dependency of rural family forms on their physical environment (see Fig. 1). There are great differences in soil and climate—and therefore also differing types of local economies. The prevailing terrain is mountainous. In the east-Alpine area we can find varying types of mountain-peasant economies. Due to the different forms of Alpine pasture, extremely high regions in the mountains are exploited, and the exploitation of woodland resources is of great importance in the Alpine area. The different mining regions have a very specific character. There are three main types of exploitation and processing, which influence the respective areas: salt mining districts, iron ore mining districts, and the districts where precious metals are mined. An entirely different type of economy than that in the Alpine zone can be found in the mountainous areas of the Waldviertel and the Mühlviertel north of the River Danube. Soil and climate favour flax growing in these regions. While the mountain peasants of the Alps are engaged in cattle-raising, the peasants of the plains of the sub-Alpine zone (*Alpenvorland*) specialize in grain-farming because of the favourable conditions of the physical environment. The same situation obtains in the east at the border of the Pannonic area. In some parts of the valley of the River Danube, in the so-called *Weinviertel* in Lower Austria, around the city of Vienna, in the Burgenland, and in eastern and southern Styria the conditions of the physical environment enable viniculture as a specialized form of single-crop farming. Thus very different economic regions adjoin each other in the area of research, and this forms a good basis for a comparison of the ecological conditions in which different family forms exist.

SOURCES

The historical sources are also well-suited for a study of family forms in relation to different economic areas in the territory of Austria. Many surviving lists contain detailed information on constellations of age and family roles in household communities and domestic groups, especially in the nineteenth, and sometimes even dating back to the seventeenth century. Such sources are

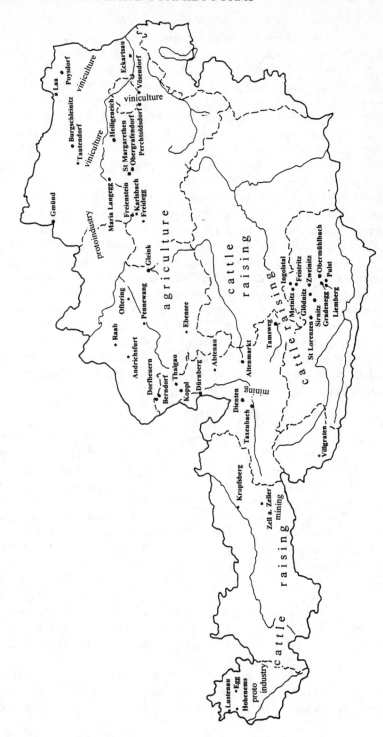

Figure 1: Locations of the investigated districts, Austria

available for almost all types of economic regions. A special feature of the Austrian census sources are serial listings—annual counts of persons living together in one household—which makes it possible in some cases to observe changes in household composition for six or seven decades. In recent years several hundred such census lists have been collected and interpreted in the Institute of Economic and Social History of the University of Vienna. Parts of this source material were made machine readable and can be used in the Vienna Data Base on European Family History (Ehmer, 1985; Held, 1982, p. 235; Schmidtbauer, 1983, p. 348; Mitterauer, 1986, p. 187; Eder, 1990, p. 10). The analytical results of this material form the basis for the present discussion, but complementary information comes from a type of source totally different from the ones mentioned above. Parallel to the collection of census type listings, a collection of autobiographies was organized at the Institute of Economic and Social History. To date, this collection has come to include more than 900 life stories, especially of persons from the rural milieu (Weber, 1987; 1990; Hämmerle, 1991). These autobiographies provide much interesting information on the topic of the family and labour, which permits generalizations to be drawn about the dependency of family forms on the local economy. Another type of source used in this article stands between the quantitative and qualitative kind. This is the so-called *Historische Topographien* (historical topographies) describing specific conditions of labour and the local economy, not from the point of view of the individual (as in the case of autobiographies), but from a collective view and including the characteristic economic features of a whole region.

THE ECOTYPE APPROACH

The theoretical approach, used in this article to discuss the relations between rural family forms and the conditions of their natural environment, is centred on the concept of peasant ecotypes as developed by the Scandinavian scholars of cultural anthropology. Orvar Löfgren defines ecotype as a pattern of resource exploitation within a given macro-economic framework (Löfgren, 1976, p. 100). In this view of the peasant economy, more than just a specific form of adaptation to the physical environment is seen. On the contrary, the model also considers forms of supra-regional division of labour, as reflected in the local economies. The diversity of possible modes of adaptation to a specific physical environment is brought into play, so that there is no danger of obtaining a static view. To avoid a static view, it is particularly important to try to integrate the ecotype concept into the history of rural family forms.

Compared with the ecosystem concept frequently used in historical studies, the ecotype concept has some clear advantages. The ecosystem concept was borrowed in the 1960s by neo-functionalistic anthropologists from biological models (Viazzo, 1989, p. 46). It focuses attention on patterns of functional interdependencies between human populations, social institutions, and the natural environment. For the purposes of analysis, an ecosystem must be closed. Because of this, its application to human ecology presents serious difficulties. As in the biological model of an ecosystem, also from an anthropological view the successful local population is one that adjusts its numbers in such a way as to maintain local resource stability. Thus the model over-emphasizes demographic questions. Another problematic point involves monocausal explanations of social institutions by reference to the environment, whereas the ecotype concept is more open to explanation by other factors.

In the history of the family, the notion of the peasant family economy is often used in too simple a way, especially in analytical traditions stemming from evolutionistic conceptions of family sociology. Since the mid-1970s, the theory of protoindustrialization has favoured such a view (Medick, 1976; 1977). In formulating the so-called protoindustrial family as a special type of family structure, some protagonists of this theory describe the peasant family as a homogeneous entity, contrasting it to the protoindustrial (Rosenbaum, 1978; Sieder, 1987). This is not, however, consistent with historical reality. Challenging all unilineal conceptions, the ecotype approach can help to demonstrate the great variety of different rural family forms and the great variety of alterations caused by economic changes in rural society. The process, which is the subject of protoindustrialization theory, has its place in an ecotype concept. The growth of the different branches of domestic industry is a very important process of economic change in rural areas—change that related to ecological conditions—but it is only one kind of change among many others.

A very important contribution of protoindustrialization theory to the history of the family was to focus attention on the family forms of non-peasant groups. This approach should be maintained and developed further. The ecotype concept of the Scandinavian cultural anthropologists also ascribes outstanding importance to non-peasant groups and their special economy based on marginal resources (Löfgren, 1976, p. 106). But it is difficult to distinguish between peasant and non-peasant groups in rural populations. In the Austrian area of research dealt with here, the evidence regarding this point is very diverse (Mitterauer, 1986, pp. 198, 240). On the one hand we find regions with a clear difference between peasants and cottagers: on the other, areas where distinctions are difficult to make. Different kinds of economy do not always correspond to different sizes of property, and for the most part, cottagers are forced to do non-agrarian work (Wopfner, 1954, p. 359; Mitterauer, 1981). Such differences between peasant and non-peasant work must be taken into account when elaborating rural ecotypes. In some cases an ecotype can be characterized by reference to only one type of production, as, for example, in the case of viniculture. In central European regions of viniculture, as a rule the whole population does the same kind of work (Landsteiner, 1990, p. 101; Mitterauer, 1986, p. 221). But in most cases it is necessary to characterize ecotypes by two or more economic activities, the one corresponding with the peasant population, the others with the non-peasant groups. For example, we can find an ecotype of cattle-raising by mountain peasants in combination with mining or with woodcutting, or another ecotype with the focus on grain-harvesting connected with small-scale iron industry (Table 1). Even formulated in such a complicated way, these categories characterize only the dominant mode of economy relevant to the family forms of the majority, but not for the whole population of the region. The group of the rural craftsmen supplying local demand always occupies a special position—the bakers, millers, butchers, innkeepers, tailors and shoemakers. Their family forms are also influenced by modes of production in a specific way, but individually, and not collectively, as it would be ecotype (Mitterauer, 1986, p. 284).

The concept of ecotypes is based on the premise that the local dominance of different modes of production is dependent on the exploitation of specific natural resources of the physical environment. This dependency on nature, however, varies greatly. Viniculture, for example, in the north of the Alps is possible only in a limited area with very special conditions such as a specific sandy soil (the so-called *Löß*), suitable slopes, and arid climate. Where the environment is suitable for viniculture, this form of single-crop farming predominated, because of its high profit relative to all other kinds of agriculture as well as cattle-raising. This ecotype is dependent on nature in an extreme way and is not transferable to areas with other conditions of physical environment. The dependency is more complicated if the kinds of soil exploitation are connected with different steps of subsequent industrial treatment. For example, we can find textile domestic industry in the territory of Austria mostly in areas with good conditions for flax growing. As for viniculture, so also for flax growing the conditions of habitat are of great importance for the quality of the product (Marks, 1970, p. 19; Vonwiller, 1970, p. 37). The conditions for flax were especially favourable in the regions of heavy precipitation in the Rhine Valley and in the Bregenzer Wald in Vorarlberg (Fitz, 1985, p. 35). The linen merchants of St Gallen in Switzerland insisted that for products of high value only yarn from that region was to be used. The ecotype at first was only characterized by flax cultivation and by spinning, the first step of processing. In later times linen weaving also became customary in this area. Finally, cotton weaving was introduced. In this manner the region developed into the most important area of domestic industry in the territory of modern Austria. The production of cotton, by contrast, had no immediate connection to the physical environment. Although one can characterize an ecotype by reference to a mode of production, dependency on the natural environment is more complex if there is a transition from domestic industry to the peddling of wares so produced. In Austria, we can find this phenomenon especially in areas where mining had flourished, and where after the decline of mining, people had to look for new sources of income. In the Defereggen Valley in the Eastern Tyrol for example, men started to produce dishes made from the wood of the cembra pine, which is widespread in the

Table 1

District	Province	Census Year	Dominant Characteristic of Economic Structure	Inhabitants	Servants %	Lodgers %
Pulst	Kärnten	1803	cattle raising	770	44.0	13.3
Ingolsthal	Kärnten	1757	,,	374	39.0	15.0
Metnitz (Umland)	Kärnten	1757	,,	2,217	36.0	5.0
Liemberg	Kärnten	1757	,,	195	34.4	9.2
Taxenbach	Salzburg	1799	cattle raising and timber	1,430	34.1	15.0
		1622		1,273	24.6	12.9
St Lorenzen-Reichenau	Kärnten	1757	cattle raising	820	33.9	7.6
Feistritz	Kärnten	1757	,,	738	33.6	5.0
Obermühlbach	Kärnten	1757	,,	1,386	33.0	20.0
Sirnitz-Glödnitz	Kärnten	1757	,,	1,460	31.8	10.5
Andrichsfurt	Oberöst.	1813	large-scale agriculture	820	30.3	6.0
		1823		806	29.1	5.0
		1833		811	29.4	5.0
		1842		748	27.4	7.7
		1853		698	27.3	6.0
		1863		702	27.7	8.4
		1873		650	28.5	5.8
		1883		648	27.4	4.2
		1896		632	29.7	6.4
		1909		622	22.7	7.5
		1947		539	14.1	5.8
Raab (Umland)	Oberöst.	1816	agriculture	1,841	27.4	11.2
		1834		1,882	24.4	9.4

Table 1. cont. (1)

District	Province	Census Year	Dominant Characteristic of Economic Structure	Inhabitants	Servants %	Lodgers %
Zweinitz	Kärnten	1760	cattle raising	1,202	29.4	3.3
		1770		679	27.7	10.3
		1786		608	22.0	10.4
		1798		641	24.8	9.0
		1811		676	24.9	6.8
Altenmarkt (Umland)	Salzburg	1755	cattle raising, timber	1,725	25.3	8.0
		1733		2,002	23.2	8.7
		1762		1,978	22.8	8.6
Gradenegg	Kärnten	1757	cattle raising	311	25.1	6.1
Abtenau	Salzburg	1790	cattle raising, timber	3,916	22.4	15.5
		1632		4,112	12.7	19.1
Vösendorf	Niederöst.	1695/6		1,146	21.6	
Oferting	Oberöst.	1703				
St Margareten a. d. Sierning	Niederöst.	1887	large-scale agriculture	785	20.9	11.1
		1810		506	17.2	3.6
		1831		687	16.0	4.7
		1851		717	19.7	9.9
		1871		763	20.2	8.5
Koppl	Salzburg	1805		538	20.5	6.4
		1647		645	14.3	20.3
Thalgau	Salzburg	1750		2,570	19.6	8.8
		1648		2,949	13.4	11.7

Table 1. cont. (2)

District	Province	Census Year	Dominant Characteristic of Economic Structure	Inhabitants	Servants %	Lodgers %
Freienstein	Niederöst.	1695/6		1,122	16.8	3.5
Gleink	Oberöst.	1856	especially fertile grain	922	15.7	27.9
		1799	region, some pasture	1,054	15.2	20.1
		1807	and cattle raising	1,018	14.6	21.6
		1818		1,104	14.9	27.1
		1828		1,111	15.6	29.5
		1840		1,091	15.5	29.8
Gericht Kropfsberg	Tirol	1637	cattle raising, mining	8,304	16.4	high
Eckartsau	Niederöst.	1766		1,324	15.5	16.6
Dorfbeuern	Salzburg	1862	agriculture, many cottagers	804	15.5	3.2
		1772		747	13.3	6.1
		1648		988	10.1	5.7
Karlsbach	Niederöst.	1695/6		1,140	15.1	1.5
Berndorf	Salzburg	1649		1,783	15.0	20.4
Dienten	Salzburg	1711	cattle raising,	677	14.5	18.0
		1756	woodworking, mining,	516	12.6	13.8
Perchtoldsdorf	Niederöst.	1754	wine-growing,	1,685	14.3	high
		1857	strongly commercial	2,930	10.3	–
Zell am Ziller	Tirol	1779	cattle raising, mining	2,581	13.7	26.8
Freidegg	Niederöst.	1695/6	peddling	1,599	13.4	24.0

Table 1. cont. (3)

District	Province	Census Year	Dominant Characteristic of Economic Structure	Inhabitants	Servants %	Lodgers %
Tautendorf	Niederöst.	1835		795	12.1	8.4
		1805		766	11.4	4.2
		1815		728	11.1	8.7
		1825		750	11.9	6.5
		1844		863	7.4	11.9
		1855		897	7.5	7.7
		1864		860	7.2	6.4
		1874		790	9.6	8.4
Heiligeneich	Niederöst.	1800	wine growing,	1,341	11.9	18.1
		1790	agriculture, strongly	937	10.5	24.9
		1820	commercial	1,547	11.1	14.0
		1840		1,672	11.5	15.3
		1853		1,715	11.0	15.8
		1874		1,354	10.3	10.9
		1884		1,549	9.7	9.7
Maria Langegg	Niederöst.	1808	mixed economy,	543	10.4	12.1
		1788	woodcutting	530	7.9	11.3
		1798		470	10.4	6.7
		1818		556	8.8	10.9
		1828		616	7.9	15.9
		1840		523	9.0	15.5
		1848		801	10.6	24.3
		1856		639	9.1	14.2
		1875		625	5.8	23.7
Villgraten	Osttirol	1781	cattle raising	3,420	10.8	5.6

Table 1. cont. (4)

District	Province	Census Year	Dominant Characteristic of Economic Structure	Inhabitants	Servants %	Lodgers %
Poysdorf	Niederöst.	1890	wine-growing, market district	3,113	10.1	–
Obergrafendorf	Niederöst.	1787	textile industry with home spinning, trade in central market district, agriculture in surrounding area	1,980	9.9	14.0
Burgschleinitz	Niederöst.	1876	small peasantry	831	9.0	6.4
		1802	agriculture, stone	611	4.1	4.1
		1822	quarrying and stone	770	7.5	5.1
		1839	cutting	857	7.6	5.8
		1862		847	6.7	6.3
Laa	Niederöst.	1867		2,161	7.8	
Dürrnberg	Salzburg	1647	salt mines, tiny cottages tied to agriculture	510	6.9	18.5
Ebensee	Oberöst.	1809	woodcutting, salt	857	5.8	high
		1829	cottage industry.	1,069	5.9	high
		1848	woodworking	1,228	4.8	high
		1864		1,185	3.5	high
Gmünd (Umland)	Niederöst.	1840	home weaving.	1,543	5.1	22.0
		1801	agriculture	1,054	4.9	10.5
		1807		1,140	3.7	9.7
		1818		1,166	2.7	7.5
		1828		1,348	4.3	14.6
Lustenau	Vorarlberg	1837	textile industry	2,980	0.5	–
Hohenems	Vorarlberg	1837	textile industry	3,436	0.2	–
Egg	Vorarlberg	1754	textile industry	1,194	0.2	–

Alpine mountains (Kröll-Stemberger, 1985, p. 192; Wopfner, 1954, p. 344). Later they themselves became pedlars of these products. Even later the peasants of Defereggen bought little carpets made of cattle hair, which were produced in a valley nearby, and travelled to different markets all over Europe to sell them. Finally they specialized in peddling straw hats made in Krain (Slovenia) and clocks from Switzerland. A similar shift from selling of local products to trade in others can be observed in the Zillertal in Northern Tyrol, which was suitable for the pedlar's trade in the same way as Defereggen was by its geographical position near mountain passes (B. Weber, 1837, p. 528; Troger, 1954, p. 43; Wopfner, 1954, p. 393). This process also began with the decline of mining. The most important article which the men of Zillertal peddled was at first the so-called *Mithridat*, a medicine or drug made from different substances of Alpine herbs and produced in the valley itself. Then they also sold the so-called *Steinöl*, a mineral oil made in the neighbourhood. Finally, the trade of these mountaineers included gloves and canary birds. Although these different kinds of peddling had no direct connections with the exploitation of natural resources, we can call this form of local economy an ecotype.

It is worth considering whether we should define the ecotype concept in a wider sense to include also other factors related to the exploitation of natural resources. For example, rural settlement patterns are influenced by ecology as well as by economy. But it is not obvious that in settlement patterns economic needs are determinate. For example, in some areas of the sub-Alpine region that are characterized by isolated farmsteads, we can frequently find little cottages nearby (Ortmayr, 1984, p. 107; 1986, p. 341). Probably they were originally used as dwellings for day-labourers working on the corresponding farmstead. They could maintain this function for a long time, but conversely they would lose it in times of declining demand for day-labourers. Perhaps the cottage changed its function and became the dwelling of a rural craftsman. Such examples show that sometimes settlement patterns reflect the economic needs of earlier times. By their permanence, rural settlement patterns continue to have a long-term influence. They are also relevant to family forms, but it is better to define them as a special case separated from the local economy, because they do not operate in the same way. This thought can also be applied to the size of holdings, proprietary rights, or rules of inheritance. They all are connected very closely with different modes of production. But it would expand the notion of ecotype too much if we included all these factors. The concept would lose its value as an instrument of interpretation in a comparative analysis of the condition in which family forms exist.

ECOTYPES, LABOUR ORGANIZATION AND FAMILY FORMS

The decisive link in the causal connection between ecotypes and rural family forms is the demand created by the organization of labour. The needs of labour organization determine the structure of the family (Mitterauer, 1986, p. 255).

They play an essential role in rural family economies by influencing decisions about whether farmhands are taken in, whether children stay at home or leave when they have reached a certain age, and in the case of widowhood, whether remarriage is economically necessary. In an indirect way, the labour force demand of the family forms also influences the structure of households not organized as family economies, especially those of the cottagers. The needs of labour organization determine not only family structure, but also family relations. Power balance within and other aspects of family life are influenced strongly by forms of cooperation within the family. Family forms are more than just a number of people living together in one household, as we can find them in census lists. They also include specific patterns of personal relationships, which are influenced partly by labour relationships (Ortmayr, 1986, p. 390).

With respect to additional labour force demand, we can differentiate between two main types of rural societies: those employing farmhands and those employing day-labourers (*Gesindegesellschaften* and *Taglöhnergesellschaften*) (Mitterauer, 1986, p. 198). The first type is characterized by full integration of additional labour into the family for one year or more. Farmhands participate in all activities of family life. The latter type is characterized by short contracts. There is no full family integration. If the day-labourers dwell in the same house as the peasant for whom they work, they usually have the status of lodgers (*Inwohner*) and are members of the domestic group. The relationship, however, is not as close and as personal as that involving farmhands. Nowhere can both types—'farmhand societies' and 'day-labourer societies'—be found in their pure form. They appear always as a mixture, in which one or the other group is more dominant. Combining types of additional labour with rural ecotypes, we can see a remarkable correspondence between family economies with farmhands and cattle-raising, on the one hand, and day-labourers and viniculture, on the other. The different ecotypes of grain-farming have a position between these two (see Table 1).

The functional explanation of the correspondence between cattle-raising and family economies with farmhands is to be found in the specific requirements for handling cattle. Permanent workers are necessary to take care of the animals. In cattle-raising there are many activities requiring continuous work: feeding, milking, and cleaning the animals and the stables. The work is carried out daily and is performed not only during the daytime but sometimes also at night, as in cases of illness among animals or when cows are calving (Walleitner, 1948, p. 15). In cattle-raising a sound knowledge of the peculiarities of each animal is very important (Waß, 1988, p. 28; Passrugger, 1989, p. 127). Milkers must know the cow very well to get the best yield. Taking care of horses correctly also requires the long experience produced by continuous work (Ortmayr, 1986, p. 379). On the other hand, in cattle-raising there are no seasonal peaks that cause a sharp additional demand for labour. Only hay making requires more workers for a short time.

The ups and downs of labour demand during the working year seem to be the main reasons why grain-farming peasants need not only farmhands but also day-labourers (Platzer, 1904, pp. 96, 266; Mitterauer, 1986, p. 213). Because of the differing amount of obligatory work at harvest time and during winter months, it is reasonable and economical to have permanent workers occasionally. The labour force demand in viniculture is even more irregular during the year than that of grain-farming. Therefore, it is not rational to have farmhands as permanent workers. It is for this reason that workers not integrated with families are the dominant type in vine-growing areas (Landsteiner, 1990, p. 107).

In addition to these ways of coping with the labour needs of the family economy, there is another interesting alternative to be found in the Austrian research area. In some Alpine valleys, labour force demands are met by retaining relatives in the family (Wopfner, 1931; 1932; Mitterauer, 1986, p. 209). In these regions siblings remain on the farmstead and are sometimes allowed to marry, producing complex family forms. The reason for the development of large families of this kind is not a specific kinship or marriage ideology. There is no structural analogy here to the *zadruga* of south-eastern Europe. A more probable explanation of this phenomenon can be found in manorial conditions. Another cause, in these upland communities, might be the difficulty of getting servants from the lowlands. We know from autobiographies that it was very difficult and sometimes nearly impossible for lowland-people to do the work of mountain peasants, while there were no similar obstacles in the other direction. This factor can explain the downward migration frequently found in Alpine areas (Viazzo, 1989, p. 41; Mitterauer, 1986, p. 303). Whatever the cause, these examples suggest that there is no one-way relationship between the ecotype of mountain area cattle-raising and a specific pattern of the peasant family.

In comparison with extended or complex family forms, the model of the family economy that makes use of farmhands is more flexible, because the labour force can be balanced every year. If children grow up and become fit to work, farmhands have to go. If adult children leave the house, new farmhands are taken in. (As an example of this replacement of servants by adult children and vice versa, see Fig. 2 and Gruber, 1984, pp. 220, 251.) Such a balance by age and sex is not possible in families with a continuous labour force. The need for a fixed stock of permanent workers is especially high for farmsteads in detached settlements. In villages it is easier to get help from neighbours in an exchange arrangement. Thus there are fewer farmhands in areas where villages are the predominant form of settlement.

Ecotypes involving the work of farmhands affect rural lower strata less than ecotypes involving the work of day-labourers. Societies of mountain peasants sometimes have only a small group of cottagers, mostly rural craftsmen (Mitterauer, 1986, p. 248). A strong lower class develops there only if non-agrarian income is available from, for example, woodcutting or mining, which

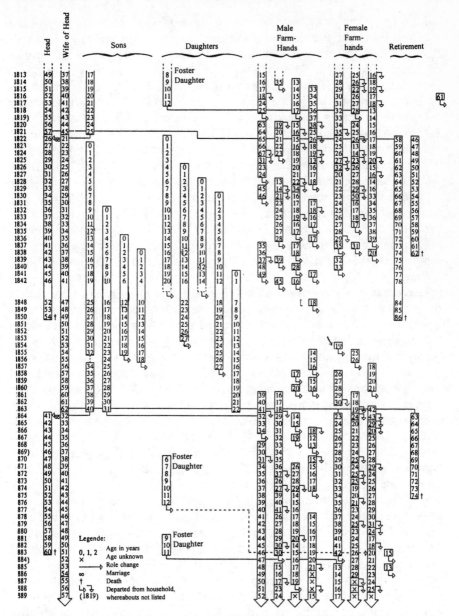

Figure 2: Developmental Cycle of the Hof Blingansing Household, Parish Andrichs-furt, Upper Austria

very often occur together. An extremely high percentage of lower-class persons can be found in silver or gold mining regions. Iron mining, on the other hand, tended to integrate farming and mining, at least in the territory of research. The labour force working in iron mining and the subsequent processing of the iron ore was sometimes integrated in very large households or house communities (Mitterauer, 1974, p. 286). In Austrian iron-mining districts the so-called *Radmeister* employed miners, smelters, woodcutters and carters. All or some of these groups lived in *Radmeister* houses. Similar structures were to be found in the homes of the so-called *Hammermeister*. These *Hammermeister* were the owners of big hammer mills employing many workers, who regularly lived together with the Meister. Such mills were a type of rural handicraft very closely connected to the ecotype of iron mining. This example shows that rural handicrafts supplying supra-regional markets could produce very different family forms. The family economies of the *Hammermeister* with many workers and farmhands provide a good contrast with the family economies of rural textile industry working mostly without additional labour.

In contrast to cattle-raising mountain peasants, the grain-farming peasants on the plains needed a corresponding group of agricultural day-labourers. There was a system of reciprocity: the independent cottagers or the lodgers living in the farmstead or in a little house nearby were required to help the peasants if they needed workers for a short time, especially during the harvest (Ortmayr, 1984, p. 111; 1986, p. 341). The peasants, on the other hand, loaned cottagers draught animals, tools and also dwellings and land. The farmhands of the peasants were recruited mostly from the children of the cottagers and lodgers (Ortmayr, 1984, p. 127; 1986, p. 333; Mitterauer, 1986, p. 229; Th. Weber, 1984, p. 33; 1985, p. 14; Gremel, 1983; Kreuztragen, 1984, pp. 18, 67; Waß, 1985, p. 23). Through this there were many personal connections between peasant and non-peasant families, sometimes with family-like aspects.

Because of the labour obligations of peasants, rural lower-class families were never fully occupied with one task. Their activities included different kinds of wage work, industrial production, and cultivation of their own plots. The economy of these groups was characterized by variable constellations of mixed earnings (Ortmayr, 1984, p. 107; Mitterauer, 1981, p. 331). None of these activities made it necessary to take on farmhands or other types of servants. Only in cases when handicraft work predominated was it necessary to have apprentices or journeymen in the house. It made no difference whether the family economy of such a craftsman supplied a supra-regional market. But in the textile domestic industry using the putting-out system, we can find very different constellations in the area of research. There are protoindustrial zones without any farmhands, apprentices, journeymen or other workers in a servant-like position (Fitz, 1985, p. 46). On the other hand, sometimes weavers in protoindustrial areas employed many apprentices (Mitterauer,

1986, p. 232). Due to this variety, the picture of the protoindustrial family without any additional labour should not be generalized. Figure 3 gives an example of a rural weaver in the Waldviertel taking in an apprentice for only a short time, similar to his old father who continued working as a weaver in retirement.

Regardless of market relations, the same rule applies to all rural handicrafts: other than in peasant farmsteads, these kinds of family economies feel no pressure to balance the labour force. Children leaving the house are not replaced by other workers, and neither is there any replacement of journeymen by grown-up children. We cannot find any effort to balance the labour force in line with the developmental cycle of the craftsman family.

THE FAMILY AS A WORK-GROUP

The presence of farmhands is a good indicator that the family has the character of a work-group. In households which take in female or male farmhands, there are not enough relatives to do all the work. The character of rural families as work-groups differs, according to ecotypes, in the peasant and non-peasant groups. In a simplified way, one might say that in all types of peasant families there exists a certain labour relationship between the majority of the family members and all of its members. The situation is different in the sub- or non-peasant groups. There are strong differences according to ecotypes. On the one hand, a dominant mode of local economy can cause the total disintegration of family ties; on the other hand there can also be family cooperation which is stronger than in peasant households. A disintegrating effect is caused by such ecotypes as peddling, itinerant work, transport, and also by outdoor activities such as mining or woodcutting. Pedlars might sometimes be away from home for periods of more than one year (Wopfner, 1954, p. 392). Rural wage workers employed in the building trade left their families early in springtime and returned in autumn (Fitz, 1985, p. 30). Some agricultural workers wandered from the plains up to the mountains in response to the different periods of harvesting and were absent for many weeks (Gremel, 1983, p. 16). A similar pattern existed among the so-called *Störhandwerker*, itinerant rural craftsmen who went from farmstead to farmstead, working in each for a few days (Eder, 1990, p. 91; Waß, 1985, p. 41). Miners and woodcutters were absent for shorter times (Mitterauer, 1974, p. 240; Waß, 1985, p. 190). Nevertheless, these forms of labour affected fatherless families, because in most cases it was the father who did outdoor work, sometimes together with adult sons. In the area of research there was virtually no female outside work comparable to these forms of male work (B. Weber, 1837, pp. 528, 531). An interesting case of outdoor child labour involving long-distance travel was the so-called *Schwabengängerei* in the Tyrol and Vorarlberg (Uhlig, 1978; Fitz, 1985, p. 31). Children and young people of rural families went to southern Germany to work as cowherds or as nursemaids. Also, the fathers of these children had to work outside the country in

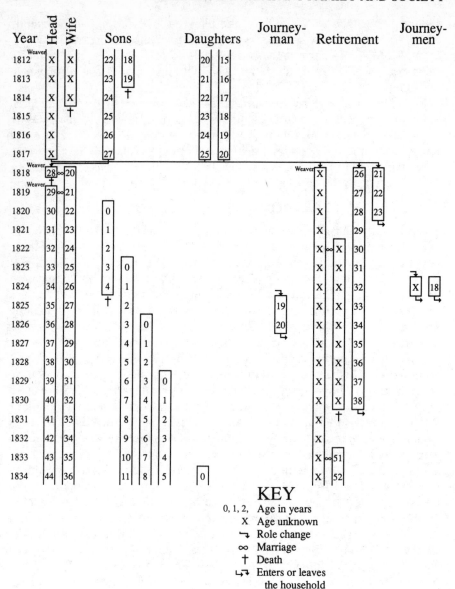

KEY

0, 1, 2,	Age in years
X	Age unknown
↱	Role change
∞	Marriage
†	Death
↳↴	Enters or leaves the household

Figure 3: Family life-course of a protoindustrial weaver, Böhmzeil, Waldviertel, Lower Austria

summertime, and so the mother remained at home with the infants, cultivating the family's land. The whole family was not reunited until autumn. It is clear that, in such areas, the rise of rural domestic industry was an important change. Now, the family could stay together the whole year, especially if it was involved in the textile industry that intensified family life by providing the family with work in the same place. If all family members participated in the textile industry by weaving, spinning, or reeling, family cooperation was more intensive than in peasant family economies. In the area of research, this type of family work in the textile industry was neither unique nor predominant. In many cases protoindustrialization concerned only the women of a certain region, as, for example, the women of salt miners and silver miners, and also of smallholding peasants who themselves worked only in agriculture. In other cases men helped in the textile industry only in the winter months (Fitz, 1985, pp. 73, 194; Mitterauer, 1986, p. 259; 1989, p. 874). In these cases the family was a protoindustrial work-unit for only a given period. But there were also activities in domestic industry performed exclusively or predominantly by men. In the textile domestic industry, machine embroidery was such a male activity (Fitz, 1985, p. 62). Such pluralism of activities is to be expected in a discussion of protoindustrial family economy.

Gender-specific division of labour in rural family economies is important in several ways with regard to the interrelationship between ecotype and family form. Family composition is dependent on ecotype conditions of labour division. Where the work domain of men and women is strictly separated, a widowed person has to remarry quickly. There is economic pressure to have family role completion (*Rollenergänzungszwang*). This pressure is absent if male and female work roles are balanced. An ecotype characterized by strict separation of work roles can be found among the mountain peasantry. Certain important tasks cannot be taken over by women: bringing in mountain hay, for example, is men's work (Sint, 1986, p. 181). This work is very dangerous and needs a kind of training that girls do not receive. Such tasks of the family economy cannot be handled by the widow of a mountain peasant and she has to remarry if there is no adult son or male farmhand to help. The situation is completely different in the family economy of winegrowers. The widow is able to manage the work without any partner. The work roles are more balanced in viniculture. The woman can accomplish nearly all labour tasks. Households of widows can be found frequently in wine growing regions. The situation is similar in the textile domestic industry.

Another important problem concerning the relationship between ecotypes, family forms, and sexual division of labour concerns gender roles and power balance in marriage. Protoindustrialization theory assumes that levelling work tasks in the family economy means levelling gender roles (Medick, 1977, p. 136; Sieder, 1987, p. 90). As has been said before, protoindustry did not create equal work tasks for men and women in all cases in our area of research. If there is any demonstrable relationship between equal tasks in work and equality in gender roles (Mitterauer, 1989, p. 879), that model should be transferable to other ecotypes. Perhaps there are analogies in viniculture. We can find some hints in our area of research that in vine-growing regions patriarchy was less strong than in cattle-raising regions. It is possible that this could be explained by more balanced work roles. The different approaches of protoindustrialization theory could be tested by the example of viniculture because there are many structural analogies between the vine-growing economy and rural domestic industry.

OTHER INFLUENCES OF ECOTYPES ON FAMILY FORMS

The dependence of family forms on ecotypes, mediated through labour organization, is very clear. With respect to other factors there is much less certainty. Surely we have to take into account mediation by dwelling conditions. As we have seen, there were connections between dwelling types and labour organization. Wherever rural wage work developed in our area of research, we can find, on the one hand, day-labourers living as cottagers, and, on the other, day-labourers living as lodgers who have to fulfil working obligations instead of paying rents (Ortmayr, 1984, p. 105; Gremel, 1983, p. 15). The number of cottagers and lodgers is extremely high and corresponds to such ecotypes as mining, viniculture and textile domestic industry that use the putting-out system. All three modes of production can be characterized as capitalistic going back to medieval times (Mitterauer, 1974, p. 273; Land-steiner, 1990, p. 108; Fitz, 1985, p. 35). All three created a very early highly developed money economy, through which they mobilized the market for housing and landed property. The ownership of cottages particularly changed more frequently (Sieder and Mitterauer, 1983, p. 312). Transmission of property by inheritance became rare, and neolocality became the rule. The highest mobility was in the group of lodgers not possessing land. The consequence of this mobilization was a trend towards neolocal residence among the rural lower classes, which contrasted sharply with the patrilocal patterns of well-to-do peasants. As a consequence of the shorter stay of the family in the same dwelling, family constellations with coresident parents or siblings became less frequent in cottager families than in peasant families. Lodger families were even more unstable because they changed dwellings. Often a child was separated from the family when there was a change of dwelling. Occasionally the result was the disintegration of the whole family.

Sometimes the dependence of family forms on modes of production is seen to be mediated by generative behaviour. Protoindustrialization theory places particular stress on the influence of rural domestic industry on demographic development (Medick, 1977, pp. 120, 161). The connection is established, on the one hand, by the interest protoindustrial family economies have in a large number of children as a means of enlarging the family's labour force; and on the other hand, by a lower marriage age which is made possible by earning power at an earlier age. With respect to the territory of Austria, it can be said that there is no hint of a close connection between the value of children for the family economy and a larger number of children, even in protoindustrial regions (Mitterauer, 1986, p. 300). An immediate dependency of generative behaviour on ecotypes seems to exist in another way. Sometimes fertility differs very clearly between neighbouring upland and lowland communities (Troger, 1954, p. 75; Mitterauer, 1986, p. 303). As discussed earlier, it was very difficult for mountain peasants to get additional labour from immigrants because of the difficult nature of their work. Maybe the high fertility of communities located at high altitudes is a reaction to this difficulty. Fernand Braudel characterized mountains as *fabriques d'hommes à l'usage d'autrui*. The need for high levels of self-reproduction because of the problem of getting sufficient labour can provide an explanation of this much discussed phenomenon of Alpine historical demography (Viazzo, 1989, p. 91).

In an analysis of the condition in which different family forms arise, we have to mention that there are clear limits to the interpretative value of the ecotype approach. Two examples will illustrate this point. With respect to the rural inheritance patterns, the only correspondence to an ecotype can be found in wine-growing regions. In Austrian territory, in nearly all the areas where viniculture is conducted on the basis of single-crop farming there is partible inheritance, although in the surrounding areas impartible inheritance prevails (Kretschmer, 1965; Feigl, 1967, p. 167). Viniculture enables a family to live within a very small holding. Partible inheritance is very rare elsewhere in the area of our research. This pattern predominates only in the extreme east in the Burgenland and in the extreme west—in the western parts of the Tyrol and in Vorarlberg—in both cases as an extension of large areas of partible inheritance outside Austria (Kretschmer, 1965). These legal conditions have a strong influence on the family and cannot be attributed to economic factors. In adjacent regions there may be the same ecotype but a different rule of inheritance. Probably the historic cause of differing inheritance patterns in regions with the same ecotype is the manorial framework, which stipulates transmission to one heir in one region and equal division in another (Feigl, 1967, p. 161). Another legal factor originally created by the manor, and of great importance for family forms, is the institution of retirement (*Altenteil, Ausgedinge*) (Schmidt, 1920; Held, 1982). No clear correspondence can be found between retirement patterns and ecotypes. For example, in Carinthia the retirement of old peasants is absent in the plains as well as in the mountains, but in the Waldviertel, in Lower Austria, retirement appears not only in peasant families but also in the families of protoindustrial weavers. This element of family life exerts its influence by other means than through ecotypes.

CONCLUSION

The ecotype approach is of relatively high value for interpreting the differences in family forms in our area of research. Perhaps the influence of economic conditions was stronger there because certain non-economic factors were absent that determine family forms elsewhere. In this context it is essential to understand that there were no rules of kinship strictly limiting the development of family forms. This can be seen when comparing the area of our research with adjacent regions. In areas of Southeastern Europe, for example, patrilineal complex families were very widespread in former times (Mitterauer, 1981; Mitterauer and Kagan, 1976, p. 128). The needs of rural production had to be met by family groups assembled on the basis of agnatic kinship ties. By comparison, in our research area there was the possibility of greater variety in family composition. Even taking in of farmhands provided more flexibility. In sum, the different ways in which family forms depend on ecotypes, as discussed here, have to be considered within the framework of structural conditions that open a wide range of adaptations to economic needs.

References

EDER, FRANZ (1990), *Geschlechtsproportion und Arbeitsorganisation im Lande Salzburg*, Vienna.

EHMER, JOSEF (1985), 'The Vienna Data Base on European Family History', In E. A. Allen (ed.), *Data Bases in the Humanities and Social Sciences*, Osprey, 113–116.

EHMER, JOSEF and MICHAEL MITTERAUER (eds.) (1986), *Familienstruktur und Arbeitsorganisation in ländlichen Gesellschaften*, Vienna.

FEIGL, HELMUT (1967), 'Bäuerliches Erbrecht und Erbewohnunheiten in Niederösterreich', *Jahrbuch fur Landeskunde von Niederösterreich*, NF 37, 161–83.

FITZ, ARNO J. (1985), *Die Frühindustrialisierung Vorarlbergs und ihre Auswirkungen auf die Familienstruktur*, Dornbirn.

GREMEL, MARIA (1983), *Mit neun Jahren im Dienst. Mein Leben im Stübl und am Bauernhof 1900–1930*, Vienna.

GRUBER, BEATUS (1984), 'Kindheit und Jugend in vorindustriellen Hausgemeinschaften', In Hubert Ch. Ehalt (ed.), *Geschichte von unten*, Vienna, 217–57.

HÄMMERLE, CHRISTA (1991), 'Les Archives "Recits de vie" à Vienne', In *Cahiers de semiotique textuelle 20 (Archives Autobiographiques. Publié sous le direction de Philippe Lejeune)*, Paris, **10**, 103–13.

HELD, THOMAS (1982), 'Rural Retirement Arrangements in Seventeenth to Nineteenth-Century Austria: A Cross-Community Analysis', *Journal of Family History*, 7, 227–54.

KRETSCHMER, JOSEPH BENEDIKT (1965), 'Bäuerliches Erbrecht', *Kommentar zum österreichischen Volkskundeatlas*, 2/17, Vienna.

KREUZTRAGEN (1984), Vienna.

KRÖLL, HEINZ and GERT STEMBERGER (1985), *Defereggen. Eine Landschaft in Tirol*, Vienna.

LANDSTEINER, ERICH (1990), 'Weinbau und Gesellschaft in Mitteleuropa', In Helmut Feigl and Willibald Rosner (eds.), *Probleme des niederösterreichen Weinbaus in Vergangenheit und Gegenwart*, Vienna, 99–139.

LÖFGREN, ORVAR (1976), 'Peasant Ecotypes: Problems in the Comparative Study of Ecological Adaptation', *Ethnologia Scandinavica*, 1976, 100–115.

MARKS, ALFRED (1970), 'Leinengewerbe und Leinenhandel in Oberösterreich bis zum die Zeit Maria Theresias', In *Webereimuseum Haslach, Oberösterreich*, Linz, 175.

MEDICK, HANS (1976), 'Zur strukturellen Funktion von Haushalt und Familie im Übergang von der traditionellen Agrargesellschaft zum industriellen Kapitalismus', In Werner Conze (ed.), *Sozialgeschichte der Familie in der Neuzeit Europas*, Stuttgart, 254–82.

MEDICK, HANS (1977), 'Die Proto-industrielle Familienwirtschaft' and 'Strukturen und Funktion der Bevölkerungsentwicklung im proto-industriellen System' In Peter Kriedte, Hans Medick and Jürgen Schlumbohm (eds.), *Industrialisierung vor der Industrialisierung*, Göttingen, 90–154 and 155–93.

MITTERAUER, MICHAEL (1974), 'Produktionsweise, Siedlungsstruktur und Sozialformen im österreichischen Montanwesen des Mittelalters und der frühen Meuzeit', In Michael Mitterauer (ed.), *Österreichisches Montanwesen*, Vienna, 234–315.

MITTERAUER, MICHAEL (1981a), 'Komplexe Familienformen', *Ethnologia Europaea*, **12**, 47–86.

MITTERAUER, MICHAEL (1981b), 'Lebenstormen und Lebensverhältnisse ländlicher Unterschichten', In Herbert Matis (ed.), *Von der Glückseligkeit des Staates*, Berlin, 315–38.

MITTERAUER, MICHAEL (1986) 'Formen ländlicher Familienwirtschaft. Historische Ökotypen und familiale Arbeitsorganisation in österreichischen Raum', In Joseph Ehmer and Michael Mitterauer (eds.), *Famlienstruktur und Arbietsorganisation in ländlichen Gesellschaften*. Vienna, 185–324.

MITTERAUER, MICHAEL (1989), 'Geschlechtsspezifische Arbeitsteilung und Geschlechterrollen in ländlichen Gesellschaften Mitteleuropas', In Jochen Marttin and Renate Zoepffel (eds.), *Aufgaben, Rollen, und Räume von Frau und Mann*, Vol. 2., Freiburg im Brg, 819–914.

MITTERAUER, MICHAEL and ALEXANDER KAGAN (1976), 'Russian and Central European Family Structure', *Journal of Family History*, **4**, 257–84.

ORTMAYR, NORBERT (1984), 'Beim Bauern im Dienst. Zur Sozialgeschichte des ländlichen Gesindes in der ersten Republick', In Hubert Ch. Ehalt (ed.), *Geschichte von unten*, Vienna, 95–141.

ORTMAYR, NORBERT (1986), 'Ländliches Gesinde in Oberösterreich 1918–1938', In Josef Ehmer and Michael Mitterauer (eds.), *Familienstruktur und Arbeitsorganisation in ländlichen Gesellschaften*, Vienna, 325–60.

PASSRUGGER, BARBARA (1989), *Hartes Bort. Aus dem Leben einer Bergbäuerin*, Vienna.

PLATZER, JOHANN (1819), *Das Herzogtum Salzburg*, Linz.

ROSENBAUM, HEIDI (1978), *Formen der Familie*, Frankfurt.

SCHMIDT, KARL (1920), *Gutsübergabe und Ausgedinge. Eine agrarpolitische Untersuchung mit besonderer Berücksichtigung der Alpen- und Sudetenländer*, Vienna.

SCHMIDTBAUER, PETER (1983), 'The Changing Household: Austrian Household Structures from the Seventeenth to the Early Twentieth Century', In Richard Wall, Jean Robin and Peter Laslett (eds.), *Family Forms in Historic Europe*, Cambridge, 247–378.

SIEDER, REINHARD (1987), *Sozialgeschichte der Familie*, Frankfurt am Main.

SIEDER, REINHARD and MICHAEL MITTERAUER (1983), 'The Reconstruction of the Family Life Course: Theoretical Problems and Empirical Results', In Richard Wall, Jean Robin and Peter Laslett, *Family Forms in Historic Europe*, Cambridge, 309–46.

SINT, OSWALD (1986), 'Buibm und Gitschn beinand is ka Zoig', *Jugend in Osttirol*, Vienna.

TROGER, ERNEST (1954), *Bevölkerungsgeschichte des Zillertales*, Innsbruck.

UHLIG, OTTO (1978), *Schwabenkinder aus Tirol und Vorarlberg*, Innsbruck.

VIAZZO, PLER PAOLO (1989), *Upland Communities. Environments, Population, and Social Structure in the Alps since the Sixteenth Century*, Cambridge.

VONWILLER, RUDIGER E. (1970), 'Die Industrielle Entwicklung der Weberei im Mühlviertel', In *Webereimuseum Haslach, Oberösterreich*, Linz.

WALLEITNER, JOSEPH (1948), *Der Knecht. Lebens- und Volkskunde eines Berufstandes im Oberpinzgau*, Salzburg.

WASZ, BARBARA (1985), *Mein Vater, Holzknecht und Bergbauer*, Vienna.

WASZ, BARBARA (1988), 'Für sie gab es immer nur die Alm', *Aus dem Leben einter Sennerin*, Vienna.

WEBER, BEDA (1837), *Das Land Tirol*, 3 vols., Innsbruck.

WEBER, THERESE (ed.) (1984), *Häuslerkindheit. Autobiographische Erzählungen*, Vienna.

WEBER, THERESE (ed.) (1985), *Mägde. Lebenserinnerungen an die Dienstbotenzeit bei Bauern*, Vienna.

WEBER, THERESE (1987), 'Schreibmotivationen von Autoren lebensgeschichtlicher Aufzeichnungen', *Beiträge zur historischen Sozialkunde* **17**, 5–9.

WEBER, THERESE (1990), 'Einleitung: Religion in Lebensgechichten', In Andreas Heller et al. (ed.), *Religion und Alltag*, Vienna, 9–27.

WOPFNER, HERMANN (1931), 'Eine siedlungs- un volkskundliche Wanderung durch Villgraten', *Zeitschrift des deutschen und österreichischen Alpenvereins*, (1931), 246ff; (1932), 263ff.

WOPFNER, HERMANN (1954), *Bergbauernbuch. Von und Leben des Tiroler Bergbauern in Vergangenheit und Gegenwart*, Innsbruck.

Chapter 4

LATE MARRIAGE: CAUSES AND CONSEQUENCES OF THE AUSTRIAN ALPINE MARRIAGE PATTERN[1]

NORBERT ORTMAYR

THE MAID MARIA K.—AN ALPINE BIOGRAPHY

Maria K. was born in 1916 as an illegitimate child in Meiselding, in the St Veit district of Carinthia (interview with Maria K., 22 August 1988). Her mother was a maid, her father worked as a groom on a farm in the neighbourhood. Being poor, they could not get married, and so Maria K. was forced to stay with her mother on the farm. Her mother, however, had little time for her child, except for mealtimes. The rest of the time little Maria was looked after by the farmer's wife. There were many children on the farm, both those belonging to the farmer and those of the maids. It was a large farm with ten servants—six male and four female—all living under one roof. It was one household, but the question is: how many actual families were there? The modern term 'family' does not seem to be applicable in this case. There was no clear division between the farmer's family and the maids with their illegitimate children. It could also be the case that, because of our preconceptions, we are no longer able to perceive such a division. In any case, if such borders were present, they are definitely not those which separate the 'simple' family as we know it today.

In addition, the division was not a static one, but rather one which could change according to the time of day. In the evening the division was more recognizable, when the servant girls retired and looked after their children. In the morning, this division was no longer visible as both servants and members of the farmer's family sat down to breakfast together. After breakfast, the maids handed their children over to the farmer's wife because they had to go off to work.

Maria K. lived with her mother on the farm for a year, and at the end of that year her mother was pregnant once again. Yet another illegitimate child, yet again no chance of marrying, even though she had reached the age of twenty-seven. Unfortunately, two children proved to be too much of a burden for Maria's mother, who was forced to send Maria away to foster parents. Maria

1 Financial support for this article was provided by the Austrian Fonds zür Förderung der wissenschaftlichen Forschung.

soon became more attached to her foster mother than to her own. She remained in her new home for nine years. Then, at the age of ten, she was forced to leave again. She was needed by her godparents to look after the cows. She had to get up at half past five, take her godmother's cow up to the meadow, look after it and bring it down again before rushing off to school. At three in the afternoon she had to rush home and again take the cow up to the meadow. Five years went by, and she was then old enough to become a maid herself. She then returned to the farm where she had been born and where her mother had worked. She spent the next forty-five years as a servant for different farmers. These were also years of moving around between various farms and villages. During that time she herself gave birth to three children, all of whom were illegitimate. At her last farm she stayed for fifteen years and then retired. Today she lives with her daughter's family. She never married.

Maria K.'s life is typical of Alpine society in the nineteenth and early twentieth centuries. In the latter part of the nineteenth century, 68 per cent of all children born in the St Veit district of Carinthia were illegitimate. Similarly, 61 per cent of those living in the district never had the chance to get married and start a family (Schimmer, 1875, p. 156). Starting a family in the Alpine regions of Austria had always been a problem. My research so far has shown that the Alpine regions of Austria had the highest age of marriage in Europe and the highest proportions never married. In the nineteenth century the average age of marriage for men in some Alpine regions was as high as 38 or 39, and the proportion of men who were still single between the ages of 45 and 49 was on average 30 to 60 per cent (Hajnal, 1965, p. 101; Platter, 1883, p. 56; Guenther, 1930, p. 192).[2]

THE ALPINE MARRIAGE PATTERN

In order to place the Austrian Alpine marriage pattern in a broader geographical perspective, I will also now include a description of the Austrian lowlands in our discussion of Austrian marriage patterns. Using the census data for 1880, it is possible to make a rough division of three regional types in Austria:

1. Regions with high age of marriage and high proportions never married, the latter proportions being 30 to 60 per cent for men. From 75 to 90 per cent of men aged 25 to 29 were still single. This pattern was typical of the Alpine regions of Tyrol, Salzburg, Carinthia and Upper Styria.

2. Regions in which between six and 30 per cent of the population never married. These were the regions north and south of the Alps, the 'Waldviertel' and 'Mühlviertel', as well as the protoindustrial regions of Vorarlberg and the district of Waidhofen/Thaya. Between 60 and 75 per cent of the 25 to 29 year old men were still single.

2 In Austria, Josef Ehmer was the first to draw attention to this exceptionally high proportion of people who never married.

Table 1: *Percentages never married of population aged 45–49 by district, 1880*

District

St Veit (K)	61.8	Vöclabruck (O)	24.5
Murau (St)	49.6	Feldkirch (V)	23.5
Judenburg (St)	48.9	Reutte (V)	23.0
Lienz (T)	48.1	Perg (O)	22.7
Zell/See (S)	45.0	Steyr-Umgebung (O)	21.0
Wolfsberg (K)	44.7	Neunkirchen (N)	20.9
Klagenfurt-Umgebung (K)	43.4	Leibnitz (St)	20.1
Liezen (St)	41.7	Scheibbs (N)	19.7
Imst (T)	40.6	Rohrbach (O)	19.5
St Johann (S)	40.2	Wels (O)	19.0
Völkermarkt (K)	39.5	St Pölten (N)	18.6
Kufstein (T)	38.8	Linz-Umgebung (O)	18.5
Tamsweg (S)	38.4	Freistadt (O)	18.5
Gröbming (St)	38.3	Braunau (O)	18.2
Schwaz (T)	37.9	Radkersburg (St)	17.9
Graz-Umgebung (T)	37.7	Gmunden (O)	17.6
Leoben (St)	37.7	Feldbach (St)	17.1
Spittal (K)	37.1	Wr Neustadt (N)	15.7
Bruck/Mur (St)	35.9	Baden (N)	14.3
Landeck (T)	35.4	Bruck/Leitha (N)	14.3
Innsbruck-Umgebung (T)	34.2	Sechshaus-Hietzing (N)	14.0
Kitzbühl (T)	33.6	Hernals-Währing (N)	13.2
Villach (K)	30.2	Krems (N)	13.2
Hermagor (K)	27.9	Horn (N)	12.0
Salzburg-Umgebung (S)	27.2	Zwettl (N)	11.9
Bregenz (V)	27.1	Korneuburg (N)	9.8
Deutsch-Landsberg (St))	26.9	Groß-Enzersdorf (N)	9.2
Lillenfeld (N)	26.7	Waidhofen/Thaya (N)	6.3
Ried (O)	26.6	Oberhollerbrun (N)	6.1
Hartberg (St)	26.3	Mistelbach (N)	4.7
Kirchdorf (O)	25.3	Vas (U)	6.9
Bludenz (V)	25.0	Moson (U)	5.5
Schärding (O)	24.9	Sopron (U) ⁻	4.5
Amstetten (N)	24.8		

Notes: K = Carinthia; N = Lower Austria; S = Salzburg; T = Tyrol; O = Upper Austria; St = Styria; V = Vorarlberg; U = those Hungarian 'komitate' of which parts are now in the Austrian province of Burgenland.
Source: Österreichische Statistik, Bd. 1, Budapest, 1882.

3. Regions with early and almost universal marriage. The proportion never married was less than seven per cent. This pattern was common in Burgenland and in the Weinviertel area of Lower Austria (Tables 1 and 2).

Table 2: *Mean age at first marriage in selected alpine communities*

Community	Year	Male	Female
Innervillgraten	1700–1749	27.6	25.0
(Eastern Tyrol)	1750–1799	34.1	29.7
	1800–1849	36.1	31.8
	1850–1899	37.0	32.7
	1900–1949	37.8	32.1
Hopfgarten	1789–1800	30.5	25.5
(Eastern Tyrol)	1801–1850	30.7	26.8
	1851–1900	37.6	30.2
	1901–1950	33.8	29.4
Ötz	1801–1825	33.1	30.3
(Tyrol)	1826–1850	34.8	31.2
	1851–1875	37.1	33.0
	1876–1900	35.8	30.8
	1901–1925	33.7	29.5
Baumkirchen	1740–1799	36.0	29.4
(Tyrol)	1800–1849	35.3	30.2
	1850–1899	34.4	29.9
	1900–1939	33.0	27.9
Weichselboden	1775–1799	30.8	–
(Styria)	1800–1849	29.5	26.1
	1850–1899	30.4	26.3
	1900–1934	31.5	27.5

Source: Alge (1975); Kraler (1970); Stecher (1970); Keiter (1940); Fliri (1948).

In the urban centres of Austria, the proportions never married varied from 15 to 25 per cent. The only clear exception was Klagenfurt in Carinthia, where the proportion never married reached 38.9 per cent and was certainly a direct result of the pattern typical of the surrounding area.

The only other European countries with relatively high proportions never married were Ireland and Finland. Between 1841 and 1926 the proportion of men in Ireland between 40 and 44 years of age who were still single rose from 10 to 40 per cent, while the average age of marriage for men was between 30 and 32 and for women between 26 and 28. In Finland in 1930 the proportion of single men between 40 and 44 years of age was 30 per cent, with the average age of marriage for men being 27.4 years (Knodel and Maynes, 1976, p. 131; Dixon, 1978, p. 451; Dixon, 1971, p. 215). In the nineteenth century the average age of marriage in Austria rose, reaching a peak in 1857 (Mitterauer, 1982, p. 262); however, the average age of marriage in the Alpine regions continued to rise until the end of the century (see Table 2).

In addition, it is significant that the urban-rural ratio of those never married in Austria was exactly the reverse of the pattern existing in almost all other European countries, with the exceptions of Switzerland, Bavaria and Belgium (Knodel and Maynes, 1976, p. 131).

REASONS FOR THE MARRIAGE PATTERN

In order to understand the reasons for the exceptional demographic behaviour in the Alpine region, it is necessary to describe the social and economic structure of this society. The Alpine regions were areas of low population density, yet were overpopulated relative to the amount of arable land that was available (Wutz, 1939, p. 4). Since the late Middle Ages people have settled at extreme altitudes up to 1,800 metres. Furthermore, the Alpine regions were areas with a low level of local division of labour. Economically, the two dominant factors were cattle breeding and forestry. The farmers had a low level of market integration. The only areas where dairy and cheese products were marketed were a few regions in Vorarlberg (Bregenzerwald). The small amount of cereal crops grown were exclusively for the farmer's own consumption. Only in a few suitable basin areas (Klagenfurter Becken, Krappfeld in Carinthia) were cereal crops produced for the market.

As far as inheritance patterns are concerned, we differentiate two types of regions: those with partible land inheritance (Western Tyrol, Vorarlberg) and those with impartible inheritance (all other regions) (*Österreichischer Volkskundeatlas*, 1985, map 2/7). The social structure of the peasantry was linked directly to the inheritance patterns. In Western Tyrol and Vorarlberg the partible inheritance pattern led to small-sized farms (Wolf, 1970). On the other hand, regions with impartible inheritance were characterized by the dominance of medium- and large-sized farms. One could make a further subdivision within the Pinzgau area, Upper Styria and the St Veit/Glan district in Carinthia, which had predominantly large-sized farms. In early modern times abandoned farms were attached to existing farms (known as *Zulehen* or *Zuhuben*), resulting in farms having one hundred or more hectares. These were also the regions with the highest proportions of farm servants. In the early twentieth century these large farms had up to 30 or 40 servants (*Seelenbuch der Pfarre Bruck*).[3]

This brings us to the rural family structure. Here we can also make a rough division into two regional types. In the areas with impartible inheritance there were large peasant holdings with many unrelated servants. Hence the family structure was characterized by frequent cohabitation of unrelated persons in one household. Since both male and female servants only worked in one place for one or two years, there was a high level of mobility between the households. On the other hand, the family structure in Western Tyrol and Vorarlberg was completely different. In these areas servants were hardly ever

---

3 In the Traunergut in 1846 there were 24 male and 14 female farmhands.

used. Similarly, unrelated lodgers are rarely to be found in the census lists. These were indeed family oriented societies, characterized primarily by the fact that all members of a household were related. What was also missing was the movement of the servants between the households, which was typical of the regions with partible inheritance. The mobility here was less between households than between the village and the outside world. What this means is that there was seasonal work involving both teenage and adult men. Every spring they left home to work in Switzerland, Germany and France, mostly in the building trade. Even children were involved in such seasonal work (*Schwabenkinder*) (Uhlig, 1978). In the eighteenth and nineteenth centuries Alpine societies experienced slow population growth. Whereas, for example, in the period 1754–1850 Burgenland's population grew by 53 per cent, the population of Salzburg province increased by only four per cent (Klein, 1973, p. 105).

To summarize, the Alpine regions showed no uniform social structure. The individual regions differed essentially in inheritance patterns, farm size, family structures and their feudal past (the structure of the manorial system). It is important that, although on the one hand the family structures were influenced by inheritance patterns and farm size, on the other hand these factors had no important effect on the age of marriage and the proportion never married. Therefore we must ask: just what factors caused this marriage pattern to be prevalent in the Alpine regions? As far as I can determine, the Alpine marriage pattern was mainly dependent on the following two factors. First, the dominance of family and/or servant labour combined with the lack of local agricultural labour, and secondly, the absence or very slow progress of the agricultural revolution in the Alps in the nineteenth century. The search for reasons for the late marriage pattern also gave contemporary statisticians a number of headaches. What is important in the context of our own inquiry is the work of von Zwiedeniek-Suedenhorst in the periodical *Statistische Monatsschrift* in 1895. He carried out a survey of the age of marriage in two different agrarian regions with the following results.

Upper Styria, an Alpine region mainly concerned with cattle breeding, was characterized by extremely large farms, on average 60 hectares, yet had only a small number of people who could exist on daily wages alone. Cottage families were forced to live off their wages as either craftsmen or forestry workers. The degree of transfer of ownership was also limited, and it was therefore difficult to start a new life by purchasing or leasing land. The other significant factors were high proportions of servants and late retirement on the part of the farmers. This all led to late marriage or non-marriage.

The economic structure of Lower Styria was completely different. It was a fertile region with a high concentration of vineyards and cereal crops, a high proportion of day-labourers and high levels of market integration and changing of land ownership. The average farm size was only 9.3 hectares. All of these factors made the establishment of a new household much easier.

Whereas between 1883 and 1887 a quarter of all bridegrooms in Upper Styria were under 30, in lower Styria almost 60 per cent were under that age. Hence we have late or non-marriage caused by high proportions of servants, large-sized farms, small numbers of cottagers and a low level of market integration. On the other hand, the chances of marrying and starting a family were higher in areas with low proportions of servants, a high level of ownership transfer, small-sized farms and a high level of market integration.

What, then, was the situation in Western Tyrol, which was an Alpine region with few servants, a high proportion of small farms, yet with a high age of marriage and high proportions of inhabitants who never married? The answer lies in the fact that agriculture was not so intensive, while pastoral agriculture dominated and local day labour was insignificant. Family labour and the exchange of labour between peasant holdings were the two chief types of agricultural work. As a result of partible inheritance there was no social differentiation between peasants and cottagers; it was a relatively egalitarian type of rural society. This meant that the decisive variables which regulated the demographic figures of 'age of marriage' and 'proportions never married' were the intensity of agriculture and the extent of wage labour available in a local society. If there was enough agricultural day labour, it was possible for a large class of cottagers and lodgers to establish itself. In the nineteenth and early twentieth centuries these rural lower classes made up at least two-thirds of the total rural population of those areas with cereal crops and vineyards. In the Alps the cottager class had always been smaller and lodger families were always rare, since agricultural day labour did not exist to the same extent as it did in the lowlands. In places where day labour was readily available in forestry, in the so-called wood-cutter villages, e.g.,- the community of Weichselboden, the age of marriage was lower (see Table 2). Thus the decisive factor was the percentage of cottagers and lodgers.

So much for the first structural explanation for the difference in marriage patterns between the Alpine areas and the lowlands. In the nineteenth century this structural imbalance was enhanced further by the lack of an agricultural revolution in the Alpine regions. The growth in population in the eighteenth and nineteenth centuries was made possible by an agricultural revolution, which resulted in an expansion in agricultural production. Until the eighteenth century, agricultural progress had always been hindered by the fact that cereal production could not be increased due to the lack of manure. This was the chief limiting factor in the agrarian economic system (cf. Pfister, 1988, p. 126). From the late eighteenth century onward this stagnation, which had lasted for centuries, could be overcome by three innovations in the non-Alpine regions. These innovations were the introduction of the potato, the cultivation of clover, and the stall feeding of cattle in the summer. The numbers of livestock could be increased considerably, thus compensating for the lack of manure. Cereal production expanded and total agricultural production increased enormously (Sandgruber, 1978a, p. 195).

The situation was completely different in the Alpine regions. Here, cattle farming predominated, and cultivation played only a marginal role. Attempts to increase the number of livestock always failed because of the acute lack of fodder during winter. In the autumn either the cattle had to be sold at the markets or they survived the winter on reduced supplies of fodder. According to oral reports from Salzburg, the cattle had lost so much weight by the spring that they sometimes had difficulty getting up to the mountain pastures (Interview with B. Wass). Therefore hay was the limiting factor in the system. It is also important to note that in contrast to the lowlands, fodder supplies could not be increased in the Alps. The cultivation of clover, like the cultivation of cereals, was insignificant in this respect. Neither was it possible to convert the corn fields to pasture because they were needed for the production of rye. Also, summer stall feeding was never introduced. The only real innovation in the Alps was the introduction of the potato. This too met with problems in some Alpine regions. In Salzburg, for instance, in 1904 the area of land used for the cultivation of potatoes made up only 1.7 per cent of the area of arable land. In contrast, 10.2 per cent of arable land was used for potatoes in Lower Austria (Sandgruber, 1978a, p. 216). Consequently there was stagnation in the numbers of livestock. Between 1840 and 1910 livestock numbers decreased by 4.1 per cent in the Alps, whereas in Upper and Lower Austria, livestock increased by 34.3 per cent (Wohlschlägl, 1978, p. 185). For example, in Salzburg in 1850 there were 134,800 cows, whereas in 1910 there were only 70,700 (Sandgruber, 1978b, p. 201). There was a similar reduction in the number of goats, which was a clear indication that there were no new resources for rural lower-class families, and therefore no basis for population growth (Wohlschlägl, 1978, p. 181).

Agricultural progress stagnated and the potential productivity of the agricultural revolution could not be exploited because of the environmental conditions of the Alpine regions. The trades also stagnated (Hoffmann, 1972). The Alps, which had been characterized by intensive mining, suffered massive deindustrialization in the eighteenth and nineteenth centuries. Nor was there any development in the textile industry. Therefore it was impossible for either the supply of food to be increased or for employment opportunities in the secondary sector to be created. It remained only to constrain the growth in population by restricting the possibilities of marriage. The Alpine marriage pattern was thus a cultural adaptation to this situation wherein the economic potential was completely exploited. It was only in the twentieth century that the demographic-economic stagnation of Alpine society could be changed considerably by the growth in tourism.

CONSEQUENCES OF THE MARRIAGE PATTERN

What then were the consequences of late marriage and non-marriage? I differentiate between the consequences for family structure, the demographic pattern, and the general socio-cultural situation.

Consequences for Family Structure

Late marriage and non-marriage have only been considered with reference to their demographic effects—the birth rate, population growth, and illegitimacy—and not with regard to the consequences for family structure. However, the Alpine marriage pattern described above was also coupled with a high proportion of non-typical family structures in comparison with other cultures. These were:

(1) Pure sibling households (unmarried brothers and sisters);
(2) Households with unmarried siblings of one or both married partners;
(3) 'Families' without co-residence;
(4) Service as a life-long phenomenon.

Pure sibling households (i.e. households where only unmarried brothers and sisters lived together) were a typical development in the Alpine areas of divided land inheritance in Western Tyrol and Vorarlberg. They have been documented by historical sources since the eighteenth century and made up approximately 10 to 30 per cent of all households. This type of household, which in the 'Hammel-Laslett schema' appears in the category 'no family', was, however, significant in the poverty cultures of Western Tyrol and Vorarlberg. Unmarried siblings owned and jointly ran a small farm. When they died, they consequently appeared in the parish register as 'unmarried farmer' or 'unmarried owner' (*Sterbematrik Fliess*, 1850; *Sterbematrik Bad Schönau*, 1850). It was quite different in the areas with impartible land inheritance. Those who died unmarried were registered as 'poor' or 'landless'. This type of household was connected structurally with the practice of partible inheritance of land and an economic environment of small sized-farms, where further division was not possible. Additional sources of income apart from agriculture were insufficient. In Table 3, which records the proportion of sibling households in three communities with different economic structures, this connection is clearly recognizable. The community of Lustenau in Vorarlberg had the lowest proportion of sibling households. Lustenau was characterized by relatively intensive agriculture, early agricultural reforms (the early introduction of maize and potatoes in the eighteenth century), as well as protoindustrialization. The community of Egg in the Bregenzerwald was situated in the middle. It was characterized by protoindustrialization, but less intensive mountain farming. The highest proportion of this type of

Table 3: *Proportions of sibling households*

Lustenau	1806	3.5%
Egg	1752	12.5%
Fliess	1911	24.0%

Source: Fitz (1985, pp. 111, 123); Volkszählung, Fliess, 1911.

household was found in the community of Fliess, 1,200 metres up in the West Tyrolean Alps, where apart from the less intensive cattle farming no other resources existed.

Households with unmarried siblings of one or both married partners were typical of the Austrian areas with impartible land inheritance, although such households could also be found in the regions with partible inheritance. As a rule the whole of the property was inherited by just one son, while the other brothers and sisters often had to be satisfied with a small sum of money. For many of them marriage was not possible because of economic circumstances. Unmarried brothers very often left the family farm after their elder brother's marriage and worked as farmhands. Sisters often stayed at home as unmarried aunts. As a rule, apart from the right of residence they owned nothing and were usually not paid for their labour. Their social status was very low. In the regions with partible inheritance the social status of the unmarried brothers and sisters was quite different. Here the unmarried siblings who lived with their married brother's or sister's family did own property. They owned land, which they ran together with the family with which they lived.

Families without co-residence is a term which I take to mean those social systems that included an unmarried mother, her illegitimate child, and the child's father. It is clear that these social systems were not families in the modern sense of the word, particularly when seen from an institutional perspective. As a rule the parents did not marry. Nevertheless, they constituted a biological and social form with limited family functions. In addition they were so significant in Alpine society that they should be considered as an independent type of family.

This type of family was found primarily in those Alpine regions that also had high rates of illegitimacy. This type of family had its own particular characteristics. The mother, father and child did not live together. In most cases the father lived separately, and it was more common for the mother and child to live together. However, this was not always the rule. Three sub-types can be identified: (a) the mother and child lived together, the mother usually serving as a maid while the father lived apart from the mother-child group; (b) the father, mother and child each lived in separate households; and (c) the father and child lived together, while the mother lived separately. The father in this case was usually married to another woman.

This type of family continually adapted its structure to other family life cycles. When there was room in a peasant household for the mother and child, they could stay together; when that was not the case, the child was taken in by foster parents. It often happened that a change in the location of work meant the separation of the mother and her illegitimate child, because there was no room for a maid's child at the new work place. The child was then 'given away' (*ausgestiftet*); when the child was sent to new foster parents, it was 'resettled' (*umgestiftet*). This shows that the local dialects had their own terms for the circulation of foster children, a clear indication of a collective experience.

In general the structure of rural lower-class families was always complementary to peasant families. The families without co-residence were the most extreme example of this pattern. When the mother and child lived together they formed a sub-system within a peasant household. There were boundaries between the social system of the peasant household and the sub-system, but they were not static ones. Families without co-residence were to be found not only among rural lower-class families, but were also present in the peasant class, usually as a transitional phase before marriage. This was always the case when the old farmer did not want to retire and therefore the child's father could not marry. In such a case the mother and her illegitimate child lived with her parents until the child's father had inherited the farm and marriage was possible.

With regard to foster parents, in the non-Alpine regions the illegitimate children of the maid were usually brought up by the maid's parents, whereas in Alpine society this was seldom the case, because the grandparents were most often landless unmarried servants. Therefore the illegitimate children were placed with peasants, where possible, in particular stages of the family life cycle where they might best fit. This was also often the case with the family of the natural father.

It is important to discuss the family functions of this non-cohabitant group (Mitterauer, 1979). Reproduction was obviously one of the functions of this group, while the parental function of the social placement of the child was also evident. The maid's illegitimate child was not placed according to the social status of the farmer in whose household it lived, but followed the status of the mother—and not that of the father. The functions of socialization and production were not so clear in this case. This type of family had only a limited socialization function. The mother was more often the agent of socialization than the father. When the child was with the mother, she was one agent of socialization. In addition, other members of the peasant household, such as the farmer's wife and other peasant children, played an important role in bringing up the child. This type of family was obviously not a productive unit. On the other hand, it partially carried out a protective function. The elderly mother was very often looked after by one of her illegitimate children.

A further consequence of the Alpine marriage pattern was that service lost its character as a phenomenon restricted to the youth as life cycle servants (Hajnal, 1983). For a greater part of the farmhands and maids, service became a life-long occupation. Together with the high illegitimacy rate, this meant that servants were no longer simply from a particular age group, but to a certain extent had become a self-reproducing social class.

Demographic Consequences

In addition to slow population growth, the high rate of illegitimacy was also an important demographic consequence of the Alpine marriage pattern. The

Eastern Alps formed the region with the highest illegitimacy rate in the whole of Europe. In the nineteenth century the Alpine regions with impartible land inheritance had average illegitimacy rates of between thirty and fifty per cent (Mitterauer, 1979). Without doubt the restricted opportunities for marriage were the main cause. However, we also have Alpine regions which show a high age at marriage and high proportions never married, but which also have a minimum level of illegitimacy. These are the areas of partible inheritance in the Western Tyrol, Vorarlberg, and East Tyrol. The reason for this phenomenon is to be found in the number of servants. Late marriage and non-marriage led to a high rate of illegitimacy only in those areas with a high proportion of servants. Working as servants meant that people who were not related, and were therefore not in danger of incestuous relationships, lived together in the same household. Service also meant the circulation of unmarried people between the households. Therefore the servant's sexual behaviour could not be watched over by parents or by peasants, as was the case with the peasants' own children. In regions with fewer servants, the more frequent cohabitation of relatives resulted in a stricter check on sexual behaviour.

In addition, other social and cultural factors played an important role. Carinthia, the province with the highest illegitimacy rates in Austria, also had a long tradition of secret Protestantism, and in some areas an anti-clerical attitude and a relatively low proportion of priests (Mitterauer, 1979, Table 4, p. 184). The Tyrol was just the opposite; it had the highest proportion of clerics in the whole monarchy and Catholicism was widespread and deeply rooted. The reason for this was that in the Tyrol the radical counter-reformation in the seventeenth and eighteenth centuries, combined with extreme poverty, provided a solid foundation for rigid sexual morals in all classes of the population. Even in the 1930s girls who were expecting illegitimate children had to go to the altar in front of the entire community at Sunday mass and beg for forgiveness. We also have reports from Salzburg on similar rituals of confession. Until the early twentieth century pregnant girls had to stand in front of the congregation wearing a straw garland as atonement for the guilt of pregnancy out of wedlock (Wass, 1985, p. 63).

Socio-Cultural Consequences

The other socio-cultural consequences of the Alpine marriage pattern are much more difficult to identify than the demographic or family structural consequences. The fact is that in the eighteenth and nineteenth centuries Alpine society was to a great extent a society of unmarried people. Remaining single always presented a problem in agrarian societies. Adult status was only achieved when one had undergone the rite of passage of marriage. What happened then to those who, because of economic barriers, could not undergo this rite of passage? Were they subject to a reduced status? This would have been plausible if non-marriage had remained the problem of a social minority. Remaining unmarried was not, however, a phenomenon of the minority in Alpine Austria, but was experienced by a greater part of the population.

A second factor was also involved. In Ireland, another region in Europe with comparably high rates of non-marriage, this phenomenon was restricted to a relatively brief period (1850–1940), that is to say two or three generations. In Austria, however, the same pattern reached much further back (Klein, 1988, p. 1293). It must therefore have had a much stronger influence on society as a whole. One could then ask the question: how did society cope with this demographic challenge? My hypothesis is that, on the one hand, society provided alternative rites of passage and alternative career possibilities, while, on the other hand, there was a religious re-evaluation of unmarried status through the expansion of the cult of the Virgin Mary.

The clerical profession offered such an alternative career. It is certainly not a coincidence that the Alps contained the highest proportion of priests, monks and nuns in the whole monarchy. In the late nineteenth century in the western half of the Austro-Hungarian Monarchy, for each 1,000 inhabitants there was an average of 1.5 clerics; in Salzburg the number was 5.77, and in the Tyrol, 5.8. The highest rates were found in the Landeck district of Western Tyrol, with 7.4 clerics per 1,000 inhabitants, and in the Vorarlberg district of Bregenz, with 8.18 (Table 4). Entering a monastery or the priesthood were the traditional channels of social advancement for the rural lower classes. In such a case, remaining unmarried did not lead to a loss in status, but, just the opposite, to social advancement. It should also not be forgotten that Catholicism offered some legitimacy to the celibate state by defining a nun as 'bride of Jesus Christ'.

At the same time, the unmarried status came to be revalued in religious terms through the cult of the Virgin Mary in the nineteenth century. The worship of the Virgin Mary has had a long tradition in theology. Among the people, the cult of the Virgin Mary only gained in popularity in the nineteenth century, which continued into the twentieth century. Only in the nineteenth century did the Virgin Mary become such a central national and supranational cult figure. This cult figure then replaced the enormous variety of local religious cults which had survived into the eighteenth century. The cult of the

Table 4: *Priests per 1000 inhabitants, 1869*

Lower Austria	1.9
Upper Austria	2.1
Salzburg	4.7
Carinthia	2.2
Styria	1.7
Tyrol and Vorarlberg	5.8

Source: Bevölkerung und Viehstand (1872, p. 102).

Virgin Mary counted as one of these supranational cults, as did the cult of the guardian angel and the cult of the heart of Jesus (Schieder, 1987).

Since the late nineteenth century, the medical examination for military service has been a special day for teenage boys, and this, too, can be seen as an alternative rite of passage. On this day most of the boys were declared fit for military service and thus were seen as having become grown men. Was this ritual now an alternative rite of passage to full adult status in place of marriage? There are many indications that this was true. For example, there were also parallels between the customs connected with this day and wedding customs (Gaal, 1976, p. 258). And perhaps this is the reason why in the nineteenth century, in a relatively short time, the military developed from an institution that had been despised for centuries to one which was socially accepted to a very high degree. All these are vague thoughts, perhaps they are even wrong, and perhaps the phenomena described are only parallel phenomena with no direct causal connection. I think, however, they deserve more consideration.

References

ALGE, G. (1975), *Bevölkerungsgeographische Untersuchungen im Defreggental. Hopfgarten in Defreggental*, Innsbruck.

Bevölkerung und Viehstand der im Reichrathe vertretenen Königreiche und Länder (1872), pt. 5, Vienna.

DIXON, R. B. (1971), 'Explaining Cross-Cultural Variation in Age at Marriage and Proportions Never Married', *Population Studies*, 25.

DIXON, R. B. (1978), 'Late Marriage and Non-marriage as Demographic Responses: Are they Similar?', *Population Studies*, 32.

FLIRI, F. (1948), *Bevölkerungsgeographische Untersuchungen im Unterinntal*, Innsbruck.

GAAL, K. (ed.) (1976), *Tadten*, Eisenstadt.

GUENTHER, A. (1930), *Die alpenlaendische Gesellschaft*, Jena.

HAJNAL, J. (1965), 'European Marriage Patterns in Perspective', In D. Glass and D. E. C. Eversley (eds.), *Population in History*, London.

HAJNAL, J. (1983), 'Two Kinds of Pre-Industrial Household Formation Systems', In R. Wall (ed.), *Family Forms in Historic Europe*, Cambridge.

HAMMEL, E. A. and LASLETT, P. (1974), 'Comparing Household Structures Over Time and Between Cultures', *Comparative Studies in Society and History*, 16.

HOFFMANN, A. (1972), 'Die Agrarisierung der Industriebauern in Österreich', *Zeitschrift für Agrargeschichte und Agrarsoziologie, 20.*

KEITER, H. (1940), 'Weichselboden. Geburt, Ehe und Tod im steierischen Gebirge', *Volk und Rasse, 10.*

KHERA, S. (1981), 'Illegitimacy and Mode of Land Inheritance among Austrian Peasants', *Ethnology*, 20.

KLEIN, K. (1973), 'Die Bevölkerung Österreichs vom Beginn des 16. bis zur Mitte des 18. Jahrhunderts', In H. Helcmanovski (ed.), *Beiträge zur Bevölkerungs-und Sozialgeschichte Österreichs*, Vienna.

KLEIN, K. (1988), 'Bevölkerung und Siedlung', In H. Dopsch and H. Spazenegger (eds.), *Geschichte Salzburgs, 2*, Salzburg.

KNODEL, J. and MAYNES, M. J. (1976), 'Urban and Rural Marriage Patterns in Imperial Germany', *Journal of Family History*, 1.
KRALER, P. (1970), *Kulturgeographie von Villgraten. Landschaft und Mensch in einem extremen Bergbauerngebiet*, Innsbruck.
MITTERAUER, M. (1979), 'Familienformen und Illegitimität in ländlichen Gebieten Österreichs', *Archiv für Sozialgeschichte*.
MITTERAUER, M. (1981), 'Marriage without Co-Residence', *Journal of Family History*, 5.
MITTERAUER, M. (1982), 'Auswirkungen der Agrarrevolution auf die bäuerliche Familienstruktur in Österreich', In M. Mitterauer and R. Sieder (eds.), *Historische Familienforschung*, Frankfurt.
Österreichische Statistik. Ergebnisse der in den Laendern der ungarischen Krone am Anfang des Jahres 1880 vollzogenen Volkszaehlung samt Nachweisung einiger nutzbarer Haustiere, (1882), 1, Budapest.
Österreichischer Volkskundeatlas (1985), Vienna.
PFISTER, C. (1988), *Klimageschichte der Schweiz 1525–1860*, Bern.
PLATTER, J. (1883), 'Trauungen und Geburten in Tirol und Vorarlberg in den Jahren 1751–1874', *Statistische Monatsschrift*, 1883.
SANDGRUBER, R. (1978a), 'Die Agrarrevolution in Österreich', In A. Hoffmann (ed.), *Österreich-Ungarn als Agrarstaat*, Vienna.
SANDGRUBER, R. (1978b), *Österreichische Agrarstatistik 1750–1918*, Vienna.
SCHIEDER, W. (1987), 'Religion in der Sozialgeschichte', In W. Schieder and V. Sellin (eds.), *Sozialgeschichte in Deutschland*, 2, Göttingen.
SCHIMMER, G. (1875), 'Die unehelich Geborenen in Österreich', *Statistische Monatschrift*, 2.
Selenbuch der Pfarre Bruck, Parish Archive Bruck, Pinzgau.
STECHER, A. (1970), *Das Ötztal. Eine bevölkerungsgeographische Studie*, Dissertation, Innsbruck.
Sterbematrik Bad Schönau (1850), Parish Archive, Bad Schönau, Lower Austria.
Sterbematrik Fliess (1850), Parish Archive, Fliess, Tyrol.
UHLIG, O. (1978), 'Die Schwabenkinder aus Tirol und Vorarlberg', *Tiroler Wirtschaftsstudien*, 23.
Volkszählung der Pfarre Fliess, 1911, Pfarrarchiv Fliess.
VON ZWIEDENIECK-SUEDENHORST, O. (1895), 'Die Illegitimität in der Steiermark', *Statistische Monatsschrift*, 21.
WASS, B., Interview in Kuchl (Salzburg).
WASS, B. (1985), *Mein Vater—Holzknecht und Bergbauer*, Vienna.
WOHLSCHLÄGL, H. (1978), 'Das Wachstum der landwirtschaftlichen Produktion in Oesterreich im 19. Jahrhundert: Der Viehstand', In A. Hoffmann (ed.), *Österreich-Ungarn als Agrarstaat*, Vienna.
WOLF, E. R. (1970), 'The Inheritance of Land among Bavarian and Tyrolese Peasants', *Anthropologica*, 12.
WUTZ, A. (1939), *Landwirtschaftsatlas der Ostmark*, Berlin.

Chapter 5

SOCIO-ECONOMIC CHANGE, PEASANT HOUSEHOLD STRUCTURE AND DEMOGRAPHIC BEHAVIOUR IN A FRENCH DEPARTMENT

JAMES R. LEHNING

HOUSEHOLD STRUCTURE AND THE ECONOMY

Students of population behaviour have long been convinced that a relationship exists between social and economic conditions and population behaviour. Classical economists such as T. R. Malthus and William Nassau Senior were concerned with the relationship between the production of an economy and population growth (Malthus, 1959; Senior, 1828). The coincidence in time of significant changes in family formation in the nineteenth century and the process of industrialization furthered the conviction by many observers and later scholars that the two facts were connected. Critics of industrialization and urbanization saw these changes in terms of moral degradation: industry and the cities it spawned destroyed the basic values on which society had been built. The end result was the decay of authority within the family, fewer children, higher illegitimacy, and improvident 'beggar marriages' (Le Play, 1871).

The articulation of the theory of the demographic transition after the Second World War meant the adoption by modern social scientists of similar views, albeit without many of the moral overtones of nineteenth-century critics of changes in family formation. Frank Notestein wrote that 'Birth rates were not reduced largely by means of contraception, but in response to drastic changes in the social and economic setting that radically altered the motives and aims of people with respect to family size' (Notestein, 1945; 1953; Coale, 1973; Beaver, 1975). Earlier marriage and the rise of the nuclear family ideal were also attributed to industrialization, urbanization, or a vague modernization (Goode, 1963). The connections drawn between industrialization and these changes in family formation were sometimes obscure, but the conviction has remained that economic development had 'caused' the West European demographic transition and would 'cause' a similar transition in the developing countries of Latin America, Asia and Africa (World Population Plan, 1975).

The relationship between economic development and demographic change has most recently led to an emphasis on the household as the locus of decision-making. Drawing on the theory of the firm as an economic unit, the 'new household economics' views the household as a decision-making unit that seeks to maximize the use of scarce resources. Children, in this scheme, are seen as consumer goods, and the number of children in a family is the result of rational decisions aimed at maximizing the use of resources. Rises in income, therefore, lead to an increase in the number of children. But consumption theory also includes consideration of tastes and values about consumer goods, and it is assumed that increases in income lead to changes in these factors, reducing the number of children desired. Variations in the theory have taken into account the competition between children and other consumer goods for family resources, as well as the distinction between the quantity and the quality of children. Such concerns as the expected costs of raising a child, the expected contribution of the child to family income, and the demand of a child on the mother's time have been raised as a consequence of this way of viewing demographic decision-making (Simon, 1974; Becker, 1960; 1981; Easterlin and Crimins, 1985; Caldwell, 1982; Lindert, 1978; see also Lesthaeghe, 1980; Smith, 1986).

It has been suggested that one route through an explanatory framework of family formation is from broad societal changes through households to demographic behaviour, most frequently by demographic transition theorists such as Frank Lorimer (1954) and Kingsley Davis (1955). In their view, economic development led to a convergence of household systems towards universal nuclear structure, but that different household structures were associated with different demographic systems. Extended family systems and corporate kinship groups tend to be associated with early and frequent marriage, high marital fertility, and therefore high levels of overall fertility. Stem and nuclear family systems, on the other hand, should have low overall fertility brought about by either restricted marriage or limitation of fertility within marriage (Burch and Gendell [1971] summarize this literature). Since this work from the 1950s and 1960s, historians have suggested that household structures were associated with different kinds of social and economic structures. Extended households have been tied to the requirements for labour imposed by agricultural tenure systems: the classic stem family system described by Frederic Le Play was essentially a way of connecting household structure, impartible inheritance, and a family-sized farm (Le Play, 1871; Berkner, 1972; Collomp, 1972; Peyronnet, 1975). Joint households, similarly, have been connected to the requirements of maintaining a viable farm in the face of partible inheritance (Lemaître, 1976; Shaffer, 1982). Finally, nuclear households have been seen as particularly compatible with the demands of an industrialized economy (Goode, 1963; Parsons, 1943). Most 'household economics' theorists do not pay much attention to household structure,[1] but on

---

1 In general, demographers who have considered the question do not, strictly speaking, mean the residential household but rather, in John Caldwell's words, 'those groups of close relatives who share economic activities and obligations' (Caldwell, 1978, p. 553; Burch and Gendell, 1971, p. 88).

the basis of these considerations, we might expect uncontrolled fertility within marriage (to produce labour) and restricted marriage (to hold on to labour) in extended household systems, while nuclear households, which have less use for the labour of children, should exhibit restricted marital fertility and more frequent marriage. One might, in fact, argue that vertically extended households are evidence of wealth flows from children to parents, while a characteristic of nuclear households is a net wealth flow from parents to children (Caldwell, 1982).

Advocates of extended households, such as Frederic Le Play in the nineteenth century, have also insisted that there was more to an extended household than just the presence of kin outside of the conjugal pair. Extended households were the repositories of morality, values that led to a willingness to subordinate individual desires to the needs of the family. Nuclear households, on the other hand, reflected individualism. Since the decline of extended households and the rise of the nuclear household were also tied to the evil effects of economic development, a clear line was drawn between the individualism of nineteenth-century capitalism, the nuclear family, and demographic effects such as limited fertility and more frequent marriage (Le Play, 1870).

Different ways of viewing family formation therefore lead to different hypothetical relationships between family structure and demographic behaviour, and one can raise questions about both approaches. The modernization assumptions inherent in demographic transition theory are open to criticism, and the household economists have had difficulties in operationalizing such concepts as the future benefits or the emotional costs of children. These problems not only lead to different possible outcomes, but also to conceptual and methodological difficulties in analysing the problem (Burch and Gendell, 1971; but see Berkner and Mendels, 1978). Nonetheless, the possibilities are enticing enough that, as a part of a larger examination of family formation in a French department, it seems worthwhile to examine the role of household structure in determining demographic behaviour (Lehning, 1983; 1984a; 1984b; 1988).

THE DEPARTMENT OF THE LOIRE

The focus of this essay will be the ways in which household structures filtered economic changes to affect the processes of family formation in the rural parts of the French department of the Loire in the second half of the nineteenth century. The Loire, located in the south-east of France near Lyon, is shaped as a rectangle standing on its short side and bounded on the south, east and west by low ranges of mountains. Its centre, in contrast, is a plain, marshy at the beginning of the nineteenth century but drained and turned to productive agricultural use by mid-century. Pre-industrial manufacturing sectors marked some parts of the department in the early nineteenth century: in the south, around Saint-Etienne, the largest city in the department, skilled urban artisans and unskilled peasants wove silk ribbons. In the eastern *Monts du Matin*, peasants wove silk goods for merchants in Lyon and the smaller city of Tarare in the neighbouring Rhône. Further to the north, a domestic cotton weaving and spinning industry existed in the countryside around Roanne, the second largest city in the department. There was also substantial economic development during the nineteenth century: the valley that centred on Saint-Etienne became the home of a major steel and coal complex, profiting from the existence of deposits of both coal and iron ore close to the surface, and the cotton industry of the Roannais left the countryside and became concentrated in factories in the city. As a consequence of this industrial development, the countryside lost some long-standing by-employments: silk and cotton weaving no longer recruited a substantial labour force in the countryside, and most peasants who sought employment in these industries now had to move to Roanne, Saint-Etienne, or the more distant Lyon. In exchange, however, the countryside was opened to new influences: railroads were built and roads improved, marketing networks developed that brought the countryside closer to the cities, and primary school systems were established. Nevertheless, the agrarian structure of the Loire remained much the same in 1900 as it had been in 1800: the mountainous periphery was marked by small family farms, while the centre, becoming more productive by the middle of the century, was an area of larger farms frequently rented to peasants on share-cropping leases (Guillaume, 1963; Gras, 1906; Pariset, 1901; Dechelette, 1910; Cayez, 1978; Lehning, 1980; A.D.L., 1852; 1892).

The department of the Loire was not among the earliest French departments to begin its fertility decline, but this was under way by the middle of the nineteenth century (see Coale and Treadway, 1986 for the following measures). Marital fertility between 1851 and 1891 fell from a level indicating uncontrolled fertility ($I_g = .646$) to one indicating widespread use of family limitation ($I_g = .478$). Overall fertility also declined, as I_f decreased from .332 to .251. Nuptiality patterns were also in flux. Some change had occurred by 1891 (I_m increased from .483 in 1831 to .498 in 1891). In spite of a reversal of the trend immediately after the First World War, by 1961 I_m for the Loire had risen to .631 (Coale and Treadway, 1986. p. 100). As with France as a whole, therefore, the changes in nuptiality in the second half of the nineteenth century occurred at the same time as the decline of marital fertility, the first sign of a major shift in marriage patterns that became more obvious in the twentieth century.

Household structures were also changing in the second half of the nineteenth century, at least if the rough measures that can be calculated have any validity (see Parrish and Schwartz, 1972; Berkner, 1977).[2] Both Adults per

2 As Berkner notes (1977), these measures are only rough estimates of household behaviour, capturing only the aggregate behaviour of the village at a single point in time. They are useful only insofar as they provide a means of summarizing behaviour.

Household (A.P.H.) and Marital Units per Household (M.U.H.) were relatively elevated throughout the department at mid-century, with a band of very high levels of both measures in the western mountain cantons, including virtually the entire western border of the department in M.U.H. and the isolated cantons of the Monts du Forez for A.P.H.

Some sense of change over time in these patterns can be gained from a sample of 33 villages in the department in both 1851 and 1891. The mean value of Adults per Household increased between 1851 and 1891 (2.22 to 2.41), while Marital Units per Household decreased (1.04 to .94). In terms of its structure, then, the household moved towards a nuclear structure with a vengeance, as multiple marriage households became less frequent in the population. The number of adults in each household, however, increased, and this can only be through increased co-residence of unmarried men and/or women (relatives, servants, boarders) with married couples. There was, however, a tendency towards greater uniformity in both aspects of household structure in the department, as the size of standard deviations decreased in the forty years under consideration.

It is apparent, then, that even as the families in the rural Loire were changing their reproductive behaviour, by marrying more frequently and controlling fertility within marriage, they were also changing the structure of the residential family group. How were these patterns of household organiz- ation related to the social and economic structure of the department? How did the changes in the department's economy affect households? And, most importantly, how did these changes in households affect demographic behav- iour in the Loire countryside?

HOUSEHOLD STRUCTURES

We can begin to find some answers to these questions by using data accumulated for a sample of 33 rural villages (see Appendix 1 for a description of the data). Essentially we need to examine two sets of relationships, with household structure as the centrepiece. The first set involves the relationship between the socio-economic structures of these villages and the patterns of household structure within them. We would anticipate that landholding would be associated with more complex households, while indicators of economic development would be associated with movement towards more nuclear household structures.

The second series of relationships are between household structure and demographic behaviour, and these are somewhat ambiguous. The two measures of household structure are to some extent a sliding scale in which lower to higher values imply shifts from nuclear to stem to joint household systems. The range of values in the sample used here, however, falls primarily in the nuclear and stem part of the scale, suggesting that households were rarely joint in the Loire (see the next section and Lehning, 1980, Ch. 7 for confirmation of this). Because of this, it is possible that we will not find a relationship between household structure and overall fertility, since both nuclear and stem household systems may be associated with less than maximum fertility. The possible association of nuclear households with wealth flows from parents to children suggests, however, that nuclear households may be associated with lower levels of overall fertility than stem households. Further, stem and nuclear families arguably work through different paths to overall fertility: stem families, which require heirs to the farm, should maintain high fertility within marriage but limit overall fertility by restricted nuptiality. Nuclear families may operate in this way as well, although the imperatives for an heir seem weaker. But both the direction of wealth flows and the individualism associated with nuclear households suggest that they would be associated with restricted marital fertility and possibly with more widespread marriage.

Table 1 gives the results of the first of these analyses, concerning the socio-economic determinants of Adults per Household and Marital Units per Household. None of these equations is particularly impressive, not surprising given the roughness of the measures of both household structure and of socio-economic structures. But several conclusions do seem to emerge. First, M.U.H. and A.P.H. are not related to the same socio-economic variables. A.P.H. in 1851 is significantly related only to the distance from a railroad, a measure of the isolation of the village from the communication networks developing in the nineteenth century. By 1891, this has disappeared, and A.P.H. is not related to any available measure of socio-economic structure.

Table 1: *Multiple regression results (betas), independent socio-economic variables and dependent household structure variables*

	M.U.H. 1851	A.P.H. 1851	M.U.H. 1891	A.P.H. 1891	D.A.P.H.	D.M.U.H.
Foncier/Cap.	.06	−.00	.03	.00	.00	.05
Patent/Cap.	.11	.07	−.33**	−.04	.18	.54***
Personnel/Cap.	−.18	−.01	−.08	−.08	.08	−.14
Prop. Pct.	−.07	.10	−.24	.19	−.09	.18
Fermiers Pct.	.03	−.03	.09	.15	−.26*	−.07
Text. Pct.	−.32*	−.14	−.29*	−.22	.07	−.10
RR Distance	.18	.52**	−.06	.30	.45**	.33
City Distance	.23	.13	.44**	.02	.18	−.20
Multiple R	.57	.64	.71	.51	.69	.55
R Square	.32	.41	.50	.26	.48	.31

* = significant at .05 level
** = significant at .01 level
*** = significant at .001 level

Table 2: *Multiple regression results (betas), household structure variables independent, demographic variables dependent*

	Adult/H.H.	Marital Units/H.H.	Multiple R	R Square
I_g 1851	.28	.05	.33	.107
I_g 1891	.67***	−.31	.53	.286
DIG	−.30	−.04	.33	.108
I_m 1851	−1.06***	.63***	.73	.531
I_m 1891	−.70***	.59***	.56	.317
DIM	−.33	.08	.30	.090
RIF 1851	−.09	.06	.06	.0041
RIF 1891	.05	−.16	.13	.02
DRIF	—	−.25	.25	.06

*** = significant at .001 level

M.U.H., in contrast, was related in 1851 to a measure of occupational structure, namely the percentage of textile workers in the village. The negative direction of this relationship suggests that this protoindustry helped reduce the frequency of complex households. The same relationship exists in 1891, and the percentage of textile workers was joined by patent per capita and the distance from a major city. All three significant relationships are in the direction suggested by modernization studies of the family (Goode, 1963): greater commercial activity, the former presence of exposure to cottage industry, and proximity to a major city meant less complex households, and half of the variance in M.U.H. in 1891 is accounted for by these variables. In contrast, there is no significant relationship between landholding (Prop. Pct.) and household structure, as Le Play argued there should be and as Parrish and Schwartz found for France at the departmental level (Le Play, 1871; Parrish and Schwartz, 1972).

It is apparent, then, that there is some socio-economic basis for the variations in household structure that are measured by A.P.H. and M.U.H. In particular, those aspects of the social and economic structure that suggest exposure to the developing economy of the nineteenth century were associated with the movement towards a nuclear household system. In contrast, isolation from these characteristics was associated with patterns of household complexity, especially the presence of several married couples in the same household.

The multiple regression results testing the relationship between household structure and demographic behaviour are presented in Table 2.[3] It is first of all apparent that no significant relationships existed between household structure,

3 Illegitimate fertility was negligible in the department and therefore has not been considered here.

on the one hand, and overall fertility after the effects of marital fertility and proportions married are taken into account (R.I.F.). Thus any effects on overall fertility must operate through its two principal components, marital fertility and proportions married.

The results with regard to marital fertility are ambiguous. In 1851, when most of the sample villages were operating under a system of uncontrolled fertility within marriage, household structure does not seem to have a measurable impact on differences within this regime of natural fertility. In 1891, in contrast, there is a positive relationship between A.P.H. and I_g, accounting for more than a quarter of the variation in I_g. The positive direction of the relationship is as expected: the high level of unmarried adults in households is related to high marital fertility. Childcare problems may have been reduced by the presence of unmarried adults and it is also possible that the attitudes towards the family that led to accepting unmarried siblings into the household also encouraged high marital fertility and helped resist the adoption of family limitation.

It was through nuptiality behaviour, however, that the household system primarily worked. In 1851 and 1891 both A.P.H. and M.U.H. were significantly related to proportions married, and in both instances the relationships are in the expected direction. Here we see the direct influence of the system of household formation on the ways women married. Adults per Household was inversely related to proportions married: where households provided a place for unmarried women, proportions married were low. In contrast, where nuclear households were the rule, proportions married were high. A direct relationship existed between Marital Units per Household and proportions married, suggesting that marriage was easier when the need to establish a separate household immediately after marriage was not a part of the system. Where separate residency was required—in areas of nuclear households— proportions married remained low. These results are similar to those found for French departments in 1856 (Berkner and Mendels, 1978).

This analysis suggests, then, that the principal path by which household residency rules influenced demographic behaviour was through nuptiality. But it also shows that this influence was diminishing over time, as the rural population of the Loire moved from a system of reproduction marked by restricted marriage and natural fertility within marriage to one of more widespread marriage and family limitation. In 1851, more than half of the variance in I_m could be 'explained' by A.P.H. and M.U.H.; by 1891 this had dropped to just under one-third. In terms of the statistics, this seems to be the result of the fact that both measures of household structure were decreasing in variance themselves between 1851 and 1891. In terms of the family system of the rural Loire, this suggests that as household rules became less idiosyncratic from place to place in the department, other factors began to affect nuptiality.

VILLAGE ANALYSIS

A better understanding of the relationship between rural industry and household structure can be gained by examining two villages in the Loire, one agricultural, the other with a protoindustrial sector (Mendels, 1971) in its economy. The two communes examined are Verrières, an agricultural village of around 1,000 people in the mid-nineteenth century; and Saint-Hilaire, a smaller commune of about 700 people. Verrières, located in the canton of Montbrison in the foothills of the western Monts du Forez, was dominated by family farmers. Most heads of household listed themselves as *propriétaires-cultivateurs* in the 1851 census, but their farms were probably composed of both their own land and share-cropping *domaines*. According to the 1852 *Enquête Agricole Décennale*, a majority of farmers were able to piece together farms of 10–20 hectares that produced cereals (especially rye) and livestock. While much of the cereal produced was probably for local consumption, livestock was a valuable cash product that provided income for payment of rents, taxes, and expansion of holdings (A.D.L., 1852).

By the end of the nineteenth century, a significant change had occurred in the agrarian structure of Verrières. The *metayage* leases that were omnipresent in 1852 had disappeared, and most farms were cultivated by *propriétaires* with the help of their family or others. This change in land tenure was accompanied by some reduction in the size of farms: whereas in 1852 most farms were between 10 and 20 hectares, only 17 per cent were over ten hectares in 1892. Almost half (48 per cent), however, were between five and 10 hectares (A.D.L., 1892). It is difficult not to see a relationship between the end of *metayage* and the fragmentation of farms: as John Shaffer noted in the Nivernais, share-cropping spared the share-cropping family from the necessity of dividing property among several heirs in each generation (Shaffer, 1982). Proprietorship, however, exposed the farm to division and, over time, could lead to reduced farm size. In the place of share-cropping, therefore, Verrières had become a village of family farms which, while smaller in size than the *domaines* of mid-century, were still of substantial size for this part of France and still demanded a substantial labour force to work. Nonetheless, the changes in land tenure placed long-term pressures on family behaviour in the commune.

Saint-Hilaire, in contrast, was in the mountainous canton of Charlieu in the north-eastern corner of the department. Landholding was more divided here than in Verrières, and most farms were less than five hectares in size, too small to employ more than a few family members and not productive enough to provide for the needs of an entire family. Agriculture was supplemented in Saint-Hilaire by silk and cotton-weaving for merchants in Thisy and Lyon in the neighbouring department of the Rhône (A.D.L., 1852).

Saint-Hilaire did not experience significant changes in the system of land tenure or size of farms between the mid-nineteenth century and the beginning of this century, and in fact it was spared the complete de-industrialization that was the lot of many protoindustrial villages in late-nineteenth-century Europe. Nonetheless, the economic outlook for Saint-Hilaire was not bright by the end of the century. Returns on seed in wheat improved, although those for the other major crop, oats, did not. Fragmentation of landholding, however, continued to make it difficult for a family to employ many family members in agriculture: probably no more than two adults could profitably be used on the majority of farms, and almost half of the farms that were under one hectare were little more than gardens. Indeed, by the time of the 1901 census, most heads of household were listed as *fermiers* rather than *propriétaires*. In these circumstances the wage sector of the economy was a vital part of the family economy, and there was an increase in the proportion of households working entirely in the textile sector. But the last part of the nineteenth century and the beginning of the twentieth was a period of stagnation for the Roannais cotton industry, and mechanization was proceeding rapidly, concentrating the industry in Roanne and its suburbs (Lequin, 1977, pp. 93–94; Dechelette, 1910, p. 48). Wages are difficult to judge in such a dispersed industry. But it is difficult to believe that textile work could support a family at the turn of the century better than, or even as well as, at mid-century. The textile industry remained in Saint-Hilaire at the turn of the century, and this was a positive factor in the family economies of the residents of the village. But mechanization and stagnation were the principal features of the industry, and these suggest that it was a tenuous way to make a living.

Indices of demographic and household behaviour in Verrières and Saint-Hilaire are presented in Table 3. Both communes at mid-century seem to fit most characteristics of a pre-transition demographic regime, with uncontrolled fertility within marriage, restricted marriage, and moderate levels of overall fertility. Mortality in Verrières was somewhat lower than in Saint-Hilaire, and this, combined with the level of fertility, meant that out-migration was an important way of relieving pressure on resources. In Saint-Hilaire, in contrast, higher mortality was accompanied by lower levels of out-migration. Household structure in Verrières was more complex than in Saint-Hilaire: it is apparent that a significant number of households in Verrières were complex in some way, whereas nuclear household structure was more frequent in Saint-Hilaire.

In both communes a movement towards more frequent marriage, control of fertility within marriage, and a nuclear household system occurred in the second half of the century. I_m increased between 1851 and the end of the century, I_g decreased (in the case of Saint-Hilaire, dramatically), and Adults per Household and Marital Units per Household decreased. However, while in Saint-Hilaire these changes led to a much lower level of overall fertility (I_f), this measure actually increased in Verrières. Mortality also showed some improvement in Saint-Hilaire, which in combination with the dramatic decline in reproduction meant that *in*–migration was necessary to maintain the

Table 3: *Summary of demographic and family changes in Verrières and Saint-Hilaire between 1851 and 1901*

	Verrières	*Saint-Hilaire*
I_g 1851	.792	.959
I_g 1901	.499	.284
I_h 1851	.000	.000
I_h 1901	.014	.000
I_m 1851	.382	.416
I_m 1901	.498	.459
I_f 1851	.302	.399
I_f 1901	.339	.130
APH 1851	2.62	2.26
APH 1901	2.40	2.02
MUH 1851	1.190	0.980
MUH 1901	1.004	0.866
CDR 1851	14.5	25.4
CDR 1891	15.5	18.1
CDR 1901	19.8	19.7
MIGR 1841–1851	−32.1	−21.2
MIGR 1886–1891	−10.3	2.5*

* Positive rate indicates in-migration.

population. In Verrières, in contrast, mortality remained at about the same level (albeit still lower than in Saint-Hilaire) and, with overall fertility even higher than it had been at mid-century, out-migration remained an important part of the demographic mechanism. In general, while Saint-Hilaire appears, in this span of two generations, to have entered full tilt into a twentieth-century pattern of demographic and family behaviour, Verrières, although somewhat closer to this behaviour in 1851 than was Saint-Hilaire, moved more gradually in that direction during the fifty-year period.

A Protoindustrial Village: Saint-Hilaire

In Saint-Hilaire the overwhelming majority of households were nuclear in structure.[4] Almost two-thirds of all households in 1851 consisted only of parents and their unmarried children. This pattern was most marked when the head was in young adulthood (ages 25–34), when almost three-quarters of all households were nuclear. Among older heads of household there was some

---

4 Because of their length, I have not included the tables cross-tabulating the age of the head of household with household structure for Saint-Hilaire or Verrières. I hope that sufficient data have been included in the text to make up for this omission.

decline in the percentage of nuclear households, but even when the head was over 65, 56 per cent of households were nuclear.[5] The predominance of nuclear household structure is even more striking when households that included only the conjugal pair, their children, and a non-kin servant are considered. This group (nuclear plus servant) was the second most important category of households in the village, containing more than 10 per cent of all households.

Complex households made up a very small proportion of the total in Saint-Hilaire in 1851, with only 14 per cent including kin from outside the conjugal family. No particular form of household complexity stands out: there were only a handful of households in each category. The range of kin from whom peripheral household members were drawn was very narrow: there were no household members more distant from the conjugal pair than niece or nephew, and most were siblings. This suggests again the importance of nuclear household structure in the family system in Saint-Hilaire: household complexity did not follow any clear pattern, such as the stem family found in Austria or the joint households found in central France (Berkner, 1972; Shaffer, 1982). Instead, the kind of complexity was virtually random. For most Saint-Hilairiens, therefore, marriage meant the formation of a new household separate from both sets of parents.

This household system was closely linked to the family economy. There were two different patterns of family economy in Saint-Hilaire (Lehning, 1983). In one, agricultural families supplemented the agricultural labour (and earnings) of some members with the industrial labour (and earnings) of other members of the household. This is a reflection of the smallholding prevalent in the village, with most farms less than five hectares in size, below the minimum needed to provide for a family and not requiring the entire family as a labour force. Agriculture, therefore, does not appear to have been productive or profitable enough to provide an adequate basis for a family in Saint-Hilaire. There was excess labour as well as a need for additional income in each of these households, and rural industry provided a supplement to agricultural work and income. A second pattern is also apparent, in which rural industry was the sole means of support. These households (20.9 per cent of the total) did not have access to land, and the entire household, not just some of its members, supplied labour on which rural industry could draw.

Were there differences in household formation and structure between these two types of rural industrial families? Among the households totally dependent upon rural industry, there was a clear tendency towards nuclear household structure: 31 out of 35 were nuclear (one with a co-residing

---

5 I am, of course, considering a cross-sectional source, the nominal census list, as if it reflects longitudinal experience. The lack of a true longitudinal source leaves no other choice, but in any event the slowness of changes in household behavior suggests that this should not create a serious problem.

servant), and only one was complex. In this instance, then, we can see in Saint-Hilaire the reflection of the earlier examination of villages at the aggregate level, as cottage industry was related to nuclear household structure.

The situation is more complicated with the families sharing agricultural and industrial work, but a marked preference for nuclear households is evident. Three-quarters of these families lived in nuclear households, and the remaining households were scattered over a number of different types of household complexity. In Saint-Hilaire, therefore, both concentration on rural industry and the small-holding agriculture that forced people to resort to rural industry as a by-occupation were associated with nuclear household structure. The nuclear system found in Saint-Hilaire suggests the results of the poor prospects for agriculture—graphically underscored by the complete absence of exclusively agricultural families—as well as the ability of rural industry to provide the economic basis for a household. Certainly none of these families were prosperous, and what emerges from this evidence is a population dependent on different kinds of makeshift family economies (Hufton, 1974, Chs. 3 and 4).

There was little change in this household system by the end of the century. A substantial number of households (69.8 per cent) were nuclear, either with or without servants. About the same proportion of households as in 1851 were complex, and these households again showed no clear pattern but were scattered almost randomly over the different forms of complexity. One notable change, however, is that in 1901 there were substantially more households in spite of the smaller population of the village—almost 25 per cent more than in 1851. A large part of this increase is in the number of households without any family; that is, those consisting of unrelated persons or, most often, of a single individual. These households were composed primarily of either the young or the old. If any fact were to underline the essentially nuclear character of the family system in Saint-Hilaire, it is this. The household of origin was not able to hold on to young adults as they grew up, nor did it provide an occupation or shelter for the elderly. Statistical data shed only dim light on emotional aspects of family and household life, but the fact that by 1901 in Saint-Hilaire most individuals left home when they could and did not depend on their adult children for care in old age suggests that the household as a collective institution was under severe strain.

As in 1851, this household system in 1901 in Saint-Hilaire found clear roots in the village economy. Smallholdings and the presence of weaving in particular encouraged independence from the family of origin: exclusively agricultural households did not need much labour outside the conjugal pair and their children to work the family farm and, while as in 1851 some households supplemented the agricultural work of the household head with weaving, these were overwhelmingly nuclear in structure (47 out of 54, only two of which had servants). The households with no related persons in them were able to exist because of the opportunities provided by weaving: ten out of 35 were exclusively dependent on weaving for their livelihood, and even those dependent on agriculture were *cultivateurs* or *ménagères* rather than *proprié-taires*. Indeed, it is apparent that, other than the *curé*, *instituteur*, and a few *rentiers*, those who lived in this kind of household were overwhelmingly drawn from the lower range of the social structure of the village: those dependent on some kind of wage labour or on rented land for their livelihoods. The proletarianization that was a consequence of the social and economic structures of Saint-Hilaire in the second half of the nineteenth century thus found its echo in a fragmented household structure.

Change in the family and household system of Saint-Hilaire had, therefore, been modest between 1851 and 1901, but it was certainly in the direction of emphasis both in practice and, possibly, in attitudes towards individualism. While in both census lists the nuclear household system appears closely tied to the economic structure of the village, the opportunities for employment outside family farming seem particularly important in this village. In these circumstances, smallholding and the stagnation of the Roannais cotton trade in the last decades of the nineteenth century placed heavy pressures on the household.

The relationship of the predominantly nuclear household system of Saint-Hilaire to the demographic changes of the second half of the nineteenth century in the village cannot be shown definitively, but some associations seem apparent between the ways the household responded to the economic pressures of the late nineteenth century and the changes in demographic behaviour in the village. While even in 1851 nuclear households predominated in the village and there is not much evidence of kin outside the conjugal pair playing an important role for the household, a kind of 'household fragment-ation', with young and old—precisely those that we would expect to see in complex or extended households—establishing their own households, had occurred by 1901. Children had ceased to act as old-age insurance, if they had ever functioned that way for parents, and they became an increasingly heavy burden even as improving mortality meant that more children would live to adulthood. Thus the pressures on parents to limit the number of their children increased. From the perspective of the child reaching adulthood, the family of origin could do little to set them on their way, and marriage became more of an individual decision. Whether or not the nuclear household system of Saint-Hilaire transmitted individualistic attitudes, it was itself rooted in the wage economy of the village and, along with that wage economy, it must have encouraged family formation decisions based on individual considerations.

An Agricultural Village: Verrières

The household system in Verrières presents a striking contrast to the overwhelmingly nuclear pattern in Saint-Hilaire. Certainly a majority of households were nuclear in structure (61.5 per cent, including those with servants). But almost one-third of all households in 1851 were complex in some way. Many of these complex households included several conjugal pairs

(42 of 203 households), and households headed by older parents and including married children made up the majority of these.

Most households were nuclear when the head was young and in middle age, peaking when the head was in the 45–54 age group—that is, just before his own children began to marry. As the head grew older, however, nuclear households became less frequent, until in the 65+ age group only 28.9 per cent of all households were nuclear. Of increasing importance in these age groups were complex households, especially those involving the co-residence of a married child with his/her parents. In the 65+ age group, this kind of multiple household included 38.5 per cent of all households. In Verrières, therefore, a clear pattern of multi-generational household complexity appears. Much less frequently than in Saint-Hilaire did marriage mean the establishment of a separate household, independent of parents. Instead, many men and women remained in a subordinate position even after their marriage.

This household system was closely connected to the agricultural economy in Verrières, and especially to one of the forms of land tenure in the village, *metayage* (Shaffer, 1982). The composition of farms in Verrières at mid-century—a small plot owned by the farmer plus a share-cropped *domaine* probably 10–20 hectares in size—affected the peasant household in several ways. In the first place, the fact that the greater part of the land worked was not owned but held under a *metayage* lease meant that the peasant had no control over the ultimate disposition of the land. Thus, holdings were not divided with each inheritance, but remained grouped together into relatively large farms. These farms also demanded relatively large amounts of labour in order to be worked. While some families had recourse to domestic servants (17.7 per cent of households), kin were more frequently used (30 per cent of households). The complex families in Verrières therefore were labour-sharing groups that made it possible for a family to rent and work a *domaine*. The absence of alternative employments in the village, such as the rural industry available in Saint-Hilaire, no doubt strengthened the position of parents as they sought to keep a child working for them even after marriage. But the most important point about this household system was that it made it possible for the tenants in Verrières to work large share-crop farms. As John Shaffer has shown in the neighbouring Nivernais, *metayage* contracts required the family to provide sufficient labour to work the *domaine*. While servants were a possibility, kin— and especially adult children—were a solution to this problem. In contrast to the restrictions on family size placed by the limited economic possibilities in Saint-Hilaire, the system of *metayage* in Verrières encouraged large, extended households.

Household complexity remained an important part of the family system in Verrières in 1901. A smaller proportion of households were nuclear (55.1 per cent *vs.* 61.5 per cent) in 1901, and there was some increase in the proportion of households consisting of unrelated or single persons (15.2 per cent *vs.* 8.4 per cent). But while this increase in non-family households was to some extent at the expense of complex households, almost one-fifth of the households in the village were vertically extended (19.3 per cent).

The importance of complex households in Verrières in 1851 and in 1901 suggests that household change in that village occurred at a slower pace than in the rest of the rural communes of the department, and the contrast with the overwhelmingly nuclear household system of Saint-Hilaire remains apparent even at the beginning of the twentieth century. But there were some changes: the proportion of complex households declined, while that of non-family households increased. Many of these non-family households were made up of older people: in fact, more persons aged over sixty-five lived by themselves than in complex households (10 *vs*. 11). As in Saint-Hilaire, the number of households increased even though the population of the village declined.

It seems, then, that even in Verrières the complex family was losing its strength. The labour needs of the smaller family farms were still greater than on the miniscule farms of Saint-Hilaire, but increasingly these needs could be met from within the nuclear family. As a consequence, by 1901, many people as they grew older either chose or were forced to live by themselves.

It is apparent that the pace of economic, household, and demographic change was slower in Verrières than in Saint-Hilaire. Certainly marriage became more frequent by 1901; family limitation also became more frequent. But the levels of the measures of these aspects of family formation, as well as the *rise* in overall fertility, suggest that a significant number of families in the village continued to follow the practices of mid-century. Indeed, the continuation of a systematic form of extended household structure, tied to the labour needs of the agricultural system, meant that for those families that continued in this type of agricultural activity, the imperatives were for extended households, restricted marriage and high fertility within marriage.

The households found in Saint-Hilaire and Verrières were extremely flexible. Households in Saint-Hilaire, with family members working in silk and cotton-weaving and few kin outside of the conjugal family, reflected the exigencies of a socio-economic structure built on small, unproductive farms but with non-agricultural employment available. In Verrières, by contrast, the availability of land for rent and the ability of the household to expand to include married children coincided to make it possible for families to work the large farms the *metayage* preserved in 1851. By the end of the century, the decline of *metayage* had placed pressures on the household system; in these circumstances, the household changed towards a more nuclear structure. All of these households responded to the opportunities and demands that the economic structure—reflected in the size of farms, the forms of land fenure, and the possibilities of industrial work—presented to the members of the family. Family members were clearly actors in the process, but their households were firmly enmeshed in the system of social relations that surrounded the land and rural industry in the department.

CONCLUSIONS

This essay has focused on the relationship between social and economic structure and household structure on the one hand, and household structure and demographic behaviour on the other. While one might hope for stronger results, the analysis has nevertheless provided some insight into the factors that determined household structure and demographic behaviour. In terms of both the aggregate analysis of a sample of rural villages in the department of the Loire and the two villages in the department more closely examined, it is apparent that labour needs imposed on the household by the economy helped to determine the structure of that household, and that, especially by way of nuptiality, such considerations could also affect reproduction. By the nature of such kinds of analysis, there is far less convincing evidence about the role of attitudes in such relationships. Nonetheless, the comparison of Verrières and Saint-Hilaire seems to suggest that these systems of economic structure, family structure, and demographic behaviour were part of a culturally determined moral economy (Smith, 1981, p. 618). Wage labour in Saint-Hilaire and capitalistic land ownership in Verrières helped undermine this moral economy in the second half of the nineteenth century, leading in turn to changes in demographic behaviour.

Nonetheless, it would be pressing the evidence much too far to suggest that only household structure determined demographic behaviour. Social and economic organization—types of agriculture, the extent of industrialization, urbanization, and market development—can play an independent role in determining fertility and nuptiality behaviour even without the mediation of household structures and their imperatives. Cultural factors, such as literacy, education, and religious belief and secularization, may have independent influences on the decisions of individuals to marry and families to reproduce. By way of conclusion, then, we might consider how the relationships on which this essay has focused fit into a larger explanatory framework of demographic behaviour.

For the purposes of this analysis, we will return to the aggregate data on 33 sample villages in the Loire for 1891, by which time, as we have already seen, these villages and the department had moved substantially towards a demographic system of increasingly frequent marriage and limitation of fertility within marriage. Table 4 presents in summary form the results of three different explanatory models for I_g and I_m in 1891. The first, a socio-economic model, includes a number of measures of the socio-economic structures of the villages; the second utilizes solely household structure variables; the third includes measures of cultural factors: 0,-literacy and schooling, linguistic particularism, and secularization.[6]

6 The socio-economic model included the following independent variables (see Appendix for a full explanation of them): FONC, PAT, PERS, PROPPCT, FERMPCT, TEXTPCT, RRDIST, CITYDIST. The household structure model included: APH, MUH. The cultural model included:

Table 4: *Values of R square for three explanatory models for I_g and I_m in 1891, sample of villages in Loire*

	I_g 1891	I_m 1891
Socio-economic model	.61	.43
Household structure model	.29	.32
Cultural model	.68	.51

It is evident that, of the three models, the Household Structure Model, while significant, is the least satisfactory for both marital fertility and proportions married. Thus, while we should not ignore the significance of household structure in determining demographic behaviour—and that is the basic point of this essay—we need to include other factors in a full explanation. What is most striking about these results is that in the case of both marital fertility and proportions married, the socio-economic model is less satisfactory than the cultural model. A complete explanation of the demographic changes that occurred in the Loire and throughout Europe in the nineteenth century must therefore consider not only economic development, but also the independent influence of such factors as household structure, literacy, education, secularization, and the erosion of linguistic particularism (see Lehning, 1984a; 1984b; 1988; Cleland and Wilson, 1987).

Appendix 1: Variables Used in the Analysis 0*-

The variables used in this analysis are drawn from data found in five sources: (1) the nominal lists of the 1851 and 1891 censuses of the population, which provide age and marital status distributions of the population and the number of households in each commune (A.D.L., 1851; 1891), as well as (in 1851) occupational summaries for each commune; (2) the *Mouvement de la population*, 1849–1853 and 1889–93 (A.D.L., 1851), which gives the number of legitimate and illegitimate births and the number of deaths in each commune (where necessary, these have been supplemented by the registers of the *état civil* for 1849–1853, found in A.D.L. 3E; (3) the *Annuaire du département de la Loire pour 1846* (1846, pp. 134–45; 184–93; 236–45), which provides tables with the assessments for each of the four principal direct taxes (the *foncier* on land, the *personnel* on personal property, the *patente* on businesses, and the *portes et fenêtres* on doors and windows) for each commune; (4) the vital registers of the *état civil* for the periods 1846–55 and 1883–92, including marriage acts that indicate those spouses able to sign their names; (5) the

MALE LITERACY 1891; FEMALE LITERACY 1891; MALE SCHOOL ATTENDANCE IN 1860; FEMALE SCHOOL ATTENDANCE IN 1860, SOUTH, EUVERT PCT.

returns for each commune for the election of 1885 to the Chamber of Deputies (A.D.L., 3 M 21–22).

Each of the variables has been constructed from these data as follows: *Foncier*/Cap (FONC): the per capita assessment for the land tax (*impôt foncier*) using the 1851 population as the base. The absence of evidence for significant agricultural change in the period between 1851 and 1891 argues that this variable as well as the next one should remain relatively valid at the later date as well; Pat: the per capita assessment for the *patent*, the tax on business establishments, using the 1851 population as the base.

Pers: the per capita assessment for the *impôt personnel*, the tax on personal property, using the 1851 population as the base.

Proppct: the percentage of the 1851 population whose occupations were listed in the census as proprietor;

Fermpct: the percentage of the 1851 population whose occupations were listed in the census as *fermiers*.

Textpct: the percentage of the population in 1851 whose occupations were listed in the census as in the textile industry. Since the principal textile regions in 1851 (Roannais, centre-east, and Stephanois region) were either in decline or concentrating production in factories by 1891, this measure indicates areas of rural industry in 1851, but areas of recent de-industrialization in 1891;

RR distance: the distance in kilometres of the commune from the nearest principal railroad, either the line from Lyon to Le Puy through the Stephanois valley in the south or the Roanne to Saint-Etienne line that ran north-south along the western side of the department;

City Distance: the distance of the commune from the closest of the two major cities in the department, Saint-Etienne or Roanne.

South: a value of one indicates that the commune falls into the southern linguistic region of the department as described in Gardette (1943); zero indicates that it does not;

APH: the total number of adults aged 25 and over divided by the number of households.

MUH: the number of married males plus the number of widowed or divorced males plus the number of widowed or divorced females divded by the number of households.

DAPH: the change in Adults per Household between 1851 and 1891.

DMUH: the change in Marital Units per Household between 1851 and 1891.

I_g: a measure of marital fertility, which measures the marital fertility of the subject population as a proportion of the marital fertility of the Hutterites;

I_m: a measure of female proportions married, weighted by the marital fertility of the Hutterites;

I_f: a measure of overall fertility, based on the marital fertility of the Hutterites;

I_h: a measure of illegitimate fertility, based on the marital fertility of the Hutterites;

DIG: the change in marital fertility (I_g) between 1851 and 1891;

DIM: the change in proportions married (I_m) between 1851 and 1891;

RIF: the residual of I_f after the effects of I_g and I_m have been taken into account;

DRIF: the change between 1851 and 1891 in the residual of I_f after the effects of I_g and I_m have been taken into account.

Male Literacy 1891: the percentage of men married 1883–92 able to sign their certificate of marriage;

Female Literacy 1891: the percentage of women married 1883–92 able to sign their certificate of marriage;

MAT 60: the percentage of males aged 7–13 attending school in 1860;

FAT 60: the percentage of women aged 7–13 attending school in 1860;

Euvert %: the percentage of those voting in 1885 who voted for the conservative Euvert list.

MIGR 1841–50: the annual net migration rate between 1841 and 1850;

MIGR 1886–91: the annual net migration rate between 1886 and 1891.

References

ARCHIVES DÉPARTEMENTALES DE LA LOIRE (A.D.L.) (1846), *Annuaire du Département de la Loire en 1846*, Montbrison. (1851), 48 M 23–130 *Mouvement de la Population, 1847–1893*. (1852), 55 M 10 *Enquête agricole quinquennale de 1852*. (1892), 55 M 44–46 *Enquête agricole décennale de 1892*. (1851), 49 M-72–96 *Liste nominative de recensement de 1851*. (1885), 3 M 21–22 *Elections législatives 1885*. (1891), 49 M 252–261 *Liste nominative de recensement de 1891*. (1901), 49 M 341–354 *Liste nominative de recensement de 1901*.

BEAVER, S. E. (1975), *Demographic Transition Theory Reconsidered: An Application to Recent Natality Trends in Latin America*, Lexington, Mass.

BECKER, G. S. (1960), 'An Economic Analysis of Fertility', In *Demographic and Economic Change in Developed Countries*, Princeton, 209–31.

BECKER, G. S. (1981), *A Treatise on the Family*, Cambridge, Mass.

BERKNER, L. K. (1972), 'The Stem Family and the Developmental Cycle of the Peasant Household: An Eighteenth Century Austrian Example', *American Historical Review*, **77**, 398–418.

BERKNER, L. K. (1977), 'Household Arithmetic: A Note', *Journal of Family History*, **2**, 159–63.

BERKNER, L. K. and F. MENDELS (1978), 'Inheritance Systems, Family Structure, and Demographic Patterns in Western Europe, 1700–1900', In C. Tilly (ed.), *Historical Studies of Changing Fertility*, Princeton, 209–24.

BURCH, T. K. and M. GENDELL (1971), 'Extended Family Structure and Fertility: Some Conceptual and Methodological Issues', In S. Polgar (ed.), *Culture and Population: A Collection of Current Studies*, Cambridge, Mass., 87–104.

CALDWELL, J. C. (1978), 'A Theory of Fertility: From High Plateau to Destabilization', *Population and Development Review*, **4**, 553–77.

CALDWELL, J. C. (1982), *Theory of Fertility Decline*, New York.

CAYEZ, P. (1978), *Métiers jacquards et hauts fourneaux: aux origines de l'industrie lyonnaise*, Lyon.

CLELAND, J. and C. WILSON (1987), 'Demand Theories of the Fertility Transition: An Iconoclastic View', *Population Studies*, **41**, 5–30.

COALE, A. J. (1973), 'The Demographic Transition', In *International Union for the Scientific Study of Population, Liege, 1973*, Liege, 53–71.

COALE, A. J. and R. TREADWAY (1986), 'A Summary of the Changing Distribution of Overall Fertility, Marital Fertility, and the Proportion Married in the Provinces of Europe', In A. J. Coale and S. C. Watkins (eds.), *The Decline of Fertility in Europe*, Princeton, 31–180.

COLLOMP, A. (1972), 'Famille nucléaire et famille élargie en Haute-Provence au XVIIIe siècle (1703–1734)', *Annales. Economies. Sociétés. Civilisations*, 969–75.

DAVIS, K. (1955), 'Institutional Patterns Favoring High Fertility in Underdeveloped Areas', *Eugenics Quarterly*, **2**, 33–39.

DECHELETTE, C. (1910), *L'Industrie cotonnière à Roanne*, Roanne.

EASTERLIN, R. and E. CRIMINS (1985), *The Fertility Revolution*, Chicago.

GOODE, W. (1963), *World Revolution and Family Patterns*, New York.

GRAS, L.-J. (1906), *Histoire de la rubannerie*, Saint-Etienne.

GUILLAUME, P. (1963), 'La Situation économique et sociale du département de la Loire d'après l'Enquête sur le travail agricole et industriel du 25 mai 1848', *Revue d'histoire moderne et contemporaine*, **10**, 5–34.

HUFTON, O. H. (1974), *The Poor of Eighteenth-Century France 1750–1789*, Oxford.

LEHNING, J. R. (1980), *The Peasants of Marlhes*, Chapel Hill.

LEHNING, J. R. (1983), 'Nuptiality and Rural Industry: Families and Labor in the French Countryside', *Journal of Family History*, **8**, 333–45.

LEHNING, J. R. (1984a), 'The Decline of Marital Fertility: Evidence from a French Department, la Loire, 1851–1891', *Annales de démographie historique*, 201–17.

LEHNING, J. R. (1984b), 'Literacy and Demographic Behavior: Evidence from Family Reconstitution in Nineteenth Century France', *The History of Education Quarterly*, Winter, 545–59.

LEHNING, J. R. (1988), 'The Timing and Prevalence of Women's Marriage in the French Department of the Loire 1851–1891', *Journal of Family History*, **13**, 3.

LEMAÎTRE, N. (1976), 'Familles complexes en Bas-Limousin. Ussel au début du XIXe siècle', *Annales du Midi*, No. 127, 219–24.

LE PLAY, F. (1870), *L'Organisation du travail*, Tours.

LE PLAY, F. (1871), *L'Organisation de la famille*, Paris.

LEQUIN, Y. (1977), *Les Ouvriers de la région lyonnaise (1848–1914)*, Lyon.

LESTHAEGHE, R. (1980), 'On the Social Control of Human Reproduction', *Population and Development Review*, **6**, 527–48.

LINDERT, P. (1978), *Fertility and Scarcity in America*, Princeton.

LORIMER, F. (1954), *Culture and Human Fertility*, Paris.

MALTHUS, T. R., (1959), *First Essay on Population*, Ann Arbor.

MENDELS, F. F. (1971), 'Protoindustrialization: The First Phase of the Industrialization Process', *Journal of Economic History*, **32**, 241–61.

NOTESTEIN, F. (1945), 'Population—The Long View', In Theodore W. Schultz (ed.), *Food for the World*, Chicago.

NOTESTEIN, F. (1953), 'Economic Problems of Population Change', In *Proceedings of the Eighth International Conference of Agricultural Economists*, London, 13–31.

PARISET, E. (1901), *Histoire de la fabrique lyonnaise*, Lyon.

PARRISH, W. and M. SCHWARTZ (1972), 'Household Complexity in 19th Century France', *American Sociological Review*, **37**, 154–73.

PARSONS, T. (1943), 'The Kinship System of the Contemporary United States', *American Anthropologist*, **43**, 22–38.

PEYRONNET, J.-C. (1975), 'Famille élargie ou famille nucléaire? L'Exemple du Limousin au début du XIXe siècle,' *Revue d'histoire moderne et contemporaine*, **XXII**, 568–82.

SENIOR, W. N. (1828), *Two Lectures on Population*, London.

SHAFFER, J. (1982), *Family and Farm: Agrarian Change and Household Organization in the Loire Valley 1500–1900*, Albany.

SIMON, J. (1974), *The Effects of Income on Fertility*, Chapel Hill.

SMITH, R. M. (1981), 'Fertility, Economy and Household Formation in England Over Three Centuries', *Population and Development Review*, 7, 595–622.

SMITH, R. M. (1986), 'Transfer Incomes, Risk and Security: The Roles of the Family and the Collectivity in Recent Theories of Fertility Change', In David Coleman and Roger Scholfield (eds.), *The State of Population Theory*, Oxford, 188–211.

WORLD POPULATION PLAN (1975), *Population and Development Review*, I, 163–81.

Acknowledgements

Research for this article was supported by Grant No. 1 F32 HDO 54 17–01 from the National Institute of Child Health and Development, and by grants from the American Council of Learned Societies and the University of Utah Research Committee. I am grateful for the comments made by participants in the Conference on the European Peasant Family and Economy at the University of Minnesota, 7–8 October 1988.

Chapter 6

THE STEM FAMILY, DEMOGRAPHY AND INHERITANCE: THE SOCIAL FRONTIERS OF AUTO-REGULATION

ANTOINETTE FAUVE-CHAMOUX

Since the pioneer essay of John Hajnal appeared about the European marriage patterns of the past (Hajnal, 1965), historians and demographers have been trying to understand human reproduction processes: the Malthusian 'positive checks' (wars, famines etc.) had been the main regulators, but mortality was not the only controller of growth. Societies had been controlling their size, to avoid subsistence crises and keep social order, by regulating both nuptiality and fertility (Fauve-Chamoux, 1984a; 1984b; 1987b). Those 'preventive checks' concerned mostly access to marriage and property. The stem-family system is one of the ways some societies elected to allow for those preventive checks.

Access to resources and land was strictly regulated by social norms in rural pre-industrial societies. Post-feudal France—as a patchwork of different dialects and cultures (Breton, Basque, Norman, Flemish, Alsacian, Savoyard, Provençal, Languedocian, Catalan, Gascon, Auvergnat. . .), of different origins and traditions—seems to present a mosaic of diverse inheritance systems (Le Roy Ladurie, 1976). Sometimes parents' property was equally divided amongst the surviving children, while at other times a privileged heir was designated as a successor, the other children being excluded from land inheritance, with or without financial compensation.

The inegalitarian transmission of patrimonial property—land, house and goods—so common in European aristocratic societies of the past (French *droit d'aînesse* regime or Spanish *majorat* [Clavero, 1974]), was usual amongst landowner peasants in southern France of occitanian tradition. In the middle of the nineteenth century, the social reformer Frederic Le Play invented the concept of the 'stem-family' (*famille-souche*) to describe this kind of transgenerational family behaviour in which he saw a perfect model of social organization. The domestic and economic unit was transmitted to a lone heir (a privileged child) who lived with his parents in a multi-generational household, with his spouse and children, from amongst whom he would himself choose an heir. This mode of social reproduction allowed the familial group to keep on living in and on a 'house', with the subsequent constant transmission of knowledge between the generations. This situation also served as a strict control on the number of autonomous rural estates, assuring permanency of an autonomous unit and consequently good equilibrium between population and resources. In case of population pressure, extra individuals had either to leave or to stay unmarried in the native house where they worked as if they were domestic servants. Controlling population growth was a constant worry in those societies where nonegalitarian modes of transmission were practised.

If high rates of celibacy and migration were observed in western Europe within those stem-family societies, and if controlling fertility by some kind of family limitation happened to be efficient, particularly in south-west France (Henry, 1972), it is nevertheless certain that a clear population increase took place during the eighteenth century and that collective behaviour had to adjust to important demographic changes.

Our purpose in this essay is to look, through a Pyrenean example, at the typical stem-family society of the Baronnies, at how the rigidity of nonegalitarian transmission faced demographic pressure and how it confronted the main cultural mutation which the egalitarian French Revolution tried to impose. When the social ideal is auto-regulation and permanence within a conservative system, is it nevertheless possible for some changes to occur and for some kind of innovation to be seen?

THE CONSERVATIVE OCCITAN STEM-FAMILY

Pre-industrial rural western societies were basically organized, socially, economically and technically, into familial working groups of co-residents. The domestic unit in their occidental Old World generally consisted of a couple and the children. This was true all over Europe, as the Cambridge group studies have shown (Laslett and Wall, 1972; Wall, 1983), in areas where partible inheritance was the common practice, but the proportion of complex households remained high (sometimes more than 40 per cent) in some regions, for example southern France or central Europe, where impartible inheritance had been usual Peter Laslett, defending a 'nuclear hardship model' (Laslett, 1972; 1978; 1983), was unwilling to recognize anything other than a recessive model in the resistant real and demystified stem-family system he was confronted with in some regions, especially the mountainous areas of Europe (witness his fascinating debate with L. K. Berkner [Laslett, 1978]). With the passage of time it now seems clear that this debate lacked basic precise historical data concerning integral property transmission of the *Hof* (and its connected land) in Lower Saxony or Austria (Berkner, 1972; 1976; 1977), and did not explore clearly and nominatively the developmental cycle of the domestic group. This is why, although difficult to believe, it still remained to be proved, in the late 1970s, that the presence of the stem family was definitely associated with practices of impartibility, and was not only an aristocratic or gentry model. Indeed, within the peasantry, where 'a new kind of household developed between the 1690s and 1760s' (Berkner, 1977, p. 64), the general implications of European family mutations for industrialization, urbanization and socio-demographic changes were already clear (Berkner and Mendels, 1976).

Working in a parallel direction, anthropologists and ethnographers began in the meantime to study precisely the kinship networks in European rural societies, as they used to do in exotic ones, analysing matrimonial and successoral systems as a set of regulations, customs and oriented choices, within a specific lineage or group (Pingaud, 1971; Segalen, 1972; 1985) or between groups, which all tended to protect, conserve or improve the position of the original group (Bourdieu, 1962; 1972). The concept of 'house' (*maison*) as an economic and social unit of residence (production, consumption and reproduction unit) was rediscovered by historians, be it in southern France the *domus* of Montaillou (Le Roy Ladurie, 1975a; 1975b; 1976), the Lozerian or Rouergan *oustal* (Claverie and Lamaison, 1982), the Provençal *casa* (Collomp, 1983), the Basque *etchea* (Douglas, 1969; Rodriguez Hernandorena, 1988) and the gasco-Pyrenean *maysou* (Augustins, 1981; 1989; Fauve-Chamoux, 1981; 1984a; 1985; 1987a). It appeared then as evidence that Le Play's 'stem family' was, in the light of these recent studies, a true archetype of the occitan *house* (Assier-Andrieu, 1984), a genuine peasant system of reproduction, characteristic of a post-feudal *roturière* society (defending the integrity of the *manse* against the seigneurial right of *mainmorte* in case of escheat) (Maurel, 1900; Ourliac, 1956; Poumarède, 1970; 1979; Ragon, 1931), influenced by Roman antique laws (freedom of will), and finally in charge of applying what we could call a complex set of Malthusian 'preventive checks'. Le Play had seen perfectly the difference between the 'stem family' he discovered in Pyrenean Lavedan and the mythical 'patriarchal family', or other kind of familial community of co-residents.

The 'Real Model' Authority and Discipline

For Le Play, the 'stem family' ('real model'—Le Play, 1875) differs fundamentally from the ancient 'patriarchal family'—be it Greek, Jewish or mythical—and from the modern urban and miserable 'unstable family'. He compares the French southern-occidental rural and sedentarized stem family with the German *Stammfamilie* (or *Stammhaus*) presented by Dr Schaeffle from the University of Tübingen[1] (Le Play, 1878, vol. 3, p. 11). He apparently did not know Wilhelm H. Riehl's book, *Die Naturgeschichte des Volkes als*

---

1 F. Le Play (1878, vol. 3, p. 11) refers to contemporary studies about the German *Stammfamilie* (Dr Schaeffle, *Zeitschrift für die gesammte Staatswissenschaft*, XXI, p. 303; and *Das gesellschaftliche System der menschlichen Wirthschaft*) 'recently published', which certainly led him to forge the neologism 'famille-souche'. He says: 'The word *Souche*, better than *Stamm* (trunk, stem) expresses the distinctive quality of a family which is united and fertile in descendance: it is consequently useful to re-establish the use of this word in our literature, to facilitate the reappearance of the institution in our society'. Through the Bible, the Jewish tradition refers to *houses* and *tribes*, in German, *Stammhäuser* and *Stämme*.

Grundlage einer deutschen Socialpolitik (*Natural History of the People as the Base of a German Social Policy*), whose volume 3 was a perfect presentation of the German traditional family, living in a 'total house' (*Ganzes Haus*), a 'house' system very close to Le Play's 'stem family', characterized by cohabitation of successive generations, stability of private property, non-egalitarian transmission, exclusion of non-heirs (with eventual assistance and protection in case of crisis), and strict authority of the head of the household (Sabean, 1990, p. 89).

Authority and discipline are basic features of the stem-family organization: only one heir, who will get married and stay in the house with his spouse and children, is designated by the parents. The other children, *cadets* and *cadettes* (boys and girls) receive a dowry (or at least are supposed to), and leave the native house or stay there unmarried. In any case, they agree to withdraw from other forms of inheritance. With the French Civil Code and its egalitarian dispositions (Goy, 1988), long indivisions of property and pseudo-partitions which, after enforcement of the Code, became common practice, were patiently but officially followed in south-west France by a reconstitution of the entire patrimonial land by the heir, to whom his brothers and sisters were supposed to sell their part. Cheating with the law was a great game for lawyers in charge of written and legal arrangements—in Tyrol (Berkner, 1976, p. 72) as well as in southern France. Many transactions were still oral and traditionally based on exchanges and credit recognition, avoiding whenever possible money payments. Compensation of dowries between families exchanging their children at marriage could go without a penny (Augustins, 1981), so that a family debt could last a long time—in some cases a generation or more. In any case, the head of the house was the only one to decide roles and schedules, and the parents finally 'give a share of their authority to their adult child whom they consider to be the most suited for working together with them and then for continuing with the development of the family after their death' (Le Play, 1875).

Male primogeniture was respected in southern France: the heir was usually the oldest son. However, integral primogeniture (i.e. a boy or girl automatically inheriting when he or she was the first born) was rarely the norm. This has certainly been attested to in some Central Pyrenean regions, such as Andorre, the Barèges valley (Maurel, 1900; Leybold, 1979; Rieu-Gouy and Sauzeon-Broueilh, 1978), Lavedan (Le Play, 1875) or Ossau (Butel, 1894): for example, 40 per cent of the transmissions in the Soule Valley concerned an heiress (Poumarède, 1970). But in other Pyrenean villages, primogeniture goes with masculinity, following the aristocratic Roman custom. In the Pyrenean Baronnies we have studied, the heir will be a girl if a son is missing or if the boy is too young or considered not suitable for succession (20 per cent of the transmissions went to an heiress during the eighteenth century [Fauve-Chamoux, 1993]).

Impressed by the situation in the Lavedan, Le Play considered that a female heir brought harmony to the peasant house. He had observed in the Melouga stem-family that the inheriting daughter was living without problems with her father and mother, whereas in other cases a daughter-in-law would be expected to meet conflictual situations with her mother-in-law (Le Play, 1875). The heir or heiress had to be trained, more or less, by familial education, to accept the traditional customs and submission to the older generation's authority.

The choice of the heir was usually officialized at his marriage, when a contract was concluded with the chosen partner who was to 'enter' the house. The heir (son or daughter) clearly declares in the document that he or she will serve the interests of the house and assume the continuity, finding agreements with his or her parents and kin. In case of infertility, the heir would of course resign heirship. The marriage of the heir (not the death of the father) is the real moment of transition in the life of the stem family, the moment when the modalities of the transmission of the house are pronounced, the responsibilities expressed by the heir when he takes his partner in the house, a choice with consequences tacitly accepted by all the family members and known in the village community. There is no change of headship at this moment. It may take a long time before mastership is achieved. Some heirs never reach this point. Now that the family consensus is public about individual and collective roles, the heir has only acquired recognition of his *potential* authority over his brothers and sisters. While his parents are alive, he has no real authority: he has heavy charges concerning others' subsistence and dowries and an obligation to procreate. His or her partner is like a new servant in the house. The partner even loses his or her family name on entering the house.

THE STEM FAMILY AND IDENTITY

The identity of the house is so marked in the Pyrenean society that each house has a proper name. Le Play did not miss this important fact when describing the *Melouga* 'stem family', Melouga being the name of the house and not the patronym of the father, the head of the household. This house was three times transmitted to a female successor, a son-in-law entering the house at each generation, with his own patronym, given legally to his wife and children, and inscribed in the written civil archives. But those children were socially identified as *Melouga*'s children, 'said Melouga' for administrative purposes. In the Pyrenean Baronnies, the name of the house plays a major role in personal and familial identity within the peasant community (Augustins, 1981; Bonnain, 1986a). In Esparros, the *maysounyme* helps in following over three centuries, generation after generation, all the members of the house, whether native born in the house or 'adopted' (spouses) (Fauve-Chamoux, 1984; 1987). This name is a visible sign of the perpetuity of the family. In Basque society, amongst peasant landowners, as in the Baronnies, the name of the house (*etche*) is transmitted with the same modalities of personal hereditary identification (Rodriguez Hernandorena, 1988), both in the oral and in the written sources. It is even used for rented farms, in the Landes region, where every family entering the farm by contract takes the name of the house (meaning estate) which does not belong to them (Larroque, 1984).

But when looking carefully at family histories, we may detect formation of new houses. Those instances of family formation occurred with population pressure, when the Pyrenees, like many other regions of western Europe, enjoyed better living conditions and were witnessing the beginning of the agricultural revolution in the late eighteenth century (increased production of corn and potatoes). Historians wondered how those new houses could survive and be tolerated, given the rules controlling the stem family. There is indeed some evidence in Lomné, a small village of the Baronnies studied by Augustins, that the number of exploitations did not vary much during the time of the eighteenth century given the agricultural improvements taking place and population pressure of the end of the century: 36 houses in 1793, 42 in 1826. On the contrary, there were 61 in 1851 (Augustins, 1989, p. 198). In the 1840s and 1850s new houses were created. Families were supported by some degree of craftwork, but the new houses did not last long. Emigration was severe in the 1870s for this new marginal group in Lomné, whereas most of the old houses, respecting for their part the nonegalitarian transmission, stayed intact. This fascinating, and quite ideological, ethnographic interpretation that there were great changes taking place (not only in the population), but that nothing was happening structurally in a stem family quasi-immobile society, was as disturbing for the historical demographer, confronted with another reality in Esparros, as was Peter Laslett's 'nuclear hardship model', claiming the 'recessiveness' of the stem family (Laslett, 1978, p. 99) which is still prevalent today, whereas still nowadays we observe a persistence of this model, at least in the mentalities. It cannot be taken as read that the stem family was a specific resistant model that could not be included, as an intermediate form, in a bi-polaric view of the simple household/joint household. Hajnal, for his part, did not take the stem family into account in his brilliant essay about European models of household formation (Hajnal, 1983). Nor did it fit into the four sector schematic domestic group organization proposed by Laslett (1983).

No serious conclusions could be given about the stem family's conservative properties without a monographic study (in this case a study of a large Pyrenean community), including eighteenth-century family histories. In the framework of the interdisciplinary study on the Baronnies (Chiva and Goy, 1981), the families of Esparros had already been reconstructed from the Revolution to the First World War (Fauve-Chamoux, 1981). I decided to go back as far as possible into the past, using tax lists (beginning in 1713), cadasters (1668, 1773) and parish registers (beginning in 1662), for a broad perspective. This was the only way to understand what really took place in the stem families of the Baronnies at the end of the eighteenth century and the beginning of the nineteenth.

THE STEM FAMILY ELASTIC RESISTANCE

Research confirmed that the Pyrenean Baronnies were a perfect choice for a large interdisciplinary study involving all kinds of historical approaches including medical, linguistic, ethnographic, demographic, etc. (Chiva and Goy, 1981, 1986), about an occitan rural community where the stem family prevails—the non-egalitarian handing down of the patrimony, primogeniture and cohabitation of the married heir with his parents were customary practices.

The Pyrenean Baronnies: A Privileged Observatory

The particularities of traditional rural life have been exceptionally well preserved in the Baronnies, due to the fact that the region was not subjected to the changes occurring in the Pyrenean valleys in the nineteenth century (industrialization, railways etc.). The geology of the region even gave it a specific circumscribed unity which the main transport routes by-pass, be it to the east in the vallée d'Aure or to the west the vallée de Campan. To the north, the plateau de Lannemezan, like a badly closed lid, forms a veritable frontier. When its glacis was formed in geological times, the alluvium ran north, leaving the Baronnies untouched, like an island protected by its own private mountain (Signal de Bassia: 1,921 metres) (Peron, 1986). Fertile and wet enough (watered both by the rain and by the river Arros), the countryside has been cultivated since neolithic times by prosperous agricultural and pastoral communities. The mountain not only offered rich pasture (land and large forests), but also accessible outcropping ferruginous soil. In fact, the economic development of the population is attested well before the Roman invasion. It seems clear that the fortunate and prosperous community situated on the sunny slopes at the foot of the mountain (the peasants of Esparros [with three neighbouring villages], forming a democratic assembly of heads of households) played a leading role in the past, at least since the middle ages. Under the feudal regime, the Community of the 'Baronnie of Esparros' successfully bargained for customary 'privileges' from the landlord (the Baron of Esparros), securing free access to and free exploitation of the mountains in return for taxes and administrative or even military protection (mainly from the recurring and aggressive pretensions which the neighbouring valleys expressed for the Baronnean mountains).

The history of the whole 27 parishes ('the Baronnies', a region economically dependent on 'the Baronnie of Esparros', whose assembly kept control of the mountains), explains the strong social and cultural identity of the local population. They belong to a specific, very democratic rural society, both pastoral, 'artisanal' (a very modest textile and wood protoindustry existing, supplying a local handicraft market) and agricultural (poly-cultural). Still today, the 'Baronnies' are locally understood as a regional concept which, since feudal times, has never been administratively recognized: twenty-seven villages sharing the same eco-system, the same landscape ('a garden'), the same way of life (a very rich cuisine), a specific occitan language (an archaic gascon) and very strong family traditions, based on a pure stem-family mentality.

The 'Baronnie of Esparros', the *seigneurie* which gave its name to the regional entity (the Pyrenean Baronnies), covered four villages, belonging to the same *seigneur* (landlord) during the Ancien Régime: Esparros (the largest parish), Laborde and Arrodets (extensions which used to be dependent), and Labastide (traditionally annexed). Situated at the foot of more than 2,000 hectares of mountainside whose collective use and exploitation it has always managed to safeguard, this community of four very similar parishes made up, with its 250 houses, 22 per cent of the Baronnian population (which just exceeded 5,000), or 27 parishes, at the time of the Revolution, in 1793. At the beginning of the nineteenth century, the Pyrenees as a whole experienced a great demographic expansion, followed by a severe rural exodus lasting from about 1850 to the present day. In 1846, the Baronnies (still consisting of 27 villages) had more than 10,000 inhabitants, their population having therefore doubled since the Revolution. Today, as we approach the end of the twentieth century, the Baronnies support only 3,000 inhabitants. This population depression has had a strong impact on people's attitudes. Modern-day peasants frequently refer to a better time in days gone by, when the village was active and the farms full of children.

The demographic history of the Baronnies over the last three centuries does not include what we would call a 'stable' population. Neither do the figures concerning changes in the number of houses or vital records contain any evidence of a 'stable' society. Let us consider the data for the village of Esparros (Fig. 1), comparing the evolution of the population since the end of the seventeenth century and the number of houses (the house here refers specifically to just one household) in the censuses and in the tax records leading up to the present times.[2]

We can clearly see that the creation of houses began at least as early as the beginning of the eighteenth century, at a time when control of stem families' growth was very efficient, although population pressure was growing increasingly stronger. With the egalitarian nature of the *Code Civil* (1804), the new

---

2 We were lucky to discover in the local archives (Communal Archives) reliable sources for Esparros' demographic and family history: a long series of pre-Revolutionary tax lists (capitations), three cadastres (1668, 1773 and 1821), and nominative censuses from 1846 to the present. Nominative lists of the period of the Revolution were found for 21 villages of the Baronnies region in Tarbes (Departmental archives), for 1793 ('Year II'). The four villages of the 'Baronnie of Esparros' were missing. The large village of Bourg-de-Bigorre was chosen as a similar locality, to replace Esparros.

A general family reconstitution was also conducted with parish registers and civil registration sources, from 1660 to 1914. The CASOAR program (Bardet and Hainsworth, 1981) was used for tabulations, adhering strictly to Louis Henry's historical demography procedures.

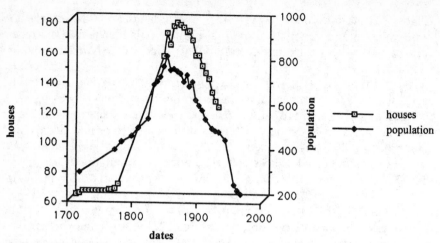

Figure 1: Population growth and number of houses in Esparros (sources: Esparros data bank; censuses, cadasters and fiscal data)

houses foundation process continued or even increased its pace. Population growth stopped in Esparros after 1851, reaching a maximum of 844 inhabitants, but for another twenty years young couples were still building new houses in the town, with a maximum of 774 houses being reached in 1886. Now we must accept that, during the hundred years from the 1780s to the 1880s, the stem family's strict system of reproduction was strongly attacked. In many families the children rejected non-egalitarian transmission and obtained enough land, goods and money to establish a new house, marrying in contravention of a customary practices. These facts seem to be contradictory in view of others' conclusions about the stability and conservative permanence of the stem families and the regularity of non-egalitarian inheritance in the Baronnies. A complete reconstitution of the family histories (and houses) of Esparros would help us understand how this situation developed. Was it a demographic revolution? A social revolution? A cultural revolution? How was it that such a surge in the figures (i.e., the growth mentioned above) had for so long been overshadowed by the well-known and still visible fall in population and the declining number of houses?

From this perspective, the history of the stem-family model had to be seriously revised—not an easy task. By the 1970s, many new eighteenth- and nineteenth-century houses had already disappeared: both from the landscape and from people's memories. The iconoclast *cadets* had gone to South America before the First World War. Now, in contemporary times, many houses were dying, because the ancestral patrimony no longer offered enough for a family to live on, because the Baronnean type of agriculture was dying and the world had changed. Heirs could no longer find a good native wife to keep the farm running. Some houses were even sold to strangers as holiday houses. Many barns were ruined. Most of the remaining peasants were old, poor and dependent upon the welfare state. Depopulation in the 1970s was not felt in the Baronnies to be a new problem.

From Marginality to Rural Exodus: The Rise of Non-Conformism

Recent and present depopulation had been masking, for Le Play as for modern and contemporary commentators, a century of population growth and a long period of anti-conformist household formation in the middle of gasco-bearnais stem-family pseudo-resistant society. Discussing my first results concerning Esparros (Fauve-Chamoux, 1981), I had to face the criticism that this community was not representative of the history of the Baronnies. This accusation was easily refuted in the light of Figure 2, where population growth in the Baronnies (Peron, 1986, p. 8) is shown to be identical to—even earlier than—that in Esparros.

It has been shown that the population of Lomné (Augustins, 1981; 1990), or Laborde (Bonnain, 1986b, p. 139) nearly doubled between 1773 and 1840 at the same rate as in Esparros. However, these newly constructed houses were nevertheless seen by Augustins and Bonnain as a rather marginal and temporary social phenomenon (with a clear parcellization of patrimonial land and evidence of a rapid pauperization of the new households), most of the 'good families' succeeding in preserving the integrity of the patrimonial house. Both authors' final conclusion was that the elite of the stem families maintained their traditional behaviour. If the others (the poor houses) were said to 'fall' (Bonnain, 1986c, p. 166), their social decline and frequent

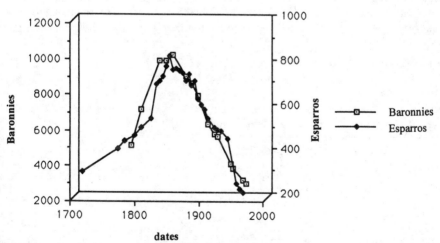

Figure 2: Population of the Baronnies and population of Esparros (sources: Esparros data bank; censuses, cadasters and fiscal data)

economic collapse was said to be due to their marginality in relation to the
stem-family norm.

When we considered for our part the histories of all the new houses in
Esparros (since 1700), it appeared that their failure did not occur automatically. The family reconstitution, drawing on parish registers, civil registration,
censuses, tax lists and cadasters, provided evidence that 'non-conformist
marriages' of a *cadet*, forming a new house with a *cadette*, the couple staying in
the village, heading a new entity, was not so rare and could not be neglected: at
the end of the Ancien Régime, one out of five excluding all those married in
the village who did not take residence in Esparros but including all residing
couples, even those married outside the village. The name of the house—new
or old—always mentioned in the reference data, was a permanent indication of
the presence of the familial entity—the house.

During the revolutionary and Napoleonic periods (1790–1809), as many as
47 per cent of new couples did not follow the stem tradition and established a
new household. The introduction of egalitarian partition of the patrimony
therefore had serious consequences on family establishment. Many *cadets* and
cadettes asked for their part of the family inheritance, refused traditional
emigration or celibacy in the native house and decided to stay in Esparros.
Until then, only one *cadette* could expect to be married to an heir, and one
cadet had a (very) small chance to enter another house as son-in-law (few
heiresses were available—only between a third and a quarter of the successions
chose a female heir in the Baronnies). The change of legislation after 1790
created genuine local social change which had enormous consequences on the
demographic figures. But this represented a 'non-conformist earthquake'
rather than a 'total revolution' because the stem-family modes of transmission
and exclusion customs remained in existence. A third of the stem families still
refused to divide up patrimony between 1700 and 1914. However, the other
two-thirds turned their backs on custom, dividing the patrimony on more than
one occasion.

Although traditional rules of family formation were deeply modified,

Table 1: *Frequency of 'stem-marriages' and 'non-conformist marriages' (all resident
couples, Esparros, eighteenth and nineteenth centuries)*

Period of marriage	Heir (male or female) (=stem marriages)	Non-heir x cadet/cadette (= non-conformist marriages)	Total
1700–1789	78 %	22 %	100 %
1790–1809	53 %	47 %	100 %
1810–1849	58 %	42 %	100 %
1850–1899	65 %	35 %	100 %

Sources: Esparros data bank. Family reconstitution linked with fiscal and patrimonial archives.

Table 2: *Frequency of successoral situation for males and females (all resident couples, Esparros, eighteenth and nineteenth centuries)*

Marriage	Heir	Cadet	Heiress	Cadette	Total Male	Female
1700–1789	59 %	41 %	19 %	81 %	100%	100%
1790–1809	46 %	54 %	7 %	93 %	100%	100%
1810–1849	46 %	54 %	14 %	86 %	100%	100%
1850–1899	48 %	52 %	17 %	83 %	100%	100%

Sources: Esparros data bank. Family reconstitution linked with fiscal and patrimonial archives.

marriage was still not open to everybody and did not become a universal option. Celibacy and emigration did not disappear at all: only one *cadet* ended up getting married, which meant that two boys in every family are becoming heads of a household! Other children were of course able to get married elsewhere, to emigrate to other towns or to the colonies, to start a new home away from their birthplace, as had always been the case.

Marriage remained a selective process in the native village. Thus the question arises about the age at which marriage took place: could the non-conformist *cadets* get married whenever they wanted? Did they have to wait longer than the heir or heiress to attain marriageable age? The concept of stem family is often associated with an early age at marriage for those children who have access to reproduction (Cheysson, 1875, p. 263).

Hereditary Differentiation in Age of Marriage

Early marriage within the stem family is part of its disputable ideology. After 1650, late marriage was the norm in the Pyrenees as everywhere else in France. However, in the Baronnies, 14 per cent of brides got married before they were 20 years old during the period 1700–1789, while in the Barèges valley, that figure stood at 22 per cent during the first part of the nineteenth century (Rieu-Gouy and Sauzeon-Broueilh, 1978). During that same period, the number of brides marrying before they were 20 years old stood at 15 per cent in the Alpine Queryas (Espagnet, 1976), whereas 40 per cent were still marrying at a very young age in Uri, Switzerland (Zurfluh, 1986; 1988). This means that in our case there were a large majority of late marriages. This shift to late marriage may have been a relatively recent phenomenon and may have occurred in the Pyrenees in the early seventeenth century, as 60 per cent of early marriages were found in Bigorre, close to the Baronnies, between 1618 and 1650 (Guy, 1989). In any case, the pre-revolutionary mean age at first marriage was late in the Pyrenees, with an overall age of 29 for grooms and 25 for brides, giving a difference of at least four years between spouses (see Table 3).

Table 3: *Mean age at first marriage, by period of marriage (Esparros, 1700–1899)*

Period of marriage	Grooms	Brides
1700–1789	29.1	24.8
1790–1809	29.3	24.5
1810–1849	29.1	24.3
1850–1899	30.0	25.9

Sources: Esparros data bank. Parish registers and civil registration, marriages.

Male age at marriage was usually much later for non-heirs: between 27 and 29 for heirs, and over 30 for non-heirs. Around 1800, with the change in marriage selection, the gap virtually disappeared before returning with the process of depopulation and ageing of the population in the course of the nineteenth century. On the female side, as most of the *cadettes* who married in the local countryside used to marry an heir before the Revolution, the age difference between girls was small. However, this changed during the nineteenth century, the heiresses becoming younger and younger (23 in the 1800s), and the *cadettes* older and older (26.5 in the 1880s) (see Table 4).

Cadettes marrying an heir, as part of a familial strategy, were much younger than non-conformist *cadettes* who married a non-inheriting *cadet*: heirs had a large choice and preferred younger spouses—or they were preferred by them. To marry against the custom does not mean earlier marriage, neither for men nor for women, but rather later marriage. Money was necessary for household establishment, familial arrangements took time, and *cadets* and *cadettes* choosing to stay in Esparros (or to come back to the village, after years of work outside, to settle in a new house) had to wait to get their share (or part of their share) of the inheritance, and/or work hard to accumulate sufficient finances. This is clear if we observe the crossed situation at first marriage, considering the resident couples only, to avoid emigration bias (see Table 5).

Table 4: *Mean age at first marriage according to successoral situation, by period of marriage (Esparros, 1700–1899)*

Period of marriage	Grooms		Brides	
	Heir	Cadet	Heiress	Cadette
1700–1789	27.5	31.5	24.5	24.9
1790–1809	28.9	29.6	25.0	24.4
1810–1849	26.9	30.8	23.5	24.4
1850–1899	29.0	30.9	23.1	26.4

Sources: Esparros data bank. Family reconstitution.

Table 5: *Mean age at first marriage according to successoral situation of the residing couple, by period of marriage (Esparros, 1700–1899)*

Period of marriage	Heir x cadette		Cadet x heiress		Cadet x cadette	
1700–1789	27.5	24.7	29.6	24.6	33.1	25.1
1790–1809	28.9	24.2	30.0	25.0	29.6	24.7
1810–1849	26.9	23.0	28.1	23.5	31.8	25.9
1850–1899	29.0	26.3	29.9	23.1	31.4	26.7

Sources: Esparros data bank. Family reconstitution.

Changes in age at marriage in Esparros have to be considered in terms of establishment possibilities: birth order of surviving children, besides gender considerations. In a highly controlled situation, where the stem family prevails, it is not surprising to find a strong differentiation between age at marriage of heirs and non-heirs. When non-heirs in principle acquired access to local marriage, age at marriage fell slightly for *cadets* and increased for heirs, following the change from customary impartibility to legal partibility of the patrimonial house. Age at marriage also decreased slightly for all women. Within the stem family, arranged marriage meant that reproduction was possible at a relatively younger age. As marriage for non-conformists was always bound to their capacity for financial non-dependency on their native house, freedom of choice never meant an earlier decision to start a family. Did the non-conformist houses form a recognized 'sub-society' in the Baronnies? We could call it 'cadettery' (a *junioral* society), growth of which created a social disequilibrium in the traditional *senioral* stem-family society. This social dichotomy did not mean that the behaviour of the new group was totally unconventional—they simply did not feel bound by the same constraints.

Cadettery, Bastardy and Social Dichotomy

When the primogeniture rules of transmission were not respected and new houses were established, the name given to the new household had a certain significance in the community. The name of the new house was often a female one, the name of the spouse of the founder. The female name was usually reserved in the Baronnies to small houses where unmarried mothers used to live independently with their illegitimate offspring. The specific mode of female repetitive illegitimate reproduction, so well identified by Peter Laslett (1977; 1980), was common in the early nineteenth-century Baronnies. Illegitimacy could also anticipate marriage, when a non-conformist marriage was delayed. This is shown in Figure 3, where age at marriage of non-heiresses is compared with illegitimacy ratios: the older the *cadette* when she marries, the higher the illegitimacy rate. Illegitimacy followed general demographic changes, reflecting population pressure and decline, in anticipation of the

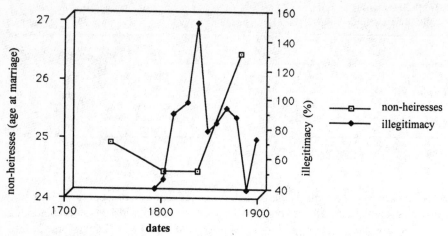

Figure 3: Illegitimacy ratios (per thousand) and mean age at first marriage of non-heiresses in Esparros (sources: Esparros data bank; family reconstitution)

number of houses available. We agree here that the increase in illegitimacy can be linked to the increase in age at marriage (Laslett, 1977; Alberra and Viazzo, 1986; Viazzo, 1986; 1989), but in the Baronnies it is more a reflection of the changing situation of the *cadettes* and consequently not related to a higher rate of celibacy, *cadettes* marrying in the village more easily than previously when they had been obliged to remain unmarried at home or to emigrate.

The family reconstitution project shows that births occurring out of wedlock are due to *cadettes'* sexual habits. Heiresses never faced bastardy because they married younger and because their wedding was a familial arrangement. There was no place for illegitimacy for a girl who found herself at the first level of the stem-family reproduction process. Sexual freedom was not allowed, but a socially controlled pre-marital sexual relationship with the designated future groom was acceptable: a kind of 'trial marriage', as attested in the Basque region, both French and Spanish (Valverde, 1989). The social marriage, with its associated familial responsibilities, is more important than the subsequent religious recognition. Checking the fertility of both partners charged with reproduction could be part of the strategy.

In the Baronnies, overall pre-marital conception remained at a high level during the nineteenth century: 27 per cent during 1792–1839, 30 per cent for 1870–1904 with a remarkable peak of 50 per cent between 1835 and 1839, when the possibility for non-conformist new family establishment faced considerable difficulties. Frequent pre-marital conception and illegitimate births do not, however, mean that there was ignorance regarding contraception.

Marital behaviour can be observed through family reconstitution and differential fertility rates by age at marriage. In Esparros, fertility control appeared early and was in evidence during the eighteenth century. If we consider marital fertility rates by age at marriage and by marriage duration, the younger a woman was at marriage, the lower was her fertility, even before the Revolution. Early Malthusian behaviour was not, however, specific to French urban areas. While it was present in towns, like Rouen (Bardet, 1983), Rheims (Fauve-Chamoux, 1988) or Châtillon-sur-Seine (Chamoux and Dauphin, 1969), family limitation was also in evidence in some rural populations, especially in mountain regions, during periods of population/subsistence pressure (Fine-Souriac, 1977).

The sub-fertility of women in south-west France, with their prolonged periods of breastfeeding and particularly lengthy inter-birth intervals (Henry, 1972; Fine, 1978) may correspond, however, to another type of fertility control than that which we can observe in the Pyrenean Baronnies. There, for the period 1720–1789, a 'definitive' phase of contraception was observed by women aged over 35 years, particularly after 10 years of marriage. This pattern of birth control can be observed in stem-families, as there were relatively few non-conformist couples to be taken into consideration towards the end of the Ancien Régime. The main question which I am not prepared to answer is whether the drastic cessation of reproduction after 35 years of age was due to contraception or to abortion.

In Esparros, fertility rates varied significantly during the Ancien Régime (1720–1789) with the age of the spouses, signifying a voluntary practice of family limitation (see Fig. 4). During the period after the Revolution, overall

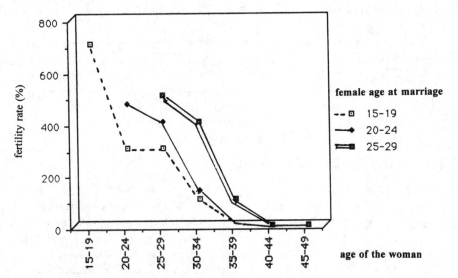

Figure 4: Legitimate fertility rates by age at marriage and age of the woman (Esparros, periods of marriage: 1720–1789, completed families)

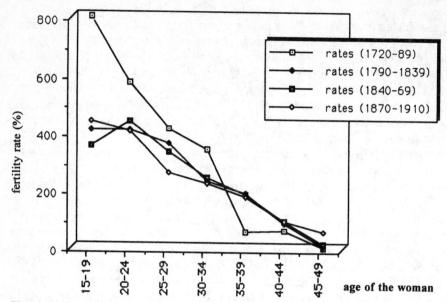

Figure 5: Evolution of legitimate fertility rates, all ages at marriage, by age of the woman, successive periods of marriage (Esparros, completed families)

legitimate fertility rates fell, showing still more efficient controls on procreation, but this reduction does not conform to the earlier model. After the Revolution Esparros saw a wider incidence of women giving birth after the age of 35 (see Fig. 5).

Conjugal fertility control remained constant (fertility restrictions occurred immediately after marriage) but children came to be accepted much later in a woman's period of fertility. We have to recognize in this a radical cultural change compared with the end of the Ancien Régime. Were all couples changing their reproductive practices in the same way and for the same reasons? Let us look carefully at differential fertility rates for those couples married during the years 1790–1839 (see Fig. 6).

Other Family Regulations, Other Priorities

For couples married after the Revolution but before 1840 (i.e., before the beginning of the population depression), the difference between the fertility of women married young and of those married late is striking. Women who married late were *cadettes* forming non-conformist couples when measured against stem-family behaviour. Non-conformist couples were much more fertile than their stem counterparts. Heiresses and women marrying an heir limited their descendance as did their mothers, following the stem-family rules of severe auto-regulation, reducing births when the family had grown large

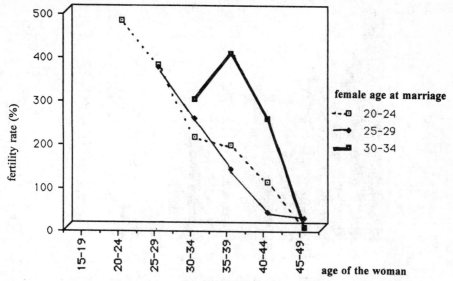

Figure 6: Legitimate fertility rates by age at marriage and age of the woman (Esparros, period of marriage: 1790–1839, completed families)

enough, after 10 years of marriage. New houses had other priorities. Those families generally did not live off agricultural resources, but from some kind of industry or commerce. They had less need to count how many 'mouths' they had to feed, or calculate how many helping hands they needed. They managed to live either with or without children. When the crisis came, after 1850, they managed to make a living elsewhere. Non-conformists were less attached to their family land, to their patrimony. Nevertheless they may have had close links with their native roots, such as their language, and with their ancestral access to the mountains (communal land, forest and pasture), their original small craftwork (making wooden goods or textile products), and with their 'house'. But *junioral* mentality differs in terms of fertility behaviour: children are accepted from a beloved and chosen spouse, under different conditions than in the 'good' stem families, at a different age, within or outside wedlock. *Cadets* and *cadettes* were neo-individualists. Their optimistic (imprudent) behaviour at the beginning of the nineteenth century shows in their family size: women married in their early thirties, and would raise 3.4 children (compared with just one in the previous period, in the stem families). This is a significant difference (see Fig. 7).

We need to look at the attitudes towards reproduction, not just of women, but also of men. Moheau recognized in 1778 that 'Already, the deadly secrets unknown to all animals but Man have penetrated the countryside: Nature is being deluded in the very villages'. Here, he was referring to the practice of *coitus interruptus*, which could be used to prevent or to space births. *Cadets*

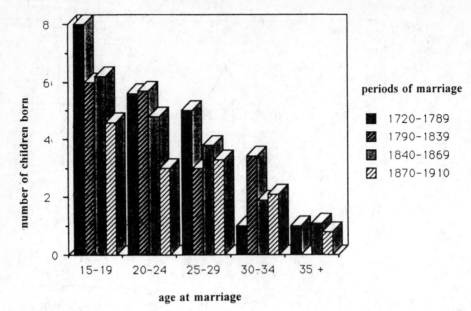

Figure 7: Mean number of children born, in completed families, by female age at marriage, by periods of marriage (Esparros)

adopted the practice. They may have learned it outside the village, when in domestic service or apprenticeship in towns or in military service. It seems that non-conformist couples did not approach the question of procreation in the same way that stem-family couples used to. Had the non-conformists, being mobile before starting a family, reached a different cultural level? Were they, for example, more literate than their conformist counterparts? This was not the case. The cultural and social changes observed in Esparros were unrelated to literacy, as the population of the Baronnies as a whole was mostly illiterate.

Pyrenean Culture and Orality

Literacy rates in Esparros were amongst the lowest in the whole of France. In Esparros, before the Revolution, only eight per cent of men could sign their name on the day of their wedding (none of the women could do so). Between 1790 and 1830, 18.5 per cent of men could sign their marriage certificate, while still no woman was capable of doing so. Between 1830 and 1870, 68 per cent of men knew how to write their name, as did eight per cent of the women. Finally, from 1870 to 1914, 91 per cent of men could write their signature, as compared with only 16 per cent of women. The nearby Béarn region was much more literate (Frezel-Lozey, 1969). Here, 93 per cent of men could sign their names by the end of the nineteenth century and 99 per cent of women while, in the eighteenth century, these figures were 74 per cent and 4 per cent respectively.

Between 1800 and 1870, 91 per cent of men and 16 per cent of women could write their names. The Pyrenees, therefore, lagged far behind as far as literacy was concerned, especially with regard to girls, whereas in the Alps, in Queyras during the eighteenth century, 95 per cent of men could sign their name and 76 per cent of women knew how to hold a quill (Espagnet, 1976).

Consequently, literacy and contraceptive practice must be totally unrelated. In the Pyrenean village under study, we are dealing with an illiterate society up to the year 1830, where the women who got married before 1870 were all illiterate, but could nevertheless control their births efficiently, this having been the case since at least the end of the seventeenth century. This behavioural model differs completely from the French urban model of the eighteenth century. What is at stake is a completely different civilization, a peasant and mountain civilization, with specific values and practices, which at least in its behaviour submits neither to the authority of the Church, nor to the central northern government. The Baronnies formed an independent occitan region, a kind of cultural *isolat*, but not closed, in the sense that the stem family created a permanent and strong trend towards emigration. The economic equilibrium of the region implies a permanent contact with the valleys, which functioned as a market for selling and buying goods and where seasonal work was to be found, in both France and Spain. Transactions were not written; all contracts were based on faith, word and honour. Pyrenean culture was oral.

The stem-family type of transmission was part of customary practices that were oral in nature. Regional customs were not written and published until very late, during Enlightenment times. The Pyrenean *Coutumes de Barèges et du pays de Lavedan* were even published as late as 1837. The custom, says the jurist 'constated by the memory of facts and by oral declarations of competent men' form 'a set of rules imposed on public life by tradition' (Ourliac, 1956, p. 258). The local traditional model of reproduction was far from the legal schema imposed by the Revolution (no more freedom of will) and the dispositions of the Napoleonic Code of 1804. In fact, the two were incompatible. The tension between legality and custom was also faced with European economic change and an enormous cultural change which the peasants could not ignore. The *cadets* (both men and women) had always formed a linkage between the village and the outside world, as mobile elements of society. They looked for domestic service, for salaried work in the neighbouring villages, in the valleys and the distant cities (such as Bordeaux). If still unmarried, they used to return to their home village. Emigration was felt to be temporary. We saw that after the Revolution, *cadets* decided to settle in the Baronnies, asking for a family plot to build a house, or squatting on communal land. The final result was a rapid proletarianization of the new non-conformist group, living mostly from non-agricultural labour (except for cattle raising). Their proletarian mobility was structural and usually did not allow a state of literacy to be achieved.

Exclusion, Individualism and Proletarianization

The stem-family mentality did not ignore individualism. Individuals who were not directly involved in the reproduction process were free to go where they pleased. Geographical and social mobility were part of the occitan nonegalitarian model of reproduction. Domestic service, military service, commercial and industrial activities, colonial adventure and religious service offered all kinds of possibilities. The stem family 'conciliates, in just measure, the father's authority and children's freedom, stability and improvement of conditions' (Le Play, 1878, p. 12).

The stem-family regime of exclusion could have significant consequences on society in general. It created centrifugal population movements within dynamic non-married age groups (male and female). Adventurous, successful 'cadets de Gascogne' are both part of French history and its mythological cultural background. The romanesque view of a seditious, charming *cadet*, free to risk his life but keeping his honour at all times, is a direct result of stem-family continuity and moral reference, on a simili-aristocratic level. Self-individualism was permitted within set moral boundaries; some degree of respect towards women was part of the code of honour. Upward social mobility was accepted if money-making was honest. Most of the time it was permitted by non-rural strategies of alliance. For the Baronnians, the chance of success was small; the mobility network, in every direction (Gers region, Spain, Toulouse, Bordeaux, America, Paris) existed at a low cultural level.

When discussing the origins of the European proletariat, two components are often presented for north-western society: expropriation and development of wage labour (Mendels, 1981; Smith, 1981; Tilly, 1984). The demographic growth of southern France also meant growth of the landless classes. This group was made up of the usual surplus of *cadets*. Its size was affected, as happened everywhere, by a reduction of the mortality rate during the eighteenth century, and by local uncustomary access to family formation. Marriage possibilities also increased at the same time, while the fertility of this group was soon to increase as well, accounting for the population boom in the Pyrenees. But on one important point the Pyrenean model differed from the contemporary components of growth: born into the stem-family controlling society, the *junioral* society retained a very high age at marriage with no evidence of a shift toward earlier marriage. To settle in a small new house was not a straightforward task. The *cadets* were not simple landless proletarians: they were family *cadets*. They contributed to land parcellization in a mountain society of small independent farms. This represented deconcentration of capital. They were given a legitimate part of their patrimonial land and were not totally dependent on wages. Before the boom, they were given money (*la legitime*, a kind of dowry), never land. Now they wanted a plot and to be able to save on their earnings (not only wages) to settle down properly. Non-conformist couples adopted different approaches to household formation than stem couples, but the need for a 'good' household was still there. Many tried to 'make stem', some with success.

Previously, unsuccessful *'cadet'* society during the Ancien Régime had generally contributed to the formation of a proletarian (or marginal) society outside the village, in an urban or non-rural society. The situation in Esparros at the end of the Ancien Régime was different. It provides us with a new vantage point on a mutation, a change in the modalities of transmission in a specific society, the rise of a social group in the heart of its own culture. What is revolutionary is precisely the fact that many *cadets* continued to stay in the village, instead of moving out. They fought for egalitarian rights inside their own group. This struggle was not new. Many egalitarian battles had apparently been lost in the Pyrenees in the sixteenth and seventeenth centuries, where customary practices had proved stronger than those of the squatters. In fact we can see that in Esparros some new houses founded in the seventeenth and eighteenth centuries did in fact survive. This can be seen from the number of houses and the cultivation of new land. After the 1800s in French northern culture, the written law was on the *cadets'* side in their struggle against an anti-revolutionary tradition of 'droit d'aînesse'. Seen from Paris, this privilege was aristocratic, and the father's decision of transmission anti-democratic. Napoleon was to restore the authority of father and husband (he was born in Corsica, in a Mediterranean society), reduce the rights of women, but retain egalitarian transmission, as it gave control to the state and destroyed the power and independence of the big estates. As such, it broke both aristocratic and peasant power.

It is fascinating to observe in some detail the reproduction strategies in the *cadets'* society. Two sub-groups can easily be identified here. First, there are *cadets* who produced a stem family as soon as they could and did their best to avoid egalitarian partition. These would survive. The second group, who had many children, left their houses. The pauperization of the second generation would be dramatic. The whole society of Esparros would pay for their anti-customary individualism.

Nuclearization: Recessiveness or Invisibility of the Stem Family?

After 1850 depopulation began in the Baronnies and in the Pyrenees as a whole. The rural exodus affected all families. Even some designated heirs resigned their inheritance and left for South America, for Argentina, as did Basques and Bearnais who also emigrated on a massive scale during the same period in the 1880s (Douglas, 1971). Consequently, a general reduction in household size occurred.

The mean household size (MHS) stood at around five persons at the beginning of the eighteenth century (MHS = ratio of population to households), rising to 6.6 persons before the great increase in household formation took place (see Fig. 1), with the stem family resisting increased population pressure. Then, around 1800, mean household size began to fall as new

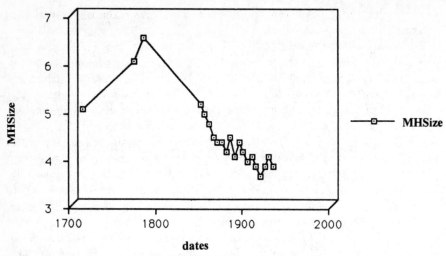

Figure 8: Mean household size (MHS) in Esparros, since 1700

conjugal units appeared. It continued to fall during the whole of the nineteenth century, dropping to just four around 1900. This figure remained between four and 3.5 persons after 1900 (see Fig. 8).

The size of the stem family is not so variable. The number of people who need to be fed is controlled. Like an accordion, the family has moments of expansion and moments of shrinkage. Family reconstitution files were linked with census data, nominatively, for the second part of the nineteenth century when the rural exodus was severe. We are therefore able to follow, in each household, every five years, the changes in family size and the successive changes in its composition, according to all kinds of family events: births, deaths, marriage, remarriage, emigration, immigration (Fauve-Chamoux, 1984a). Domestic service was not important in Esparros. *Cadets* and *cadettes* may have been servants, but most of the time they were outside the Baronnies. Late marriage was not a consequence of local domestic employment.

The proportion of boarders and servants was negligible for tne eighteenth and nineteenth centuries in Esparros. Domestic service and non-familial living arrangements were rare occurrences. A domestic servant was taken in when the mother died and the children were too young, and only if an aunt, grand-mother or sister-in-law was not available. In case of crisis, the neighbours had a duty to help (Bonnain, 1981); services were usually exchanged and not paid for in the nonegalitarian and customary inheritance regime. In this sense *cadets* also had duties and not rights. Crises were solved by returning home if the heir died and extra hands were needed. Thus there was constant family regulation of the workforce. The presence of a servant did not imply a financial problem but a problem of exchange strategy and compensation between families (stem families): they exchanged their children. The family reconstitution exercise showed familial relations with the native houses of servants. This could also be an economic arrangement, and some economic arrangements had familial consequences: with the dramatic rise in marriage possibilities at the beginning of the nineteenth century, *cadets* were marrying girls from the valleys where they used to go to help with the harvest.

The complexity of the stem family is only visible during certain phases of its development which most frequently followed a thirty-year cycle in the absence of any minor interfering factors. I have suggested that, for the stem family to be the social norm, it would be sufficient for a quarter of households to be simultaneously composed of three generations in the locality under observation (Fauve-Chamoux, 1984a). Let us consider the frequency of family types in the Baronnies, using, for convenience and to allow comparative views, the Cambridge group classification (Laslett, 1972) (see Table 6).

The high percentage of complex families (both extended and multiple) indicates, in successive censuses, the extent to which the stem family was found in the region. The methodological problems inherent in the study of family structures have been discussed now for many years (Laslett and Wall, 1972; Wall, 1983). I am convinced that the stem family has to be understood in its processes of dynamic reproduction and continuity, the perpetual changes in its form being part of its specificity. The Pyrenean family system, such as can be seen in the Baronnies, constitutes a well defined, yet much more complicated model than Le Play thought it to be. It is an elastic model capable of adapting to demographic circumstances and to the most unfavourable situations. In 1881 almost 15 per cent of households in Esparros were made up of a solitary person, living alone (Fauve-Chamoux, 1994), a phenomenon accompanied by a rapid halving of the number of complex families (a drop from 43 per cent to 21 per cent between 1793 and the end of the nineteenth century). This change

Table 6: *Frequency of types of households in Bourg-de-Bigorre and Esparros*

Types	Bourg-de-Bigorre 1793 (%)	Esparros 1846 (%)	Esparros 1881 (%)
1. Solitary	0	2.5	14.7
2. No structure	6.7	5.0	4.9
3. Conjugal	50.0	55.5	58.2
4. Extended	28.8	23.0	17.0
5. Multiple	14.5	14.0	4.9
TOTAL	100	100	100
Complex families (type 4 + type 5)	43.3	37.0	21.9

Sources: Esparros data bank. Censuses.

in the frequency of family structures reveals a profound economic and demographic crisis but, in spite of all this, the stem family was still in existence, was functioning and was perceived in its society as the norm, the dominant cultural model.

CONCLUSION: THE STEM FAMILY REINVENTED

Following on from the above, I do not think that the term 'recessiveness' (Laslett, 1978) is suitable for the Pyrenean stem family observed in the Baronnies at least before 1900. The occitan stem-family system was not disappearing during the nineteenth century, even if it was suffering from egalitarian practices of inheritance (between 1770 and 1870) and if emigration and ageing led after 1850 to diminution in the proportion of complex households. Heirs and most of the founding *cadets* still considered this system to be standard. The *cadets* wanted to soften, not to change radically, their native society, and to stay in it. They partly failed. Either they had to leave, en masse, after one or two generations, or they adapted to the strict stem-family rules.

But after 1900, the traditional agricultural society was already dying, and population was ageing. Heirs felt they were being sacrificed to the patrimonial house and secular custom. They became jealous of the *cadets*' non-conformism and freedom of choice. Le Play had perfectly understood that the stem family was a way of life. He did not realize that it was changing in front of him, the same way that Malthus understood a society whose main parameters were in mutation, with industrialization and the traditional auto-regulating mechanisms already out of date (Fauve-Chamoux, 1984b).

In Pyrenean society, the socio-economic parameters changed late. The occitan culture did, nevertheless, survive in the Baronnies, keeping to this day its value if not its demographic visibility. The honour of the stem family is still not dead. This is why it was so interesting to combine, in the Pyrenean Baronnies, ethnological and historical approaches.

References

ALBERA, D. and P. VIAZZO (1986), 'Population, Resources and Homeostatic Regulation in the Alps: The Role of Nuptiality', In M. Mattmuller (ed.), *Itinera* (special issue) *Economies et sociétés de montagne*, Berne, 182–231.

ASSIER-ANDRIEUX, L. (1984), 'Le Play et la famille-souche des Pyrénées: politique, juridisme et science sociale', *Annales E.S.C.*, **39**, no. 3, 495–513.

AUGUSTINS, G. (1981), 'Maison et société dans les Baronnies au XIXe siècle', In I. Chiva and J. Goy (eds.), *Les Baronnies des Pyrénées*, vol. 1: 'Maisons, mode de vie, société', 21–117.

AUGUSTINS, G. (1989), *Comment se perpétuer. Devenir des lignées et destins des patrimonies dans les paysanneries européennes*, Nanterre.

BARDET, J.-P. (1983), *Rouen aux XVIIe et XVIIIe siècles*, Paris.

BARDET, J.-P. and M. HAINSWORTH (1981), *Logiciel CASOAR, Calculs et analyses sur ordinateur appliqués aux reconstitutions*, Paris.

BERKNER, L. K. (1972), 'The Stem Family and its Developmental Cycle of Peasant Household: An Eighteenth Century Austrian Example', *American Historical Review*, **77**, 398–418.

BERKNER, L. K. (1976), 'Inheritance, Land Tenure and Peasant Family Structure: A German Regional Comparison', In J. Goody, J. Thirsk and E. P. Thomson (eds.), *Family and Inheritance. Rural Society in Western Europe 1200–1800*, Cambridge, 71–95.

BERKNER, L. K. and MENDELS, F. F. (1976), 'Inheritance Systems, Family Structure and Demographic Patterns in Western Europe 1700–1900', In C. Tilly (ed.), *Historical Studies in Changing Fertility*, Princeton, 209–23.

BERKNER, L. K. (1977), 'Peasant Household Organization and Demographic Change in Lower Saxony (1689–1766)', In R. D. Lee (ed.), *Population Patterns in the Past*, New York, 53–69.

BONNAIN, R. (1981), 'Les bonnes maisons', In I. Chiva and J. Goy (eds.), *Les Baronnies des Pyrénées*, vol. 1: 'Maisons, mode de vie, société', Paris, 123–68.

BONNAIN, R. (1986a), 'Les noms de maison dans les Baronnies', In I. Chiva and J. Goy (eds.), *Les Baronnies des Pyrénées*, vol. 2: 'Maisons, espace, famille', Paris, 179–200.

BONNAIN, R. (1986b), 'Nuptialité, fécondité et pression démographique dans les Pyrénées, 1769–1836', In I. Chiva and J. Goy (eds.), *Les Baronnies des Pyrénées*, vol. 2: 'Maisons, espace, famille', Paris, 87–121.

BONNAIN, R. (1986c), 'Droit écrit, coutume pyrénéenne et pratiques successorales dans les Baronnies, 1769–1836', In I. Chiva and J. Goy (eds.), *Les Baronnies des Pyrénées*, vol. 2: 'Maisons, espace, famille', Paris, 157–77.

BOURDIEU, P. (1962), 'Célibat et condition paysanne', *Etudes rurales*, **V–VI**, 32–135.

BOURDIEU, P. (1972), 'Les stratégies matrimoniales dans le système de reproduction', *Annales E.S.C.*, **27**, nos. 4–5, 1105–25.

BUTEL, F. (1894), *Une vallée pyrénéenne, la vallée d'Ossau*, Paris.

CHAMOUX, A. and C. DAUPHIN (1969), 'La contraception avant la Révolution Française: l'exemple de Châtillon-sur-Seine', *Annales E.S.C.*, **24**, 662–84.

CHEYSSON, E. (1875), In Le Play, *L'organisation de la famille selon le vrai modèle signalé par l'histoire de toutes les races et de tous les temps*, 2nd edition, 1st Appendix, Tours, 211–89.

CHIVA, I. and J. GOY (eds.) (1981), *Les Baronnies des Pyrénées*, vol. 1: 'Maisons, mode de vie, société', Paris.

CHIVA, I. and J. GOY (eds.) (1986), *Les Baronnies des Pyrénées*, vol. 2: 'Maisons, espace, famille', Paris.

CLAVERIE, E. and P. LAMAISON (1982), *L'impossible mariage. Violence et parenté en Gévaudan, XVIIe–XVIIIe et XIXe siècles*, Paris.

CLAVERO, B. (1974), *Mayorazgo Propriedad feudal en Castilla (1369–1836)*, Madrid.

COLLOMP, A. (1983), *La maison du père*, Paris.

DOUGLAS, W. (1969), *Death in Murelaga: Funerary Rituals in a Spanish Basque Community*, Washington.

DOUGLAS, W. (1971), 'Rural Exodus in Two Spanish Basque Villages: A Cultural Explanation', *American Anthropologist*, **LXXIII**, 1100–14.

ESPAGNET, M. (1976), *Saint-Veran en Queyras (1735–1815): étude de démographie historique*, Paris (mimeo).

FAUVE-CHAMOUX, A. (1981), 'Population et famille dans les Hautes Pyrénées aux XVIII–XXe siècles: l'exemple d'Esparros', In J. Goy and C. Bobinska (ed.), *Les Pyrénées et les Carpates (XVIe–XXe siècles)*, Cracovie, 43–63.

FAUVE-CHAMOUX, A. (1984a), 'Les structures familiales au royaume des familles-souche: Esparros', *Annales E.S.C.*, **39**, No. 3, 513–28.

FAUVE-CHAMOUX, A. (ed.) (1984b), 'Introduction', *Malthus hier et aujourd'hui*, Paris.

FAUVE-CHAMOUX, A. (1985), 'Vieillesse et famille-souche', *Annales de Démographie Historique*, Paris, 111–25.

FAUVE-CHAMOUX, A. (1987a), 'Le fonctionnement de la famille-souche dans les Baronnies des Pyrénées avant 1914', *Annales de Démographie Historique*, Paris, 241–62.

FAUVE-CHAMOUX, A. (1987b), 'Introduction', In A. Fauve-Chamoux (ed.), *Evolution agraire et croissance démographique*, Ordina, Liège, 11–22.

FAUVE-CHAMOUX, A. (1988), 'Les structures familiales en France aux XVIIe et XVIIIe siècles', In J. Dupâquier (ed.), *Histoire de la population française*, Paris, vol. 2, 317–47.

FAUVE-CHAMOUX, A. (1993), 'Mariages sauvages contre mariages-souche: la guerre des cadets', In M. Segalen and G. Ravis-Giordani (eds.), *Au miroir des cadets, l'ordre des familles*, Paris, 183–96.

FAUVE-CHAMOUX, A. (1994), 'Aging in a Never Empty Nest: The Elasticity of the Stem-family', In T. K. Hareven (ed.), *Aging and Generational Relations* (in press).

FINE, A. (1978), 'Mortalité infantile et allaitement dans le Sud-ouest de la France au XIXe siècle', *Annales de Démographie Historique*, Paris, 81–103.

FINE-SOURIAC, A. (1977), 'La famille souche pyrénéenne au XIXe siècle, quelques réflexions de méthode', *Annales E.S.C.*, **32**, 478–87.

FRESEL-LOZEY, M. (1969), *Histoire démographique d'un village en Béarn: Billères d'Ossau, XVIIIe–XIXe siècles*, Bordeaux.

GOY, J. (1988), 'La Révolution française et la famille', In J. Dupâquier (ed.), *Histoire de la Population française*, Paris, vol. 3, 84–115.

GUY, Y. (1988), *Saint Savin, démographie d'un village bigourdan, 1618–1975*, Paris.

HAJNAL, J. (1965), 'European marriage patterns in perspective', In D. V. Glass and D. E. C. Eversley (eds.), *Population in History*, Chicago, 101–40.

HAJNAL, J. (1983), 'Two Kinds of Pre-industrial Household Formation System', In R. Wall, J. Robin and P. Laslett (eds.), *Family Forms in Historic Europe*, Cambridge, 65–104.

HENRY, L. (1972), 'La fécondité des mariages dans le quart sud-ouest de la France de 1720 à 1829', *Annales E.S.C.*, **27**, No. 3, 612–40; **27**, Nos. 4–5, 977–1023.

LARROQUE, M.-T. (1984), *Contrats de mariage et vie familiale en pays d'Orthe (1816–1914)*, Paris (mimeo).

LASLETT, P. (1977), *Family Life and Illicit Love in Earlier Generations*, Cambridge.

LASLETT, P. (1978), 'The Stem-family Hypothesis and its Privileged Position', In K. W. Wachter and P. Laslett (eds.), *Statistical Studies of Historical Social Structure*, London, 89–111.

LASLETT, P. (1983), 'Family and Household as Work Group and Kin Group: Areas of Traditional Europe Compared', In R. Wall, J. Robin and P. Laslett (eds.), *Family Forms in Historic Europe*, Cambridge, 513–63.

LASLETT, P., K. OOSTERVEEN and R. SMITH (eds.) (1980), *The Bastardy and its Comparative History*, London.

LASLETT, P. and R. WALL, (1972), *Household and Family in Past Time*, Cambridge.

LE PLAY, F. (1875), *L'organisation de la famille selon le vrai modèle signalé par l'histoire de toutes les races et de tous les temps*, Tours, 2nd edition with Appendices (1st edition 1871).

LE PLAY, F. (1878), *La réforme sociale*, Tours, 6th edition (1st edition 1864, 4th edition 1872).

LE ROY LADURIE, E. (1975a), 'La domus à Montaillou et en Haute-Ariège au XIVe siècle', In D. Fabre and J. Lacroix, *Communautés du Sud*, 167–223.

LE ROY LADURIE, E. (1975b), *Montaillou, village occitan*, Paris.

LE ROY LADURIE, E. (1976), 'Family Structures and Inheritance Customs in Sixteenth Century France', In J. Goody, J. Thirsk and E. P. Thomson (eds.), *Family and Inheritance. Rural society in Western Europe 1200–1800*, Cambridge, 37–70.

LEYBOLD, M. (1979), *Le système social d'une vallée pyrénéenne, droit coutumier, population, groupe domestique à Grust, Hautes Pyrénées*, Paris (mimeo).

MAUREL, P. (1900), *L'organisation de la famille et le principe de la transmission des biens de souche sous l'emprise des diverses législations qui ont régi la vallée de Barèges*, Toulouse.

MENDELS, F. (1981), *Industrialization and Population Pressure in Eighteenth Century Flanders*, New York.

MOHEAU (1778), *Recherches et considérations sur la population de la France*, Paris (Montyon is the real author of the book).

OURLIAC, P. (1956), 'La famille pyrénéenne au Moyen Age', *Recueil d'études sociales publié à la mémoire de Frédéric Le Play*, Paris, 257–63.

PERON, Y. (1986), 'Paysan témoin, paysage acteur d'une société pré-montagnarde sur la défensive', In I. Chiva and J. Goy (eds.), *Les Baronnies des Pyrénées*, vol. 2: 'Maisons, espace, famille', Paris, 11–61.

PINGAUD, M.-C. (1971), 'Terres et familles dans un village du Châtillonnais', *Etudes rurales*, **XIII**, 52–104.

POUMAREDE, J. (1970), *Les successions dans le Sud-Ouest de la France au moyen-âge, géographie coutumière et mutations sociales*, Paris, PUF.

POUMAREDE, J. (1979), 'Famille et tenure dans les Pyrénées du moyen-âge au XIXe siècle', *Annales de Démographie Historique*, Paris, 347–60.

RAGON, H. (1931), *Le droit d'aînesse en Bigorre*, Bagnères.

RIEHL, W. H. (1855), *Die Naturgeschichte des Volkes als Grundlage einer deutschen Sozialpolitik*, 2nd edition, Stuttgart and Augsburg: vol. 3 'Die Familie'.

RIEU-GOUY, A. M. and M. L. SAUZEON-BROUEILH (1978), *Le choix du conjoint et la transmission du patrimonie dans la vallée de Barèges: les communes de Betpouet et Gedre*, Toulouse (mimeo).

RODRIGUEZ HERNANDORENA, A. (1988), *Mating Patterns and Fertility in a Basque Shepherding Community, 1800–1975* (Saint Engrace), PhD, Oxford (mimeo).

SABEAN, D. W. (1990), *Property, Production, and Family in Neckarhausen, 1700–1870*, Cambridge.

SEGALEN, M. (1972), *Nuptialité et alliance dans une commune de l'Eure*, Paris.

SEGALEN, M. (1985), *Quinze générations de Bas-Bretons. Parenté et société dans le pays Bigouden Sud, 1720–1980*, Paris.

SMITH, R. M. (1981), 'Fertility, Economy and Household Formation in England over Three Centuries', *Population and Development Review*, **7**, No. 4, 595–622.

TILLY, C. (1984), 'Demographic Origins of the European Proletariat', In D. Levine (ed.), *Proletarianization and Family History*, New York, 1–85.

VALVERDE, L. (1989), *Illegitimacy in Spain*, Alicante (mimeo).

VAN DE WALLE, E. (1978), 'Alone in Europe: The French Fertility Decline until 1850', In C. Tilly (ed.), *Historical Studies of Changing Fertility*, Princeton.

VIAZZO, P. (1986), 'Illegitimacy and the European Marriage Pattern: Comparative Evidence from an Alpine Area', In L. Bonfield, R. Smith and K. Wrightson (eds.), *The World we have Gained*, London, 100–21.

VIAZZO, P. P. (1989), *Upland Communities: Environment, Population and Social Structure in the Alps since the Sixteenth Century*, Cambridge.

WALL, R. (ed.) with the collaboration of J. ROBIN and P. LASLETT (1983), *Family Forms in Historic Europe*, Cambridge.

ZURFLUH, A. (1986), 'Gibt es den Homo alpinus? Eine demographisch-kulturelle Fallstudie am Beispiel Uris (Schweiz) im 17–18. Jahrhundert', In M. Mattmuller (ed.), *Itinera* (special issue) *Economies et sociétés de montagne*, Berne, 232–81.

ZURFLUH, A. (1988), *Une population alpine dans la confédération. Uri aux XVIIe–XVIIIe–XIXe siècles*, Paris.

Chapter 7

THE PROTOINDUSTRIAL HOUSEHOLD ECONOMY: TOWARD A FORMAL ANALYSIS

ULRICH PFISTER

The association between internationally active urban merchants and dispersed handicraft producers located in the countryside is usually considered a basic feature of European industry in the early modern era (Kellenbenz, 1974; Kriedte et al., 1981; Mendels, 1984). Thus, understanding the structure and dynamic of rural households engaged in handicraft industries has become a central objective of protoindustrial theory, the main paradigm for investigating rural industry before mechanization.

Based on the writings of Medick (1976), Kriedte et al. (1981, chs. 2 and 3), Levine (1977) and Braun (1978; 1990), the protoindustrial household has initially been considered to be small and of simple composition, work roles were thought to be characterized by weak age and sex differentials, and it was surmised that family organization would foster rapid demographic growth. More recent studies, however, have presented material which contradicts some or all of these statements, the most notable ones being those by Lehning (1980) and Gullickson (1986) on two French textile regions (cf. also Spagnoli, 1983; Gutmann and Leboutte, 1984). Does this imply that the concept of protoindustrialization is without relevance and that it should be discarded from our vocabulary (Coleman, 1983)?

The present study argues for the contrary case. In my opinion, the problems of protoindustrial theory reside less in a fundamental weakness of the concept than in a priority of phenomenological over structural analysis. Efforts have mainly gone into a description of processes and corollaries of cottage industry, rather than into a formal analysis of the basic structural elements of protoindustrial growth and the conditions under which they might produce different types of processes.[1] What follows is an attempt to provide such a structural and, to a certain degree, formal analysis for the topic under discussion, namely the organization of the protoindustrial household economy.

The paper starts by presenting a simple model of the decision-making process by which rural households allocate their labour between the agricul-

---

[1] The 'definitions' and 'hypotheses' proposed by Mendels (1984, pp. 988–94) are a good example of this kind of phenomenological analysis.

tural and industrial sectors. It allows the formulation of several hypotheses regarding the size and composition of households, as well as the demographic corollaries of protoindustrialization (cf. the summary given in Appendix 1). In this part, the analysis assumes that household labour is a homogeneous input. The later sections relax this restriction by discussing, first, the differentiation of work roles with regard to sex and age, and, second, the allocation of labour over time spans of different lengths, such as seasons and life cycles. Throughout, I will try to keep the formal discussion simple; the main thrust consists of an attempt to integrate the wide and, at first sight, often contradictory range of empirical evidence into a coherent interpretative framework.

LABOUR ALLOCATION AND SOCIAL STRUCTURE

Two features are usually considered distinctive of the household economy of protoindustrial producers in the countryside. First, peasant households engaged in cottage industry tended to split their labour over agriculture and industry. Such a combination of agrarian and industrial activities made it possible for merchants to pay relatively low wages and thus assured the competitive advantage of protoindustrial areas located in north-western Europe over the older town-based systems of the Mediterranean (Medick, 1976, pp. 299–300; examples in Deyon, 1972 and Rapp, 1975). Second, the production of individual households was oriented toward an inter-regional or international market. As a consequence, demand for industrial goods was clearly beyond the control of an individual household, which thus was essentially a price taker. This feature distinguishes the protoindustrial household economy from that of rural handicrafts serving a restricted local clientele, in which case the behaviour of individual producers may affect prices.[2]

What follows is a simple model of the labour allocation process in the protoindustrial household as it can be conceived against the background of these two structural features. It is assumed that households seek to maximize family income by optimally allocating their labour between the agricultural and protoindustrial sectors. Initially, it is also assumed that agricultural labour (as well as protoindustrial work) is equally distributed over the year and that no labour market exists, so that the amount of labour is fixed by the size of the family. In addition, labour is considered to be homogeneous, so that amounts of labour can be split continuously over tasks of different types. All these restrictions are at least partially relaxed in the further course of the analysis. Finally, work in the manufacturing sector is supposed to be available to an

---

2 This point is directed at Schremmer (1981), who argues that protoindustrialization should be considered simply as a part of a general ruralization of crafts, be they export-oriented or not. The model presented below would look quite different if the relationship between the labour supply of oligopolistic or monopolistic producers in small markets and the prices of the respective goods had been taken into account.

Figure 1: Allocation of household labour over the agricultural and manufacturing sectors (vmp$_f$, vmp$_i$: value of marginal product in the agricultural and industrial sectors, respectively; L: labour supply; A, T: agricultural and total household labour force; r: reproduction cost of labour).

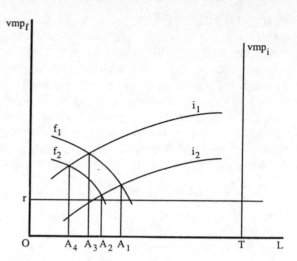

unlimited extent to all households throughout, i.e. the whole analysis applies only to protoindustrial contexts.[3]

Figure 1 presents several configurations of the base model. The horizontal axis measures the amount of labour (L) devoted either to agricultural or protoindustrial tasks. The total amount of labour available is constrained by the size of the individual household (T). Labour devoted to agriculture is measured from the left axis, protoindustrial work from the constraint T to the left; A/T and (T–A)/T are the respective shares of household labour devoted to agriculture and protoindustrial work. Each type of labour has its specific marginal product (vmp). The left axis measures the value of the marginal product of labour obtained by the household through cultivating its own land (vmp$_f$=price P_f times marginal product mp$_f$ in the agricultural sector); the line through the labour constraint T measures the value of the marginal product of household labour obtained by using rooms, tools and possibly circulating capital to produce manufactured goods (vmp$_i$=P_i· mp$_i$). Concrete functions of the value of the marginal product of labour on the level of individual households are represented by f_1 and i_1 in the respective sectors. The surface beneath them represents the amount of the household's income. Additionally, r is the cost of reproducing labour; given the absence of a labour market, this amount basically embodies the provision for subsistence needs. The income surface above r represents the rents accruing to the household. On the one

---

3 The base model is strongly inspired by Ho (1984). The main difference to Ho is that I do not, at this stage at least, differentiate between the labour requirements during different seasons of the year, and that I provide an explicit discussion of the labour supply schedule whereas Ho seems to assume a backward-bending curve of labour supply. Furthermore, Ho's unit of analysis is the region, and not the individual household (although problems of aggregation are not discussed explicitly). Other relevant sources are Hymer and Resnick (1969), Nakajima (1969), Mokyr (1976) and Mendels (1978).

hand, it receives a capital rent for providing soil, tools and working space necessary for both agricultural and protoindustrial production.[4] On the other hand, the household derives a rent from its labour input. It is assumed that the rent income as a whole accrues mainly to the household head.

The basic result of Figure 1 is the determination of the optimal distribution of labour over agricultural and industrial activities. It is given by the intersection between the production functions of the two sectors: A_1 in the case of f_1 and i_2. At this point household income attainable with given resources and family size is maximal.

A first variable which may be investigated is the level of the productivity function in the agricultural sector, reflecting variability in the amount of land available to a household as well as the productivity of agricultural labour (f_1 and f_2 in Fig. 1). Here, f_2 represents a case in which the values of the marginal product of labour derived from agriculture are lower than in the case of f_1 because of a smaller surface area or lower fertility of the land cultivated by the household. This implies that the point of optimal labour allocation between the agricultural and industrial sectors (A_2) is farther to the left than in the case of f_1 (A_1). From this follows the hypothesis that—industrial earnings held constant—households disposing over land of small surface area or of low fertility tend to devote a larger share of their labour to protoindustrial than to agricultural tasks compared with households with larger surface areas and higher productivity (statement 1). This hypothesis is far from novel, of course. It has been advanced frequently, both for the levels of individual households (Medick, 1976, p. 297) and for inter-regional comparisons (Jones, 1968, p. 64; Gullickson, 1983). Accordingly, a great number of studies provide at least qualitative evidence that cottage industry was most widespread among land-poor households. Systematic quantitative evidence is available for some English and pre-alpine contexts (Levine, 1977, pp. 50f; Tanner, 1982, pp. 79 and 259; Pfister, 1992, pp. 281–85).

Of course, the function for the marginal product of protoindustrial labour may vary as well. Weaving, for example, is usually associated with a higher marginal product than spinning (cf. i_1 vs. i_2 in Fig. 1). As a consequence, a greater share of the household labour force is devoted to work in the manufacturing sector in this case (see A_1 vs. A_3 or A_2 vs. A_4). Temporal variations in piece rates will have a similar effect.

---

4 Some of my discussion partners have been reluctant to view protoindustrial activities as subject to diminishing returns at the level of the individual household; in fact, Mokyr (1976, pp. 10–11 and 137–44) explicitly develops a similar model based on the assumption that labour was the only relevant input in protoindustry and that, therefore, it was not subject to diminishing returns. Nevertheless, I consider the rents that rural households derive from the disposition over working space and—depending on the degree of penetration of a putting-out organization into production—over tools and circulating capital as relevant elements of the protoindustrial household economy. The later discussion of the mutual relationship between the productivity schedules in the agricultural and industrial sectors and its implications on the demographic corollaries of protoindustry as well as other related topics is crucially based on this assumption.

More interesting than looking at the separate variation of the values of the marginal product of labour in the two sectors is the consideration of a possible correlation between the two. In fact, it can be argued that, under certain circumstances, the ability of a household to engage in protoindustrial activities depends on its endowment with agricultural resources. Thus, if local raw materials are being processed—such as in the linen industry—and markets for raw or intermediate goods are lacking, there exists a positive linear relationship between the levels of the functions for the marginal product of labour in the two sectors. But even if the access to factor inputs for protoindustrial production is less restricted, a correlation between the levels of the two production functions is possible: the rents derived from activities in any of the two sectors considered can be saved and invested. High returns in agriculture which surpass labour reproduction costs can be used as circulating capital to bridge production periods, to acquire expensive tools, to build houses with sufficient space to place them and thus to engage in highly productive and remunerative protoindustrial activities. Conversely, rents derived from protoindustrial production can be used to purchase land and thus to increase the productivity of agricultural labour.

The argument that the levels of the productivity functions in the protoindustrial and the agricultural sectors may be correlated with each other across individual households because each sector may provide relevant factor inputs (raw materials, capital) for production in the other has several implications (statement 2).

First, the negative relationship between the marginal product of agricultural labour and the share of family labour devoted to protoindustrial activities (cf. statement 1) is not of universal validity. Rather, it is confined to branches which require few inputs other than labour on the part of an individual household, such as spinning, and in which markets for raw and intermediate goods are readily accessible (statement 2.1). Where such markets are lacking, protoindustrial production suffers from a constraint on inputs which is basically determined by the size of the agricultural concession. The level of the productivity function in the protoindustrial sector is thus related to the one in the agricultural sector by a positive linear relationship whose slope approaches unity. As a consequence, the share of protoindustrial labour remains largely constant across households characterized by their differing endowments with land (statement 2.2).

A third constellation emerges when both agricultural and protoindustrial activities require considerable amounts of capital inputs on the part of individual producers. In this case, it is the mutual relationship of the *capital* productivity schedules in the two sectors which determines the structure of household labour (statement 2.3). If the two intersect at a positive value of capital inputs, a curvi-linear relationship between investment capacity (which reflects the position of a household within the social hierarchy of a village) and the share of protoindustrial labour emerges. Thus, in contexts of extensive agriculture the marginal product of capital at lower input levels may be higher in the protoindustrial than in the agricultural sector. Relatively poor peasants will therefore choose to increase their labour productivity in the proto-industrial sector—for example by buying a weaving loom and by shifting part of their labour force from spinning to weaving—rather than in agriculture. The result is illustrated in Figure 1 if it is assumed that configurations f_1 and i_1 with A_3 and f_2 and i_2 with A_2 represent two households which differ by their investment capacity. Although f_1 is superior to f_2—for example because the first household has more land than the second—the first household records a higher share of protoindustrial labour than the second (A_3 vs. A_2). This is because the difference between i_1 and i_2 is largely superior to the one between f_1 and f_2, reflecting differences in the marginal product of capital in the two sectors. However, it is probable that the marginal product of capital declines faster in the protoindustrial than the agricultural sector: after all household members of working age have been provided with a weaving loom, few productive investments can be made in the protoindustrial household sector, whereas opportunities to improve factor inputs (purchase of new seeds, improvement of soils) cause the marginal product of capital to fall less steeply in the agricultural sector. For the labour allocation process depicted in Figure 1 this implies that, from some point on,[5] i rises less quickly than f if one moves to configurations marked by a higher investment capacity of the household (i.e., towards the top of the figure), implying a renewed shift of A to the right.

To put this in simpler terms, it is argued that, in protoindustrial branches that require a certain investment capacity on the part of the individual household and in contexts marked by extensive agriculture, the highest share of protoindustrial labour is expected to prevail among the rural middle classes, whereas both farmers and poor households devoid of any investment capacity will record lower proportions of protoindustrial household labour. However, as already mentioned, such a curvi-linear relationship between the structure of household labour and the position within the hierarchy of rural society will only materialize if the capital productivity schedules of the two sectors intersect, presumably in areas characterized by extensive agriculture. If this is not the case, a linear relationship, as exposed in statement 1, will be present even for protoindustrial branches requiring a certain amount of capital on the part of individual producers. Such a situation can be expected to prevail in areas of intensive agriculture (wine-growing regions, for example) where even small investments by land-poor peasants can increase labour productivity by considerable amounts.

The most explicit empirical discussion of a curvi-linear pattern between land ownership and the share of protoindustrial household labour so far is Schlumbohm's (1982, pp. 324–29) study of linen weaving in the Ravensberg

---

5 This point is defined by the intersection between the functions for the marginal product of capital in the two sectors.

area east of Bielefeld (Germany). While no large farmers engaged in weaving, this activity was more common among the smallholders than among the completely landless. Furthermore, landless weavers disposed of fewer looms and were more frequently dependent on a putter-out than weavers who had some land. Further data on indebtedness show that land was a critical provider of security guaranteeing access to credits which could be used as circulating capital, i.e. to bridge the time gap between the purchase of yarn and the selling of cloth. The same study also presents material from another region (Osnabrück) where a rigid agricultural structure assured close control over the labour of the poor by farmers and precluded the formation of an open market for yarn. Hence, the amount of critical inputs for the production process such as flax and yarn were dependent on the size of an agricultural concession. Accordingly, as postulated above for circumstances of this kind, a positive linear relationship between land and linen production emerged: farmers were bigger sellers of cloth than smallholders and the landless (cf. statement 2.2; Schlumbohm, 1982, pp. 319–21).[6]

Another good example of a curvi-linear relationship between land and the share of protoindustrial household labour is the silk ribbon weaving industry in Marlhes (Stephanois, France; Lehning, 1980). A ribbon weaving loom constituted a relatively heavy investment for a peasant family and, because of its bulkiness, required considerable space. Hence, ribbon weaving was most frequent among farmers whose concessions were slightly below the level sufficient for fulfilling subsistence needs, whereas virtually landless households recorded far fewer weavers; even large farmers displayed shares of protoindustrial workers which were not much below those of the landless.[7] Similar results have been obtained in local case studies for the wool textile industry of the Haut-Givaudan (France; Claverie and Lamaison, 1981, p. 212) and a large parish dominated by linen weaving in Wurttemberg (Southern Germany; Medick, 1983, Table 8, pp. 288–90).[8] Finally, material from Zurich (Switzer-

---

6 Readers may be confused by the fact that I argue both for the *absence* of a relationship between land size and the *share* of protoindustrial labour and for a *positive relationship* between the *absolute amount* of protoindustrial production and land size. By saying this I assume that the size of the household labour force is positively correlated with land size. This relationship, whose actual existence can be easily documented, will be dealt with in more detail below.

7 Lehning (1980, Table 3, p. 42). My interpretation deviates from the one given by Lehning, who argues that during the cottage industry phase 'weaving was . . . practised without regard for the amount of land held by the family' (p. 40). However, a statistical analysis of his table for 1851 suggests a statistically significant relationship between the amount of land held by a household and the frequency of ribbon weavers (Chi^2=9.54, df=2, p<.01).

8 Again, my interpretation differs slightly from the one given by the author. In Table 8 of Medick's study—a cross-tabulation of the profession and the taxable property of household heads—the share of weavers among all household heads is lowest among the richest and the poorest groups; the shares differ only slightly among the other categories. The relationship is statistically significant with Chi^2=22.46, df=5, p<.001.

land) suggests that, while wool and cotton spinning was most frequently practised by landless households in a number of parishes, a curvi-linear relationship between land and silk or cotton weaving prevailed in villages marked by extensive agriculture, but not in regions of intensive wine cultivation (Pfister, 1992, pp. 281–89).

The argument for a possible relationship between the values of marginal product in the agricultural and protoindustrial sectors holds not only for the analysis of individual households but for the comparison between adjacent regions as well. Thus, in the West Riding region of Yorkshire, the upland parts, where soils were bad and weak manorial control permitted the emergence of a virtually landless proletariat, developed a putting-out system based on the production of cheap worsted. Many households engaged only in spinning and carding. By contrast, in the more fertile valleys to the east where manorial control remained stronger and agricultural units were larger, there occurred a specialization in the production of heavy woollen cloths by large households organizing most production processes autonomously (Hudson, 1986, pp. 61–70). Likewise, a cross-sectional analysis of Irish counties suggests that flax spinning was concentrated in relatively poor regions where smallholders were numerous and soils were of bad quality, while linen weaving was not (Almquist, 1979, correlations between variables 1, 2, 16, 17 and 18 on p. 711).

The second main conclusion to be derived from the potential relationship between the product functions in the agricultural and manufacturing sectors, respectively, refers to the implications of protoindustrialization for agriculture. If the marginal product of protoindustrial labour increases—for example as a result of higher piece rates—labour devoted to agriculture will decline if no offsetting rise in agricultural productivity occurs (cf. A_1 vs. A_3 or A_2 vs. A_4 in Fig. 1). Thus, marginal soils will be abandoned and possibly be converted into woodland or pasture, and the remaining territory may be cultivated less carefully. This seems to have happened in regions where manorial or communal regulations inhibited investment in the agricultural sector by individual households. Arthur Young made this observation on the 'Linen Triangle' of Ulster and the Pays de Caux (Normandy, France). His views are commented on rather sceptically by present-day historians, however (Gullickson, 1986, p. 49; Clarkson, 1990, p. 257). It appears nevertheless that, in the protoindustrialized areas of the flatter parts of the Canton of Zurich, rigid communal regulations can be held responsible for a negative influence of protoindustry on the labour inputs into agriculture (Braun, 1990, pp. 129f; Pfister, 1992, pp. 453–56).

By contrast, where manorial and communal regulations are absent or conducive to agricultural innovations, the rent derived from work in the manufacturing sector may be saved and invested in the improvement of agricultural techniques, that is, in enclosures, new seeds (clover), improvement of soils, the purchase of cattle, and so on (statement 2.4). The process is well documented for Flanders (Mendels, 1975), but a number of other protoindustrial regions are known to have developed a highly productive commercial agricultural sector, usually in branches other than grain production. Examples are the development of livestock farming in parts of England and of pre-alpine Switzerland, or of Mediterranean cash crops in the lower Languedoc (Thirsk, 1961; Mendels, 1980; Mattmüller, 1983; Pfister, 1992, pp. 444–52).

The next step in the analysis consists in the relaxation of two restrictions present in the base model: fixed family size and the absence of a labour market. For this purpose, Figure 2 expands the model by introducing the wage rate of rural labour (day labour, servants; w) as an additional parameter. Accordingly, the focus of the analysis shifts from the implications of the positions of the respective production functions on the labour allocation process to their implications on household size and composition. The consideration of a labour market implies that households can optimize their size by recruiting new members or by inducing present members to leave the household. The configuration marked by the constraint of the amount of familial labour (F) and the location of f_1 and i_1 is sub-optimal in the sense that the value of the product of the marginal unit of labour (A_1) is above the wage rate. Thus, the employment of servants increases the household's utility until the intersection of the two production functions reaches the wage rate (A_1', amount of servants: $T-F$). Increasing household size by the employment of wage labour produces an additional rent for the household by the amount delineated by A_1, w, $T-(F-A_1)$, i'—which is simply i shifted to the right—and f_1. On the other hand, households with low labour productivity will have to reduce their size and send some of their labour to other households. For example, the configuration marked by f_2 and i in Figure 2 designates a household with an optimal size of the familial labour force (A_2 intersects with w). If family size

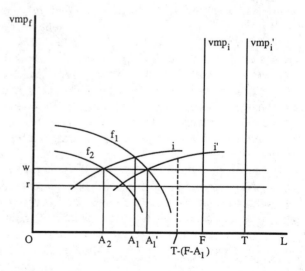

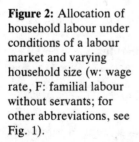

Figure 2: Allocation of household labour under conditions of a labour market and varying household size (w: wage rate, F: familial labour without servants; for other abbreviations, see Fig. 1).

increases beyond F, for example, because children become able to work, surplus labour will have to leave the household.

Several conclusions regarding household size and structure can be deduced from Figure 2. The most general one is that household size depends to a large extent on the level of the function for the marginal product of overall household labour, i.e. regardless of sectoral differences (statement 3). In so far as there are many situations in which land-poor households are most frequently engaged in manufacturing, this statement resembles Medick's (1976, pp. 301–02) assertion that the nuclear family was the predominant household structure among protoindustrial households. In fact, a number of studies show comparatively low household size and complexity among the protoindustrial lower classes (cf. Levine, 1977, pp. 50–53; Tanner, 1982, ch. 8; Pfister, 1989a, pp. 87 and 98; on an aggregate level Fitz, 1985, pp. 105–83). However, if the production of manufactured goods is concentrated among the rural middle classes, the size of protoindustrial households (along with the level of overall productivity of labour) can be considerable. In Marlhes, for example, households containing ribbon weavers were more frequently extended than the rest of the population during the cottage industry period; and the same appears to have been true of Irish linen weavers and of cotton weavers in the Austrian Waldviertel (Lehning, 1980, pp. 106–07; Collins, 1982, p. 134; Mitterauer, 1986, p. 237). Thus, depending on the outcome of the labour allocation process discussed above, the size of households engaged in protoindustry will vary more frequently than other peasant groups.

While it is impossible to attribute a predominant size or type to households engaged in protoindustry beyond the general relationship mentioned in statement 3, it can be argued that manufacturing introduces a stabilizing factor into peasant households of different social status measured by land size. This holds especially in situations where the productivity functions in the proto-industrial sector differ little between individual households (as in the case of spinning, for example). Thus, in Figure 2 the absolute amount of labour allocated to protoindustry does not vary between the two configurations marked by different marginal products in the agricultural sector ($F- A_2=T- A_1'$). This means that optimal household size varies less among households with different agricultural production functions than under circumstances where no protoindustrial employment opportunities are available and where the optimal household sizes are A_2 and A_1', respectively ($A_2/A_1'T/F$). While few studies have explicitly analysed this point, it corresponds with the general notion that households from the protoindustrial lower classes are larger than those of rural labourers in purely agrarian contexts; parents can tie grown-up children to their homes until a higher age than labourers who have to send their children into domestic service (Medick, 1976, p. 302).

Figure 2 also allows some issues related to income distribution within the household to be tackled. It has been argued above that households receive rent on both labour ($w-r$ in Fig. 2) and capital (land, buildings, tools; income surfaces above w), and that these rents accrue essentially to the household head. Withholding the labour rent from other family members is only possible as long as the latter are dependent on the household head in terms of protection and, notably, inheritance. If this situation does not apply, the household head has to renounce exclusive rights on the labour rent and provide other family members with an income corresponding to the wage rate to keep them at home. In terms of Figure 2, this implies that F shifts dramatically to the left (being restricted to the household head and his wife) and that the presence or absence of both servants and other family members is actually governed by market forces.

This argument holds true particularly for the rural lower classes who, because of the low level of capital inputs involved in both agricultural and protoindustrial production, fulfil the condition of a low relevance of inheritance and other, non-material criteria. Hence, it is among these households that employment-like relationships between parents and children develop during favourable periods (i.e. when w exceeds r considerably). There is evidence that in these situations, children made ample use of their bargaining power and readily chose to board with other households if their parental household should prove uncompetitive. This has originally been suggested for the Canton of Zurich (Braun, 1990, pp. 54–59), and a recent comparison of life cycles in various English communities suggests that a great incidence of lodging among young adults was a distinctive feature of protoindustrial communities (Wall, 1987, pp. 84–87). The inability of household heads among rural lower classes to acquire the labour rent from at least a section of their family members hampered their ability to save and invest, and was thus a factor which contributed to keeping them in persistent poverty.

DEMOGRAPHIC COROLLARIES OF PROTOINDUSTRIALIZATION

The degree to which children can autonomously dispose of their labour rent is crucially linked to the process of household formation, and this brings us to the topic of the relationship between household structure and the demographic corollaries of protoindustrialization. In the existing literature it is argued that the spread of cottage industry led to a significant increase in population size by creating employment opportunities outside agriculture, which in turn led to an increase in marriage and fertility rates (Mendels, 1972, pp. 249–53; Fischer, 1973; Levine, 1977, pp. 11–12; Kriedte et al., 1981, ch. 3; Braun, 1978). In the light of the conflicting evidence available, however, there is a need to formulate more qualified hypotheses.

Positing a direct link between protoindustrial employment opportunities presupposes that youths can exert autonomous control over their labour rent and/or that households largely devoid of agrarian resources can be formed. As the previous section has shown, these conditions are by no means fulfilled in every case. Rather, according to the possible configurations of the values of the marginal product of labour in the agrarian and protoindustrial sectors on the aggregate level, three main variants of demographic corollaries of protoindustry should be distinguished (cf. statements 4.1–3):

(a) *Low marginal product of protoindustrial relative to agricultural labour* (cf. i_2 and f_1 in Fig. 1)—*demographic growth* (if present at all) *through declining mortality*. In this configuration, the share of protoindustrial labour in total household activities is low, as is its contribution to family income. Hence, working capacity in the protoindustrial sector cannot serve as security for lenders in the context of household formation and, likewise, the ancillary or part-time character of protoindustrial work makes it easy for household heads to appropriate the labour rents of youths, thus hampering their saving capability. As the control of a minimal amount of land remains a prerequisite for the foundation of a new household, variations in piece rates in the protoindustrial sector cannot constitute a decisive element in the decisions of young people to marry; a pattern of rising marriage and fertility rates is not to be expected in this case. Rather, a modest demographic expansion may result from the fact that protoindustrial incomes, small as they are in this case, foster the investment capacity of rural households (cf. statement 2.4). This may improve levels of nutrition and contribute to lower mortality rates, thus favouring population growth.

In practice, this pattern seems to have been quite frequent among populations engaged in spinning in marginal areas or during periods of modest employment opportunities. As low remunerations in comparison with urban labour are considered a distinctive feature of rural protoindustry, this fact is probably of a conceptual significance which has not been fully recognized so far. Results on the pre-alpine region of the Entlebuch (Switzerland), whose population was integrated as spinners of linen and cotton yarn into more developed production systems farther to the north and west, show that it was one of the first regions to adopt potato cultivation in that area. At the same time, it displayed a slow decline of mortality throughout the eighteenth century, whereas marriage age and fertility do not seem to have altered significantly (Bucher, 1974, pp. 106–07, 227–33). A similar tendency has been found for a village in the Swiss Jura engaged in lace-making (Sorgesa Miéville, 1992, pp. 126–31). The careful juxtaposition of figures on daily earnings and life events in the Pays de Caux suggests that marriage rates remained largely constant while weaving constituted predominantly a seasonal side-activity for men and women who were confined to spinning (Gullickson, 1986, pp. 70, 80–81, 139–42). Finally, in the upland parts of the Canton of Zurich which were dominated by the spinning of cotton and, earlier, wool, the relationship between marriage rates and fluctuations in textile exports remained weak before the onset of the cotton boom around the middle of the eighteenth century. Demographic growth in excess of the neighbouring agrarian areas was mainly due to lower death rates (Pfister, 1989b, pp. 648–51; 1992, pp. 471–77, 487–88). It is not quite clear whether the wool producing region around Verviers (Belgium) conformed to this pattern as well. Low prices in the industrial sector during the eighteenth century seem to have tied industry closely to agriculture, thus precluding an immediate reaction of marriages to industrial business cycles (Gutmann, 1987, pp. 166–71; 1988, pp. 88, 160–65).[9] The wool producing areas of the Black Forest (Germany), where stable population patterns combined with a modest amount of land poverty have been observed, may also belong to this variant (Ogilvie, 1990, pp. 79, 82, 93).

(b) *High levels of labour productivity in both sectors* (cf. i_1 and f_1 in Fig. 1)— *demographic growth through declining mortality, possibly to a lesser degree through rising marriage and fertility rates*. It has already been noted that several protoindustrial activities associated with high labour productivity are strongly tied to an agrarian resource base through capital or primary input requirements (cf. statements 2.2/3). As in type (a), the foundation of a new household of this type requires a considerable investment effort, and the relevance of the agrarian resource base still enables household heads to withhold the labour rent from youths in exchange for the prospect of inheritance. Only the fact that engagement in a highly remunerative trade can serve as a security to lenders may foster marriage rates during periods of favourable price relations. However, the primary factor behind population growth in configurations marked by high labour productivity in both sectors is declining mortality rates. It has been shown above that households of the present type are those which are most likely to save and invest protoindustrial incomes in improvement of agricultural techniques. Even more than type (a) they are, therefore, characterized by an improvement of nutrition and a corresponding decline in mortality.

It may well be that this pattern is the dominant one among the 'rich' industries. Gutmann and Leboutte (1984, p. 604) suggest that the high investments in human capital necessary in the coal and iron industry contributed to the stability of marriage rates in the Basse-Meuse (Belgium). Vallorbe, a small centre of the iron industry in the Swiss Jura, has been shown to have grown primarily by spectacularly low rates of mortality in the eighteenth century (Hubler, 1984, pp. 273–82). Low mortality was the primary and high fertility the secondary factor behind eighteenth-century population growth in the silk ribbon weaving area of Basle—which, at the

---

9 In the passages quoted, Gutmann stresses his inability to replicate Mendels' (1972, pp. 250f) claim for a relationship between the number of marriages and the ratio between industrial and grain prices, as well as the strong interrelationship between agriculture and protoindustry. The very high marriage age of spinners lends additional support to this interpretation (Gutmann, 1988, p. 169). However, in other instances Gutmann documents shares of landless households (*circa* 50 per cent) which are rather high in comparative perspective and suggests that weavers married without acquiring land (Gutmann, 1988, pp. 163, 170–72). Likewise, the tables presented in Gutmann (1987, pp. 167–70) are in complete support of Mendels' hypotheses, contrary to the text of that article. In a personal communication Professor Gutmann, however, has kindly made available revised tables. My tentative re-analyses of them suggest support for the cautious reasoning given in the text above. In my view, no definitive interpretation of this large and interesting body of material can be offered at present.

same time, was quick in adopting agricultural innovations—and possibly, albeit to a lesser degree, of the Stephanois (Mattmüller, 1983, pp. 50–51; Lehning, 1980, p. 61). The same configuration prevailed during the last upsurge in linen weaving in eastern Switzerland during the late seventeenth century (Tanner, 1982, p. 127). Likewise, relatively low mortality rates combined with a slow fall in marriage ages seem to explain the demographic expansion in the parish of Belm in the linen weaving district of Osnabrück (Schlumbohm, 1992, pp. 189–92).

(c) *High remuneration for protoindustrial activities requiring few inputs on the part of individual producers* (cf. i_1 and f_2 in Fig. 1)—*demographic growth through rising marriage and fertility rates in accordance with protoindustrial-agrarian price relations*. A situation of high relative prices in the industrial sector, rendering viable a household economy whose labour force is predominantly engaged in protoindustrial activities, is the primary precondition for the existence of a direct relationship between protoindustrial business cycles and marriage rates (in contrast to type [a]). The absence of investment requirements on the part of individual producers, which may act as a barrier against flexible individual decisions, is a secondary precondition (cf. type [b]). However, it should be noted that not under all circumstances is there an increase of marriage and fertility rates in the present configuration. The argument says that there is a linear positive correlation between the marriage rate and the position of the production function of industrial labour (i in Fig. 1). Hence, marriage rates rise only if real prices in the protoindustrial sector (measured, for example, by the ratio of cloth to grain prices) rise too. Situations characterized by a stagnation or a slow evolution of the proto-industrial sector cannot, even in the present case, produce a rise in marriage and fertility rates.[10]

Pattern (c) was first documented by Mendels, who has demonstrated a relationship between the frequency of marriages and the ratio of linen to rye prices in a sample of linen-producing villages of eighteenth-century Flanders.[11] From a wider perspective, this type of demographic evolution seems to apply mainly to relatively 'poor' industries during boom phases, such as the rapid expansion of the cotton industry during the second half of the eighteenth century. Two Swiss examples amply bear out this point. During this era, the

---

10 This applies, for example, to the Pays de Caux during the second half of the eighteenth century, where the number of cloth pieces seems to have remained largely on the same level after 1750 (Gullickson, 1986, p. 63). Similarly, Gutmann and Leboutte (1984, p. 604) admit that coal mining and metal works expanded rather slowly in the Basse Meuse.

11 Mendels (1972, pp. 250–51) finds that the relationship existed only in years which saw an increasing linen-rye price ratio, a result to which Medick (1976, pp. 304–05; Kriedte et al., 1981, ch. 3.1) has paid great attention. In the light of methodological doubts (expressed in Pfister, 1989b, p. 649, note 42), as well as the findings of Levine (1977, pp. 62–63), Gullickson (1986, pp. 137–43) and Pfister (1989b, p. 648), which all suggest a decline in marriage and fertility levels during periods of crisis, not much weight should be attributed to this result.

regions of the Canton of Zurich with a strong presence of cotton spinning experienced a transition to rapid increases in marriage and fertility which can be satisfactorily explained by the ratio between textile export taxes (as a proxy for the availability of employment and the level of piece rates) and wheat prices, i.e. a measure for real protoindustrial incomes (Pfister, 1989b, pp. 648–51). At the other end of the production process, a village on Lake Neuchâtel experienced a phenomenal reduction in marriage age after its inhabitants began to work in a newly-established calico-printing manufacturing nearby (Caspard, 1979, p. 124). In both instances, investment requirements on the part of individual households were minimal and remuneration was good, so that young persons could easily celebrate 'beggar weddings' (Braun, 1978, p. 314). Another instance emanating from the cotton boom is the Pays de Caux, where the availability of machine-spun yarn temporarily increased the demand for weavers. It became possible to form household economies based exclusively on the industrial work of both spouses. This led to a drastic fall in marriage ages (Gullickson, 1986, pp. 139–42, 208). Outside the cotton industry, mention should be made of the spread of framework knitting from London into Leicestershire, which is known to have produced a similar effect in the course of the eighteenth century. As frames were often rented from putter-outs, no investments were necessary on the part of individual households; as production was partly centralized in small shops, not even working space was required (Levine, 1977, pp. 20–25, 62–64).

In sum, the foregoing discussion suggests the presence of a considerable variety of demographic patterns among protoindustrial populations which can be systematically linked to specific configurations of the functions for the values of the marginal product of agricultural and protoindustrial labour. This general finding has an important macro-economic implication, namely, that the supply of household labour is non-elastic with respect to prices in the manufacturing sector in a majority of situations. As long as the level of technology does not permit substitution of labour by capital, this implies that protoindustrial systems have to expand geographically in order to increase production. As has often been pointed out, this results in mounting transportation and organization costs along with increasing difficulties of quality control and supervision. These, in turn, are conducive to a centralization and rationalization of production, preparing the ground for later industrialization (cf. Kriedte et al., 1981, ch. 4).

SEX- AND AGE-SPECIFIC WORK ROLES IN THE HOUSEHOLD ECONOMY

So far, the analysis has assumed that labour is a homogeneous input factor. This is, of course, a very generous abstraction; in reality, labour is differentiated by sex- and age-specific work roles as well as by time units. Labour allocation over different activities and the regulation of household size always involves the definition of social roles among persons closely connected by material interests, social institutions and emotions. By studying the patterns of age- and gender-specific work roles—the topic of the present section—we can grasp in a more specific manner the processes underlying the optimizing strategies discussed above. In addition, optimizing behaviour regarding the structure of household labour does not derive from an abstract rationality but is embedded into specific temporal horizons of action. By focusing on the latter, the next section will tackle the issue of the social rationale of the protoindustrial household economy.

Before the advent of bourgeois family ideology during the late eighteenth century, the positions of the two sexes were defined by status rather than by contrasting innate characteristics which were supposed to render men apt for public, productive activities and women for reproductive home tasks. Instead, male authority derived from control over primary productive resources (such as land and cattle) while women were allotted productive tasks associated with the provision of food and the home economy in general. The latter entailed the participation of women in the production and marketing of goods produced beyond immediate subsistence needs, such as eggs or milk, or an engagement in side-activities, such as brewing, retail trade or textile work, which would bring cash into the household. However, the small size of the family economy as well as the sequential order of many tasks often limited role differentiation and necessitated a continuous cooperative effort between spouses. This introduced a considerable element of flexibility into actual gender roles (cf. Segalen, 1980, ch. 3; Hanawalt, 1986, chs. 1, 7–10). This general pattern can be shown to bear heavily on work roles in protoindustrial textile manufacturing (statement 5).

Where several types of protoindustrial activities are available, individuals maximize their own labour productivity by engaging in the activity whose work pattern best suits the role they perform in the rest of the household economy (statement 5.1). This means, on the one hand, that women generally tend to engage in activities that provide continuous employment whereas men choose activities that can be performed as side-activity along with agriculture. As for women from different social strata, on the other hand, the wives of farmers, who have to perform a variety of tasks in the agricultural sector of the household economy, tend to engage in protoindustrial activities with flexible work patterns which can be performed as side-activities. In contrast, women of lower-class origin and living in households with a small agricultural interest tend to engage in activities providing full-time employment. This principle of the maximization of individual productivity and the issue of the flexibility of specific activities it raises may constitute an additional factor, apart from the relative productivity of labour (cf. statements 2.2/3), explaining the class-specific patterns of protoindustrial activities.

These general points can be illustrated by a juxtaposition of some contrasting examples. In the Pays de Caux, cotton spinning was an important activity for women while men of lower-class origin often combined day-labouring with temporary weaving before the end of the eighteenth century. Only when yarn became abundant after the introduction of machine spinning, did women also become involved in weaving (Gullickson, 1986, pp. 80–83, 99, 108–13). On the other hand, in one protoindustrial village of the Canton of Zurich where a dense commercial network rendered cotton yarn amply available, weaving was done primarily by the wives and daughters of small farmers. Their sons, if they engaged in the textile trade at all, mainly performed the ancillary tasks of spinning, combing and spooling (Pfister, 1989a, pp. 100–01). It is the temporal considerations rather than the actual nature of the types of work involved which seem to explain gender-specific work roles in these two cases.

In one village of the wool textile region around Verviers, a number of farmers' wives were spinners, whereas weaving seems to have been performed primarily in the households of smallholders. Looms were often rented from entrepreneurs and, therefore, did not constitute an investment requirement for individual households (Gutmann, 1988, pp. 165, 172). Dependence on employers may have made weaving an activity with a fairly rigid time schedule, rendering it unsuitable for the wives of farmers. The argument can be made more explicit by looking at the results from Hirzel (Canton of Zurich, Switzerland), whose population by the late seventeenth century was already engaged in a variety of protoindustrial trades, ranging from cotton and wool spinning to the weaving of silk gauze. The latter was directly organized by urban putter-outs, and it was therefore predominantly performed by lower-class women whose husbands were weavers themselves and thus went on periodical errands to the town in order to deal with urban merchants. By contrast, cotton spinning was organized as a *Kaufsystem* by local pedlars and small traders in which the spinners usually purchased the raw material. Cotton spinning, therefore, was not subject to a fixed schedule and could easily be performed as a side-activity. This explains why it was most commonly found among the wives of farmers who often span only during winter. The spinning of wool represents an intermediate case as it was organized by small local putter-outs who were dependent on urban merchants. Accordingly, it was most common among the rural middle strata of the wives of artisans and small-holders (Pfister, 1992, pp. 370–76). Individuals obviously tried to combine activities whose work patterns complemented each other.

The degree of flexibility of individual work roles depends on the local structure of the protoindustrial sector as a whole, of course. Where the range of possible activities is narrow, the differentiation of the household economy among the landless strata—where the configuration of relevant production functions permits their emergence—is modest, too. Hence, the differentiation of work roles as well as the degree of labour division will be slight in this case; a kind of 'wage-earning co-residence' ensues (statement 5.2; cf. Levine, 1977, p. 27; Medick, 1976, pp. 310–14). Good examples for this thesis are contexts where trades requiring little capital input were performed by land-poor households. In Shepshed (England), framework knitting (the frame was usually rented from putters-out) was often performed by several persons in the same household, and in an area of the Canton of Zurich where cotton spinning provided the sole form of protoindustrial employment, a group of households can be identified in which virtually all members of working age were engaged in this activity (Levine, 1977, pp. 27–29; Pfister, 1989a, pp. 89–92). These are also the regions in which a relative improvement in the status of women occurred; in the uplands of the Canton of Zurich, where cotton spinning domi-nated, *veillées* and taverns were turned into meeting places for young persons of both sexes. On the other hand, in the Pays de Caux, where the proto-industrial workforce consisted primarily of women during the eighteenth century, women's earnings stabilized a pattern of public consumption by men in *cafés* and *veillées* (Braun, 1990, pp. 83–93; Gullickson, 1986, pp. 84–85).

The relaxation, or even removal, of traditional sex-based work roles among certain lower-class households, by requiring males to abandon field work and return to the home to do what had traditionally been women's work, entailed a potential loss of status for adult men. A frequently chosen strategy of lower-class males to evade this situation was simply to withdraw from the family labour force. This is suggested by Hufton's (1975, pp. 14–17) short account of lace-making around Le Puy in the French Massif Central. Although it became the main source of income for most lower-class families in the region, it remained an exclusively female industry. While women assumed new positions of authority within the household, males remained unemployed and simply hung around if they did not choose to emigrate, at least temporarily. Similar, albeit less dramatic, evidence comes from the area of the Canton of Zurich where cotton spinning was, at first sight, practised by both sexes among the offspring of the protoindustrial lower classes. However, boys around the age of ten would work less frequently and attend school more often than girls. Likewise, young men left the parental household at an earlier age than girls, probably to become agricultural servants (Pfister, 1989a, pp. 93, 95). A comparison between parishes characterized by varying levels of sectoral productivity of labour in both agriculture and protoindustry suggests that, the higher agricultural relative to protoindustrial productivity, the more farmers were able to keep their sons at home and even attract young men from lower-class backgrounds as servants (Pfister, 1992, pp. 387–88). Tentatively, similar patterns of sex-specific circulation between different rural strata have been suggested by a comparison of a number of English parishes. On average, the households of farmers displayed higher ratios of sons over daughters than those of other strata; widows, who often engaged in a textile trade, on the other hand, found it easier to retain daughters than sons (Wall, 1987, pp. 93–94, 96–98).

As for the work roles of children, it can be argued that they correspond to the comparative advantage of individuals set by age, rather than by sex. This means that children, as they grow, move from ancillary tasks like spinning or spooling, which usually start around the age of five or shortly after, to work requiring more strength and skill such as weaving, which usually starts between 12 and 15 years of age or after, and later to agriculture. From this it follows that children are generally more frequently employed in the protoindustrial sector than adults. Likewise, it can be implied that many men, during the transition from adolescence to adulthood, will experience an occupational mobility from the protoindustrial to the agricultural sector, whereas women will continue to engage in protoindustrial trades throughout their lives.[12]

I conclude the discussion of age- and sex-specific work roles by pointing to the implications of protoindustrialization for the organization of household labour and the role of servants. If the structure of protoindustrial production favours the emergence of labour division within the household economy, it follows that stable role patterns emerge within individual families. This means that variations in household size and structure have to be restricted and that role patterns have to be held constant. Thus, as in purely agricultural contexts, households have to recruit servants to make up for the lack of elder children or to replace a deceased household head or his spouse (statement 6.1; cf. Kussmaul, 1981, p. 26).

Little systematic information pertaining to this hypothesis is available at this time. In the West Riding of Yorkshire, household size may have corresponded to a certain degree to the technical requirements of cloth production; at the same time, the areas producing heavy cloth were characterized by household units which were larger and employed more journeymen and apprentices than the households in the Kersey area (Hudson, 1986, pp. 63–64). Likewise, Collins (1982, pp. 133–34) reports that Irish linen weavers employed winders and spinners as substitutes for children in reaching optimal production units. The silk industry seems most consistently to have been associated with a complex family structure or a high incidence of lodgers. The ribbon weavers of Marlhes often lived in extended households (Lehning, 1980, p. 107), while Chilvers Coton (Warwick county, England; Wall, 1987, pp. 85, 87), where the same industry prevailed during the late eighteenth century, displayed a very high incidence of lodging. In the Canton of Zurich, lodging was also most common among households of the middle strata which contained many family members engaged in silk weaving. These households probably contained some free working space and may have tried to exploit fully the working capacity of younger children performing ancillary tasks for adult weavers (Pfister, 1992, pp. 312–14, 349–53). These examples suggest that strategies designed to

---

12 Evidence of the contribution of children to the household economy is scarce and dispersed. For example, Mendels (1978, p. 782) cites evidence suggesting an age of 15 as the transition to a net contribution to agriculture; Tanner (1982, p. 256) mentions a contemporary source which puts this age at 12 in the cotton weaving and embroidery sectors. Evidence from household listings in the Canton of Zurich giving detailed information on the activities of all persons suggests the ages given in the text (Pfister, 1989a; 1992, ch. 4.4). Information on the evolution of activities over the life cycles of men and women is contained in the same material (cf. also Pfister, 1989a).

provide for a stable role configuration in the household economy only make sense in cases of reasonably differentiated role patterns. They do not apply to situations in which individuals perform parallel tasks and where the household economy degenerates into a 'wage-earning co-residence'.

SEASONS, FAMILY TIME AND LIFE TIME

Units of labour involved in the allocation process described in the first part of this study are not only differentiated by sex and age, but by time as well. Time itself is not an absolute quantity, but acquires its meaning in relation to social units embodying temporal horizons of action. The working day, the season, the family cycle and the time of life are all temporal horizons of action which individuals use in different situations. Thus, the model elaborated so far can be extended by arguing that individuals do not maximize their immediate, but rather their permanent, utility (cf. Ghez and Becker, 1975).

Even very short-time work patterns sometimes experienced significant change with the introduction of cottage industry. By the use of a flexible combination of different activities as described in the previous section, labour efforts, by continuously shifting between agricultural, protoindustrial and other activities, could assume a more constant level. Furthermore, a transition to abstract work patterns determined by forces largely beyond the command of the family economy took place in households largely devoid of land (Braun, 1990, ch. 5; Thompson, 1967, pp. 69–74; Kriedte et al., 1981, ch. 2.6).

In order to investigate the implications of seasonal variations in family labour requirements, Figure 3 extends the model of Figure 1 to a situation of two seasons with different functions for the value of the marginal product of

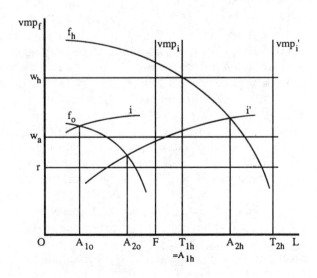

Figure 3: Allocation of household labour with seasonal variations in the marginal product of agricultural labour and wage rates (f_h, f_o: value of marginal product in the agricultural sector during the period of cultivation and harvest and the slack period, respectively; w_h, w_o: wage rates during the respective seasons; for other abbreviations, see Fig. 1).

agricultural labour. During the first season (the cultivation and harvest season), the function for the marginal product of agricultural labour assumes high values (f_h), whereas during the second season (the slack season), it adopts very low values (f_o). For the sake of simplicity, it is assumed that both seasons are of equal length, so that total annual household income amounts to the sum of the two optimal income surfaces (for instance, the area enclosed by f_o, i' and T_{2h} plus the one delineated by f_h, i' and T_{2h}). In addition, the presentation considers a labour market with two different wage rates. During the high-productivity season, short-term labour, such as day labour for harvesting, is paid at the rate w_h; the wage rate for year-long contracts, such as for servants, is lower, namely w_a (both rates are standardized values for one seasonal production period). The difference between the two rates measures in part the costs of circulating capital that landless peasants require to bridge the slack season, whereas these reproduction costs are taken over by the farmer household in the case of annual contracts.

A first and rather trivial conclusion which can be derived from Figure 3 is that households employ a higher share of their labour in the protoindustrial sector during the slack season than during the cultivation period (cf., for example, A_{2o} and A_{2h}). That cottage industry was almost universally practised to a greater extent in winter than in summer is commonplace and needs no explicit documentation. In fact, as this result can also be derived from the analysis of Figure 1 above, seasonality does not constitute a separate element in the protoindustrial household economy (cf. Mokyr, 1976, pp. 141–42 in contrast to Mendels, 1972, p. 242).

A new element, particularly with respect to the function of protoindustrial work in farming households, is introduced by the consideration of two different wage rates during the respective seasons. Consider a household with a family labour force of size F. Employing only temporal labour during the heavy work periods of cultivation and harvest means paying a high wage (w_h) and taking on only a small amount of additional labour ($T_{1h}-F$). An optimal solution is to tie servants, lodgers partially working in the family economy, kin or elder children permanently to the household by granting them an income equivalent to the wage rate of annual labour contracts (w_a). In this case, the size of the optimal household labour force amounts to T_{2h}, which is reached where the average product of the marginal labour unit is equivalent to the annual wage rate ($w_a=[vmp_{A2o} \ vmp_{A2h}]/2$). By permitting the exploitation of the high level of labour productivity during the cultivation season, this solution can considerably increase annual household income (by the surface delineated by w_h, F, w_a, T_{2h}, i' and f_h minus the surface delineated by F, i, f_o and i'). This income is a rent the household derives from providing continuous shelter and food, thus saving the capital costs that land-poor people incur by reproducing themselves during the slack season (statement 6.2).

Different institutional patterns of tying persons or groups of people permanently to the household through a combination of agricultural and protoindustrial work can be observed. In so far as these relationships restrict the room for manoeuvre of certain categories of dependent groups of persons, the solutions to the problem of stabilizing a reservoir of dependent labour are constitutive for the household as a decision-making unit. Actual patterns range from tying only individual persons to tying a large number of dependent households to the decision-making unit. The former end of the continuum is represented by areas where access to land and the formation of new holdings is comparatively easy. Thus, in the parts of the Canton of Zurich which were characterized by extensive agriculture, daughters of farmers regularly span and, in one extreme case, virtually all children in all classes were engaged in silk weaving (Pfister, 1989a, p. 93; 1992, pp. 309, 349–50). It seems that farmers employed part of their family labour force, particularly women, in protoindustry during most of the year to keep them available for the few labour peaks in agriculture. These are also the regions where dual occupation of servants in both agriculture and protoindustry can be observed (see Mitterauer, 1986, p. 232, on the Waldviertel; Pfister, 1992, pp. 304–14, for the Canton of Zurich).

An intermediate case is provided by the linen weaving areas of Osnabrück and (to a lesser degree) Ravensberg, where the number of holdings was largely fixed and landless households (*Heuerlinge*) were closely tied to the households of individual farmers through an exchange of labour services (including servants) and a dependency regarding the granting of leases. Hence, proto-industry remained strongly tied to the seasonal patterns of agricultural production, and—despite the presence of a sizeable landless class—demo-graphic patterns seem to correspond to the configuration expected among a population where protoindustry is combined with significant farming activities (Schlumbohm, 1983, pp. 96–117; cf. above for demographic patterns).

The other end of the continuum is characterized by a sizeable portion of Russian protoindustry. There, seasonal employment in the manufacturing sector was often simply a strategy to increase the profitability of large estates. As only dependent labour was employed and capital profits accrued to owners who were often absentee landlords (and not to individual self-employed households), most statements advanced so far cannot hold for this context; despite the presence of manufacturing activities, the protoindustrial household economy as conceived in the present study simply did not exist (Rudolph, 1985, esp. pp. 61–62).

Not only does the need to balance household labour over seasonal fluctuations of agricultural work create linkages between agriculture and protoindustry, but so does the time horizon of the life cycle, the last topic addressed in this study. If individuals maximize their permanent utility over the life cycle, it can be argued that there exists an inverse relationship between the level of the productivity of their labour and the propensity to save and invest, on the one hand, and the devotion of time to consumption and leisure on the other. In the phases in life during which labour productivity is high, labour supply and the propensity to save are high, too. Conversely, the propensity to consume and to spend time on leisure is highest when the marginal product of labour is low. This relationship holds at a zero interest rate, that is, when it is easy to build up savings for old age or to accumulate the social capital to derive revenues of age later on. If, however, the interest rate is high and opportunities for saving are lacking, the temporal substitution between consumption and working periods disappears, and consumption is highest when wages reach their peak (statement 7; for an overview, see Modigliani, 1980; cf. also Ghez and Becker, 1975, ch. 1, notably pp. 15–16).

Within the space of action of protoindustrial households as it has been described above, this implies that household heads will use life phases of high labour productivity to move the household economy in a direction which allows them to tie other persons to the family in order to derive high rents on capital, as well as to appropriate even part of the rent on their labour, thus assuring an income in old age. In practice, this implies that peasants who start their family cycle with limited means try to acquire land and engage in highly qualified protoindustrial activities through recursive and incremental steps of saving and investment following the logic discussed (in a more static manner) in the first section of this paper (statement 7.1). For example, young couples, poor in land and involved in spinning, may profit from a favourable business cycle and be able to acquire a small plot of land to produce hay or to temporarily fatten a calf. The income derived from this may again be saved and invested in the purchase of a weaving loom and a corresponding enlargement of the house, whereas later stages in this accumulation cycle may include the purchase of more meadows, the permanent acquisition of cattle and, finally, the purchase of fields.

Empirical studies on the life-cycle-specific dimension of protoindustrial activities are extremely rare. Evidence on age-specific occupations, career mobility and indebtedness from the regions of the Canton of Zurich, where the predominance of dairy and livestock farming, together with easy access to land through a functioning real estate market, supported incremental accumulation strategies, suggests that life cycles of the type just described were in fact fairly common. However, the situation was found to differ in protoindustrial areas dominated by arable farming, where the foundation of a functioning agricultural unit was linked to heavy investments and where, partly because of strict communal regulations, the real estate market was rather discontinuous. As this precluded incremental strategies of saving and investment, a pattern of generalized intra-generational upward mobility could not materialize (Pfister, 1989a, pp. 97, 103; 1992, pp. 368–86). The compatibility of agrarian structures with incremental strategies of accumulation is important in the present context, as it bears heavily on certain elements of household formation. The perspective of a family cycle marked by incremental accumulation may be crucial for the motivation of young individuals to save in the prospect of marriage, as well as for the possibility to obtain the necessary credits for founding a new household without a substantial base in agriculture. The demographic implications of the life-cyclical aspects of the protoindustrial household economy are borne out by the fact that, in the Canton of Zurich, the rigidity of communal regulations regarding new settlements mediated the relationship between the expansion of protoindustry and the level of fertility rates in individual parishes (Pfister, 1989b, pp. 653–59).

This brings us to the cultural limits of utility-maximizing behaviour, that is, the type of action presupposed by the whole previous analysis. At least two situations can be conceived in which a maximization of permanent utility makes no sense to protoindustrial households (statement 7.2). First, as just described, the structure of agriculture may render the saving of small amounts of cash by land-poor peasants virtually impossible, thus undermining the precondition of permanent utility maximization. Second, incomes from protoindustrial activity may be so low as to preclude any savings, thus rendering the prospect of incremental accumulation illusionary. Under these circumstances, the protoindustrial lower classes can undergo a process of sub-cultural differentiation which separates them culturally from the rest of rural society. The fact that, given the impossibility of permanent utility maximization, actual consumption has to match actual income implies that the type and level of consumption assumes a distinctive significance in social intercourse, as postulated by Braun (1990, pp. 68–72). And if piece rates in protoindustry temporarily fall below the reproduction cost of labour, self-exploitation and a backward bending curve of labour supply will emerge, as suggested by Medick (1976, pp. 298–99; Kriedte et al., 1981, chs. 2.2 and 2.6).

Again it must be stated that empirical research on these topics is still extremely scarce. Some statistical analyses document the greater exploitation of female and child labour in lower-class households than among other rural strata (Saito, 1981, pp. 643–46; Pfister, 1989a, pp. 91–92). But no study has yet systematically investigated the variables explaining the presence of utility-maximizing behaviour and of subsistence orientation under different circumstances.[13] However, one general point should be made in concluding this section. The classical works of Braun (1990) and Medick (1976) both draw heavily on sources from the early nineteenth century in the pertinent passages, that is, from an era during which mechanization had already made significant inroads into many domains of protoindustrial employment. This suggests that the sub-culture of proletarian households wholly engaged in manufacture was perhaps rather a phenomenon of the transition to industrialization than of protoindustrialization as such.

---

13 In Pfister (1992, pp. 384–86) I try to show that the areas of the Canton of Zurich marked by different patterns of life cycles (as described in the text above) also displayed differences with respect to several elements of popular culture—at least in the descriptions of contemporaries—which correspond to the thesis advanced in statement 6.2.

CONCLUSION

Taken together, the foregoing discussion suggests that protoindustrial theory must be more abstract to be more concise. Rather than making concrete statements on how the protoindustrial household and demography take shape, the present analysis starts from the simple and hardly controversial notion that the emergence of cottage industry introduced a new element in the labour allocation process of rural households. The main line of enquiry, then, is to ask what variables explain the different patterns in the crucial dimensions of the share of household labour devoted to protoindustry, the demographic corollaries of protoindustry, and the allocation of labour to persons of different sex and age as well as during the course of the life cycle. Variables which have been found to be of particular relevance are the relationship between the production functions for labour and capital in the agricultural and protoindustrial (household) sectors in the case of the share of protoindustrial family labour (statement 2) and, likewise, in the case of the demographic corollaries of protoindustrialization (statement 4); second, the compatibility of the labour requirements and work patterns of specific protoindustrial activities with gender roles in explaining the labour division between household members of different sex (statement 5.1); and, finally, the availability of investment opportunities in terms of a flexible market for agricultural inputs in the case of variations in life cycles (statement 7).

In presenting the above analysis, care has been taken to build a parsimonious model. This means that a number of potential ramifications have not been considered systematically. This is particularly true for the institutions that set the framework of action for individual households, such as communal regulations, the *demesne* economy (fixation of concessions, serfdom) or corporate regulations (cf. Ogilvie, 1990). Likewise, little attention has been paid to contexts of transition between home-based cottage industry and continuous wage labour as they have been analysed by several recent studies (e.g., Wall, 1986; Rose, 1988). To take account of such a situation might require introducing a third sector characterized by external wage labour (and from which households derive no rent on capital) into the decision model developed at the outset of this study.[14]

It may be appropriate to briefly contrast the analytical framework of the present study with the classical conceptual discussion of the protoindustrial household economy by Medick (1976; Kriedte et al., 1981, chs. 2 and 3). A first difference refers to the way of theorizing: Medick develops an ideal-type of the

---

14 I found Wall's (1986, p. 265) notion of the 'adaptive family' of little help in interpreting the transition from a family to a family wage economy. In fact, as the concept is defined by the expectation 'that families would attempt to maximize their economic well-being by diversifying the employments of family members', the protoindustrial household economy (as conceived by the present study at least) can be considered as an adaptive family *par excellence* (cf. statement 5.1).

protoindustrial household economy consisting of functionally closely related parts. Despite the relative paucity of in-depth studies available in the mid-1970s, he discusses a considerable range of actual patterns, but (perhaps precisely because of the ideal-type approach) pays little systematic attention to the variables discriminating between these different patterns. This may also be the reason why critical discussions have often ignored these ramifications of the 'classical' model.[15] A second, more fundamental difference concerns the fact that Medick relies strongly on the economics of subsistence as they have emerged from Chayanov's seminal work, whereas I hold that most relevant issues can be adequately structured by fairly conventional neo-classical economics.[16] However, I see clear limits to utility-maximizing behaviour: thus, the very existence of the protoindustrial household economy as a decision-making unit hinges on the institutional autonomy of individual households, which is clearly not given under certain conditions, notably under serfdom. Furthermore, gender-specific work roles are conceived to be strongly influenced by normative forces. Finally, households for which a strategy of permanent utility maximization makes no sense economically are considered to display behaviour oriented towards maintaining a specific standard of subsistence.

I wish to conclude with a brief reflection on the implications of the present analysis for future research. In fact, several variables which have often received insufficient attention in individual case studies have been demonstrated to be of crucial relevance. Considering the pace of protoindustrial expansion, the rough relationships between the production functions for labour and capital in the agricultural and protoindustrial sectors appear to be of decisive importance if one wishes to approach an adequate interpretation of a specific situation (cf. also Gutmann and Leboutte, 1984, pp. 603–07). Likewise, knowledge of class-specific differences regarding the structure of family labour may be indispensable for the formulation of significant conclusions in many instances. All this implies that research projects have to become both more specific and more sophisticated. Investigating contexts in

15 Good examples are the discussions of extended or complex families among protoindustrial populations and the occurrence of demographic patterns marked by high ages at first marriage ('cottager marriage pattern'; Medick, 1976, pp. 307–09; Kriedte et al., 1981, ch. 3.2). The latter is said to occur in circumstances where protoindustrialization affects only a segment of rural society—a situation which is almost always the norm, so this variable can be of little discriminatory power.

16 Whether it is useful to play off the two approaches against each other can be questioned, of course; Nakajima (1969), for instance, provides a neo-classical analysis of subsistence farming. The difference which is relevant here is that neo-classics assume actors to be utility maximizers throughout, whereas some authors writing on subsistence economies see the fulfilment of relatively static subsistence needs through sequential work tasks which leave little room for choice as the basic framework of action. The best historical treatment of the subject is still Thompson (1967).

which only part of the relevant variables can be covered by empirical data will make little strategic sense. Likewise, a number of theoretical statements can be critically assessed solely on the basis of a comparative research design. Only if empirical research and theoretical model building jointly evolve toward a more general and more concrete level alike can protoindustrial theory remain a viable paradigm for the analysis of early manufacturing production.

Appendix 1: Summary of hypotheses and statements

1. The *lower the level of the function for the value of the marginal product* (vmp) *of agricultural labour in a household* (i.e. mainly the size and the fertility of the land it controls), the *larger is the share* of the labour force it devotes to *protoindustrial activities*.

2. *The levels of the functions for the protoindustrial and agrarian vmps can be correlated* across different households because rents derived from activities in each sector may provide relevant factor inputs (i.e. raw materials and capital) for production in the other. Hence:

2.1. *Qualification of statement 1*: A negative linear relationship between the level of the function of agrarian vmp and the share of household labour devoted to protoindustrial activities is essentially *limited to branches requiring few inputs* on the part of the individual household and to contexts in which *markets for primary and intermediate inputs* exist.

2.2. In situations where *raw materials or intermediate goods have to be provided by the agrarian resource base of individual households*, *the levels* of the functions for the vmp of labour in the protoindustrial and the agricultural sectors *share a positive linear relationship* whose slope approaches unity. As a consequence, the *share of protoindustrial labour does not vary between households with different agricultural resource endowments*.

2.3. Protoindustrial activities *requiring capital inputs* on the part of individual producers may be *more frequent among those with control over land of medium size and productivity* than among both the landless and wealthy farmers (*a curvi-linear relationship* between land size and the share of protoindustrial household labour). This holds only where the marginal product of capital in the manufacturing sector exceeds that in agriculture in the lower part of the productivity schedule (i.e. in regions character-ized by extensive agriculture).

2.4. Among households with both high levels of agrarian and industrial vmp, the rent derived from the production of manufactured goods may be *invested in improving agricultural techniques or expanding the amount of land owned*, leading to an increase in agrarian vmp; the share of agricultural labour will not decline in these households as a result of rising vmp of protoindustrial labour. This holds *only if manorial or communal restrictions do not inhibit investment* in agriculture by indiv-idual households. *On the other hand*, an increase in the vmp of protoindustrial labour will lead to a *decline of labour inputs into agriculture*.

3. Within a given system of family organization, *household size and complexity will decline* along with the *level of the vmp of labour overall*, i.e. regardless of sectoral variations. As there are households with relatively high levels of functions for vmp in both the agrarian and the protoindustrial sector, it is impossible to make a general statement on household size and structure concerning protoindustrial households.

4. Depending on the ratio between the levels of the functions for the vmps of protoindustrial and agricultural labour, three patterns of demographic growth can be associated with protoindustrialization:

4.1. A *low level of vmp for protoindustrial relative to agricultural labour* implies that savings derived from protoindustrial incomes are small, meaning that the foundation of households with scant agrarian resources is largely impossible. Rather, the labour rents of youths tend to be appropriated by the heads of existing households in exchange for the prospect of inheritance. These (small) rents can be saved and invested in improving agricultural techniques (cf. statement 2.4). Hence, *if there is demographic growth at all*, it comes about *primarily through declining mortality* due to improved nutrition.

4.2. Protoindustrial *activities associated with high vmps of labour and requiring inputs* of capital or raw materials *tend to be concentrated in households with medium or even high vmps of agricultural labour* (cf. statements 2.2/3). Hence, the reasoning behind statement 4.1 applies here, too. As rents derived from production in the protoindustrial sector and, correspondingly, savings increase, *demographic growth fuelled by declining mortality* tends to be more vigorous. In addition, as future savings derived from high protoindustrial incomes can serve as security for lenders, *high marriage and fertility rates may play a secondary role* in demographic growth.

4.3. Only *if protoindustrial activities requiring few inputs* on the part of individual households *are combined with high vmps of labour* (because of high prices, notably) does it become possible to form lower-class households largely devoid of agrarian resources and based solely on protoindustrial activities. In this situation, *high marriage and fertility rates are the prime movers of demographic growth* and are associated with the fluctuation of real protoindustrial incomes.

Note that in all three cases, demographic growth is associated with a high or rising value of the marginal product of labour in the protoindustrial sector. If the latter does not experience growth (in terms of prices and/or employment opportunities), no demographic expansion is expected.

5. *Gender-specific work roles* tend to be *differentiated along normative role conceptions* ascribing to women the tasks associated with the home economy and to men those associated with control over primary

productive resources (notably land). With respect to protoindustrial activities, this implies:

5.1. *If different activities are available, individuals maximize their own labour productivity by choosing the activity whose work pattern suits their role in the rest of the household economy.* This may result in a modification of class-specific patterns of protoindustrial activities as they have been described in statements 2.1–3.

5.2. *If only a single activity is available, role differentiation is small*; if the configuration of the vmps of agricultural and protoindustrial labour suggests the *presence of lower-class households devoid of land*, all family members of working age are engaged in the same occupation. As this results in male work roles which are contrary to normative role images, males try to withdraw from such household economies.

6. In principle, *servants play a similar role as in a purely agrarian context*; however, where *protoindustrial activities are only slightly integrated* (cf. statement 5.2), their status may *approach that of a lodger*.

6.1. If protoindustrial production at the household level requires a *fixed configuration of work roles, servants or lodgers can substitute* for appropriate family members (lack of children of working age, deceased parents, etc.).

6.2. If *labour peaks in agriculture are short and extreme*, it is more profitable for individual farming households to *employ a large family as well as servants most of the year in protoindustry* and use it as agricultural labour in the peak season instead of relying on short-term labour contracts during the peak seasons.

7. *Permanent income hypothesis*: *savings are highest* in those phases of the life cycle during which *labour productivity is highest*, and *consumption is highest when labour productivity is lowest*. This holds under circumstances in which *an effective capital market* renders it easy to invest and de-invest small amounts of income; in the contrary case, *consumption matches actual income* at a given stage of the life cycle. In the case of the rural lower classes, the *relevant capital market is the one for agricultural inputs* (land, cattle, fruit trees, etc.).

7.1. Where a *flexible market for agricultural inputs exists*, protoindustry supports life cycles marked by an *incremental strategy of accumulation*. Households try to improve their labour productivity in both agriculture and protoindustry by repeated cycles of production, saving and investment over their family cycle.

7.2. A *continuous market for agricultural inputs may be lacking* due to structural or institutional reasons, or *protoindustrial incomes may be too low to permit savings*. This situation *is conducive to a sub-cultural differentiation of protoindustrial lower classes* from the rest of rural society: cash incomes are converted into status consumption, and the labour supply schedule may slope backwards.

References

ALMQUIST, E. L. (1979), 'Pre-famine Ireland and the Theory of European Protoindustrialization: Evidence from the 1841 Census', *Journal of Economic History*, **39**, 699–718.

BRAUN, R. (1978), 'Early Industrialization and Demographic Change in the Canton Zürich', In C. Tilly (ed.), *Historical Studies of Changing Fertility*, Princeton, 289–334.

BRAUN, R. (1990), *Industrialisation and Everday Life*, Cambridge and Paris (originally published as *Industrialisierung und Volksleben: Die Veränderungen der Lebensformen in einem ländlichen Industriegebiet vor 1800 [Zürcher Oberland]*, Erlenbach, 1960).

BUCHER, S. (1974), *Bevölkerung und Wirtschaft des Amtes Entlebuch im 18. Jahrhundert*, Luzern.

CASPARD, P. (1979), 'Die Fabrik auf dem Dorf', In D. Puls (ed.), *Wahrnehmungsformen und Protestverhalten: Studien zur Lage der Unterschichten im 18. und 19. Jahrhundert*, Frankfurt a.M., 105–42.

CLARKSON, L. A. (1990), 'The Environment and Dynamic of Pre-factory Industry in Northern Ireland', In P. Hudson (ed.), *Regions and Industries: A Perspective on the Industrial Revolution in Britain*, Cambridge, 252–70.

CLAVERIE, E. and P. LAMAISON (1981), 'Der Ousta als Produktions-und Wohneinheit im Haut-Gévaudan im 17., 18. und 19. Jahrhundert', In N. Bulst and J. Hoock (eds.), *Familie zwischen Tradition und Moderne: Studien zur Geschichte der Familie in Deutschland und Frankreich vom 16. bis zum 18. Jahrhundert*, Göttingen, 202–13.

COLEMAN, D. C. (1983), 'Protoindustrialization: A Concept Too Many', *Economic History Review*, **36**, 435–48.

COLLINS, B. (1982), 'Protoindustrialization and Pre-Famine Emigration', *Social History*, **7**, 127–46.

DEYON, P. (1972), 'La concurrence internationale des manufactures lainières aux XVIe et XVIIe siècles', *Annales, E. S. C.*, **26**, 20–32.

FISCHER, W. (1973), 'Rural Industry and Population Change', *Comparative Studies in Society and History*, **15**, 158–70.

FITZ, A. J. (1985), *Die Frühindustrialisierung Vorarlbergs und ihre Auswirkungen auf die Familienstruktur*, Dornbirn.

GHEZ, G. R. and G. S. BECKER (1975), *The Allocation of Time and Goods Over the Life Cycle*, New York and London.

GULLICKSON, G. L. (1983), 'Agriculture and Cottage Industry: Redefining the Causes of Protoindustrialization', *Journal of Economic History*, **43**, 831–50.

GULLICKSON, G. L. (1986), *Spinners and Weavers of Auffay: Rural Industry and the Sexual Division of Labour in a French Village, 1750–1850*, Cambridge, Mass.

GUTMANN, M. P. (1987), 'Protoindustrialization and Marriage Ages in Eastern Belgium', *Annales de démographie historique*, **1987**, 143–73.

GUTMANN, M. P. (1988), *Toward the Modern Economy: Early Industry in Europe, 1500–1800*, New York.

GUTMANN, M. P. and R. LEBOUTTE (1984), 'Rethinking Protoindustrialization and the Family', *Journal of Interdisciplinary History*, **14**, 587–607.

HANAWALT, B. A. (ed.) (1986), *Women and Work in Preindustrial Europe*, Bloomington.

HO, S. P. S. (1984), 'Protoindustrialisation, protofabrique et désindustrialisation: une analyse économique', *Annales, E. S. C.*, **39**, 882–95.

HUBLER, L. (1984), *La population de Vallorbe du XVIe au début du XIXe siècle: Démographie d'une paroisse industrielle jurassienne*, Lausanne.

HUDSON, P. (1986), *The Genesis of Industrial Capital: A Study of the West Riding Wool Textile Industry c. 1750–1850*, Cambridge.

HUFTON, O. H. (1975), 'Women and the Family Economy in Eighteenth-Century France', *French Historical Studies*, **9**, 1–22.

HYMER, ST. and ST. RESNICK (1969), 'A Model of an Agrarian Economy with Non-agricultural Activities', *American Economic Review*, **59**, 493–506.

JONES, E. L. (1968), 'Agricultural Origins of Industry', *Past and Present*, **40**, 58–71.

KELLENBENZ, H. (1974), 'Rural Industries in the West from the End of the Middle Ages to the Eighteenth Century', In P. Earle (ed.), *Essays in European Economic History 1500–1800*, Oxford.

KRIEDTE, P., H. MEDICK and J. SCHLUMBOHM (1981), *Industrialization before Industrialization: Rural Industry and the Genesis of Capitalism*, Cambridge and Paris.

KUSSMAUL, A. (1981), *Servants in Husbandry in Early Modern England*, Cambridge.

LEHNING, J. R. (1980), *The Peasants of Marlhes: Economic Development and Family Organization in Nineteenth-Century France*, London.

LEVINE, D. (1977), *Family Formation in an Age of Nascent Capitalism*, New York.

MATTMÜLLER, M. (1983), 'Die Landwirtschaft der schweizerischen Heimarbeiter im 18. Jahrhundert', *Zeitschrift für Agrargeschichte und Agrarsoziologie*, **31**, 41–56.

MEDICK, H. (1976), 'The Protoindustrial Family Economy: The Structural Function of Household and Family during the Transition from Peasant Society to Industrial Capitalism', *Social History*, **3**, 291–315.

MEDICK, H. (1983), 'Privilegiertes Handelskapital und "kleine Industrie": Produktion und Produktionsverhältnisse im Leinengewerbe des alt-württembergischen Oberamts Urach im 18. Jahrhundert', *Archiv für Sozialgeschichte*, **23**, 267–310.

MENDELS, F. F. (1972), 'Protoindustrialization: The First Phase of the Industrialization Process', *Journal of Economic History*, **32**, 241–61.

MENDELS, F. F. (1975), 'Agriculture and Peasant Industry in Eighteenth-Century Flanders', In W. N. Parker and E. L. Jones (eds.), *European Peasants and their Markets: Essays in Agrarian Economic History*, Princeton, 179–204.

MENDELS, F. F. (1978), 'La composition du ménage paysan en France au XIXe siècle: Une analyse économique du mode de production doméstique', *Annales, E. S. C.*, **33**, 780–802.

MENDELS, F. F. (1980), 'Seasons and Regions in Agriculture and Industry During the Process of Industrialization', In S. Pollard (ed.), *Region und Industrialisierung*, Göttingen, 177–95.

MENDELS, F. F. (1984), 'Des industries rurales à la protoindustrialisation: historique d'un changement de perspective', *Annales, E. S. C.*, **39**, 977–1008.

MITTERAUER, M. (1986), 'Formen ländlicher Wirtschaft: Historische Ökotypen und familiale Arbeitsorganisation im österreichischen Raum', In M. Mitterauer and J. Ehmer (eds.), *Familienstruktur und Arbeitsorganisation in ländlichen Gesellschaften*, Vienna, 187–323.

MODIGLIANI, F. (1980), 'The Life Cycle Hypothesis of Saving Twenty Years Later', In A. Abel (ed.), *The Collected Papers of Franco Modigliani, Vol. II*, Cambridge, Mass., 41–75.

MOKYR, J. (1976), *Industrialization in the Low Countries, 1795–1850*, New Haven and London.

NAKAJIMA, CH. (1969), 'Subsistence and Commercial Family Farms: Some Theoretical Models of Subjective Equilibrium', In C. R. Wharton, Jr. (ed.), *Subsistence Agriculture and Economic Development*, Chicago, 165–85.

OGILVIE, SH. C. (1990), 'Women and Protoindustrialisation in a Corporate Society: Württemberg Woolen Weaving, 1590–1760', In P. Hudson and W. R. Lee (eds.), *Women's Work and the Family Economy in Historical Perspective*, Manchester and New York, 76–103.

PFISTER, U. (1989a), 'Work Roles and Family Structure in Protoindustrial Zurich', *Journal of Interdisciplinary History*, **10**, 83–105.

PFSITER, U. (1989b), 'Protoindustrialization and Demographic Change: The Canton of Zürich Revisited', *Journal of European Economic History*, **18**, 629–62.

PFISTER, U. (1992), *Die Zürcher Fabriques: Protoindustrielles Wachstum vom 16. zum 18. Jahrhundert*, Zurich.

RAPP, R. T. (1975), 'The Unmaking of the Mediterranean Trade Hegemony: International Trade Rivalry and the Commercial Revolution', *Journal of Economic History*, **35**, 499–525.

ROSE, S. O. (1988), 'Protoindustry, Women's Work and the Household Economy in the Transition to Industrial Capitalism', *Journal of Family History*, **13**, 181–93.

RUDOLPH, R. L. (1985), 'Agricultural Structure and Protoindustrialization in Russia: Economic Development With Unfree Labour', *Journal of Economic History*, **45**, 47–69.

SAITO, O. (1981), 'Labour Supply Behaviour of the Poor in the English Industrial Revolution', *Journal of European Economic History*, **10**, 633–52.

SCHLUMBOHM, J. (1982), 'Agrarische Besitzklassen und gewerbliche Produktionsverhältnisse: Grossbauern, Kleinbesitzer und Landlose als Leinenproduzenten im Umland von Osnabrück und Bielefeld während des frühen 19. Jahrhunderts', In *Mentalitäten und Lebensverhältnisse: Beispiele aus der Sozialgeschichte der Neuzeit, Festschrift for Rudolf Vierhaus*, Göttingen, 315–34.

SCHLUMBOHM, J. (1983), 'Seasonal Fluctuations and Social Division of Labour: Rural Linen Production in the Osnabrück and Bielefeld Regions and the Urban Woollen Industry in the Niederlausitz (c. 1770–c. 1850)', In M. Berg, P. Hudson and M. Sonenscher (eds.), *Manufacture in Town and Country Before the Factory*, Cambridge, 92–123.

SCHLUMBOHM, J. (1992), 'From Peasant Society to Class Society: Some Aspects of Family and Class in a North-West German Protoindustrial Parish, 17th–19th Centuries', *Journal of Family History*, **17**, 183–99.

SCHREMMER, E. (1981), 'Protoindustrialization: A Step Toward Industrialization', *Journal of European Economic History*, **10**, 653–71.

SEGALEN, M. (1980), *Mari et femme dans la société paysanne*, Paris.

SORGESA Miéville, B. (1992), *De la société traditionnelle à l'ère industrielle: Les comportements familiaux face au changement économique (Mutations démographiques d'un village horloger du Jura Neuchâtelois-Fleurier 1727–1914)*, Neuchâtel.

SPAGNOLI, P. G. (1983), 'Industrialization, Proletarianization and Marriage: A Reconsideration', *Journal of Family History*, **8**, 230–47.

TANNER, A. (1982), *Spuhlen-Weben-Sticken: Die Industrialisierung in Appenzell Ausserrhoden*, Zurich.

THIRSK, J. (1961), 'Industries in the Countryside', In F. J. Fisher (ed.), *Essays in the Economic and Social History of Tudor and Stuart England in Honor of R. H. Tawney*, Cambridge, 70–88.

THOMPSON, E. P. (1967), 'Time, Work Discipline and Industrial Capitalism', *Past and Present*, **38**, 56–97.

WALL, R. (1986), 'Work, Welfare and the Family: An Illustration of the Adaptive Family', In L. Bonfield, R. M. Smith and K. Wrightson (eds.), *The World We Have Gained: Histories of Population and Social Structure*, Oxford, 261–94.

WALL, R. (1987), 'Leaving Home and the Process of Household Formation in Pre-Industrial England', *Continuity and Change*, **2**, 77–101.

Acknowledgements

Comments offered by Jon Mathieu, Franklin Mendels, Jürgen Schlumbohm, Hansjörg Siegenthaler and by participants of the Conference on the European Peasant Family and Economy have been of great help in preparing this study and are gratefully acknowledged. Particular thanks are due to Jürgen Schlumbohm and the Max-Planck-Institut für Geschichte at Göttingen, whose hospitality has permitted the complete reformulation of this paper.

Chapter 8

FAMILY LABOUR STRATEGIES IN EARLY MODERN SWABIA

MARTHA WHITE PAAS

Among the regions whose study is enhancing our understanding of the variety and consequences of the peasant family's strategies for dealing with economic change in the early modern period, Swabia has proven to be a particularly helpful one. Augsburg, its chief city, has extensive records for this period, and from a considerable number of village charters issued in the fourteenth century and preserved in the Bavarian State Archives we know a great deal about the individual villages in the area. In an earlier study I established that the rise in population in Augsburg itself from 1450 to 1618 was due to positive net immigration, primarily from rural areas in Swabia, and to declining natural decrease as death rates abated (Paas, 1981). When we look more closely at the economic constraints on families in the rural areas, the resulting migration can be shown to have been a rational response to this population pressure. The resulting changes in labour supply and their consequences flow directly from these decisions. This interaction of factors gave rise to rural emigration for some peasants and to participation in rural industry for many who stayed on the land. The result was a more integrated labour market by 1618 and a pattern of response to market forces which differed from earlier family behaviour.

Several economic factors appear to have been responsible for the change in the rural patterns of life in Swabia in the early modern period. The first involves the system of inheritance. As in many areas west of the Elbe, there was no uniform system for changing ownership of land on the death of the copyholder. In middle Swabia, where the land was settled in early medieval times, a system of partible inheritance was in place. Eastern Swabia was settled later under the influence of powerful nobles, and there a system of primogeniture dominated. Wilhelm Abel's general model for Germany has stressed the importance of partible inheritance in identifying pressures which gave rise to cottage industry (Abel, 1955). In fact, there is evidence in Swabia that the revival of a thirteenth-century legal relationship, *Seldnertum*, which allowed non-inheriting children to build separate dwellings and to maintain independent existences, was facilitating rural industry even in areas dominated by primogeniture.

Seldner are first mentioned as *Soldner* in the thirteenth century. The origins of the word are important in discovering the origins of the *Seldner* themselves. The stem *Sold* comes from the Latin *solidus*, a Roman gold coin. Originally it meant 'money' or 'wages'. About 1150 the form had borrowed from the French and become the middle high German *scolt*, which meant 'a wage for service'. A *Soldner* was a small cottager in the thirteenth century who worked for wages, and it came to be spelled *Seldner* under the influence of the Bavarian dialect in the sixteenth century (Kluge, 1963, p. 714). This is why the term *Seldner* appears only in southern Germany. The *Seldner* were most probably non-inheriting children of medieval farmers who, because of population increase in the thirteenth century, were without land. They were given a dwelling in exchange for work on the farms (hence the root word meaning 'wages'). The crucial questions to be asked are whether *Seldner* were allowed to settle in the villages or not and under what conditions, and what was the nature of their industry.

There was great variation in the types and forms of *Seldner* holdings, for they emerged at different points of population pressure, notably in the thirteenth and sixteenth centuries. Many gained the right to till or to graze their domestic animals on some land, and/or they had, along with the farmers, rights to till some common lands. The important fact here is that there was a large increase in the number of *Seldner* in the fifteenth and sixteenth centuries in eastern Swabia, and they greatly outnumbered the copyholders. The increase, however, did not occur evenly in each village, and the question to be answered is 'why'.

Village charters provide the answer. In villages such as Gabelbachergreut, *Seldner* were never plentiful, because the village charter gives rights to the common lands exclusively to copyholders. Excluded as *Seldner* were from common lands, they were only able to be day labourers. Other villages or the city offered more opportunity for them. In villages such as Grunenbaindt or Neumunster, *Seldner* were given rights to gardens and their numbers grew. The villages which restricted the rights of *Seldner* remained purely agricultural and had no influx of new settlers. The *Seldner* who lived in them did not participate in the putting-out system promoted by the urban entrepreneur, but remained primarily agricultural labourers. Therefore, the patterns of inheritance and the legal rights of the *Seldner* which accompanied inheritance practices were fundamental in determining the options open to this growing stratum of peasants.

The second factor which shaped the strategy of the peasant family in Swabia was the nature of the rights and privileges granted to the *Seldner*. In villages where *Seldner* were allowed to pasture any cattle which they could feed over the winter, there was an incentive to increase their land holdings in order to raise fodder crops. As grain prices soared in the sixteenth century, competition for land was intense, and rents and copyhold fees rose. The *Seldner* therefore looked for other ways to acquire cash to buy fodder and to take advantage of their rights to pasture. In the fifteenth and sixteenth centuries, many of the *Seldner* turned to cottage industry, especially weaving. Their numbers were the greatest in villages where *Seldner* had pasture rights, such as Buch,

Gussenstadt and Westerstetten, rather than in the agricultural villages which restricted the rights of the *Seldner*. The price of grain and hence of land was therefore crucial in influencing the economic behaviour of the *Seldner*.

The third factor involves the interaction of low income and price inelasticities of demand for grain and the differential impact which this inelasticity had on the small producer relative to the large producer. Bad harvests in Swabia in the early modern period—1491, 1502, 1511, 1526–32, 1551, 1567, 1569–72, 1574, 1579, 1586, 1589–90, 1594, 1600, 1605, and 1614—caused a rise in grain prices. An upward trend in grain prices occurred all over Europe in this period as a result of population pressure, but inland cities like Augsburg showed greater price increases because of the lack of ready access to imported supplies. The income elasticity of demand for grain was even lower in the fifteenth century than it is today because bread was a main ingredient in the diet. A bad harvest meant a cut in supply and a rise in prices, and a good harvest meant a fall in prices.

There exists, however, a differential impact of price changes in agricultural products on the farm income of small producers as opposed to large producers. A rise in agricultural prices as a result of a bad harvest benefits large producers who have surpluses to sell above their own needs. Likewise, a bumper crop may have a much greater relative benefit to small producers than to large producers.

Abel has illustrated this principle numerically, basing his calculations on Gregory King's observation in the seventeenth century that grain prices change in greater proportion than does the volume of grain harvested (Abel, 1935, pp. 23–26). King estimated that if a grain harvest is 10 per cent below normal, the price of grain rises 30 per cent. If the harvest fails by 20 per cent, the price rises by 80 per cent; if the yield fails by 80 per cent, the price rises by 450 per cent. These estimates, while no longer verifiable for the sixteenth century, are reasonable for the early modern period when we consider the highly price-inelastic demand for grains, the high proportions of 'food budgets' devoted to grains, the low grain yields, and the relatively small percentage of grain which entered the market compared with the wheat needs for the peasants' consumption. Abel's numerical example illustrates this principle. Assume that there are three farms, A, B, and C, of different sizes and that each has an assumed amount to sell in a normal harvest year with a grain price of 20 denars per 100 kilograms (1 dz.) (see Table 1).

If we assume a bad harvest year where 20 per cent of the crop fails and the price rises by King's estimate of 80 per cent, the result is that the small farmer is left with no surplus to sell in a bad harvest and that the large farmer actually profits from the sharp rise in prices (see Table 2). In a bumper crop year, if King's estimate of a 40 per cent fall in prices attended a 20 per cent increase in grain harvested, we can calculate the result (see Table 3). The small peasant benefits from a bumper crop despite the fall in prices, while the largest farmer is a relative loser. It is just this simple principle, based on the near-subsistence

Table 1: *Normal harvest: grain price = 20 den./dz.*

		Farm	
	A	B	C
Harvest	250 dz.	500 dz.	1,000 dz.
Needed for own use	200 dz.	300 dz.	400 dz.
Offered for sale	50 dz.	200 dz.	600 dz.
Income from sale	1,000 den.	4,000 den.	12,000 den.

Table 2: *Harvest failure of 20 per cent: grain price = 36 den./dz.*

		Farm	
	A	B	C
Harvest	200 dz.	400 dz.	800 dz.
Needed for own use	200 dz.	300 dz.	400 dz.
Offered for sale	—	100 dz.	400 dz.
Income from sale	—	3,600 den.	14,000 den.

Table 3: *Good harvest of 20 per cent increase: grain price = 12 den./dz.*

		Farm	
	A	B	C
Harvest	300 dz.	600 dz.	1,200 dz.
Needed for own use	200 dz.	300 dz.	400 dz.
Offered for sale	100 dz.	300 dz.	800 dz.
Income from sale	1,200 den.	3,600 den.	9,600 den.

farming of the small peasant, which Ashton illustrates from an anonymous eighteenth-century source: 'The farmer fears a good year more than a bad. He prefers a half harvest to a full one' (Ashton, 1959, p. 41). The writer means, of course, the large farmer.[1]

An exception to this principle would be the case in which large producers

---

1 Early modern people understood the nature of price elasticity for agricultural products, as the following lines from *Macbeth* (II, 3) show: 'Who is there in Beelzebub's name?/ Here's a farmer that hang himself on the expectation of plenty'. Even the groundlings in Shakespeare's day (*Macbeth* was written in 1603) must have understood this principle in the face of several good harvests in a row in England at the turn of the century.

had lower costs, since in bumper periods their costs might fall more than prices. The major cost reduction factor in the early modern period might have been the existence of draught animals, but it would be difficult to postulate this average cost curve. Falling average costs depend on a cost function with a fixed component; as output rises, the unit cost of the fixed component declines. In this context, draught animals would not constitute an important fixed factor; to cultivate larger areas, more animals probably would have been required, and early on. Economies of scale over a substantial range of output over a longer period would possibly flow from greater specialization of tasks on the farm and from technical innovation, such that the efficient size for the farm would be larger. But here, too, neither one of these economies can be assumed to have been occurring during the sixteenth century. Thus, an assumption of nearly constant costs may be more realistic.

The implication of this for the rural Swabian peasant family is important. The *Seldner* often worked on copyholds for payment in kind or in money wages, and therefore a bad harvest did not necessarily mean starvation. But often it did mean less work as well as a smaller marketable crop from their own lands. Without money, the *Seldner* could pay neither rent nor taxes (to the extent that they were collected in money terms), nor could they buy fodder for their animals. The bad harvests far outnumbered the good harvests in the sixteenth century, and this situation is important to keep in mind as we determine the economic pressures on the cottagers. With declining real incomes, the *Seldner* increasingly turned to cottage industry, primarily weaving, to supplement their income and to provide themselves with the cash which they could not always count on from their crops.

The fourth factor which influenced family decision-making in Swabia formed the demand for labour, both from the urban trading sector and from the rural sector itself. This aspect is the only part of the model which can be seen to be demand oriented: the other factors under discussion are properly understood as supply factors. A brief summary of the scope of rural industry in Swabia may be helpful as we consider the options open to the peasant labourer.

Paper making and printing located on the numerous tributaries of the Danube which run through Swabia was one of the important rural industries. Expansion of this industry generated forward linkages to the textile industry, where printed cloth appeared in the early sixteenth century. There was in addition some iron mining undertaken in the Allgau region.

Weaving was the major rural industry in Swabia, as it was in many areas of Europe. Fustian was woven with cotton imported through Venice and with flax supplied locally. All cloth exported from Augsburg, whether woven in the city or by rural weavers, was required by the Weavers' Guild to meet identical quality standards. Beyond this requirement, the Weavers' Guild exerted no control over the rural weavers. Whereas in Hesse and Saxony, guilds had been successful in extending their jurisdiction in matters of training or limitation of entry to the rural areas, in Swabia this had not occurred. The urban landowners had blocked attempts by the Weavers' Guild to enlarge its power for several reasons: 1) they wanted to ensure the labour supplies needed seasonally in agriculture (especially for the labour-intensive flax harvest) and, therefore, they wanted rural weaving to prosper as a cottage industry; 2) they sought to preserve weaving for the peasants as a way for them to earn cash to pay their taxes and rents; 3) market taxes were a major source of revenue for the urban landowner, and thus it was in their interest to preserve local markets; and 4) in some cases, the landowner and merchant were one and the same (as in the case of the Fuggers), and the availability of cheap, skilled labour in the country forestalled the rapid rise in urban weavers' wages.

While not conclusive, there is some evidence from which to draw inferences about the course of real wages for the period. Abel, Brown and Hopkins have calculated the real wages of builders in Augsburg for most of the sixteenth century, and conclude that real wages of unskilled builders declined on balance (Rich and Wilson, 1967, p. 482; Abel, 1974, p. 27). This evidence, combined with evidence for many years of bad harvests, suggests that a decline in real income for urban craftsmen and for rural peasants was probable.

Evidence shows that this was not the case for the urban middle classes and for the larger copyholders on the land. Blendinger has shown that there was a rising middle class in the last quarter of the sixteenth century and early seventeenth century in Augsburg as long-distance trade revived for a time (Blendinger, 1972). There is also evidence that the larger copyholders were prospering at this time. We know that farm houses were larger and better furnished than they had been earlier. Rural inventories show a rising living standard in southern Germany as the copyholder's terms of trade became more favourable. It appears that rents lagging behind prices accounted for at least part of this improvement in living standards. Rural peasants must have seen the relative prosperity of the copyholders and judged migration to the city or to villages which offered an independent livelihood to be preferable to day labouring without the possibility of marriage. In turn, this labour supply, which formed an increasingly integrated labour market in Swabia, supported the brief revival of the Augsburg economy before the Thirty Years' War.

The problems facing the trading sector in Augsburg in the early seventeenth century, however, were not to be solved with lagging real wages which yielded higher profits for potential investment. The cloth trade encountered increasing competition in finer cloths from the Rhineland and elsewhere, and failed to respond competitively. Agriculture remained fragmented, and there is no evidence of the widespread adoption of the types of improvements that Kerridge describes in England in the sixteenth century (Kerridge, 1968). David's thesis of a certain threshold size of farm determined by relative factor prices developed in the context of nineteenth-century American mechanization of reaping has some relevance here (David, 1974). It may be that farmers in Swabia were approaching a certain threshold size of farm in the latter half of the century. But landholding patterns delayed it, and the Thirty Years' War cancelled that imperative altogether.

The Swabian experience presents us with several sets of economic factors which influenced the decision-making process in the peasant family. First, there were significant supply factors which helped to promote an integrated labour market in Swabia which have not been fully appreciated. Among these are the variety of inheritance patterns and village rights which offered options to the peasant. Then there were market forces which influenced the labour supply by acting on subsidiary enterprises such as animal husbandry. The rise in the price of grain and hence of land forced peasants into auxiliary undertakings in order to earn cash for fodder crops and, occasionally, for copyhold acquisition. Third, there were economic relationships which produced a differential impact on peasant incomes compared with copyhold incomes in the event of bad harvests in the sixteenth century. The number of bad harvests recorded suggests that peasants were extremely vulnerable to crop failure and did not benefit from the subsequent rise in prices. Fourth, on the demand side, it is clear that the structure of production and long-distance trade in Swabia worked to keep wages from rising either in the rural or urban areas as fast as the price level rose, and hence, real wages declined. Even the resulting profits were not sufficient by themselves to ensure the long-term economic vitality of the region since they were not invested in agricultural improvements or in industrial innovation.

Nonetheless, despite the failure of the Swabian economy to sustain growth, some fundamental structural changes had occurred which were to alter fundamentally the economic position of the peasant family. The rural community could, by 1618, properly be called a 'sector' in that it was integrated with the urban trading sector in a type of protoindustrialization. As such, the individual decision makers were beginning to respond to increasingly complex market forces rather than to tradition or command. In that sense, their economic behaviour may justifiably be termed 'modern'.

References

ABEL, W. (1935), *Agrarkrisen und Agrarkonjunktur*, Berlin.
ABEL, W. (1955), 'Schichten und Zonen europäischer Agrarverfassung', *Zeitschrift für Agrargeschichte und Agrarsoziologie*, **3**, 1–19.
ABEL, W. (1974), *Massenarmut und Hungarkrisen im vorindustriellen Europa*, Hamburg and Berlin.
ASHTON, T. S. (1959), *Economic Fluctuations in England, 1700–1800*, Oxford.
BLENDINGER, F. (1972), 'Versuch einer Bestimmung der Mittelschicht in der Reichsstadt Augsburg vom Ende des 14. bis zum Anfang des 18. Jahrhunderts', *Veröffentlichung der Kommission für Landeskunde in Baden-Württemberg*, B ser., 6g, 32–78.
DAVID, P. (1974), *Technical Choice, Innovation and Economic Growth*, Cambridge.
KERRIDGE, E. (1968), *The Agricultural Revolution*, New York.

KLUGE, F. (1963), *Etymologisches Wörterbuch der deutschen Sprache*, 19th ed., rev. Walther Mitzka, Berlin.

PAAS, M. W. (1981), *Population Change, Labor Supply and Agriculture in Augsburg, 1480–1618*, New York.

RICH, E. E. and C. H. WILSON (eds.) (1967), *Cambridge Economic History of Europe, Vol. 4*, Cambridge, England.

Chapter 9

PEASANTS AS CONSUMERS OF MANUFACTURED GOODS IN ITALY AROUND 1600

DOMENICO SELLA

After centuries of nearly total neglect at the hands of historians, the peasantry of early modern Europe has, in recent times, emerged from undeserved obscurity and has attracted unprecedented attention: the dynamics of rural demography, the structure of the peasant family, the role of the peasantry in protoindustrial production, peasant rebellions, culture and religion, are all topics on which scholars in the past twenty years or so have trained their searchlights—and the results of their labours have been impressive in terms of both quality and quantity. For all this, however, there is one aspect of the peasant experience that has not shared (or has shared very little) in this recent surge of interest, namely the role peasants played in the overall economy of their country or region as consumers of goods and services which they themselves did not produce.

The reasons behind this gap in our knowledge of rural society are not difficult to find. One is the long-held and persistent notion that the peasant household was basically self-sufficient in that it not only grew its own food, but also produced what few farming tools, cooking utensils, clothes, and footwear it needed and could afford. Another is the notion that, when it produced a marketable surplus, the peasant household had to allocate most of the receipts to the payment of rent, tithe, and taxes rather than to the purchase of consumer wares, with only a minimal fraction of its income being left for an occasional transaction within the village itself. Lastly, it has been widely assumed that, even if the peasants did make an occasional foray on to the market, those purchases were, given the peasants' dismally low income level, negligible in the aggregate—an assumption reinforced by the fact that peasant purchases of non-farm articles, if they took place at all, have left precious little trace in the records most commonly available to scholars.[1]

Some recent studies, however, have begun to crack the wall of silence surrounding the peasantry in its role as consumers of market goods. The studies of inventories *post mortem* (such as the one Jan De Vries [1975] has devoted to seventeenth-century Friesland) has shown that, in the Netherlands

---

1 It is revealing of the paucity of studies on peasant demand for non-farm goods that the otherwise excellent chapter by Walter Minchinton (1974) does not address this question.

at least, rural households did contain an assortment of articles, not all of which could have possibly been fashioned by the peasant family itself. As for England, Margaret Spufford's (1984) meticulous investigation of seventeenth-century chapmen has brought out how pervasive their presence was in the English countryside and how substantial their rustic constituency was. For her part, Joan Thirsk (1978) has persuasively argued that the remarkable growth of new (and largely rural) industries in seventeenth-century England (linen, hosiery, pinmaking and the like) reflected an expanding internal demand, especially among yeomen and farm labourers.

The purpose of this paper is to add to this burgeoning body of knowledge by presenting some fresh evidence on peasant participation in the market economy in one area of North Italy (Lombardy) around 1600,[2] and notably on the purchase of manufactured goods by peasant consumers. At the risk of treading on very thin ice I will also attempt to estimate what the aggregate peasant demand for low-grade, inexpensive manufactured articles may have been, and what it may have meant for the economy of the region as a whole.

I

To begin with, we must look inside the village community for evidence of market transactions between fellow villagers. Although, by their very nature, those transactions went unrecorded, nonetheless their existence can be legitimately inferred from what listings of inhabitants and administrative surveys tell us about occupational specialization in the village itself. Those documents often single out from the mass of the villagers those individuals, referred to as 'artificers' (*artefici*), who plied a specialized trade or craft and presumably made a living selling their goods and/or services to their neighbours. Their presence thus provides an early clue to the existence of market transactions within the village.

Here are a few of the many examples available. In 1617 the village of Cisliano on the rich, irrigated plain west of Milan was reported as containing 400 inhabitants. Of these, only three could boast a specialized trade—a blacksmith, a carpenter, and a tailor.[3] Some forty years earlier, in a large village a few miles from Milan (Mezzate), we find 589 villagers, the majority of whom were listed as either tenant farmers (*massari*) or day-labourers (*braccianti*). About two dozen individuals, however, were reported as working at non-farm jobs such as millers, innkeepers, carters, tailors, carpenters, blacksmiths and so on.[4] In a nearby community (Binasco) with twice as many

2 At the time, Lombardy was politically divided into a western, Spanish-ruled section (the state of Milan) and an eastern, Venetian-ruled section (consisting mainly of the provinces of Bergamo and Brescia). Here I will focus on the Spanish section.

3 Data obtained from the Archivio di Stato, Milan, *Feudi camerali p.a.*, 307/7, report of 13 January 1617.

4 Data obtained from the Archivio della Curia Arciveschovile, Milan, *Archivio spirituale*, Sez. X, vol. 5, listing (*status animarum*) for 1574.

people, we find a similar assortment of non-agricultural occupations plus one baker, one shoemaker, and a handful of weavers.[5] Paderno near Cremona, for its part, contained two smiths who, we are told, 'are hired by the day to do small jobs'; a few tailors of whom 'only four are worth anything'; three carpenters, two small shopkeepers who sold 'butter, salt, and eau-de-vie', and one barber.[6] In 1621 Santa Cristina near Pavia included among its 875 inhabitants two carpenters, one farrier, one cobbler, and one tailor; 'all the rest—reads our source—work the land and some of them, in wintertime, weave fabrics of flax or hemp'.[7]

The list could be extended, but unnecessarily so, for much the same pattern repeats itself rather monotonously in scores of village communities.[8] The point worth stressing is that, except in the smallest hamlets, our sources invariably reveal the presence of at least a few specialized craftsmen and tradesmen, and the nature of their skill suggests that they catered for some very basic needs of their fellow villagers, such as making or repairing farm tools and wagon wheels, shoeing horses, fashioning or, perhaps more often, mending or altering boots and garments. Our sources, in other words, reveal a dusting of diminutive non-farm activities scattered in the crevices of each rural community. Even though peasant households may have been largely self-sufficient, exchanges on a tiny scale did take place from time to time between them; in other words, elements of the market economy were present in the daily life of the village.

II

It would be wrong, however, to stop here and conclude that the contacts peasants had with the market economy were limited to an occasional transaction with the village tailor or blacksmith. For, in fact, contacts with the outside world were made possible by pedlars and itinerant craftsmen (for the role played by pedlars in early modern Europe, see Braudel [1982], pp. 75–80). These indispensable and indefatigable characters have left little trace of themselves in historical records, with the exception, it would seem, of pedlars in England: unlike the great international merchants who have often bequeathed to posterity ledgers, copybooks, bills of exchange, and legal papers on which later historians have voraciously fed, pedlars, hawkers, or chapmen have vanished, leaving hardly any trace of their passage. What

5 Data obtained from the Archivio di Stato, Milan, *Feudi camerali p.a.*, 94/7, report of 8 November 1632.
6 Data obtained from the Archivio di Stato, Milan, *Feudi camerali p.a.*, 430/1 and 430/4 bis, reports of 23 February 1649 and 27 April 1666.
7 Data obtained from the Archivio di Stato, Milan, *Feudi camerali p.a.*, 542/4, report for 24 November 1621.
8 In Archivio di Stato, Milan, *Feudi camerali p.a.*, see 500/12 (Robecco, 1656), 482/5b (Riozzo, 1632), 544/5 (S. Fiorano, 1617), 317/3 (Maleo, 1644), 415/3 (Olevano, 1631) and many other examples.

evidence has survived, however, suggests that their presence in the countryside was a normal phenomenon, although it has gone virtually unnoticed.

As far as I can tell, documentation on pedlars is virtually non-existent for seventeenth-century Lombardy, but their presence was brought to my attention almost fortuitously by two inquiries conducted during the war and aimed at identifying enemy subjects in the transient population. We can thus catch a glimpse of a number of those itinerant retailers as well as of the wares they carried in boxes slung over their shoulders as they travelled around the countryside. Some of them, we are told, specialized in the manufacture and sale of wooden spoons and scoops; others went from place to place (sometimes hundreds of miles away from their place of origin) with a box full of spindles and spools clearly intended for use in the peasant households where flax and silk were reeled and spun. Yet others were tinkers. The largest group, however, consisted of mercers, that is to say purveyors of buttons, combs, scissors, knives, and other such goods.[9]

III

An occasional visit by a pedlar did not exhaust the range of contacts with the world outside the village, for the peasants themselves are known to have gone to a market town nearby or to a country fair to fetch things they could not or would not produce at home.

The small town of Domodossola, located in the narrow, rugged valley that leads from Lake Maggiore to the Simplon Pass and into Switzerland, featured a fair on Saturdays 'where grains, cattle, cheese, linen, woolen cloth, notions, boots, and many other things are traded', and it attracted vendors and customers from the surrounding mountains.[10] Some of the local residents, we are also told, 'make a living by carrying loads of firewood and charcoal on their backs down to Domodossola', the mountain slopes being 'so steep that pack horses and mules cannot be used'.[11] On their return trip, we can presume, those sturdy mountaineers brought home some of the articles the Domodossola fair had to offer.

Down in the plain, things were no doubt easier due to the lie of the land, an adequate network of roads, and the presence of many small towns capable of offering a wide range of goods to rural customers with money to spend or goods to barter. Most of these small towns featured, as did Domodossola, weekly fairs intended primarily for people from the surrounding countryside. One such town was Codogno, 5,000 strong and right in the heart of the rich

---

9 Data obtained from the Archivio di Stato, Milan, *Militare p.a.*, 165 (Notificazioni de francesi e forestieri, 1667) and 165 bis (relazione del podestà di Vigevano, 5 January 1674).

10 Taken from the Archivio di Stato, Milan, *Feudi Camerali p.a.*, 613/11 ('Notizie intorno alla Valle, 1620').

11 Taken from the Archivio di Stato, Milan, *Feudi Camerali p.a.*, 25 (Bognanco, 3 May 1655).

irrigated plain. We are told that a cluster of villages within a three- to five-mile range depended on its commercial resources 'for the things they lack, such as clothes, cheese, spices, and so on'.[12] Gallarate, 30 miles west of Milan, provides a more telling example of a market town feeding on rural consumer demand. In 1574, according to a listing of inhabitants,[13] Gallarate numbered 2,406 inhabitants divided into 470 households. The listing fortunately records the occupation of virtually all the heads of households, and thus allows us an unusually detailed view of the town's economic structure. Only one-fifth of all households' heads are listed as working the land (whether as freeholders, tenant farmers, or day-labourers): agriculture was clearly not the mainstay of the Gallarate economy. On the other hand, roughly 60 per cent of household heads are identified as craftsmen, shopkeepers or wholesale merchants, and this large group included ropemakers, smiths, tailors, shoemakers, cobblers, furriers, hatmakers, carters, haberdashers and so on. All of these people could hardly have made a living by taking in one another's washing; obviously they must have catered to a larger constituency drawn from the surrounding countryside. And, in fact, we are told that every Saturday a fair was held in Gallarate and that 'it attracted people and wares from sundry parts'.

Similar observations would apply to the many market towns that dotted the Lombard landscape within twenty or thirty miles of each other: towns like Magenta, Varese, Monza, Desio, Lecco, all with a population in the 2,000 to 5,000 range (on Lombardy's market towns [borghi] and their economic role, see Sella, 1979, pp. 13–14 and 108–09). That their artisans and retailers served the rural population nearby is clearly borne out not only by the weekly fairs they all hosted, but also by a revealing comment found in a report describing the market town of Magenta. After recording that in Magenta lived 35 gentry families alongside 26 families headed by 'artificers', our source adds: 'all those 26 artificers work for the peasants, because the gentry do their shopping in the city of Milan'.[14]

IV

From these bits and pieces of evidence it appears that the rural communities of Lombardy were not so many separate, self-sufficient units of production and consumption, but were linked to one another and to the market towns by a web of commercial transactions. The peasantry, in other words, did generate an effective consumer demand for a variety of goods produced elsewhere (coarse fabrics, footwear, tools and utensils), a demand that village shopkeepers, pedlars, and country fairs somehow managed to satisfy.

12 Taken from the Archivio di Stato, Milan, *Feudi Camerali p.a.*, 264/1 (28 September 1640).
13 Data obtained from the Archivio di Stato, Milan, *Archivio spirituale*, Sez. X, vol. 23; see also Archivio di Stato, Milan, *Feudi Camerali p.a.*, 258/5, report for 10 May 1578.
14 Taken from the Archivio di Stato, Milan, *Feudi Camerali p.a.*, 307/7 (reports of 31 October 1609 and 11 January 1617).

The crucial question at this point is whether the aggregate demand emanating from peasant households amounted to something significant enough to make a difference in the economy of the region as a whole. In the absence of any quantitative information on the value or volume of manufactured goods that found their way into peasant households, the only way to attempt an answer to this question is to try to estimate: a) the average income earned by a peasant household; b) the portion of that income likely to be available for purchases other than food and lodging; c) the number of peasant households; and d) the aggregate amount that those households could spend on non-farm goods.

First of all, how much did peasants earn on average? This depended both on their occupational status and on their sex. Evidence drawn from five villages in the late sixteenth century indicates that approximately 35 per cent of all adult males were day-labourers (*braccianti*), 30 per cent were tenant farmers (*massari*), and 20 per cent tradesmen and artisans; no occupational label is appended to the remaining 15 per cent, most likely because they were casual workers, paupers or disabled.[15] As regards earnings, only for day-labourers do we have precise information on their daily rate of pay and circumstantial evidence on the number of days worked in a year (see Sella, 1968, pp. 19–20 and 120–24). Around 1600, their average rate of pay was 1.25 lira of Milan and it can be estimated, rather conservatively, that they were gainfully employed for about 200 days in the year. This yields an annual wage income of 250 lire per day-labourer. As for the tradesmen, craftsmen and tenant farmers, one can only make educated guesses, but I doubt very much that these petty tradesmen and artisans earned significantly more than day-labourers, and I am inclined to ascribe to them a 250 lire annual income as well. On the other hand, it is certain that tenant farmers, in Lombardy as elsewhere, enjoyed an income considerably above and probably double that of day-labourers.[16]

15 See Sella, 1987 and 1982. Those five villages were all located in the plain where most Lombards lived and where large estates specializing in commercial crops prevailed. Predictably, in the hill and mountain areas, the occupational distribution was different, with small-owners forming the largest group, followed by day-labourers and craftsmen, and with no tenant farmers. An example of this type of community (Villa d'Adda) is discussed in Sella (1987). Given the marginal, rugged nature of the land in the upper reaches of Lombardy, the wretched conditions of the residents, and the fact that many of them were forced to emigrate either seasonally or permanently and to seek employment as day-labourers in the plain or as journeymen in the towns, it is unlikely that the average income they could extract from their small holdings was significantly higher than that of *braccianti*. On conditions prevailing in the hills and mountains at the time, see Caizzi (1980), ch. 5.

16 That the *massari* who ran the large farms of the plain were wealthier than the day-labourers is suggested, first of all, by their role as employers of the latter, but also by the large houses in which they lived and the large, often multiple family households over which they presided. Their relatively high standing in rural society is vividly described, albeit for a later century, by Greenfield (1965, pp. 13–14). The correlation between family size and income in early modern Italy is discussed by Marzio Barbagli (1984, p. 144). It is more difficult to decide by how much tenant farmers were better off than day-labourers. In settling for a ratio of two to one, I have

For women of working age, the picture is even more elusive. We do know, however, that in addition to keeping house, women did work in the fields at harvest time along with the men and that, during the rest of the year, they engaged in other types of paid work, notably in the processing of flax and silk (Sella, 1968, p. 56). Their rate of pay was much lower than men's and probably about half that figure,[17] or 125 lire per year.

How many individuals belonged to each of these groups? Around 1600, Lombardy (the State of Milan) had a population of about 1,200,000, of whom roughly 900,000 lived in rural communities (Sella, 1979, p. 4). If we exclude, as we must, from the population of working age the very young (children under ten) and the very old (individuals over sixty) who, together, represented about one-third of the total, we are left with 600,000 people of working age equally divided between men and women. Among men, as indicated earlier, 15 per cent (or 45,000 individuals) apparently earned no income; 55 per cent (or about 165,000 individuals) were day-labourers, tradesmen, or village crafts-men and, with an average annual income of 250 lire, could earn, as a group, 41,250,000 lire per year. Tenant farmers, on the other hand, representing as they did 30 per cent of the male work force with a total of 90,000, each earning 500 lire a year, had an aggregate income of 45,000,000 lire. As for women, 250,000 of them presumably earned, at 125 lire each, an aggregate of 31,250,000 lire in a given year. Altogether, I would estimate the aggregate annual income of the rural population at 117.5 million lire of Milan.

Needless to say, the above figures do not claim to be anything more than very crude orders of magnitude. If, however, one accepts them as such, then one can proceed to the task of estimating how much of that aggregate income was spent on manufactured goods after food and lodging expenses, as well as taxes, had been taken care of.

The available evidence on working-class family budgets in early modern Europe is scant and widely scattered, but it consistently indicates that, in the towns, workers had to allocate up to 80 per cent of their annual earnings to food, about 10 per cent to lodging and connected expenses, and another 10 per cent to clothing and other consumer articles.[18]

---

had in mind conditions prevailing in England in the late seventeenth century: according to Gregory King, tenant farmers' households enjoyed an annual income nearly three times larger than day-labourers', but in view of the larger size of the former's households, on a per capita basis their income was roughly twice that of day-labourers. King's data are reproduced by Peter Laslett (1965, pp. 32–33).

17 A 1954 official proposal for wage regulation in the countryside near Pavia curtly stated that 'women shall receive half a man's pay'. The proposal is reprinted in Carlo M. Cipolla (1956, p. 12). In sixteenth-century Geneva, too, wage rates for women were half those for men (Mottu-Webber, 1987, p. 423). Similar differentials were found in the Rouen area in the eighteenth century (Gullickson, 1986, pp. 75, 221).

18 Data on urban workers' budgets from various European towns can be found in Carlo M. Cipolla (1980, p. 30). Since, by and large, no direct taxes were levied in the towns, those budgets do not include outlays for taxes. Carole Shammas (1983) has challenged the view that

What about rural workers? In Lombardy around 1600, day-labourers were paid roughly as much as urban journeymen (Sella, 1968, pp. 115, 121), but unlike the latter, had to pay a hearth tax amounting to about 15 per cent of a man's earnings (Vigo, 1977, p. 101) and about 10 per cent of the combined earnings of husband and wife. On the other hand, rural workers enjoyed the advantage of lower food prices and lodging expenses—a point often brought up at the time in connection with the competition urban craftsmen felt at the hands of their rural counterparts. All things considered, it is not unreasonable to assume that peasants could devote as much of their income to the purchase of non-food consumer articles as urban workers did, that is to say, about 10 per cent. In practice, this meant that a day-labourer's family in which the husband earned 250 lire a year and his wife 125 lire, something like 37 lire could be earmarked for buying manufactured articles.

For a family of four with only two bread-winners, 37 lire amounted to nine lire per capita—a paltry sum at a time when two yards of coarse cloth (the minimum amount required for a coat) sold for four lire, a pair of boots for three, and a felt hat for 1.5.[19] Clearly, the range of choices open to a day-labourer's family was very narrow indeed. Conditions must have been considerably better for the tenant farmer's family, whose annual income stood, hypothetically, at 625 lire (500 earned by the husband and 125 by the wife). If that family spent the same proportion of its income on non-essentials (and it probably in fact spent a somewhat larger proportion), this represented 62.5 lire—a definite improvement over the day-labourer's plight, and yet nothing that would leave room for extravagance.

Small though the discretionary income of the peasant family may have been, its impact on aggregate consumer demand was far from negligible, given the number of consumers involved. With an aggregate income of 117 million lire, rural consumers could presumably spend close to 12 million on non-farm articles and thus lubricate the wheels of rural commerce and fill the pockets of village shopkeepers, pedlars, and country fair merchants.

V

What difference did those 12 million or so lire make in the Lombard economy as a whole? In the absence of even the crudest estimates of Lombardy's gross national product around 1600, one can get a sense of what 12 million lire's

up to 80 per cent of the worker's income was allocated to expenditure on food and has proposed 50 per cent as a more realistic estimate. Her argument has been challenged (I believe convincingly) by J. Komlos (1988, p. 149) on the grounds that her calculations are based on the number of days worked rather than on the entire year. I would add that Shammas has considered wage-earners as isolated individuals rather than as members of a family with dependants.

19 The price quotation for boots is from Archivio della Veneranda Fabrica del Duomo, Milan *Mandati di pagamento*, on 16 May 1609; the price of a hat is for 1580 and is found in Dante Zanetti (1965, p. 22); that of low grade cloth is from Aldo De Maddalena (1949, p. 175): in 1605 'panno basso' sold for 1.4 lira per 'braccio' of 60 cm, i.e. about 2.1 lire per yard.

worth of manufactured articles really meant by translating them into some basic and widely used consumer goods such as low-grade cloth: at two lire per yard, this adds up to six million yards of cloth—no paltry figure. But, of course, peasant consumers spent their discretionary income, small though it was, on a variety of goods, of which cloth was but one. A more useful approach is perhaps to compare those 12 million lire with the known value of the output of possibly the largest, and certainly the most celebrated, industry of the time in Lombardy, namely the silk industry in Milan. In the 1590s its annual output of silk fabrics and silk-and-gold thread was reliably placed at about 10 million lire[20] or close to the estimated value of all the manufactured articles that rural consumers could afford in a year.

What the comparison between the two figures tells us is that behind peasant consumer demand, and depending on it, was a cluster of industries (textiles, shoe-making, and small-scale metallurgy) whose output was larger than that of the largest, most prosperous and world renowned manufacturing sector in Milan—the silk industry.

Does this conclusion really matter? I believe it does. For if it be true (as sixteenth-century observers claimed and modern historians have confirmed) that the Milan silk industry was a major component of the Lombard economy, then it must follow that the cluster of peasant-oriented handicraft industries could have represented another important component.

Whether, in fact, they did or not depended to a large extent on their location: were they located in Lombardy itself or was peasant demand met with imports? The answer is not in doubt: rural Lombardy harboured a variety of industries that catered for the needs of the lower layers of society. Less well-known than their more prestigious urban counterparts—silk making, high grade woollens, finely wrought suits of armour, string instruments, ceramics—that had long won an enviable reputation throughout Europe for cities like Milan, Como, Cremona, and Lodi; generally overlooked by historians and neglected, because they were inconspicuous, in government papers at the time; nonetheless, those obscure industries did exist and formed a significant segment of the Lombard economy, a sort of 'underground economy' that cannot be ignored.

In that economy we find, first of all, the cotton industry specializing in low grade fabrics known as fustians. From late medieval times such production was widely spread in the western portion of Lombardy, a classical example of rural or cottage industry, and one that remained prosperous well into the nineteenth century (Mazzaoni, 1981, pp. 62, 152, 156; for the period after 1600, see Sella, 1979, pp. 113–14, 137). The eastern portion of Lombardy, and notably the Valassina, on the other hand, was the home of a woollen industry whose

20 The figure reported by Gino Luzzatto (1955, p. 121) is 1.7 million scudi which, at six lira to the scudo, amounts to 10.2 million lire. At about the same time, the value of silk goods exported annually from Milan was placed at 6.6 million lire. The latter figure comes from Giuseppe Aleati and Carlo Cipolla (1958, p. 389).

output consisted, in the words of a seventeenth-century source, of 'inferior and inexpensive fabrics well suited to the poor'. In the plain, the making of linen by peasant weavers was a common feature and its coarse products served mainly to provide summer wear for the peasantry. As for small hardware, there is a good deal of evidence pointing to its manufacture in the mountain districts. One area (Valsassina) was well known for its nails; another (Lecco) for wire-drawing and its by-product, needles; yet another (Valcamonica in nearby Venetian Lombardy) specialized in farming tools and implements (scythes, ploughshares, horse-shoes, iron tyres, hoops for barrels, etc.) and was said to employ as many as ten thousand craftsmen (Sella, 1979, pp. 18, 113 [woollen industry], 114–16 [linen], 111–13 [iron]; on Valcamonica, see *Il Catastico bresciano di Giovanni da Lezze [1609–1610]*).

What is remarkable about those peasant-oriented industries is that, unlike their more exalted urban counterparts producing high quality, expensive articles for the international market, they experienced no decline in the course of the seventeenth century. Far from seeing their output plummet as was the case for the silk and armour industries of Milan or the wool industry of Como, low grade producers managed to weather the 'general crisis' of the seventeenth century and even expanded in the next century. More importantly, when modern industrialization and the factory system made their appearance in Lombardy, as they belatedly did in the second half of the nineteenth century, they did so in the very areas mentioned earlier where peasant-oriented handicraft industries had long been in existence.

The vitality and resilience of those industries can be accounted for with the fact that they were located outside the major towns and were thus spared the stifling control of the guilds as well as the tax collector's watchful eye. A further source of strength was the fact that they employed a cheaper kind of labour, namely peasants who, having a foot in agriculture, could afford to work at the loom or the anvil for lower pay. All this is true enough, but is not the whole story. The fortunes of those industries and their role in preparing a suitable environment for modern industrialization also reflected the fact that a large rural population, for all its poverty, continued to generate a steady demand for ordinary articles. In that sense, peasants as consumers deserve a place on the larger stage of the economic history of Lombardy.

References

ALEATI, G. and CARLO CIPOLLA (1958), 'Aspetti e problemi dell'economia milanese e lombarda nei secoli XVI e XVII', In Fondazione Treccani (ed.), *Storia di Milano*, Vol. XI, Milan.

BARBAGLI, M. (1984), *Sotto uno stesso tetto. Mutamenti della famiglia in Italia dal XV al XIX secolo*, Bologna.

BRAUDELL, F. (1982), *Civilization and Capitalism*, Vol. II: *The Wheels of Commerce*, trans. S. Reynolds, New York.

CAIZZI, B. (1980), *Il Comasco sotto il dominio spagñolo*, 2nd ed., Milan-Naples.

CIPOLLA, C. M. (1956), *Prezzi, salari e teoria dei salari in Lombardia alla fine del Cinquecento*, Rome.

CIPOLLA, C. M. (1980), *Before the Industrial Revolution: European Economy and Society, 1000–1700*, 2nd ed., New York-London.

DE MADDALENA, A. (1949), *Prezzi e aspetti di mercato in Milano durante il secolo XVII*, Milan.

DE VRIES, J. (1975), *Peasant Demand Patterns and Economic Development: Friesland, 1550–1750'*, In W. N. Parker and E. L. Jones (eds.), *European Peasants and their Markets*, Princeton.

GREENFIELD, K. R. (1965), *Economics and Liberalism in the Risorgimento*, Baltimore.

GULLICKSON, G. (1986), *Spinners and Weavers of Auffay: Rural Industry and the Sexual Division of Labour in a French Village, 1750–1850*, Cambridge.

KOMLOS, J. (1988), 'The Food Budget of English Workers: A Comment on Shammas', *Journal of Economic History*, **XLVIII**, No. 1, 149.

LASLETT, P. (1965), *The World We Have Lost*, New York.

LUZZATTO, G. (1955), *Storia economica dell'età moderna e contemporanea*, Vol. I, 4th ed., Padua.

MAZZAOUI, M. F. (1981), *The Italian Cotton Industry in the Late Middle Ages, 1100–1600*, Cambridge.

MINCHINTON, W. (1974), 'Pattern and Structure of Demand, 1500–1750', In C. M. Cipolla (ed.), *The Fontana Economic of Europe*, Vol. 2, Glasgow, 83–176.

MOTTU-WEBER, L. (1987), *Genève au siècle de la Réforme: Economie et Refuge*, Geneva-Paris.

SELLA, D. (1968), *Salari e lavoro nell' edilizia lombarda durante il secolo XVII*, Pavia.

SELLA, D. (1979), *Crisis and Continuity: The Economy of Spanish Lombardy in the Seventeenth Century*, Cambridge, Mass.

SELLA, D. (1982), 'Profilo demografico e sociale di un comune rurale lombardo: Balsamo nel 1597', In *Studi in memoria di Luigi Dal Pane*, Bologna, 333–44.

SELLA, D. (1987), 'Household, Land Tenure, and Occupation in Northern Italy in the Late Sixteenth Century', *Journal of European Economic History*, **16**, No. 3, 487–510.

SHAMMAS, C. (1983), 'Food Expenditures and Economic Well-being in Early Modern England', *Journal of Economic History*, **XLIII**, No. 1, 89–100.

SPUFFORD, M. (1984), *The Great Reclothing of Rural England: Petty Chapmen and their Wares in the Seventeenth Century*, London.

THIRSK, J. (1978), *Economic Policy and Projects: The Development of a Consumer Society in Early Modern England*, Oxford.

VIGO, G. (1977), *Finanza pubblica e pressione fiscale nello Stato di Milano*, Milan.

ZANETTI, D. (1965), 'Note sulla "Rivoluzione dei Prezzi" ', *Rivista storica italiana*, 864–96.

Chapter 10

FAMILY AND ECONOMY IN AN EARLY NINETEENTH-CENTURY BALTIC SERF ESTATE

ANDREJS PLAKANS AND CHARLES WETHERELL

For decades historians viewed the so-called 'second serfdom' through a single lens. Notwithstanding its documented diversity, historians conceptualized serfdom in eastern Europe after 1500 as a relatively uniform social and economic regime consisting of exploitive landowners and an exploited peasantry.[1] In recent years that situation has begun to change in response to a variety of pressures. Certainly Robert Brenner's sweeping interpretation of the development of agricultural capitalism has prompted historians to reassess agrarian relations during the early modern period in both western and eastern Europe (Brenner, 1976; 1985; Hagen, 1988). Likewise, the notion of proto-industrialization, the tendency among eastern European historians themselves to retreat from strict Marxian models of peasant society and culture, the continuing strength of peasant studies, and lingering questions about the dynamics of the pre-modern family have all led historians to re-examine serfdom in both the east and west from a number of new perspectives (Mendels, 1972; Medick, 1976; Levine, 1977; Gutmann and Leboutte, 1984; Gutmann, 1988; Kahk, 1982; Kula, 1976; Shanin, 1987; 1990; Scott, 1985; Tilly and Scott, 1987; Ehmer and Mitterauer, 1986; Hareven, 1991). The results of recent work defy simple summary, particularly as they pertain to peasant family life. All, save perhaps Brenner, exhibit a reluctance to embrace monolithic descriptions of the entire system. Some deliberately avoid questions of how family life relates to serfdom, while others are more adventurous in making connections among the many aspects of peasant community life. Different views of family and economy under the 'second serfdom' are bound to coexist for some time. Yet regardless of provenance, the entire field now exhibits a methodological and conceptual vitality that promises not only far-reaching reinterpretations but also continuing debates over pieces of the larger puzzle.

---

1 Blum (1957) introduced the notion of the 'second serfdom' into discussions of Eastern European, including Russian, agrarian relations. The 'second serfdom' differed from its medieval predecessor by the much more pronounced market orientation among landowners, which led to the treatment of the enserfed peasantry being treated as primarily a captive labour force. See also Chayanov (1925), Domar and Machina (1944), Domar (1970), Blum (1978), Durrenberger (1984), and Rudolph (1980; 1985).

Here we consider one such piece: the relationship between the organization of rural residential groups and corvée labour in the landed serf estate of Pinkenhof in the Russian Baltic province of Livland in the first two decades of the nineteenth century. Specifically, we examine the problems created for peasants by a labour system that placed an external burden on the family but did not eliminate the family's autonomy. We confine our discussion largely to the ramifications of the corvée because this area of peasant life permits us to pursue the question of familial autonomy in some detail. We have, on the one hand, a system of labour obligations fixed by an estate owner and, on the other hand, the reaction of enserfed peasants to it.

Although the relationship between family life and corvée labour remains critical to an understanding of serfdom in eastern Europe after 1500, few studies examine that relationship directly. Most skirt the issue or settle for inferring a connection from theories that assume certain kinds of (usually passive) economic behaviour. Historians of the Baltic area, for example, portray estate owners as trying to maximize profits by making rational market decisions, thereby exploiting peasants by appropriating a surplus agricultural product to sell. Landowners strive to create residential groups that can labour both for themselves and for the estate. Peasants, in contrast, do not or cannot engage in individual, rational, economic decision-making because they are either too communally oriented and tradition-bound or too constrained by serfdom. Their relative powerlessness renders them victims of the system because of the near-subsistence agriculture that became inevitable as agricultural surplus left the farmstead. In this view, the estate owner's economic interests are the determinative element, and the everyday life of the peasants, including their living arrangements and family life, the derivatives. The economic thinking of landowners is the phenomenon and the reactions of peasants the epiphenomena. Landowner economics overwhelms peasant society and culture.[2]

We suggest that the historical sources from Baltic serf communities reveal a much more complicated story. An examination of the nature of labour requirements and serf adaptations to them in Pinkenhof suggests among both landowners and serfs roughly similar actions that Peter Temin (1981) has conceptualized as *instrumental*, *customary*, and *command* behaviour. *Instrumental behaviour* is the self-conscious, rational, market-oriented, profit-maximizing behaviour of the agrarian capitalist of any status. *Customary behaviour* is the largely habitual behaviour that is governed by 'rules of thumb

---

2 Accentuation of the powerlessness of enserfed Baltic peasants and of the determinative role of landowners is found in virtually all interpretations of agrarian relations in the Baltic area, for reasons having sometimes to do with the fact that landowners possessed the land (the means of production); and sometimes because the landowners were Baltic Germans, Poles, or Russians (and therefore 'invaders') and the peasantry Estonians and Latvians (and therefore the 'colonized'). See, for example, Soom (1987), Dunsdorfs (1973), Strods (1984), Kahk (1982), and Liepina (1962; 1983).

that are honored as long as they produce results that provide a minimum level of organizational well-being'. Although created to describe the corporate cultures of modern business firms, the notion of customary behaviour is extraordinarily useful for examining economic behaviour in serf societies because it is not explicitly self-conscious, tends not to support hierarchical institutional arrangements, involves reciprocal action, and 'thrives' in communal settings. *Command behaviour*, surely applicable to serf societies, is 'the product of a context in which one person can order another to perform . . . a specific action and can impose penalties for noncompliance' (Temin, 1981, pp. 189, 190).

We introduce Temin's notions not in order to advance any integrated doctrine, but rather for two specific reasons. First, historians lack theoretical perspectives on economic action that incorporate both the individual, profit-oriented behaviour characteristic of capitalist market relations and the long recognized customary nature of peasant life. Second, the available evidence reveals behaviour that does not, in our view, simply document self-evident hierarchies of power. Both landlords and peasants acted and reacted in different ways as familial and economic life overlapped. Moreover, in dealing with serf communities as exemplars of a single productive system, historians lose information about the everyday deployment of labour that grand theories are meant to explain. In contrast, Temin's behavioural typology allows us to classify serf and landowner actions, and, we believe, to identify areas of peasant life where different behaviours intersect without violating the differences that existed in serfdom throughout eastern Europe.

Local arrangements in Europe's serf areas varied immensely. In Pinkenhof, an unusual blend of serfdom and local conditions prevailed. The peasantry did not live in villages as in many other parts of eastern Europe, but on dispersed farmsteads whose landholdings did not change significantly over time. A corvée labour norm was attached to these permanent residential sites, rather than to families, and the fundamental unit for reckoning labour delivery was the individual (or the individual and a horse) rather than the married couple as in the case of the Russian *tiaglo*. Although other feudal rents had diminished in importance in the Baltic by the beginning of the nineteenth century, the personal rights of serfs remained very circumscribed. Moreover, Pinkenhof was owned by the cosmopolitan centre of the Baltic region, the city of Riga, rather than by a private landowner or the Crown, and close proximity to a commercial entrepot undoubtedly exposed peasants to market relations that affected them more directly than those living on isolated estates. The question, in our view, is how these conditions shaped the behaviour of the enserfed peasants when they contemplated different strategies for meeting corvée obligations. In short, how did Pinkenhof's serfs use the system's flexibilities to their own advantage?

The historical records from Pinkenhof suggest that neither 'work' nor 'domestic group' are easily understood in isolation, and we accordingly assume that the connection between them is multi-stranded. Riga had always kept a close watch over its six patrimonial estates, of which Pinkenhof was one (Liepina, 1983). The managerialism of city authorities matured at the beginning of the nineteenth century when a new peasant law for Livland, adopted in 1804 by the provincial *Landtag*, required the creation of *Wacken-bücher*, or registers of all peasant obligations for every individual farmstead on all estates in the province (Schwabe, 1928, pp. 293–340). These registers took time to compile, since landowners had to survey (and sometimes re-survey) peasant holdings and develop formulae that balanced the value of the land serfs occupied with the value of their labour and other feudal rents. The registers for Pinkenhof were finished around 1809. In that same year an amendment to the 1804 law required estate owners to compose written regulations explaining in detail other serf responsibilities, exactly how many days of corvée labour each farmstead owed, and the manner in which labour dues were to be delivered at different times over the course of the year. Although the *Wackenbuch* contains no information about the individual residents of peasant farmsteads, we can supplement it with the 1816 Russian imperial head-tax census for Pinkenhof, which in Livland was part of a series of similar enumerations starting in 1782 and ending in 1859.

The available data for one holding, the Pehle farmstead, suggests the intricate labour-domestic group context of serfdom in Pinkenhof. In 1816, the Pehle residents included the farmstead's head (*Wirth*) Pawul, a serf aged 50, who had taken over the farm in 1812 when the former head Indrik died. The revision does not directly indicate a connection between these two men, but we can confidently infer that Pawul was Indrik's son-in-law because Pawul's 44-year-old wife, Ilse, is listed as Indrik's daughter. In any case, in 1816 Ilse and Pawul had three daughters, aged 20, six, and three, and four sons, aged 22, 15, 10, and nine. In addition to these nine, the farmstead's residents included a 23-year-old male farmhand and his 22-year-old wife, a 12-year-old foster daughter, and two widows, one 56 and the other 70. The presence of these last three persons illustrates the social service or welfare functions of farmsteads. Since there were no orphans' or old people's homes on the estate, such people tended to be distributed among existing farms.

If we assume that the economic information about the Pehle farmstead in the *Wackenbuch* (1804–1809) held true for 1816, then in that year Pawul was in charge of a farm that encompassed 102 acres which were divided into 24 acres of arable land (*Brustacker*), 77 acres of pasture (*Heuschlag*), and one acre of garden (*Gartenland*). All Pehle land was valued at 22 thalers, which meant, in terms of labour rents, that its obligatory corvée labour and dues-in-kind would be valued at the same amount. The *Wackenbuch* required that the Pehle farmstead contain a minimum labour force of three able-bodied (*arbeitsfähige*) males between the ages of 15 and 65 and two able-bodied females between the ages of 14 and 60. It also had to have on hand two horses, two cows and eight (unspecified) units of seed grain. In 1816 it had in fact four adult men and five adult women, two horses and four cows. Thus in 1816 the farm had more than the minimum labour force, or a surplus of able-bodied adults. The *Wackenbuch* also stated that Pehle farm had to provide 439.6 days of labour annually: 201.3 days of horse-team (harness) labour and 238.3 days of foot labour. Labour was to be delivered to the estate farm in varying amounts each week during the year, with the heaviest service falling in the period from St George's day (23 April) to St Martin's day (29 September), and lighter service in the winter months. Finally, the farm also had to deliver to the estate annually two units of rye, oats, and barley, four geese and hens, sixteen eggs, and 'half a sheep'.

Although the *Wackenbuch* supplies extensive evidence about Pinkenhof farms, it is by no means complete. We do not know how much labour, however measured, each of the farmsteads needed to work its own land, although we do know how much land each farmstead had at its disposal; nor do we know how much labour farmsteads had to supply to fulfil such collective peasant responsibilities as road repair and cartage. The *Wackenbuch* mentions none of these matters, although we know from the estate regulations and from the logic of the situation that these duties existed as part of the peasantry's total labour burden. Estate regulations also stated that farms of certain sizes could choose between several methods of discharging their labour obligations. For example, a 'one-and-one-half day' farmstead, which owed to the estate 78 days of harness labour during the summer months, and 38 days of foot labour during the winter months, could choose to fulfil this obligation by supplying one day one week and two days the next, or by supplying three days every two weeks. With the Pehle farmstead we can already see the danger of using any simple definition of either domestic group or labour. Even the formalized rules of the estate suggest that peasants themselves determined certain things: who exactly would live on the farm, how labour would be allocated over the course of the year, and how the labour force would be divided between the farmstead's own needs and its obligatory labour service.

In 1816, 1,032 peasants (or 74.8 per cent of the 1,380 individuals enumerated in the 1816 revision) lived on the 92 farmsteads listed in the *Wackenbuch* in 1809.[3] These 92 farms held 3,712 acres of pasture land and 1,052 acres of arable

3 The Pinkenhof *Wackenbuch*, concluded in 1809, contains information on 92 farms, with the signatures of estate officials appearing after the ninety-second entry, which suggests that the officials considered the list of 92 complete. The 1816 soul revision, however, contains information on 136 residential units in the estate, suggesting that a substantial number of these were not included in the main corvée system and that their inhabitants were not obligated by the corvée attached to farmsteads (*Bauerngesinde*); although these peasants were still required to participate in various kinds of collective work such as road repair, cartage, and upkeep of 'public' buildings such as postal way-stations. Among the residential units not listed in the *Wackenbuch* were a flour mill, a school, a hospital, the pastorate, three foresters' dwellings, five taverns, the main and two subsidiary estate farms, twenty-five additional farm plots (*Grundstucke*) and five apparently new farmsteads. We discuss the demography of Pinkenhof in Appendix 1.

Table 1: *Landholdings and corvée labour dues of Pinkenhof farmsteads, 1809*

	Mean	s	Median	Total
Landholdings (acres)				
Total	53.3	12.6	50.9	4,898
Arable	11.4	3.4	10.8	1,052
Pasture	40.4	10.7	39.3	3,712
Garden	1.5	0.7	1.3	134
Annual labour dues (days)				
Total	249.3	34.5	243.8	22,933
Horse-team	120.6	17.0	119.0	11,097
Foot	128.7	18.4	124.5	11,836
Weekly labour dues				
Total	3.8	0.7	3.8	354
Horse-team	1.5	0.2	1.5	140
Foot	2.3	0.5	2.3	214

Note: Acreage rounded to the nearest whole number. Source: Pinkenhof (1809a).

land, or 97.3 per cent of all pasture and 87.4 per cent of all arable land allocated to peasant use, according to a survey conducted earlier in the century.[4] As Table 1 reveals, the average Pinkenhof farmstead had 53 acres: between one and two acres of garden, 11 acres of arable land, and 40 acres of pasture.[5] In exchange for the right to occupy this land, the average farmstead owed the estate 250 days of labour (121 of harness labour and 129 of foot labour) a year, or four days a week—two-and-a-half of foot labour and one-and-a-half of harness labour. As Table 2 shows, the 92 farms contained an average of 11 people each. Fifty-eight per cent of the sample population were able-bodied adults (males age 15–65 and females 14–60); 39 per cent were children (males aged 1–14 and females 1–13); and 3 per cent were what the *Wackenbuch* viewed as 'retired' adults (males over 66 and females over 60) (Plakans, 1989; Plakans and Wetherell, in press).

4 All Pinkenhof peasants held a total of 1,204 acres of arable land and 3,816 acres of pasture land (Liepina, 1983, p. 64).
5 We cannot say whether these allocations were comparatively large or small. In Pinkenhof in 1816, the per capita ratio of arable acreage for the 92 farms (assuming that 25 per cent lay fallow) was 1.0, while in Hungary in 1841 it was 6.0. No such disparity exists, however, between Pinkenhof and Petrovskoe in interior Russia. Between 1810 and 1859 in Petrovskoe, there were roughly 4.6 acres per serf, while in Pinkenhof there were 4.8 in 1816. The Hungarian comparison is taken from Komlos (1988, p. 657); see also Clark (1987). For Petrovskoe, see Hoch (1986, pp. 26–27, 41).

Table 2: *Size and composition of sample farmsteads, Pinkenhof, 1816*

	Mean	s	Median	N	(%)
Size	11.2	2.8	11.0		
Adults	6.6	1.6	6.0	606	58.7
Children	4.3	2.0	4.0	398	38.6
Retired	0.3	0.6	0.0	28	2.7
Totals				1,032	100.0
Males	5.6	1.7	6.0	516	50.0
Females	5.6	1.9	5.0	516	50.0
Sex ratio	114.1	46.1	100.0		
Totals				1,032	100.0
Adult males	3.3	1.0	3.0	302	29.3
Adult females	3.3	1.1	3.0	304	29.5
Adult sex ratio	109.1	46.1	100.0		
Totals				606	58.8

Notes: We have followed the 1816 revision which classified adults, or the 'able-bodied', as males aged 15–65 and females 14–60; children as males aged 1–14 and females 1–13; and retired adults as males over 65 and females over 60. We have, however, classified the three male heads over 65 and the two females over 60 who were spouses of heads as able-bodied adults. Source: Pinkenhof (1816).

Some aspects of the Pinkenhof peasantry's life were beyond the serfs' control, but others, such as the composition of the farmsteads' populations, reflected decisions farmstead heads made themselves. The farmstead head, in fact, was the link between the estate owner and the farm: it was he (and sometimes she) who tried to translate the farmstead's obligations into a residential labour pool of a particular kind. But heads could not think in terms of the corvée alone. Both peasant and estate lands required attention by the same labour force, and how individuals were deployed among the two types of land ultimately rested on the decisions of farmstead heads. In making these decisions, heads always had to reckon with the labour needs of their own holdings and the corvée requirement. But within that framework, they enjoyed wide latitude, and could decide whom to keep on the farm on any given day and whom to send to join a larger labour crew working at the main estate farm or on dispersed *demesne* lands.[6]

6 Pinkenhof's *demesne* of 875 acres was undoubtedly dispersed, rather than consolidated, since the uneven topography of the estate would have made it difficult to establish as a single farm (Plakans and Wetherell, 1988, p. 379, Figure 2).

The fixed, sex-differentiated labour requirement in Pinkenhof meant that it was absolutely necessary for farmstead heads to prepare rationally for the year ahead. A labour force containing a certain number of able-bodied men and women had to be in place by St George's Day, the traditional date for making agreements with farmhands for the coming year. Verbal contracts were then renewed, unsatisfactory farmhands let go, and new people taken on as needed. Yet the situation was far from cut-and-dried because a farmstead population was more than a labour brigade with interchangeable members. It had a family dimension among those residents related to the head and among married farmhands, which meant that in making decisions about deploying labour a head had to consider both estate dictates and other customary obligations. In this sense, a farmstead head was caught between the responsibility of meeting the estate's demands and the expectations the familial basis of the farmstead entailed. Not meeting the first could threaten the survival of the group, but not living up to the second could easily undermine the head's moral authority.

Historians of Baltic serfdom have commented on this dilemma, and their observations can be translated into the hypothesis that farmstead heads sought to protect their own immediate families and co-residing relatives from corvée labour by employing farmhands who could be sent instead.[7] To implement such a protective strategy required heads to make rational decisions and to consider traditional behavioural imperatives associated with family and kin. Ordinarily, the head drew upon three labour pools: the head's own family of marriage, co-resident kin, and farmhands. For the most part, the 1816 Pinkenhof revision clearly states which people belonged to which group, since it designates individuals as, for example, 'son of head', 'head's brother's wife', or 'married male farmhand' (*Knecht*). The number of people in each pool, and the composition of each pool varied from farmstead to farmstead and from year to year, as did the total farmstead population. What could not change was the core of able-bodied adults that heads needed to meet the labour demands of both their farmsteads and the estate.

As a fact of everyday economic life, corvée labour has been extensively described, but its implementation has seldom been examined and evaluated. The corvée labour of Pinkenhof serfs was devoted to maintaining *demesne* lands: cultivating them, harvesting them, and carting the agricultural products that came from them. Some serfs worked entirely on the estate farm, or *Hof*, itself at various skilled and semi-skilled tasks, and some, particularly women, maintained the *Hof*'s household. Most of Pinkenhof's peasants, however, worked the estate's and their own lands. Estate authorities were clearly in a managerial frame of mind in the early nineteenth century. The *Wackenbuch* stated labour requirements not only in terms of 'ordinary' and 'extraordinary'

---

7 The question of who was sent to do corvée labour is discussed by Liepina (1983, p. 134), Strods (1987, p. 165), Svabe (1958, p. 187), Dunsdorfs (1973, p. 425), and, generally for Europe, Blum (1978, pp. 50–59).

(supplemental summer) labour, but also in terms of the required core population of adults, which ranged from a minimum of two to a maximum of five and always included persons of both sexes. Division of labour in estate agricultural tasks necessitated both men and women, with the former usually doing more field work than the latter. A mandated minimum core of two persons always meant one man and one woman; a core of three, always two men and one woman; a core of four, always two men and two women; and a core of five, three men and two women. Indeed, three-quarters of all farms were required to send more men than women.[8]

Was the corvée in Pinkenhof burdensome? With respect to the specificity of the requirements (exactly x days per week with exactly x many men and x many women), clearly the answer is yes. With respect to the totality of work diverted from farmsteads, however, a somewhat different picture emerges. The estate owner, Riga, was surely exhibiting *instrumental* thinking by creating obligations that involved proportionately more males than females. Men could arguably perform heavy agricultural labour more effectively than women, and accordingly provide the landlord with increased productivity. Yet if we compare the labour that had to be diverted from farmsteads with the total labour available, we find that by the early nineteenth century the Pinkenhof peasantry were not as badly off as generalized descriptions would lead us to believe. On a per capita basis, Pinkenhof farmsteads owed only 24 days of corvée labour to the estate; an amount virtually identical to what John Komlos has estimated prevailed in Hungary during the same period (Komlos, 1985). On average, Pinkenhof farmsteads owed the estate 250 person-days a year in corvée labour. This meant that farmsteads owed approximately 166 male-days and 83 female-days of labour, which translates loosely into two men and one woman for two days a week for forty-one weeks. If we use a five-day working week and a fifty-two-week working year, which the *Wackenbuch* for the most part did, each able-bodied adult could expend 260 days of work annually.[9] On average, each farmstead had at its disposal 825 days of male and 825 days of female labour. As a proportion of available labour then, Pinkenhof farmsteads paid an average rent of slightly less than 20 per cent of its male labour and 10 per cent of its female labour. If we assume no difference in male and female labour, the average annual rent of Pinkenhof farmsteads was 15 per cent of their productive labour.

Certainly by modern standards, where rent approaches 40 per cent of gross earned income, Pinkenhof peasants do not appear to have been heavily exploited. In fact, they appear to have had adequate labour for their own

8 The distribution of male and female labour requirements for the 92 farmsteads listed in the *Wackenbuch* are as follows: 1 M, 1 F (N = 2, or 2.2%); 2 M, 1 F (N = 67, or 72.8%); 2 M, 2 F (N = 21, or 22.8%); 3 M, 2 F (N = 2, or 2.2%).
9 Estate regulations (Pinkenhof, 1809b) reckoned harness corvée on the basis of a 50 week working year for those farms owing five or more days per week and a 52 week year for those owing less than five days per week.

Table 3: *Peasant and estate landholdings in Riga's patrimonial estates, c. 1809*

Estate	Arable Acreage			Pasture Acreage		
	Estate	Peasant	Ratio P:E	Estate	Peasant	Ratio P:E
Sala	227	655	2.9	345	1,310	3.8
Pinkenhof	386	1,204	3.1	490	3,817	7.8
Mazjumpravmuiza	338	757	2.2	281	1,071	3.8
Olaine	192	795	4.1	300	2,388	8.0
Beberbeki	154	395	2.6	293	1,419	4.8
Dreilini	71	267	3.8	54	497	9.1
Mean ratio			3.1			6.2
s			0.7			2.3

Note: P:E indicates the ratio of peasant to estate holdings.
Source: Liepina (1962, p. 64).

holdings despite the diversion of effort to the *demesne*. Table 3 shows the comparative size of the peasant and *demesne* landholdings in Riga's patrimonial estates as well as the ratios of peasant to estate land in 1809.

In Pinkenhof the ratio of peasant to estate arable land was 3:1 and for pasture land it was nearly 8:1. We can assume that estate officials tried to cultivate their land as intensively as possible, and the 23,000 man-days of labour a year deployed on 875 acres of land certainly supports the premise. The 92 *Wackenbuch* farmsteads encompassed slightly more than 4,700 acres of arable and pasture land, or 5.4 times as much land as the *demesne*. Again assuming a five-day working week and a fifty-two-week working year, Pinkenhof peasants could put in 157,560 man-days of labour on their own farmsteads, which is 5.9 times as much labour as their corvée labour dues. Moreover, farmsteads could use children and the elderly to tend pasture animals whereas the estate had to rely on adults from the corvée force. Thus we might better compare the labour advantage peasants possessed (5.9) to their advantage in arable land (3.1) rather than total land (5.4). Even if the *demesne* consisted mostly of cultivated land, Pinkenhof's peasants possessed a surplus of labour they could devote to their own holdings. Certainly there was a seasonality to corvée labour that moderated any strictly numerical advantage in man-days of productive labour that farmsteads possessed, but peasants had an advantage nonetheless (Kahk, 1982, pp. 46–47).

Why Riga allowed such apparently low rents is impossible to say. The low quality of Pinkenhof lands may have necessitated more labour-intensive cultivation than on other estates in the Baltic, and we cannot discount that possibility. Yet without an obvious structural explanation, we must seek a more particular, although admittedly hypothetical, one. It may well have been that over the course of the seventeenth and eighteenth centuries Pinkenhof's serfs had managed to negotiate corvée dues that by the nineteenth century had assumed the stature of custom which Riga's officials accepted when the *Wackenbücher* were compiled. If true, we can view the economic behaviour of estate officials as both *instrumental* and *customary*. It was *instrumental* in that the sex-differentiated corvée requirement aimed at increasing the productivity of estate agriculture. But it was also *customary* in that estate officials recognized and endorsed long standing corvée labour rents, even though they were extraordinarily low by modern standards.

However high or low, the corvée required the head to plan to divert a certain amount of labour on the farmstead to the estate's lands, and this meant thinking in terms of individual adult workers. Decisions on this score, again, could not assume interchangeability among available labourers because both men and women had to be sent and the head's family members had to be protected. Protectionism was an important question, in part because of the high incidence of complex family households in the Pinkenhof population. Some 46.2 per cent of the farmsteads in 1816 can be classified as complex, which meant that in them there was at least one person or one married couple related to the head but not part of the head's immediate family. These people were bound to claim customary preferential treatment with respect to corvée service. Residential group formation in the rural areas of the Baltic tended not to be marriage-driven. Young couples after marriage could reside on the farmsteads of parents, parents could live with children after 'stepping down' from headships, and married and unmarried brothers could co-reside after the death of their parents (Plakans, 1989, pp. 175–95).[10] This clustering of kin, a result of familial custom, was certainly helpful as a resident labour pool for the farmstead itself, but a head could not treat relatives as if they were simply hired labour.

Although we have no indication of who was actually sent to perform corvée labour, we do know the age, sex, and status of all farmstead residents in 1816, and an unequivocal statement from the *Wackenbuch* as to how many persons of each sex the estate expected there to be in each farmstead. Table 4 shows the components of the labour force on the 92 farms in Pinkenhof in 1816. Heads and other adults in their conjugal family units comprised roughly 50 per cent of the labour pool of 606 adults, resident kin 10 per cent, and farmhands 40 per cent. In the aggregate, the labour pool at risk of being sent to corvée labour first—farmhands and resident kin—amounted to 306 people or 50.5 per cent of the estate's able-bodied adults, and 86.4 per cent of the 354 needed for the corvée every week. Thus a substantial number of peasants potentially escaped corvée labour altogether.

Whether individual farmsteads met or surpassed estate labour obligations

10 In 1816, 21.7 per cent (20) of all farmsteads contained co-resident brothers, 6.5 per cent (6) of farms contained married sons and another 2.2 per cent (2) married daughters.

Table 4: *Size and composition of Pinkenhof's adult labour force, 1816*

Group	N	(%)
Heads	92	15.2
Other adults in heads' CFUs	208	34.3
Co-resident kin	61	10.1
Farmhands	245	40.4
Totals	606	100.0

Source: Pinkenhof (1816).

Table 5: *Proportions of farmstead labour groups, protected and unprotected, in Pinkenhof, 1816*

Labour pool	Protected		Unprotected		Pool totals	Share of adult pop.
	N	%	N	%	N	%
CFU						
Heads	80	87.0	12	13.0	92	
Spouses	72	93.5	5	6.5	77	
Sons	13	16.9	64	83.1	77	
Daughters	23	42.6	31	57.4	54	49.5
Subtotals	188	62.7	112	37.3	300	49.5
Kin						
Male	8	25.8	23	74.2	31	
Female	17	56.7	13	43.3	30	
Subtotals	25	41.0	36	59.0	61	10.1
Farmhands						
Male	13	11.6	99	88.4	112	
Female	57	42.9	76	57.1	133	
Subtotals	70	28.6	175	71.4	245	40.4
Totals	283	46.7	323	53.3	606	

Sources: Pinkenhof (1809a; 1816).

depended on the size and composition of their populations as well as the sex-differentiated corvée requirement. From this, we have calculated (as Table 5 displays) how many persons from each group heads could 'protect' from corvée labour, and how many remained 'unprotected'. The premise, once again, is that, if at all possible, heads would seek to keep family members and co-resident kin for labour on the farmstead and send farmhands to do the corvée. If there were an insufficient number of farmhands, then family and relatives would have to be used.

In a perfect situation, a head could protect all family members and co-resident kin. Yet we know that complete success of a 'protectionist' policy was impossible because the corvée requirement was sex-differentiated, the composition of a head's family and co-resident kin was affected by developmental cycles, and heads were not always in the position to hire the right kinds of farmhands. Less than one-third of Pinkenhof farms had a sufficient number of farmhands of the correct sex to allow heads to completely protect their families and co-resident kin. Most heads had to dip into the labour pools of family and relatives to meet their farmstead's corvée requirement, and no group could be totally protected. Nonetheless, most heads still had at their disposal a sufficiently large labour force to protect their immediate families from the corvée.

In a few cases, the vagaries of age, death, and conscription severely limited the head's options. Three (or 3.3 per cent) farms could not meet their required male labour dues. One farm was headed by a 33-year-old male who had a 30-year-old wife, two sons, aged six and two, and one daughter, aged eight. No co-resident kin and only one female farmhand and her two daughters, aged 13 and five, were present. However, one male, very possibly the spouse of the female farmhand, was listed in the revision as having been conscripted (Plakans and Wetherell, 1988, p. 367). Another farm was headed by a 60-year-old widow with two sons, aged 17 and 11, a 20-year-old daughter, and a six-year-old niece. The head appears to have lost her spouse in 1814 and a son in 1813 who would have been 23 in 1816. There was a 66-year-old male farmhand, officially retired, but who may well have worked and allowed the farm to meet its labour obligations. The third farm was headed by a 68-year-old male who had a 40-year-old spouse and a two-year-old daughter. There was a 45-year-old female farmhand and her twin daughters, aged 14. The head appears to have lost a son from a former marriage in 1811 who would have been 40 in 1816. In 1811 there had also been two adult males, probably farmhands, now 33 and 20, but who had departed by 1816 for a better deal, a less cantankerous head, or had been let go because of the quality of their work. In these cases, we can catch a glimpse, however indistinct, of the movement among farmsteads, bad demographic luck, and the always present danger of conscription that removed males from the farmsteads and placed heads at a disadvantage (Plakans and Wetherell, 1988, pp. 366–67, 374–75, 381–84).

Few farmsteads were this close to the edge, however. Most heads had at their disposal a sufficiently large labour force to protect themselves, their spouses, and some of their adult children from corvée labour. Fully eighty-one farms (88.0 per cent) had adult farmhands in residence. While nine had only male and another ten only female farmhands, sixty-two, or 67.4 per cent of all farms contained both adult male and female farmhands. As Table 6 reveals, slightly more than a quarter of Pinkenhof farms (26) had enough farmhands to meet all their labour dues. These farmsteads had a disproportionately larger share of farmhands, while they also had a disproportionately smaller share of

Table 6: *Differences between farmsteads who could and could not meet all corvée labour requirements with farmhands*

| | Farmsteads that | | | |
	Could	Could Not	t	p
Farm size	12.5	10.7	–2.8	.01
Adults				
Total	7.1	6.4	–2.1	.03
Sons	0.3	1.0	4.6	.01
Daughters	0.5	0.6	0.9	.41
Male kin	0.1	0.4	3.6	.01
Female kin	0.2	0.4	3.7	.01
Male farmhands	2.4	0.8	3.7	.01
Female farmhands	2.1	1.2	–4.1	.01
Children	5.1	4.0	2.1	.05
Age of head	37.4	44.9	2.9	.01
N	26		66	

Sources: Pinkenhof (1809a; 1816).

labour in the other pools. The reverse was true for those farms which could not completely meet their corvée labour obligations with farmhands. These sixty-six farms contained proportionately more adult sons and co-resident kin, were also significantly smaller, contained fewer able-bodied males, fewer children, and had older heads than the other twenty-six.

It is clear that the sex-differentiated nature of the corvée labour obligation would always cause problems for heads because it was so profoundly at odds with the sex ratio in Pinkenhof. The requirement was severely skewed toward males, yet the sex ratio in Pinkenhof, as in any relatively closed, demographic-ally healthy population, was balanced. Consequently, a labour norm that precluded universal substitutability in the labour force made the job of assembling the correct persons very difficult indeed. Although overall we find relatively balanced sex ratios not only in heads' families but also in those of both co-resident kin and farmhands, on individual farmsteads an imbalance could readily exist.[11] Since farmhands' families normally moved with them, a farmstead could easily find itself with a labour surplus in one category as a result of trying to meet the minimum requirement in another. The same thing would happen if a protectionist strategy succeeded. If heads tried to protect themselves and their families from corvée labour by hiring farmhands of a certain sex, then farmsteads could end up having more workers, particularly

11 The mean adult sex ratios and (*s*) for the three pools of labour are as follows: head's CFU, 125.0 (76.0); co-resident kin, 109.0 (32.6); farmhands, 99.3 (55.8).

Table 7: *Capability to meet corvée labour obligations exclusively with farmhands by household structure*

Household structure	Yes		No		Totals	
	N	(%)	N	(%)	N	(%)
Simple	20	76.9	29	44.6	49	53.8
Complex	6	23.1	36	55.4	42	46.2
Totals	26	100.0	65	100.0	91	100.0

Sources: Pinkenhof (1809a; 1816).
Notes: Household classification is that of the Cambridge Group for the History of Population and Social Structure (Laslett, 1972, p. 31). Table excludes one household classifiable as solitary. X^2 = 6.5, df = 1, p >.01.

females, than they needed to meet the corvée obligation. This we also find to be the case. On the average, the Pinkenhof farmsteads had three able-bodied adults that were not needed for corvée labour: one male and two females. All farmsteads met their female labour requirements and, in fact, eighty-seven (94.6 per cent) exceeded them. It is clear that the corvée standard, as formulated in Pinkenhof, could create intractable management problems for farmstead heads.

A second confounding element in the head's plans for an adequate labour force was the developmental cycle of the head's family.[12] As Table 7 indicates, more than three-quarters of farms that could meet their labour obligations with farmhands were headed by people whose family structure can be classified as simple (that is, married couples or single parents with children), as compared with 44.6 per cent (29 out of 65) of those who could not. Logically this all makes sense. Heads with simple family structures would tend to be younger, and have fewer adult children and collateral kin. Conversely, older heads would be more likely to have adult children and kin they could retain or recruit to the farmstead. A successful implementation of protectionism was clearly tied to the life cycle of farmstead heads and the pool of available farmhands. Because a farmstead's population had to bear some relationship to its resources, an expanding number of family members (and co-resident kin) meant a limit on the number of farmhands that could be employed, and that, in turn, constrained the protectionist policy. Ironically, the large family which Peter Czap, in his studies of Russian serfs, finds was described as the 'peasant's greatest wealth', worked in the Baltic against another valued peasant goal

12 Historians have long dealt with the many implications of the family developmental cycle in peasant life. See, for example, Plakans (1975; 1984), Kahk (1982), Kingston-Mann (1991), and Chayanov (1925).

(Czap, 1983, p. 105). If the relatively low level of the corvée suggests the relatively successful workings of *instrumental* behaviour among the Pinkenhof peasants, then family protectionism, although in many cases frustrated, is evidence for the strength of custom and the autonomy of familial life. Although favourably positioned to exercise substantial power over other peasants, farmstead heads were able to act instrumentally only within certain constraints. The point is, however, that they did act: they were not simply executors of the estate owner's will but of their own as well.

We have suggested thus far that Pinkenhof's farmhands, who in 1816 comprised 40 per cent of the labour force, were likely to bear the brunt of the farmstead heads' planning. Historians of Baltic serfdom have often referred to farmhands as the 'landless' (*bezzemnieki*) or the 'transients' (*gajeji*); some have even argued that estate authorities assigned to farmsteads those *bezzem-nieki* who could not find positions for themselves.[13] If indeed farmhands were forced to live on particular farmsteads, then we can easily envisage the tension Steven Hoch has argued existed among and within the enserfed co-resident groups in Petrovskoe in Russia proper (Hoch, 1986, pp. 160–90; 1982, pp. 233–42). On the other hand, if farmhands themselves made choices about where to work, then we can envisage an enserfed subpopulation with considerably more power than historians have conventionally attributed to it by reason of status (Strods, 1987; Svarane, 1971).

At first glance, the situation suggests a buyer's market, that is, heads making their choices entirely in terms of their own advantage. Yet the constraints on heads—the need to have a correctly balanced labour force and the desire to protect family members against corvée service—suggests bargaining rather than one-sided advantage. With heads who were young and correspondingly had few co-residing children and relatives, but who desperately needed adults to meet their farmsteads' labour obligations, farmhands might have been able to strike more favourable deals and even consider the reputations of the head as well as other farmhands before signing on. Moreover, farmhands may have chosen to live and work on particular farms to increase their chances of succeeding to the headship by increasing their proximity to a marriageable daughter, son, or widow (Svabe, 1958, p. 81). Clearly, farmhands did not live in a world where they were completely at total liberty to sell their services to the highest bidder, but the suggestion remains that their lot may well have been better than conventional wisdom holds. In any event, it seems reasonable to suggest that a large proportion of Pinkenhof's enserfed peasant population engaged in individual, rational, *instrumental* economic behaviour in the estate's labour market every year.

---

13 Both Latvian language terms (which the Pinkenhof peasantry spoke) are classificatory and undoubtedly imply a greater uniformity of condition than actually existed. There were farmhands who did not move for years as well as landless people whose plight was temporary. See Mierina (1968, pp. 14–69) and Svabe (1958, p. 83).

Our analysis suggests three things. First, in Pinkenhof there was ample opportunity for serfs to exhibit behaviour patterns analogous to those of estate owners. Although we have explored only one dimension of the relationship between familial and economic life, and that one only partially, we can see a variety of cultural values and social structures interacting in fundamental ways. Second, historians may have seriously underestimated the extent to which serfs could use the system to their own advantage, even in the Baltic where serfdom is said to have been more rigorous than elsewhere. Certainly Pinkenhof's peasants did not own their land and their legal status severely constrained their lives. Nonetheless, important areas of freedom of action existed. Estate owners dealt with farmstead heads who, in turn, dealt with relatives and farmhands. The last, conversely, could find their negotiating position improved by the phase of the developmental cycle in which the head's family found itself in the spring of each year. Third, we suggest that any approach to the relationship between family and economy under the 'second serfdom' that focuses primarily on who had ultimate control over land and labour easily overlooks the spheres of free action in which enserfed peasants could make their own will felt. In Pinkenhof an understaffed estate had to regulate the labour of more than one thousand peasants living on almost a hundred large farmsteads, with the consequence that oversight fell to a great extent on farmstead heads themselves. The sheer numbers of people involved argue against absolute estate control over every aspect of peasant life. Indeed, despite the structural uniqueness of Baltic serfdom, the Pinkenhof peasantry's familial autonomy suggests a parallel with other eastern European areas and the limits to the power landlords could effectively exert over serfs.

Historians will need to consider many more factors than we have been able to do here if an understanding of how mandatory labour obligations in the traditional corvée areas of eastern Europe were implemented is to become complete. Even Baltic scholars, who otherwise continued until recently to use dialectical materialist modes of historical explanation, have discarded simple exploitation models within the past decade. The number of actors whose decisions and negotiations determined how much work time was finally invested in the corvée now has to be expanded beyond the estate owner and his agents to include at least farmstead heads and possibly other members of the farmstead's communal group. The Latvian historian Dzidra Liepina, who has used the *Wackenbücher* extensively to study the corvée in Livland in the first half of the eighteenth century, suggests as much. Liepina believes that 'the official *Wackenbücher* stated formal requirements. They did not incorporate the inevitable permutations that arose when norms were fulfilled in specific situations . . . [T]he obligations of the *Wackenbücher*, therefore, must be interpreted as reporting basic general levels but not exchanges and innovations' that arose in practice (Liepina, 1983).

We have suggested, first, that in the welter of decisions that resulted in corvée labour actually being performed, the desire of the farmstead head to protect family members from corvée played a major role; and second, that with respect to the totality of corvée obligations, those of the Pinkenhof peasantry may have been less onerous than a general description of the distribution of power in the estate would lead us to expect. These conclusions inevitably invite consideration of James C. Scott's now-familiar concept of the *moral economy*. Scott conceives of the *moral economy* as a 'notion of economic justice' (Scott, 1976, p. 3) with which peasants invest their status by asserting rights of subsistence and reciprocity in exchange for their labour.[14] They demand and, in Scott's view, obtain constraints on exploitation that might jeopardize their subsistence. It takes little effort to imagine such a situation in Pinkenhof, particularly as it involves the relationship between family and economy we have explored. The codified level of corvée labour dues, as a proportion of potential productive labour, ensured subsistence for Pinkenhof's peasantry as well as an agricultural surplus for the estate itself, and permitted farmstead heads to extend a degree of protection to their families against having to suffer the regimentation corvée labour entailed. While we are not prepared to claim that lord-peasant relations in Pinkenhof all unfolded within a 'moral economy', we are satisfied that this concept, in postulating peasants as negotiating actors even in an unbalanced power relation, has far more potential for clarifying the often subtly articulated socio-economic relationships within the serf estate than does the notion that peasants were powerless.

Familial autonomy was an important element in the reciprocity of the 'moral economy' of Pinkenhof's peasantry. Without rights to land, Baltic serfs fashioned hierarchies of status and power in the one domain they could: familial life. For farmstead heads, meeting familial obligations meant achieving both economic subsistence and social harmony with the farmstead's domestic group. Although clearly not easy, the task entailed adopting different ways of thinking and acting as well as considerable freedom. The protectionist strategy we have suggested farmstead heads embraced also reflects Scott's 'safety first' principle of peasant behaviour. Economically, peasants avoid risk, and its attendant remunerative gain, so central to capitalist relations. In Pinkenhof, however, avoiding risk did not mean that peasants failed to think rationally or attempt to maximize their economic well-being. Within the constraints of Baltic serfdom, economically rational behaviour possessed a profoundly moral dimension that arguably centred on family life. Within the complex social domains of family and economy, Pinkenhof's serfs, just as Scott's generalized peasants, behaved rationally out of necessity and of choice. They also honoured custom and command for the same reasons.

---

14 The notion of moral economy originated with E. P. Thompson (1963; 1971). Scott's particular formulation has been extensively debated. See, especially, Popkin (1979) and Weller and Guggenheim (1982).

Appendix 1

It is difficult to construct a reliable demographic profile of Pinkenhof in the first two decades of the nineteenth century largely because the critical 1816 revision is less complete than the revisions of either 1833 or 1850; the last two are detailed enough in virtually every respect to allow us to entirely reconstruct annual series of births, deaths, migrations, and marriages. Perhaps more important, the 1833 and 1850 revisions reveal a demographic picture that looks more western than eastern European in character. In contrast, the 1816 revision reveals a population similar to others in the interior of Russia. Thus we are presented with the choice between believing either (1) that the 1816 revision is so biased that it fundamentally distorts the picture of the demographic regime in Pinkenhof that the 1833 and 1850 revisions capture, or (2) that the demographic regime changed fundamentally between 1816 and 1833. Although unlikely, the latter choice remains plausible because emancipation occurred between the years of those two revisions.

The following comparison of the populations living on the 92 farmsteads listed in the 1809 *Wackenbuch* in 1816, 1833, and 1850 helps to illustrate the point.

		1816	1833	1850
Population	Estate	1,380	1,375	1,569
	Sample	1,032	1,156	1,244
	(%)	74.8	84.1	79.3
Rate of growth	Estate		−0.02	0.78
	Sample		0.67	0.43
Farm size	Mean	11.2	12.6	13.6
	s	2.8	3.9	5.0
	Median	11.0	13.0	13.0
Sex ratio	Estate	99.0	106.1	94.7
	Sample	100.0	107.5	99.4
Age[15] All	Mean	23.3	23.2	25.8
	s	18.0	15.8	18.0
	Median	19.0	22.0	22.0
Males	Mean	23.4	23.5	24.4
	s	18.2	15.4	17.5
	Median	20.0	23.0	21.0
	N	514	599	620
Females	Mean	23.4	23.1	27.1
	s	18.2	16.2	18.4
	Median	20.0	20.0	24.0
	N	506	557	624
SMAM[16]	Males	21.2	29.9	29.0
	Females	25.3	28.0	27.2
Dependency ratio		66.9	50.3	54.0

The ages of marriage (SMAMs) in 1816 are something of an anomaly that may stem from a pronounced age heaping among females, some fundamental change in behaviour between 1816 and 1833, or both. Our reading of the 1816 revision leads us to conclude that the SMAM for males is accurate. We have no reliable way to adjust for age heaping among women, but the clear evidence of such behaviour may explain the higher SMAM for females in 1816.[17] Accordingly, we assume that the SMAM for females in 1816 is high, and that men and women married in their early twenties before emancipation and in their late twenties after emancipation. Logically, this makes sense. We might expect the age of marriage to rise as the Pinkenhof peasantry adjusted to the new system of labour rents and the ensuing impact on life plans. At the same time, we cannot dismiss potentially severe biases in the 1816 revision. On the one hand, the dependency ratio (the number of dependent or non-working persons, generally taken to be those under 15 and over 65 years of age, in the population per 100 working persons in the population) for 1816 seems high for a population with ages of marriage in the early twenties, and undoubtedly reflects some under-reporting of births and infant deaths evident in the 1833 and 1850 revisions (Plakans and Wetherell, 1988, p. 385). On the other hand, the proportion (37.1 per cent) of the population aged 0–14 years in 1816 (again with known ages) compares favourably with Mishino (38.2 per cent) in interior Russia which had similarly low ages of marriage among both males (21.0) and females (20.9) before emancipation (Czap, 1978; 1982). Accordingly, under-registration of births and infant deaths may be less extensive than one might initially expect, and the ages at marriage and the dependency ratio that the 1816 revision indicates may be close to the actual historical reality.

It may be that emancipation ushered in genuine demographic change in Pinkenhof and elsewhere in the Baltic, as peasants chose to marry later and constrain their fertility within marriage. Certainly the generally early (pre-1880) decline in fertility in the Baltic provinces of the Russian empire suggests the possibility, although we have been unable to isolate anything more than general disincentives for having large families and cannot date the decline at all (Plakans and Wetherell, 1991; Coale and Watkins, 1986; Coale et al., 1979). At this point, we simply cannot distinguish actual behaviour from biases in the evidence, but are coming to believe that the economic regime of labour rents that replaced serfdom, and which preceded peasant ownership of land, had a profound influence on familial and marital behaviour.

---

15 Sample N for 1816 (1,020) excludes twelve cases (two males and ten females) where exact ages could not be determined but in which status as an adult or child could be assigned on the basis of terminological references such as diminutives.

16 SMAM indicates the 'singulate mean age at marriage', after Hajnal (1953).

17 The age heaping index, which reveals rounding of ages, for the 671 females with known ages in 1816 was 326.1, as compared with 106.4 in 1833 and 90.5 in 1850; with no systematic rounding, the index would be 100. Shyrock, Siegel and Associates (1975, Vol. 1, pp. 205–06).

References

BLUM, J. (1957), 'The Rise of Serfdom in Eastern Europe', *American Historical Review*, **62**, 807–36.

BLUM, J. (1978), *The End of the Old Order in Rural Europe*, Princeton.

BRENNER, R. (1976), 'Agrarian Class Structure and Economic Development in Pre-Industrial Europe', *Past and Present*, **70**, 30–75.

BRENNER, R. (1985), 'The Agrarian Roots of European Capitalism', In T. H. Ashton and C. H. E. Philpin (eds.), *The Brenner Debate: Agrarian Class Structure and Economic Development in Pre-Industrial Europe*, New York, 213–27.

CHAYANOV, A. V. (1925), 'Peasant Farm Organization', In Daniel Thorner, Basile Kerblay and R. E. F. Smith (eds.), *A. V. Chayanov and the Theory of the Peasant Economy*, Homewood, Il., 1966, 29–269.

CLARK, G. (1987), 'Productivity Growth without Technical Change in European Agriculture before 1850', *Journal of Economic History*, **47**, 419–32.

COALE, A. J., B. A. ANDERSON and E. HARM (1979), *Human Fertility in Russia since the Nineteenth Century*, Princeton.

COALE, A. J. and S. C. WATKINS (eds.) (1986), *The Decline of Fertility in Europe*, Princeton.

CZAP, P. (1978), 'Marriage and the Peasant Joint Family in Russia', In David Ransel (ed.), *The Family in Imperial Russia*, Urbana, Il., 103–23.

CZAP, P. (1982), 'The Perennial Multiple Family Household, Mishino, Russia, 1782–1858', *Journal of Family History*, **7**, 5–26.

CZAP, P. (1983), ' "A Large Family: The Peasants' Greatest Wealth": Serf Households in Mishino, Russia, 1815–1858', In Richard Wall (ed.), *Family Forms in Historic Europe*, New York, 105–51.

DOMAR, E. (1970), 'The Causes of Slavery and Serfdom: A Hypothesis', *Journal of Economic History*, **30**, 18–32.

DOMAR, E. and M. J. MACHINA (1944), 'On the Profitability of Russian Serfdom', *Journal of Economic History*, **44**, 919–52.

DUNSDORFS, E. (1973), *Latvijas vesture 1710–1800 [History of Latvia 1710–1800]*, Stockholm.

DURRENBERGER, E. P. (1984), *Chayanov, Peasants, and Economic Anthropology*, New York.

EHMER, J. and M. MITTERAUER (1986), *Familienstrukturen und Arbeitsorganisation in landlichen Gesellschaften*, Vienna.

GUTMANN, M. P. (1988), *Toward the Modern Economy: Early Industry in Europe, 1500–1800*, Philadelphia.

GUTMANN, M. P. and R. LEBOUTTE (1984), 'Rethinking Protoindustrialism and the Family', *Journal of Interdisciplinary History*, **14**, 587–607.

HAJNAL (1953) in text

HAGEN, W. W. (1988), 'Capitalism and the Countryside in Early Modern Europe: Interpretations, Models, Debates', *Agricultural History*, **62**, 13–47.

HAREVEN, T. (1991), 'The History of the Family and the Complexity of Social Change', *American Historical Review*, **96**, 95–124.

HOCH, S. (1982), 'Serfs in Imperial Russia: Demographic Insights', *Journal of Interdisciplinary History*, **13**, 233–42.

HOCH, S. (1986), *Serfdom and Social Control in Russia: Petrovskoe, A Village in Tambrov*, Chicago.

KAHK, J. (1982), *Peasant and Lord in the Transition from Feudalism to Capitalism in the Baltics*, Tallin.

KINGSTON-MANN, E. (1991), 'Peasant Communes and Economic Innovation: A Preliminary Inquiry', In Ester Kingston-Mann and Timothy Mixter (eds.), *Peasant Economy, Culture, and Politics, 1800–1921*, Princeton, 23–51.

KOMLOS, J. (1985), 'The End of the Old Order in Rural Austria', *European Economic History*, **14**, 517.

KOMLOS, J. (1988), 'Agricultural Productivity in America and Eastern Europe: A Comment', *Journal of Economic History*, **48**, 657.

KULA, W. (1976), *An Economic Theory of the Feudal System: Towards a Model of the Polish Economy, 1500–1800*, trans. Lawrence Garner, London.

LASLETT, P. (1972), 'Introduction', In Peter Laslett and Richard Wall (eds.), *Household and Family in Past Time: Comparative Studies in the Size and Structure of the Domestic Group over the Last Three Centuries in England, France, Serbia, Japan and Colonial North America*, Cambridge, 1–89.

LEVINE, D. (1977), *Family Formation in the Age of Nascent Capitalism*, New York.

LIEPINA, D. (1962), *Agraras attiedcibas Rigas lauku novada vela feodalisma posma (17.–18.gs.) [Agrarian Relations in the Rural District of Riga in the Period of Late Feudalism (17–18th Centuries)]*, Riga.

LIEPINA, D. (1983), *Vidzemes zemnieki un muiza 18.gs. pirmaja puse [The Peasants and Estates of Livland in the First Half of the Nineteenth Century]*, Riga.

MEDICK, H. (1976), 'The Proto-Industrial Family Economy: The Structural Function of Household and Family', *Social History*, **1**, 291–315.

MENDELS, F. (1972), 'Protoindustrialization: The First Phase of the Industrial Process', *Journal of Economic History*, **42**, 241–61.

MIERINA, A. (1968), *Agraras attiecibas un zemnieku stavoklis Kurzeme 19. gs. II. pus [Agrarian Relations and the Condition of the Peasantry in Courland during the Second Half of the 19th Century]*, Riga.

PINKENHOF (1809a), Pinkenhof *Wackenbuch*, Central National Historical Archive, Riga, Latvia. Baltic Microfilms D91, Oekonomie Expedition d. Stadt-Cassa Collegiums IV E.1, s. 773–85, J. G. Herder Institute, Marburg a.d. Lahn, Germany.

PINKENHOF (1809b), 'Reglement Onera Publica welche die Baurenschaft . . .', Central National Historical Archive, Riga, Latvia. Baltic Microfilms D91, Oekonomie Expedition d. Stadt-Cassa Collegiums IV E.1, s. 809–17. J. G. Herder Institute, Marburg a.d. Lahn, Germany.

PINKENHOF (1816), Seventh Imperial Revision, Central National Historical Archive, Riga, Latvia. Baltic Microfilms, D112, Oekonomie-Expedition d. Stadt-Cassa Collegiums IV E.4, Revisionsliste Gut Pinkenhof, J. G. Herder Institute, Marburg a.d. Lahn, Germany.

PINKENHOF (1816), Seventh Imperial Revision, Central National Historical Archive, Riga, Latvia. Baltic Microfilms, D112 (1833), Eighth Imperial Revision, Central National Historical Archive, Riga, Latvia. Baltic Microfilms, D112, Oekonomie-Expedition d. Stadt-Cassa Collegiums IV. E.4, Revisionsliste Gut Pinkenhof, J. G. Herder Institute, Marburg a.d. Lahn, Germany.

PINKENHOF (1850), Ninth Imperial Revision, Central National Historical Archive, Riga, Latvia. Baltic Microfilms, D112, Oekonomie-Expedition d. Stadt-Cassa Collegiums IV. E.4, Revisionsliste Gut Pinkenhof, J. G. Herder Institute, Marburg a.d. Lahn, Germany.

PLAKANS, A. (1975), 'Seigneurial Authority and Peasant Family Life: The Baltic Area in the Eighteenth Century', *Journal of Interdisciplinary History*, **5**, 629–54.

PLAKANS, A. (1984), 'Serf Emancipation and the Changing Structure of Rural Domestic Groups in the Russian Baltic Provinces: Linden Estate, 1797–1858', In Robert McC. Netting and Eric J. Arnold (eds.), *Households: Comparative and Historical Studies of the Domestic Group*, Berkeley, 245–75.

PLAKANS, A. (1989), 'Stepping Down in Former Times: A Comparative Assessment of "Retirement" in Traditional Europe', In David I. Kertzer and K. Warner Schaie (eds.), *Age Structuring in Comparative Perspective*, Hillsdale, N.J., 175–95.

PLAKANS, A. and C. WETHERELL (1991), 'Fertility and Culture in Riga, 1867–1881', Paper presented at the annual meeting of the Social Science History Association, New Orleans, 31 October–2 November.

PLAKANS, A. and C. WETHERELL (1988), 'The Kinship Domain in an East European Peasant Community: Pinkenhof, 1833–1850', *American Historical Review*, **93**, 379.

PLAKANS, A. and C. WETHERELL (in press), 'Migration in the Later Years of Life in Traditional Europe', In David Kertzer (ed.), *Old Age in Past Times: The Historical Demography of Aging*, Berkeley.

POPKIN, S. L. (1979), *The Rational Peasant: The Political Economy of Rural Society in Vietnam*, Berkeley.

RUDOLPH, R. (1980), 'Family Structure and Protoindustrialization in Russia', *The Journal of Economic History*, **40**, 111–18.

RUDOLPH, R. (1985), 'Agricultural Structure and Proto-Industrialization in Russia: Economic Development with Unfree Labour', *Journal of Economic History*, **45**, 47–69.

SCHWABE, A. (1928), *Grundriss der Agrargeschichte Lettlands*, Riga.

SCOTT, J. C. (1976), *The Moral Economy of the Peasant: Rebellion and Subsistence in Southeast Asia*, New Haven.

SCOTT, J. C. (1985), *Weapons of the Weak: Everyday Forms of Peasant Resistance*, New Haven.

SCOTT, J. C. (1990), *Domination and the Arts of Resistance: Hidden Transcripts*, New Haven.

SHANIN, T. (ed.) (1987), *Peasants and Peasant Societies*, 2nd edn., Oxford.

SHANIN, T. (ed.) (1990), *Defining Peasants: Essays Concerning Rural Societies, Expolary Economies, and Learning from them in a Contemporary World*, Oxford.

SHYROCK, H. S., J. S. SIEGEL AND ASSOCIATES (1975), *The Methods and Materials of Demography*, 2 vols., Washington.

SOOM, A. (1987), *Der Herrenhof in Estland im 17. Jahrhundert*, Lund.

STRODS, H. (1984), *Zemnieku un muizu saimniecibu skaita un strukturas izmainas Latvija (18.gs.beigas–19.gs.I.puse)* [*Changes in the Number and the Structure of Landed Estates in Latvia from the end of the 18th Century to the First Half of the 19th Century*], Riga.

STRODS, H. (1987), *Kurzemes krona zemes un zemnieki 1795–1861* [*Crown Lands and Crown Peasants in Kurland 1795–1861*], Riga.

SVABE, A. (1958), *Latvijas vesture 1800–1914* [*History of Latvia 1800–1914*], Uppsala.

SVARANE, M. (1971), *Saimnieks un kalps Kurzeme un Vidzeme XIX.gs.vidu* [*Farmheads and Farmhands in Livland and Kurland in the Middle of the Nineteenth Century*], Riga.

TEMIN, P. (1981), 'Economic History in the 1980s: The Future of the New Economic History', *Journal of Interdisciplinary History*, **12**, 179–97.

THOMPSON, E. P. (1963), *The Making of the English Working Class*, New York.

THOMPSON, E. P. (1971), 'The Moral Economy of the English Crowd in the Eighteenth Century', *Past and Present*, **50**, 76–136.

TILLY, L. A. and J. W. SCOTT (1987), *Women, Work, and the Family*, New York.

WELLER, R. P. and S. E. GUGGENHEIM (1982), *Power and Protest in the Countryside: Studies of Rural Unrest in Asia, Europe, and Latin America*, Durham, N.C.

Chapter 11

FROM PEASANT SOCIETY TO CLASS SOCIETY: SOME ASPECTS OF FAMILY AND CLASS IN A NORTH-WEST GERMAN PROTOINDUSTRIAL PARISH, SEVENTEENTH–NINETEENTH CENTURIES

JÜRGEN SCHLUMBOHM

In early modern Europe, differently structured rural regions experienced quite diverse demographic and social development patterns.[1] In spite of an overall pattern of population growth, there were agrarian districts where the number of inhabitants stagnated, even as the number of peasant holdings remained constant. In Germany, examples can be found in the marshlands on the North Sea coast, where there were neither commons to be divided nor was agriculture much intensified (Norden, 1984; cf. Hinrichs et al., 1988, pp. 17–68).[2] Other rural areas experienced strong population growth, in particular those affected by protoindustrialization (Mendels, 1972; Kriedte et al., 1981, pp. 74–93). In regions of demographic growth, however, society did develop in divergent ways. Sometimes, holdings were increasingly fragmented with most families coming to own ever smaller plots of land. In a south-west German community, for example, the number of inhabitants trebled between the mid-seventeenth and late eighteenth centuries, but the degree of inequality in the distribution of property did not change (Sabean, 1990, pp. 40–41, 61–62, 454–58; cf. 256–57). In other places, holdings remained stable so that, with population growth, a new class of people without real property came into existence. In each of these cases, demographic patterns as well as family strategies must have been very different. This paper outlines a course of development of the last type mentioned.

THE OUTLINES: GROWING POPULATION, A FIXED NUMBER OF PEASANT HOLDINGS, AND THE RISE OF A PROPERTYLESS CLASS

The parish of Belm, which is the object of this study, comprised nine villages, each of which had a core of peasant holdings loosely grouped together,

1 References are kept to a minimum. Details and citations of sources can be found in Schlumbohm (1994).
2 Cf. Fauve-Chamoux (1981, esp. pp. 51–53) and Collomp (1988, esp. p. 70; 1983) for examples from southern France.

surrounded by one or more hamlets or dispersed farmsteads. Belm was situated between four and 12 kilometres north-east of the town of Osnabrück, and, until about 1800, it formed part of the prince-bishopric of Osnabrück, which in 1815 was incorporated into the kingdom of Hanover (see Fig. 1). The population of the parish trebled from the middle of the seventeenth century through to about 1830 (Fig. 2). Some 1,300 inhabitants were counted in 1651, while by 1833 the number had risen to about 3,850. After this date, massive emigration to North America (cf. Kamphoefner, 1987) brought about a degree of decline.

Concomitant with demographic growth in the parish, there was a considerable increase in the amount of land privately owned by peasants (Fig. 3). We cannot be certain whether the total area of peasant holdings really trebled between 1667 and 1723, because our source for 1667 is not completely reliable,

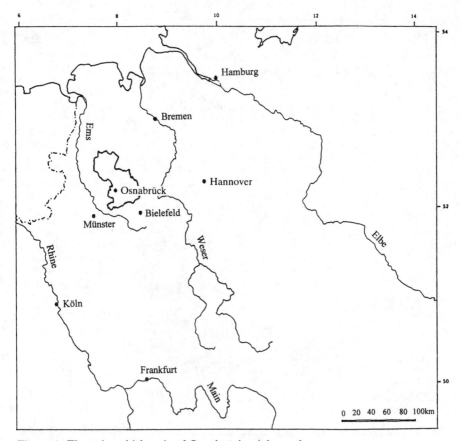

Figure 1: The prince-bishopric of Osnabrück, eighteenth century

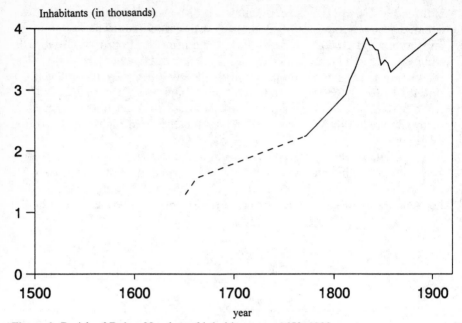

Figure 2: Parish of Belm: Number of inhabitants, *c.* 1650–1900

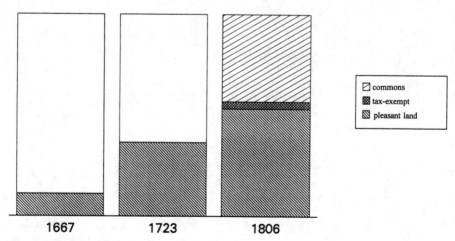

Figure 3: Parish of Belm: private peasant land as a percentage of total area, 1667, 1723 and 1806

but there must have been considerable gains. Nevertheless, only 36 per cent of the total area of the parish was privately owned by peasants in 1723. Part of the remainder belonged to tax-exempt holders like a *Rittergut* (manor) or the church (their share can be roughly quantified only for 1806). Much more than half of the total area was common land, most of which was covered by heath or coppice, with real woodland disappearing more and more due to over-use. The commons were important in complementing the peasants' private holdings: they served as pasture-ground, supplied sod as fertilizer, and produced wood for heating and building. Whenever peasants' private holdings grew, they inevitably did so at the expense of the commons. Between 1723 and the turn of the century, the total area held by individual peasants increased by nearly a half, but in 1806 the commons still accounted for 43 per cent of the total land. It was only in the course of agrarian reforms over the next thirty years that they were almost completely divided.

At first sight, all this looks like a rather smooth and balanced development. The expansion of peasants' private land more or less matched population growth. Private land would seem to be more intensively and efficiently used than common land, and agriculture would thus appear to have progressed as greater numbers had to be fed. As a matter of fact, however, this rural society neither developed calmly nor symmetrically.

From the mid-sixteenth through to the mid-nineteenth century, the total number of large peasant holdings (about 100 and called *Vollerben* and *Halberben* in this region) remained virtually unchanged (Fig. 4). The number of these holdings was neither increased by the overall extension of peasants' private land, nor decreased through fragmentation. Even more surprisingly, the number of small holdings (usually called *Erbkötter* and *Markkötter*) also stayed fairly constant, with only a minor increment in the period of the division of the commons.[3] This means that nearly all the land taken from the commons over these centuries was added to pre-existing holdings. Consequently, all the additional households formed in the course of population growth were landless households. Their share in the total number of households rose from one-third in the mid-seventeenth century to 69 per cent in 1812.

One important reason why social development took this course stemmed from the impartibility of peasant holdings. Though it is outside the scope of the present study to trace the origins of impartible inheritance in this region, it is clear that the manorial lords (*Grundherren*) and the princely authorities both showed a strong interest in impartibility. From their point of view, more rents and taxes could be collected from a limited number of large holdings than from a multitude of poor peasants. The *Grundherren* had a stronger position in the Osnabrück territory than in many other German regions west of the River Elbe, though in no village were all the peasants attached to any one lord. As a consequence of impartibility, the total number of holdings remained constant,

---

3 Cf. Mayhew (1973, pp. 122–30) for other German regions.

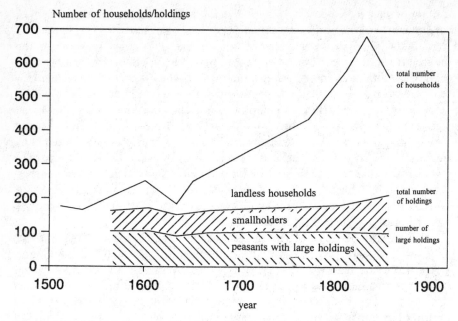

Figure 4: Parish of Belm: number of households and social stratification, *c.* 1500–1860

and, what is more, almost all the individual farms can be traced over many centuries. On an aggregate level, there was not much change from 1667 through to 1806 in the relative distribution of private peasant land between individual owners. In both eras, 50 per cent of the smallest farms accounted for only 12 per cent of private land, whereas 25 per cent of the largest farms comprised 50–60 per cent of the total. In the rank order by size of the individual holdings, too, change was rather insignificant, in spite of the expansion of the absolute size of each farm. In 1806, the large holdings (*Vollerben* and *Halberben*) had an average of 27.5 hectares with a maximum of 99 hectares, whereas small holdings averaged only 3.1 hectares.

Whether or not propertyless households should be allowed to settle was an issue fiercely contested both at the end of the sixteenth and early seventeenth centuries, and again in the mid-seventeenth century, after the end of the Thirty Years' War. The argument took place at the state level, with the prince-bishop, his officials, and the estates as participants. Perhaps even earlier the issue was discussed at the local level in the villages of the parish of Belm, where the local *Grundherren* and peasants assembled as *Holzgericht* ('court of the wood'). Again and again, peasants were forbidden to house propertyless households; exceptions were only allowed for those landless people born in that particular mark. Prince-bishop, estates and local lords were concerned that too many poor people might reduce surpluses and decrease tax and rent revenues. Equally, propertied peasants collectively appear to have worried that the commons would be over-utilized if propertyless people settled in their mark. Inevitably they would feed their geese or pigs in the commons and steal their heating there. Individually, however, some propertied peasants repeatedly took in landless people, in spite of all the decrees.

In the late seventeenth century, the whole argument came to an end. A modus vivendi was found with landless inhabitants. Neither were they expelled from local communities, nor were they allowed to found any additional small holdings. Instead, the *Heuerling* system was established, and, with several modifications, it survived well into the 1950s (Wrasmann, 1919–1921; for a neighbouring region see Mooser, 1984). Its basic features were that propertied peasants rented out to the *Heuerlinge* (derived from *heuern* = to hire) tiny pieces of land and a cottage or cabin. In turn, the *Heuerling* had to pay a money rent, and he and his wife were obliged to 'help' on the peasant's (his landlord's) farm, whenever they were called. Frequently, they were neither paid for their labour, nor was the number of days they had to work for their landlord ever specified. On the other hand, where their own resources were insufficient, they could count on some help from their landlord, for example, the use of his span of horses, for ploughing or other work that was impossible without draught animals. And though legally they had no right to the commons, they could, in fact, use them. Contracts with *Heuerlinge* were always for a limited period, usually for four years, but they could be renewed. With this system, peasants with large holdings found it advantageous to take in one or more landless households, and state authorities as well as lords came to see that propertyless people did not necessarily diminish the taxability of peasant holdings, but that even landless people could be taxed to some extent.

The total number of landless families would have remained within narrow limits, if the local economy had stayed purely agrarian. The expansion of the rural export linen industry, however, allowed the population to grow beyond these limits. There are indications as early as the late sixteenth and early seventeenth centuries that peasants in the Osnabrück countryside made linen not only for their own consumption, but for sale as well. After the Thirty Years' War ended, commercial linen production became more and more important. Increasingly, local cottage industry was integrated into the Atlantic economy. The coarse type of fabric was well known as 'osnaburg' in the Americas, and demand was enhanced by the rise of 'new colonialism' (Hobsbawm, 1954), for it was frequently used to clothe slaves. Compared with other European textile regions, the Osnabrück linen industry retained its unique character, until it fell into decay in the middle decades of the nineteenth century (Schlumbohm, 1982; 1983). In Osnabrück all the component stages of the production process were usually carried out within one household, from the planting of flax to weaving. Moreover, there were virtually no persons or households who specialized in linen production; instead it remained a second source of income for households which retained an agrarian base as well. Therefore, the manufacturing of textiles was fitted into the seasonal cycle of agrarian work, and spinning in particular, which was by far the most time-consuming part of the total production process, was done in winter. Unlike other protoindustrial regions, it was not just landless families and smallholders who were engaged in cottage industry, but, in the Osnabrück countryside, all classes of rural society participated. Households owning large farms even sold much larger quantities of linen than the *Heuerlinge* did, while smallholders occupied an intermediate position. In relation to merchant capital, all these rural producers were eager to preserve their independence and, with the support of the city- or state-controlled markets (*Legge*), the *Kaufsystem* was maintained (cf. Kriedte et al., 1981, pp. 98–101).

SOCIAL DIFFERENTIALS IN FAMILY FORMATION AND FERTILITY

The considerable population growth experienced by the parish of Belm from the mid-sixteenth through to the early nineteenth century was not due to immigration. On the contrary, there was some net emigration, even before massive migration to North America began in the 1830s. This means that local families raised increasing numbers of children who survived until adulthood and married. With every generation, the number of families became larger than it had been in their parents' time. Still, the demographic figures do not indicate a 'demographic hothouse', but allow for a steady population growth over generations.

From a European perspective, the mean age of women at first marriage was somewhat on the high side (cf. Wrigley and Schofield, 1983, p. 162; Flinn, 1981, pp. 125–26; Knodel, 1988, pp. 122–23): over the two centuries from 1651 through until 1860, the average marriage age of females was 26.5 years. From a peak of 28.4 at the end of the seventeenth century, there was a stepwise decline (interrupted, however, in the 1770s) to a minimum of 25.3 in the 1820s (Fig. 5).

The mean number of children born per marriage was not particularly high, either. An overall average of 5.5 children were born into completed first marriages. This figure climbed from 4.9 children around 1700 to 6.0 in the early nineteenth century. That these changes over time mirror the decreasing marriage age of women is what we expect when there is no deliberate fertility control in marriage. In fact, it appears that couples did not stop reproducing after they had reached a target number of children: on average, women who survived until the age of 45 had their last birth at 40.9. Interestingly, the mean age of women at the birth of their last child rose from 40.3 years around 1700 to 41.4 in the mid-nineteenth century even as the average age at marriage declined.

With rather an elevated age at first marriage for women and only a moderate number of births per marriage, we would not necessarily expect sustained population growth. Yet, one important reason that the population continued to grow was that marriage was almost universal. In spite of impartible inheri-

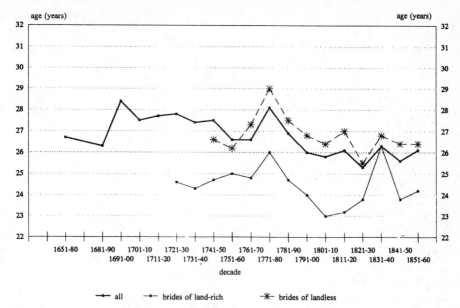

Figure 5: Parish of Belm: mean age of women at first marriage

tance, marriage was by no means limited to those who were able to acquire a holding, by marriage or inheritance. Due to the *Heuerling* system and the rise of the rural linen industry, men and women with no property rights in land were able to marry as well. A census from 1812 shows that, in a total population of almost 3,000, there were only 10 men and nine women aged 45 and more who had never been married (i.e. 3.5 per cent and 3.2 per cent, respectively, of all males and females in this age group).[4]

One needed to be single to be a servant in a household. But in the parish of Belm, the status of servant was just a phase in life. As the 1812 census reveals, the state of being a servant began at the age of 14—after confirmation as far as the Lutheran majority in the parish was concerned—and normally ended at the usual age of marriage. Among the 292 male and 312 female servants in 1812, half were less than 20 years of age (50 per cent and 53 per cent respectively), another 34 per cent and 40 per cent respectively were no more than 30 years old, and only two per cent of both sexes were 40 years or older.[5]

The *Heuerling* system provided a small piece of rented land, some employ-

---

4 Within the 'European marriage pattern', this is a very low ratio, cf. Schofield (1985), Weir (1984), Henry and Houdaille (1978–1979, part 1, esp. pp. 50f., 57f.), Imhof (1990, pp. 69f.), Ehmer (1991, p. 293, cf. pp. 123–27, 310–19).

5 In the 1812 census list, almost all unmarried people aged 14 or older were called 'servants', even those whom the family reconstitution proves to be the household head's own sons and daughters. In a census list of 1858, where this was not true, the age distribution of servants was not much different.

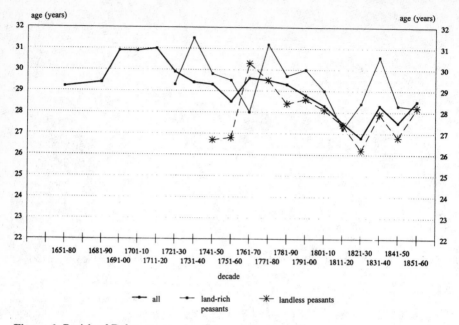

Figure 6: Parish of Belm: mean age of men at first marriage

ment as labourers, and a cottage to live in. The linen industry offered additional income, particularly in the slack season of agriculture. Consequently, almost everybody in the parish could marry. Moreover, propertyless men usually married at younger ages than landowning peasants did: males at first marriage averaged 27.9 years of age among the propertyless, 28.5 among peasants with small holdings, and 29.1 among peasants with large holdings (Fig. 6). Though there were two or three short periods of exception to this rule, it nevertheless provides a contrast to John Knodel's finding for a sample of German villages. In most of his villages, labourers used to marry later than well-to-do villagers (Knodel, 1988, pp. 130–36; cf. Schlumbohm, 1991). The contrast probably indicates that conditions for family formation in an agrarian/protoindustrial parish like Belm differed from those in other villages, as did social structure: in Belm the heirs of large holdings were likely to be obliged to postpone marriage until the impartible farm was transmitted to them. On the other hand, those who could not expect to inherit or marry into a farm found no impediment to a relatively early marriage.

In the absence of deliberate birth control among married couples, the wife's age at marriage had a much more significant impact on the number of children born than the husband's age. Social differences in terms of age at marriage were even clearer among women than they were among men, but they went in the opposite direction. Invariably over time, propertyless men married older women than propertied peasants did. Landless peasants' spouses had a mean age of 26.7; those of peasants with small holdings were on average 25.8; and those of the owners of large farms were 24.4 (Fig. 5). This means that there were marked differences in the age patterns of couples according to social status, and these differences persisted from the early eighteenth century (when sources first permit us to investigate them) well into the end of the period under study. With respect to first marriages of both partners, peasants with large holdings were usually 4.7 years older than their wives, peasants owning small farms 3.3, and landless peasants only 1.6.

Though the wives of landless peasants married at a later age than their propertied neighbours did, they neither extended child bearing to a later age nor showed any clear tendency to shorten the intervals between births. This means that they usually bore one child less than did the wives of peasants with large holdings. In first marriages unbroken by death before their 45th anniversary, the latter had a mean number of 6.4 children, while landless couples had 5.4.

Infant and child mortality was fairly low in Belm (cf. Imhof, 1990; Knodel, 1988, pp. 39–46; Wrigley and Schofield, 1983, pp. 175–80; Houdaille, 1984; Flinn, 1981, pp. 132–37). Between 1771 and 1858, 15 per cent died during the first year of life, and 70 per cent survived to the age of 15. There was no significant variation across class.

FAMILY AND SOCIAL (IM)MOBILITY

Which social positions were available for all these children? The fact that in this rural society, under manorial and state control, the number of holdings was strictly held constant was of paramount importance for the prospects of every generation. The course was set by the disproportion between the fixed number of propertied positions and the growing numbers of children.

Where could a peasant couple owning a large but impartible farm place their children? First of all, one child inherited the family farm. Local experts have pointed out that the custom varied from village to village or even from one farm to another regarding whether the oldest or the youngest son should be the privileged heir. Daughters, however, are traditionally thought to have had a chance to inherit their parents' holding only when there was no surviving male heir. A study of individual families reveals that local practice was more flexible than one might expect. There were some daughters to whom parents transmitted their farm, even though there were surviving sons. Those scholars who were close enough to the Ancien Régime were well aware 'that there is a great difference between local custom or common law (*Landgebrauch oder Gewohnheitsrecht*) and juridical theory: the former always adapt to the circumstances and combine seemingly contradictory principles, whereas the latter always seeks to implement uniform principles unconditionally' (Stüve, 1853–1882, vol. 2, p. 842). As elsewhere, choosing an heir and transmitting property did not derive from rules that were then executed, but were the result of strategies (Bourdieu, 1976).

Secondly, parents with a large holding could assume that, on average, one child could marry a partner of equal social standing. To the extent that sons were preferred as heirs, it would more likely be a daughter who left in order to be the mistress of an equal holding. Almost invariably, over time, the overwhelming majority of peasants with large holdings married daughters of their peers. Only one out of seven chose a spouse originating from a family of lower status, for a spouse's dowry depended on her (or his) parents' wealth, and a good dowry could more or less cover the compensation which the heir of the family farm owed to his (or her) siblings who were leaving it.

The gaps created by adult mortality made it possible for more than two children from families with a large farm to retain their parents' status. Death was of course an unpredictable event for individuals; still, it was part of the structure of life and marriage for the local population as a whole. Thus, in Belm, a widowed person was involved in 29 per cent of marriages. What enhanced the prospects of young men and women in the marriage market even more was the fact that 83 per cent of the widows and 87 per cent of widowers did not choose widowed, but unmarried partners, who were not much older than the mates of those who married for the first time. A young man marrying a widow with a large farm gave up his birthname and took over his wife's name or, more accurately, the name attached to the holding into which he married. His legal position depended on whether or not there were surviving children from the first marriage. If there were none, he took over the holding with full and permanent rights. As a corollary, the tie of consanguinity to earlier generations on this particular farm was frequently broken, in cases of this type. If there were children from an earlier marriage, however, the new husband was supposed to act as a temporary head of the holding just until the minor heir came of age. Nevertheless, he could count on an *Altenteil* (retirement portion) when this happened.

In spite of the additional prospects opened up by widows and widowers seeking to re-marry, parents with large holdings were unable to provide all their surviving children with social positions equivalent to their own. Some thus experienced downward mobility. For the generations marrying between 1771 and 1860, 37 per cent of the surviving children from large farms could secure the status their parents had had neither through inheritance nor marriage. Only 10 per cent were able to acquire some real property by marrying into a small farm; 27 per cent became *Heuerlinge* for the rest of their lives. Downward mobility was more extensive for daughters than for sons: 45 per cent of surviving daughters experienced declining fortunes while only 26 per cent of sons shared this fate. Downward mobility increased to some extent from the late eighteenth through to the early nineteenth century, even though there was some modest recovery after 1830. In this period, some of the disinherited children may have preferred emigration to America to becoming a *Heuerling* at home.

The children of couples with small holdings appear equally to have striven to maintain their status through marriage and inheritance. Not surprisingly, however, fewer of them were successful: more than four out of ten ended as *Heuerlinge*, i.e. almost one third of the surviving sons and more than half the daughters. On the other hand, smallholders' daughters had a 1:16 chance of marrying into a large farm, a prospect that was almost non-existent for their brothers.

In spite of the downward mobility experienced by some of the propertied peasants' children, the great majority of the *Heuerlinge* were already born into landless families by the last third of the eighteenth century. This was true of almost seven out of eight males; and more than four-fifths of propertyless men married daughters from families of equal standing. For both sexes, the trend toward self-recruitment within the landless class continued to increase. The proportion was 81 per cent for males in the generation married in the late eighteenth century and rose to 90 per cent by the mid-nineteenth century; for females it grew from 74 per cent to 88 per cent.

PROPERTIED AND PROPERTYLESS FAMILIES TIED TOGETHER: THE STRUCTURE OF PEASANT HOLDINGS

On each of the large holdings, the peasant owner lived in the main house with his family and servants. There was space enough for one or more cottages on the farmstead, or not too far from it, since the farmhouses were not densely concentrated, but only loosely grouped as villages, or even dispersed. The propertyless families lived in these cottages. A census in 1772 indicates that the mean number of landless households on a large holding was two; by 1858 it amounted to 2.8, and the maximum was nine. With a growing population, the peasant owners felt unable to build a new cottage or cabin for every additional household which they accepted as a lessee on their holding. In 1772, 72 per cent of the propertyless households shared a house and fireplace with another one. Therefore, a large holding was actually a group of households linked to a particular farm, and it housed a considerable number of people. In 1772, the mean number of inhabitants was 16; by 1858 it had risen to 23, and the maximum was 56 persons.

The household of a peasant owning a large farm and the household of a *Heuerling* were quite different in size and composition. In 1772, the mean household size for peasants with large holdings was more than double that of landless families (8.4 and 4.0 persons, respectively). By 1858, propertyless households had grown to 5.1 persons, whereas those of the owners of large farms remained constant in size (8.5). The 1772 census reveals that servants were the major reason for this difference. Peasants on a large holding had an average of 2.5 servants, half male and half female, whereas *Heuerlinge*, with very few exceptions, had no servants at all. On large farms, the owner and his family usually could not perform all the tasks on their own. Some additional labour was needed throughout the year. Such labour was best taken as servants into the peasant-owner's household. Seasonal peaks, however, were met in a much more cost-efficient way by calling upon the *Heuerlinge* and their wives who lived on the holding.

Secondary reasons for the smaller size of propertyless households derived from the smaller number of sons and daughters, and, in 1772, though not in 1858, the rare occurrence of kin. Since propertyless families usually could neither employ nor feed more than one adult male and female, virtually all their sons and the great majority of their daughters left home, beginning at the age of 14, to be servants in propertied households. One son or daughter aged 14 years or older, however, continued to live in an average peasant family with a large holding. In addition, the average size of a peasant household with a large amount of property was increased by almost one person (0.7 in 1772) by fathers, mothers or other relatives of the household head or his wife. In 1772, such extended relationships rarely existed in propertyless households (0.2 persons per household).

Smallholders' mean household size stayed between that of the propertyless and that of the holders of large farms, though it was much nearer to the former (5.0 persons per household in 1772, and 5.9 in 1858). Only some had an additional household of landless people on their farm, and usually it was not a large family. Thus, the mean number of persons living on a small farm was 6.4 in 1772 and 7.9 in 1858.

The propertied peasant and the propertyless households on a particular holding were certainly tied together by economic links. The *Heuerling* needed a cottage to live in, a piece of land to rent, and periodically the use of a span of horses. The peasant in turn wanted the rent and the labour of the *Heuerling* man and woman in peak periods. In addition to economic relations, however, were there other ties as well that bound the *Heuerlinge* and their particular peasant landlord together? It is invariably emphasized in local accounts that the landless people were essentially descendants of propertied peasant families. Growing self-recruitment among the propertyless families, however, implies that kinship relations of this kind must have become more and more remote. By linking the data of the 1858 census to family reconstitution, we can analyse fairly precisely questions of this type at the close of our period. We were able to ascertain for more than half of household heads and their wives, whether their fathers had been landless or holders of large or small farms.

In this sample, 91 per cent of landless male household heads had a father who had also been propertyless. Only six per cent were sons of a smallholder, and three per cent of a holder of a large farm. The overwhelming majority of women married to landless men were also from propertyless families (83 per cent). Among them, however, 10 per cent and seven per cent respectively had a father with a large or a small holding. By 1858, downward social mobility had thus affected a portion of the sons and daughters from propertied families. Among the heads of households and housewives who stemmed from families with large holdings, 81 per cent of the males, but only 58 per cent of the females, held large farms in 1858. Seven per cent of the males and 30 per cent of the females were propertyless, whereas 12 per cent of both sexes were smallholders. Among smallholders' descendants, 28 per cent of the males and 45 per cent of the females did not hold any real estate.

Did these disinherited sons and daughters of propertied parents stay as *Heuerlinge* on the holding from which they originated? In this case, even if they only made up a minority among the totality of landless households, they might possibly have been a stabilizing element in the overall relations between landholders and landless people. For, if one of the *Heuerlinge* on a particular farm was his landlord's brother or brother-in-law, these 'kin relationships' could 'colour other ties' between the landed and the landless families, and thus help to prevent both parties from developing 'the consciousness of class membership' (Mintz, 1973/74b, pp. 305, 319; cf. Mintz, 1973/74a, esp. p. 101). Our study reveals, however, that this can hardly have been the case in Belm by the mid-nineteenth century. The sons and daughters of propertied peasants were a tiny minority in the landless population as a whole, and even among them virtually all the smallholders' offspring had had to leave their native farm, which often was just not big enough to house more than one family. Moreover, half the disinherited sons and daughters of large property holders had left their parents' farm and were *Heuerlinge* elsewhere in the parish. Not one case could be found where a disinherited descendant of a propertied family lived as a *Heuerling* on a holding which one of his or her more fortunate siblings had acquired through marriage. This means that only in one out of ten large holdings was there a landless household whose head or housewife was an offspring of the family owning that particular farm. Ties of close consanguinity were thus a rare exception between a peasant owner and the *Heuerlinge* on his holding.

Among those born into the landless class, on the other hand, kinship ties appear to have been relevant. They may well have helped an individual to find a position as a *Heuerling*, with one sibling pulling another one behind him (or her). If we consider all groups of siblings who were heads or housewives of landless households in 1858, we find that, almost in one out of four cases, siblings were co-*Heuerlinge* on the same holding. Across the generations, the kinship network was equally relevant. Through it, aged people or young couples often found a place to live, particularly in difficult periods. In contradistinction to our findings in 1772, landless households in 1858 had a remarkable number of married or widowed lodgers. Family reconstitution reveals what the census list itself frequently conceals: with rare exceptions, these married and widowed lodgers were close kin of the head or housewife, usually either parents or sons/daughters. In addition, closer analysis shows that, in some cases, they were not biological parents or children but step-parents or step-children, or even a deceased first spouse's parent who continued to live with a remarried son- or daughter-in-law. In spite of their small dwellings and very limited resources, the percentage of landless households which accommodated one or more married or widowed relatives was 19 per cent. That is no less than with households owning large farms! In this rural society, the poor were *not* 'poor in relatives' (Bourdieu, 1976, p. 121). On the contrary, relations between generations appear to have been as strong in those families which had no real property to transmit, as they were in those which had. To be landless did not mean to be without kin.[6]

*   *   *   *   *

The way in which local landed and landless peasants organized their holdings, households and families should be viewed not only as a reaction necessitated by exogenous economic and social change, but as an active contribution to shaping demographic and social development as well. Even the way in which class was perceived and acted upon by, or hidden from, people in the past might have been influenced by the micro-structures of holdings, households, and families. Comparing our case with a seemingly remote counterpart may help to illuminate this point. On the Greek island of Karpathos, as analysed by the French anthropologist Bernard Vernier (1984), inheritance was equally impartible in the nineteenth and early twentieth centuries. Economic and ecological conditions were so poor, however, that the disinherited children usually had no means to form a household and marry. Instead, they stayed as celibate labourers in their more fortunate siblings' families. The exploited group was thus deprived of the chance to reproduce itself biologically, but they continued to think of themselves as part of the property-owning family.

In our case from early modern north-western Germany, the simultaneous development of the agrarian system and of the cottage linen industry made it possible for propertyless people to marry and have families. As a consequence, a class of rural proletarians came into existence, who comprised more than two-thirds of all households in the early nineteenth century. But these proletarians were not set free and not completely opposed to propertied peasants (cf. Mooser, 1984, pp. 255–66, 350–55). The specific agrarian social system of the region, under the fairly close control of manorial lords, estates and state officials, was not dissolved by protoindustrialization, but merely reshaped by it. The seasonal character of the linen industry, with its lack of a social division of labour, was so closely interwoven into the agrarian system that the holders of real property remained unchallenged in their predominance. What is more, they came to prevail even in the field of rural industry. Thus, unlike many other protoindustrial regions (Kriedte et al., 1981, pp. 64–73; Braun, 1990), the landless class did not become more or less emancipated from the hegemony of propertied peasants. Instead, they were divided, with a small

---

6 This finding is at odds with the view that 'in the absence of property there is little tendency to develop extended kin ties' (Sabean, 1976, p. 98). Cf. Sabean, 1990, p. 35 for a village in south-west Germany: 'Respect was due to parents because they were the source of wealth, and in terms of expressed value at least, the amount of effort . . . to be expended was directly proportional to the amount of property passed on'.

group of propertyless households on each large farm. To be sure, they had a household and an economy of their own. But their economy was so closely bound up with that of the peasant owner that it was only half-independent. Every time the holder of the farm called his *Heuerlinge* in for labour, he forced them to postpone work on their own rented field. And some work in their field could not be done without the landlord's span.

By the middle decades of the nineteenth century, protoindustrial conditions had begun to deteriorate, and the division of the commons had taken away from the *Heuerlinge* an important part of the agrarian resources. By this period, ties of close consanguinity between landless and propertied families were a rare exception. On the other hand, kin relations between propertyless families appear to have been intensified. Then there are some indications that the *Heuerlinge* began to think of themselves as a class different from, and exploited by, property-owning peasants. A farewell letter from a *Heuerling* emigrating from Belm to America in 1833 has survived, in which he tried to explain to a local state official:

. . . the whole nature of the thing, how the propertied peasants deal with the *Heuerlinge*. First, one must give them the burdensome money rents for the poor soil. Secondly, one must help them with so much work that one cannot stand it and must do one's own work at night . . . If the poor *Heuerling* wants to earn a day's pay: Oh no, you shall help me, or leave my cottage right now. And thus, the whole design is that almost all the *Heuerlinge* are poor and are bound to proceed from Germany into other countries. If you cannot change that, things will look bad . . . The propertied peasants devour the *Heuerlinge* . . .

In 1848, in addition to the choice of either complying with conditions as they were or emigrating to America, a third alternative appeared to emerge. In some parishes of the Osnabrück region, the *Heuerlinge* formed associations or rioted in order to force propertied peasants and the government to improve their situation.

References

BOURDIEU, P. (1976), 'Marriage Strategies as Strategies of Social Reproduction', In Robert Forster and Orest Ranum (eds.), *Family and Society*, Baltimore, 117–44.

BRAUN, R. (1990), *Industrialization and Everyday Life*, Cambridge.

COLLOMP, A. (1983), *La maison du père: Famille et village en Haute-Provence aux 17e et 18e siècles*, Paris.

COLLOMP, A. (1988), 'From Stem Family to Nuclear Family: Changes in the Coresident Domestic Group in Haute Provence between the End of the 18th and the Middle of the 19th Centuries', *Continuity and Change*, 3, 65–81.

EHMER, J. (1991), *Heiratsverhalten, Sozialstruktur, ökonomischer Wandel: England und Mitteleuropa in der Formationsperiode des Kapitalismus*, Göttingen.

FAUVE-CHAMOUX, A. (1981), 'Population et famille dans les Hautes Pyrénées aux 18e–20e siècles: L'exemple d'Esparros', In Celina Bobinska and Joseph Goy (eds.), *Les Pyrénées et les Carpates, 16e–20e siècles. Recherches franco-polonaises comparées*, Warsaw, 43–63.

FLINN, M. W. (1981), *The European Demographic System 1500–1820*, Brighton.

HENRY, L. and J. HOUDAILLE (1978–1979), 'Célibat et âge au mariage aux 18e et 19e siècles en France', part 1: *Population*, 33, 43–84; part 2: *Population*, 34, 403–42.

HINRICHS, E., R. KRÄMER and C. REINDERS (1988), *Die Wirtschaft des Landes Oldenburg in vor-industrieller Zeit: Eine regionalgeschichtliche Dokumentation für die Zeit von 1700 bis 1850*, Oldenburg.

HOBSBAWM, E. J. (1954), 'The General Crisis of the European Economy in the 17th Century', part 1: *Past and Present*, 5, 33–53; part 2: *Past and Present*, 6, 44–65.

HOUDAILLE, J. (1984), 'La mortalité des enfants dans la France rurale de 1690 à 1779', *Population*, 39, 37–106.

IMHOF, A. E. (1990), *Life Expectancies in Germany from the 17th to the 19th Century*, Weinheim.

KAMPHOEFNER, W. D. (1987), *The Westfalians: From Germany to Missouri*, Princeton, N.J.

KNODEL, J. E. (1988), *Demographic Behavior in the Past. A Study of Fourteen German Village Populations in the 18th and 19th Centuries*, Cambridge.

KRIEDTE, P., H. MEDICK and J. SCHLUMBOHM (1981), *Industrialization before Industrialization: Rural Industry in the Genesis of Capitalism*, Cambridge.

MAYHEW, A. (1973), *Rural Settlement and Farming in Germany*, London.

MENDELS, F. F. (1972), 'Protoindustrialization: The First Phase of the Industrialization Process', *Journal of Economic History*, 32, 241–61.

MINTZ, S. W. (1973/74a), 'A Note on the Definition of Peasantries', *The Journal of Peasant Studies*, 1, 92–106.

MINTZ, S. W. (1973/74b), 'The Rural Proletariat and the Problem of Rural Proletarian Consciousness', *The Journal of Peasant Studies*, 1, 291–325.

MOOSER, J. (1984), *Ländliche Klassengesellschaft 1770–1848: Bauern und Unterschichten, Landwirtschaft und Gewerbe im östlichen Westfalen*, Göttingen.

NORDEN, W. (1984), *Eine Bevölkerung in der Krise: Historisch-demographische Untersuchungen zur Biographie einer norddeutschen Küstenregion, Butjadingen 1600–1850*, Hildesheim.

SABEAN, D. (1976), 'Aspects of Kinship Behaviour and Property in Rural Western Europe before 1800', In Jack Goody, Joan Thirsk and E. P. Thompson (eds.), *Family and Inheritance: Rural Society in Western Europe, 1200–1800*, Cambridge, 96–111.

SABEAN, D. (1990), *Property, Production, and Family in Neckarhausen, 1700–1870*, Cambridge.

SCHLUMBOHM, J. (1982), 'Agrarische Besitzklassen und gewerbliche Produktionsverhältnisse: Großbauern, Kleinbesitzer und Landlose als Leinenproduzenten im Umland von Osnabrück und Bielefeld während des frühen 19. Jahrhunderts', In *Mentalitäten und Lebensverhältnisse. Rudolf Vierhaus zum 60. Geburtstag*, Göttingen, 315–34. (French version: 1984, 'Propriété foncière et production des toiles dans les campagnes environnant Osnabrück et Bielefeld au début du 19e siècle', In Paul Delsalle (ed.), *L'industrie textile en Europe du Nord aux 18e et 19e siècles. Actes du colloque Tourcoing 17/18 février 1983*, Tourcoing, 51–74.)

SCHLUMBOHM, J. (1983), 'Seasonal Fluctuations and Social Division of Labour: Rural Linen Production in the Osnabrück and Bielefeld Regions and the Urban Woollen Industry in the Niederlausitz, c. 1770–c. 1850', In Maxine Berg, Pat Hudson and Michael Sonenscher (eds.), *Manufacture in Town and Country before the Factory*, Cambridge, 92–123.

SCHLUMBOHM, J. (1991), 'Social Differences in Age at Marriage: Examples from Rural Germany during the 18th and 19th Centuries', In *Historiens et populations. Liber amicorum Etienne Hélin*, Louvain-la-Neuve, 593–607.

SCHLUMBOHM, J. (1994), *Lebensläufe, Familien, Höfe: Die Bauern und Heuerleute des Osnabrückischen Kirchspiels Belm in proto-industrieller Zeit, 1650–1860*, Göttingen.

SCHOFIELD, R. (1985), 'English Marriage Patterns Revisited', *Journal of Family History*, **10**, 2–20.

STÜVE, [JOHANN] C[ARL BERTRAM] (1853–1882), *Geschichte des Hochstifts Osnabrück*, 3 vols., Osnabrück and Jena.

VERNIER, B. (1984), 'Putting Kin and Kinship to Good Use: The Circulation of Goods, Labour, and Names on Karpathos (Greece)', In Hans Medick and David W. Sabean (eds.), *Interest and Emotion: Essays on the Study of Family and Kinship*, Cambridge, 28–76.

WEIR, D. R. (1984), 'Rather Never than Late: Celibacy and Age at Marriage in English Cohort Fertility, 1541–1871', *Journal of Family History*, **9**, 340–54.

WRASMANN, A. (1919–1921), 'Das Heuerlingswesen im Fürstentum Osnabrück', part 1: *Mitteilungen des Vereins für Geschichte und Landeskunde von Osnabrück*, **42**, 53–171; part 2: *Mitteilungen des Vereins für Geschichte und Landeskunde von Osnabrück*, **44**, 1–154.

WRIGLEY, E. A. and R. S. SCHOFIELD (1983), 'English Population History from Family Reconstitution: Summary Results 1600–1799', *Population Studies*, **37**, 157–84.

Chapter 12

WOMANHOOD AND MOTHERHOOD: THE ROUEN MANUFACTURING COMMUNITY, WOMEN WORKERS, AND THE FRENCH FACTORY ACTS

GAY L. GULLICKSON

Generally speaking, in eighteenth-century France, class determined whether one worked, while age and sex determined the kind of work one did. Noble men and women, not to mention noble children, by definition, did not work with their hands, and for social purposes did not work at all, although they might direct the work of others. Men, women and children in peasant, artisan and merchant families, in contrast, survived by producing crops, goods and services for sale and for the family's consumption. A sexual division of labour determined who did what tasks, but no one thought work was inappropriate or unnatural for the women and children in these families. In actuality, families might not abide by the established sexual divisions of labour in times of emergency or excessive labour demand, but these were private rather than public crossings of gender lines and did not effectively challenge or alter accepted norms of male and female behaviour.[1]

In the nineteenth century, as workers and employers grappled with the practical implications of mechanization for the organization of production and family life, the established definitions of men's and women's work crumbled, and what it meant to be a woman or a man or a child became newly problematic. New conceptualizations of gender and age that would have profound effects on the lives of women and children arose, not neatly but piecemeal, and often with unanticipated consequences. The goal of this article is to examine the evolution of these new conceptualizations of womanhood and childhood in the nineteenth-century Rouen manufacturing community. The thinking of the Rouen manufacturers is revealed in their responses to government proposals to regulate child labour in 1837 and 1867.

The question of protective legislation was a serious one for Rouen manufacturers since it involved issues not only of gender and childhood, but also of free enterprise, parental authority, and national defence. Structured by

---

1 For a more detailed discussion of women's and children's pre-industrial work in agriculture, cottage industry and artisan crafts in France, see Hufton (1975), Tilly and Scott (1978), Gullickson (1986), Segalen (1980), Lehning (1980), Duby and Wallon (1975–76), Gillis (1981), and Heywood (1988).

the questions and proposals from the national government, the Rouen reports of 1837 and 1867 do not lay out manufacturers' conceptions of age and gender systematically. They do reveal, however, that childhood and womanhood were intimately linked concepts, that manufacturers increasingly conceived of men and women as differing fundamentally and naturally, and that the practical consequences of the 1841 child labour law, rather than any coherent notions about woman's nature, provoked them to argue for restrictions on women's as well as children's labour.

Childhood was not a clearly defined concept in France before the nineteenth century. Instead, it posed a kind of Wittgensteinian problem. Childhood was a sensible concept with a clear beginning (as long as one included infancy in the concept of childhood), but it did not have such a clear end point, nor was adolescence a clearly defined stage of development. There was very little sense that it was appropriate to treat children differently from adults (or girls differently from boys), and since they began to work at young ages, children's lives were much like those of their parents. One of the interesting aspects of the child-labour legislation is that it established boundaries and stages of childhood and created new gender distinctions for the treatment of adult workers.

The impact of the 1841 law on conceptualizations of age and gender has generally gone unexamined by historians because they have divided the studies of protective legislation into two subfields. The early period (ending in 1874) has fallen under the purview of scholars interested in the history of childhood and the intervention of the state into previously private, family decisions, while the broader protective legislation that began to be passed in the 1890s has been examined by scholars interested in the history of women. Noteworthy among the studies that approach the issue from the perspective of children are recent studies by Lee Shai Weissbach, Katherine Lynch, and Colin Heywood, which have contributed significantly to our knowledge of the lives of children, the goals and assumptions of reformers, and the impact of industrialization on middle-class attitudes toward the family, children, and the role of government in society. Similarly, Mary Lynn Stewart's research has added greatly to our understanding of the impact of the later legislation on women (Weissbach, 1989; Lynch, 1988; Heywood, 1988; Stewart, 1989; [Stewart] McDougall, 1983; 1984). When one contrasts the 1837 and 1867 debates on protective legislation, one sees, however, that the passage of the 1841 law on child labour played a central role in altering the Rouen manufacturers' attitudes toward women's work, and led them to a new identification of womanhood with motherhood.

THE CONTEXT: THE ROUEN TEXTILE INDUSTRY

In the early nineteenth century, Rouen was the centre of a large semi-rural, semi-urban textile industry. Spinning mills stretched down the roads leading out of (or into, depending on one's perspective) the city. Weaving remained largely a putting-out industry, but a few workshops (soon to be factories) with mechanical looms appeared in the late 1830s. Like the spinning mills, they lined the roads leading to the old city of Rouen, as did the third branch of the textile industry, the *fabriques d'Indiennes* that dyed and printed calico.

The best mid-nineteenth-century employment figures for the Rouen textile industry come from a *statistique* on manufacturing compiled for the Seine-Inférieure in 1847–1848 (AN F^{12}4476C; ADSM 6M1100).[2] For the purpose of determining the composition of the textile labour force in the early nineteenth century, this *statistique* has several shortcomings. In the first place, the report is in very poor condition. Edges and sometimes crucial labels have crumbled, complicating the historian's task of reading, much less interpreting, the document. Secondly, information is not reported systematically. Occasionally, figures are broken down by *arrondissement*, sometimes two or more *arrondissements* are recorded together, and sometimes a column of figures is added to give a total for the department, with no indication as to which figures pertain to which *arrondissement*.

For purposes of understanding the situation in 1837, when the first debate on child labour took place in Rouen, the *statistique* was also compiled a decade too late. During that decade, the number of textile factories increased as did the total number of employees. The number of female employees particularly increased, since they dominated the expanding factory weaving labour force. On the other hand, the number of children working in mills may have decreased during the decade, as a result of the 1841 law which removed children under the age of eight from large factories using power machinery. Since this seems to be the one provision of the law to which employers paid some attention, we have to assume that the number of young children employed in spinning mills was higher in 1837 than in 1847 (AN F^{1}24713). Finally, the *statistique* defines the category of *enfant* as younger than sixteen, but that definition itself is at least partially the result of the 1841 legislation which established 16 as the age at which a worker became an adult, rather than a culturally significant line of demarcation between childhood and adulthood. Despite these drawbacks, the *statistique* provides us with the best indication we have of the gender and age composition of the textile industry in and around Rouen in the mid-nineteenth century.

The *statistique* reveals that child labour was far from a remote issue for the employers of the Rouen, Dieppe and Le Havre textile industries. In 1847, 7,843 children under the age of 16 worked in the three mechanized branches of the textile industry (cotton spinning, mechanical weaving, and calico printing) in villages and cities of the triangle formed by the three cities (AN F^{12}4476C). The spinning industry alone employed 5,596 of these children. An even larger

---

2 By 1847 there were 293 spinning mills employing 17,448 workers and 39 textile (weaving) factories employing 5,603 workers in the Seine-Inférieure. Most weavers (109,542) continued to work at home with handlooms.

Table 1: *The mechanized textile industry – employment figures for the arrondissements of Rouen, Dieppe and Le Havre, 1847–1848**

	Men		Women		Children†		Total	
Industry	No.	%	No.	%	No.	%	No.	%
Cotton spinning	6,224	36	5,628	32	5,596	32	17,448	100
Calico printing	3,880	55	1,180	17	1,940	28	7,000	100
Mechanized weaving	1,390	25	3,906	70	307	5	5,603	100
Total	11,494	38	10,714	36	7,843	26	30,051	100

*Aged 8 to 16 years.
†Figures for Yvetot, the fourth *arrondissement* of the Seine Inférieure, are not included. Sixty-three per cent of the mechanical looms in these three *arrondissements* were in Rouen.
Source: ADSM 6M1100, AN F¹²4476C.

number of children and adults worked in the cottage textile industry, but the traditional nature of their work and workplace meant that they would receive no attention from the major reformers and employers of the region (see Table 1).

CHILD LABOUR AND THE REFORMERS

The employment of children and women in the production of cotton fabric was not new in the nineteenth century. In regions like the Pays de Caux, north of Rouen, they had worked for textile merchants who put work out into the countryside for a century before the first spinning machines were built (Gullickson, 1986, pp. 68–128). What *was* new in the nineteenth century was factory work, which, among other things, made textile workers far more visible than they had been before. While increased visibility provoked little concern for adult workers, the sight of thin, ragged children trooping back and forth to the factories, plus studies that raised fears about the fitness of factory workers for army service, gradually provoked humanitarian and practical concerns about child labour in one European country after another.

First to industrialize, Britain was also the first to investigate factory work conditions and to pass protective laws. By the mid-1830s, five factory acts had been passed (1802, 1819, 1825, 1831, and 1833), all of which applied only to children (Hutchins and Harrison, 1926, rpr. 1969, pp. 14–58). Significant in their own right as the first assumption of responsibility for the health and morality of the working classes by a government (Pinchbeck and Hewitt, 1973, p. 347), the British laws also served as a model for legislation in Europe and America (AN F¹²24705; Gueneau, 1927, p. 422; *Le travail et l'enfant*, 1978, pp. 6–7; Fohlen, 1967, pp. 50–51).

By 1833 the prime characteristics of the English factory acts were: 1) their

Table 2: *Textile employees, Rouen, 1855*

| | Men | | Women | | Children | | Total | |
Industry	No.	%	No.	%	No.	%	No.	%
Spinning	3,500	47	2,500	33	1,500	20	7,500	100
Dyeing and finishing	2,500	56	500	11	1,500	33	4,500	100
Weaving*	10,000	61	4,700	28	1,800	11	16,500	100
Total	16,000	57	7,700	27	4,800	17	28,500	100

*Includes hand weaving and bobbin winding as well as mechanical weaving.
Note: Total population 100,265.
Source: ADSM 6M1103 — Renseignements statistiques sur la Commune de Rouen, 1855.

confinement to textile factories powered by water or steam;[3] 2) the establishment of nine as the minimum age for employment in such factories; 3) the establishment of maximum hours based on two age categories (nine hours for ages nine to 13; 12 hours for ages 13 to 18); 4) the requiring of schooling for children aged under 13; 5) the prohibition of night work for children under 18; 6) the mandating of meal breaks of one-and-a-half hours; 7) provisions for the whitewashing of factories; and 8) the provision of inspectors to enforce the laws. There were no restrictions for women factory workers or for children employed outside textile mills, despite testimony before various parliamentary commissions that children working in other industries, and especially those working in small workshops, were subjected to far worse conditions than those employed in the mills. Massachusetts passed legislation based on the British model in 1836 and 1838, Prussia and Austria in 1839, Bavaria and Baden in 1840, and France in 1841 (Hutchins and Harrison, 1926, rpr. 1969, pp. 14–58).

Pushed by the Mulhouse Industrial Society, which took a public stand supporting a child-labour law in 1833,[4] and the Académie des sciences morales et politiques' commissioning of the physician Louis-René Villermé to investigate the physical and moral condition of French workers in 1835 (Gueneau, 1927, p. 432; Villermé, 1840),[5] the July Monarchy began to believe a child-

3 The acts covered cotton, woollen, worsted, hemp, flax, tow, linen and silk mills. Children in lace-making and other textile-related industries like calico printing, bleaching and dyeing were not protected until the 1860s (Hutchins and Harrison, 1926, rpr. 1969, pp. 120–49).

4 For a detailed account of the Mulhouse Industrial Society's role in the passage of a child-labour law in France, see Weissbach, 1989, pp. 23–38, 50, 71.

5 Published in 1839 and 1840, Villermé's report presented data on working conditions, wages, and workers' living conditions in the cotton, wool, and silk industries in northern France, argued strenuously for protective legislation, called for a minimum age of 10 or 11 for entry into a mill, and played a role in the passage of the first child-labour legislation in France in 1841. For further information about Villermé's report, see Lynch, 1988, pp. 7, 191–92; Weissbach, 1989, pp. 35–36, 48–49.

labour law might be desirable, and set out to determine the conditions under which children were working and the restrictions for which it could garner support. In 1837, the Chamber of Peers commissioned the Bureau of Manufacturers to solicit opinions from local Chambers of Commerce, and other manufacturing and business organizations. The Bureau circulated a questionnaire, and national debate about the desirability of a child-labour law began (AN F^{12}4705).

When the French government solicited opinions about protective legislation, it had two conflicting interests. On the one hand, it was genuinely worried about the effects of factory labour on young children. On the other, it was hesitant to restrict the rights of fathers over their children, and it did not want to pass any legislation that would interfere with the ability of industry to make a profit, or with the right of older children (adolescents) to sell their labour (for more details, see Weissbach, 1989, p. 37).

The concern with children's welfare was largely, but not entirely, humanitarian. Reformers had repeatedly decried what they believed was the exposure of children to the sordid conversations of adults in the factory, the seduction of young girls by male workers and employers, the inability of factory children to attend school, and the harmful physical effects of hard labour on young children.[6] Echoing these fears, the 1837 questionnaire worried that factory children were not learning to read and write, were being weakened in body and spirit, and were being exposed in factories to 'lessons of a precocious immorality' (AN F^{12}4705).

Embedded in this humanitarian concern, however, was anxiety about the morality of the working class and the security of France. Recent efforts to enlist soldiers had resulted in the discovery that a higher percentage of recruits from industrial departments was physically unfit for military service than was the case for most rural departments. For France as a whole, the rejection rate was forty-six per cent, but for the highly-industrialized Seine-Inférieure, fifty-six per cent of the young men called for physicals were rejected for being too short, too weak, or disabled, and in the city of Rouen, sixty-three per cent were rejected. This development left the leaders of the July Monarchy worrying that the nation might not be able to defend itself against attack.[7] The

6 Reformers disagreed about the causes of immorality among the working classes. Some saw it as a direct result of urbanization and factory work, emphasizing in particular the separation of children from parents, and wives from husbands within the factory. Others lay the blame upon the working class itself, focusing on what they regarded as the drunken and debauched behaviour of adults. Even the latter reformers viewed the factory as reinforcing the corruption of the working class. See Villermé (1840, I, p. 35), Heywood (1988, pp. 183–86), Weissbach (1989, p. 24), and Lynch (1988, pp. 5, 228–36).

7 While historians have correctly pointed out that there is no consistent correlation between industrialization and the recruitment figures, and that the physical health of children who lived in the countryside was perhaps as bad as that of urban children, it is clear now, as it was in the nineteenth century, that factory work was doing nothing to improve children's health. For

government was more than cautious, however, about the age range of children it wanted to protect, and about passing legislation that might place French industry at a competitive disadvantage. It questioned the British decision to limit hours for children until they reached the age of 18 (albeit only to 12 hours a day), and suggested 15 might be a better age at which to allow workers to sell their own labour unimpeded by legislation. And while the monarchy prepared to follow the British precedent of limiting the rights of fathers to their children's labour, it did so cautiously.

The government's questionnaire asked people to evaluate the current situation—the age at which children began to work in factories, how much they earned, what hours they worked, how they were treated, and how much money their employers saved by hiring them rather than adults. It then asked what kind of limitations should be imposed on child labour and what kind of factories should be regulated. It asked no questions distinguishing girls from boys and no questions about the employment of women or the care of children outside the factory (AN $F^{12}4705$).

Three organizations in Rouen responded to the Bureau of Manufacturers' questions: the Chamber of Commerce, the Conseil des Prud'hommes, and the Société Libre pour Concourir aux Progrès du Commerce et de l'Industrie. All three were organizations of manufacturers and related occupations like merchants, financiers, and master artisans (AN $F^{12}4705$).[8] The societies agreed that children were currently being exploited by a variety of employers and that protective legislation was desirable. They disagreed, however, on the scope of the problem and the kind of law that should be enacted, with the Chamber of Commerce proposing the mildest reforms,[9] the Prud'hommes expressing the most concern about morality, and the Société Libre proposing the most radical legislation.

---

rejection figures see Villermé (1840, II, p. 399). Also see Gueneau (1927, pp. 420–503), Heywood (1988, pp. 164, 171–82), Bourcart (1827–28, p. 325).

8 The following discussion and all quotations from 1837 are from the 1837 *Rapports* located in this file. Chambers of Commerce existed in every department and were composed of five to fifteen local merchants, financiers, manufacturers and masters of coastal vessels. They were established to promote business interests, and to act as consultative bodies to the government. The Prud'hommes had a more disparate membership drawn from manufacturers (*fabricants*), foremen (*chefs d'atelier*), and licensed artisans and craftsmen (*ouvriers patentes*), but were controlled by the manufacturers who constituted one-half plus one of the members of each council. They were authorized to arbitrate industrial disputes and in a crisis could take the initiative in settling disputes. The Société Libre's membership is not revealed in any of the documents, but its purpose is clearly revealed in its title—it had been formed to facilitate progress in commerce and industry. For more information about the Chambers of Commerce and the Prud'hommes, see Newman (1987, I, pp. 183, 242–43), Bouvier-Ajam (1969, pp. 85–86).

9 The Rouen Chamber of Commerce was one of only five Chambers of Commerce (out of 24 that responded to the questionnaire) that supported any kind of child-labour law in 1837 (Weissbach, 1989, p. 45).

Both the questions posed by the government and the responses of the Rouen manufacturers reveal the impact of the British factory acts on French thinking. As in Britain, the novelty and visibility of the spinning mills made them the major target of reformers, although, as observers frequently pointed out, other, smaller industries, including non-mechanized branches of the textile industry, were far worse offenders when it came to over-taxing working children. The Prud'hommes reported that children began to work in the *lamiers* (metal-leaf workshops) as young as four-and-a-half or five, while the spinning mills did not employ them until they were six or seven. And the Société Libre, while it was very critical of practices in the spinning mills, saved its harshest comments for the *ateliers de bobinage*, where women, hired by the mills to wind thread on to bobbins, farmed out the work to children five years of age and younger. The Société Libre viewed these children as severely over-burdened, mistreated and underpaid, and the women who worked them as seriously depraved.

The societies reported that children's earnings varied according to age. Very young children (under the age of seven) earned as little as two francs a week, and the Chamber of Commerce found that even children aged eight to ten earned only 2.50 francs for six days' work in the mills. Older children (aged 10 to 11) earned four or 4.50 francs a week. By age 16 to 18, young women had hit their earning ceiling and were paid seven to eight francs a week. No matter how long they worked in the mills, they would never earn more. Experienced men over the age of 18, on the other hand, earned 14 francs a week.[10] None of these earnings were guaranteed, however, and slumps in the economy as well as shortages of raw cotton could result in unemployment and no income for anyone.[11]

The hours children and adults spent in the spinning mills were staggeringly

10 While the reports do not explain this difference in male and female earning ability, the explanation lies in the sexual division of labour which excluded women from the highest paid positions in the mill, like mule spinning, machine repairing, and supervising.

11 How much income families and individuals needed to survive was a matter of dispute in the nineteenth century, but reformers argued that even the lowest estimates could only be met in the best of times. Villermé's estimates for Rouen, published in 1839, ranged from 2.50 to 2.85 francs a day for a family of four with one child at the breast and the other six years of age (17.5 to 20 francs per week). The estimate depended upon the price of bread and housing remaining stable and low, and included no savings and less than seven francs a year per person for health care, soap and tobacco combined, a grouping that indicates that health care and soap were luxuries rather than necessities in Villermé's eyes.

While it is clear that working-class living conditions were grim in cities like Rouen, the accuracy of Villermé's and other reformers' calculations of workers' incomes and expenses cannot be taken at face value. The figures appear to have been based not on actual calculations, but created to explain the living standards reformers believed existed in particular cities. The goal of Villermé and other reformers was to provoke sympathy and alarm among the middle class and the government without making the possibility of reform appear completely hopeless (see Reddy, 1984, pp. 138–84; Heywood, 1988, p. 164; Coleman, 1982, p. 271–76). Never-thess, it remains true that wages were low and living conditions were very poor.

long by modern standards. The normal working day was 13.5 hours of work plus 1.5 hours for meals, amounting to a total of 15 hours inside the factory walls. In the summer this meant 5.00 a.m. to 8.00 p.m. In the winter, work began at dawn and continued until 15 hours later, usually around 10.00 p.m. In addition, of course, workers had to walk to and from the factory, and for many of them the distance was two to three kilometres each way. The Prud'hommes and the Société Libre thought these hours were too long for everyone and should be shortened.

To make matters worse, in the eyes of the Prud'hommes, many factories operated at night. Although children usually were not hired to work on night shifts, work stoppages during the day were frequently made up by extending work into or through the night, and children as well as adults were expected to stay in their places. Everyone agreed that children should not work at night, but they disagreed about when night began. The Prud'hommes thought no one should work after 9.00 p.m., while the Chamber of Commerce wanted to end the children's working day at 10.00 p.m., and the Société Libre at 8.00 p.m.

Everyone also agreed that very young children should be removed from the workforce and that the hours of older children should be regulated. They disagreed, however, on what the minimum working age should be. The Prud'hommes and Société Libre argued for 10, the Chamber of Commerce for nine (the 1841 law would set it at eight).[12] Following the English model, the Chamber of Commerce divided child workers into two categories (nine to 13, and 14 to 18), and suggested the first group be allowed to work no more than nine hours a day; the second, 12. The Prud'hommes and the Société Libre believed that a graduated working day for children would be impossible to institute since adults and children worked together in teams, and neither could operate the machinery without the other. Consequently, both groups recommended full working days for children, although the Société Libre said it would have recommended half days for children (hence two shifts) if the loss of wages could have been tolerated by their families. Following its liberal bent, the Société Libre recommended a reduction in the working day to 11 hours plus one-and-a-half hours for meals for everyone. The Prud'hommes suggested a 12 hour day with a similar hour-and-a-half set aside for meals.

There seems to be no reason to doubt seriously the wage, hour and child-labour data of the Rouen societies,[13] but it is important to recognize that the

12 Provisions of the 1841 law can be found in Gueneau (1927, pp. 498–501) and in *Le travail et l'enfant au XIXe siècle* (1978, p. 22).

13 Internal evidence in the reports indicates that they do not suffer from the same problems as Villermé's figures often do. For instance, when asked about the degree to which the employment of children actually saved employers money, the Prud'hommes, who reported the lowest earnings for children under eight and the highest earnings for older children, argued that the employment of children did not save employers money. In their view, only the employment of ten- to twelve-year-old children benefited employers because they had 'enough intelligence and strength' to do good work but were paid less than adults. They thought that employing children under the age of 10 achieved no real savings because they were clumsy and

reports paint an incomplete picture of working-class life since their authors were responding to specific questions rather than recording general observations. In particular, the reports do not tell us that what made the long factory hours bearable for both children and adults was the fact that neither the machinery nor the employees worked constantly. Judging from production figures, spinning machines ran only sixty per cent of the time, and some mill owners reported that children worked only four hours a day and spent the rest of the time napping behind the machinery and playing in the mills' courtyards (see Reddy, 1984, pp. 111, 238).[14] It seems likely that at least some members of the Rouen societies knew that this was the case, since many of them were manufacturers, but the reports make no mention of it, and give the impression that children and adults worked consistently during the time they were in the mills, perhaps because reformers feared that a more accurate depiction of the working day would weaken the case for reform, perhaps because this situation was too well known to merit discussion, or perhaps because what seemed most important in the early nineteenth century was not the intensity of work but the confinement of the workers in mills and factories.

The law that was passed in 1841 was weaker than any of the reforms proposed by the Rouen organizations of manufacturers and weaker than the laws in neighbouring states. A minimum age of eight was established, but only for factories using power machinery and employing 20 or more employees. A graduated working day was established with an eight-hour maximum for children aged 12 and under. Following the English precedent and the Chamber of Commerce's suggestion, the 1841 law divided children into two categories— eight to 12 and 12 to 16—and limited their daily working hours to eight and 12 respectively. As the Prud'hommes and Société Libre had warned, such a system would prove to be unworkable and unenforceable (AN F^{12}4713). Sixteen became the age at which all restrictions ended, although very few were imposed on children over the age of 12. Provisions for inspecting factories and enforcing the law were vague and fines for violations were low (see Table 3).

AGE AND GENDER IN THE 1837 REPORTS

Rouen manufacturers recorded no differences in the ages, wages, and hours of factory children based on gender, and made no arguments for differentiating between the work of girls and boys. They did, however, distinguish boys' and girls' behaviour in their responses to the government's questions about

---

unsteady workers. The Société Libre and the Chamber of Commerce, in contrast, estimated young children's earnings as slightly higher and viewed children's low wages as an advantage to employers. Such variations in figures and proposals indicate no systematic attempt to build a case based on the imagined proper figures.

14 Adults who, as children, worked in the North Carolina and other Piedmont mills in the late nineteenth and early twentieth centuries, tell similar stories about playing and resting during the work day. See Hall et al., 1987, p. 88.

Table 3: *The early factory laws in comparison*

Provisions	1833 Britain	1841 France	1839 Prussia
Apply to	textile factory power machines	power machines 20+ employees	factories & mines
Minimum age	9	8	9
Maximum hours*	9–12⁹ hrs 13–18¹² hrs	8–12⁸ hrs 13–16¹² hrs	9–16¹⁰ hrs (overtime: 1 hr. max)
Night work	none under 18 (8.30p.m.-5.30a.m.)	none under 13 (9.00p.m.-5.00a.m.)	none under 16 (9.00p.m.-5.00a.m.)
School	req. to age 13	req. ages 8–12	3 yrs req. before employ.
Sunday work		none under 16	none under 16
Inspection	paid	no provisions for pay	none

*plus meal breaks of one-and-a-half hours.

Sources: Britain: Hutchins and Harrison, 1926, rpr. 1969, pp. 19–58, AN F¹²4705; Prussia: AN F¹²4722; Villermé, 1840, p. 50; France: AN F¹²4705; F¹²4722; Gueneau, 1929, pp. 498–503.

morality. The government was concerned that children were 'imbibing lessons of a precocious immorality *in the bosom of the factory*' (AN F¹²4705; emphasis added) and asked whether children of both sexes worked together in the same rooms and what the state of their morality was. All three societies found the behaviour of boys to be worse than that of girls, and unsurprisingly exonerated the factories' workrooms as the source of the problem.

The Chamber of Commerce thought the morals of children were 'very bad in general, and particularly among the boys', but chalked this up not to co-educational work rooms (which they actually thought were rare) but to the unsupervised time children spent going to and from latrines (some of which, to make matters worse from their perspective, were shared by both sexes), going out for meals, and walking to and from work.

Similarly, the Société Libre found the morality of children left 'much to be desired, especially among the boys', but responded to the government's qualms about co-educational work rooms with the observation that children were closely supervised during work periods and could converse only with difficulty. More worrisome, they acknowledged, was the inevitable contact between boys and girls during breaks and before and after work.

For the Prud'hommes, the source of immorality lay not in mixed workrooms or in the hours children spent in the factory, although they feared working from young ages did deprive children of the time to learn right from wrong, but in the family. Parents enforced no standards of decency, exposed their children to 'indecent', 'unchaste' behaviour and provided only bad models for their children to follow so that they were already corrupted by the time they entered the factories. The corruption that began in the home was worsened by young boys being allowed to drink 'strong liquor' and to accompany adult male workers to cabarets. It was here, they suggested, rather than in the factory, that boys met corrupt men and learned 'the lessons of precocious immorality' that concerned the government. Because girls did not go to cabarets and did not drink as much as boys, the manufacturers found that both their health and their moral behaviour was better. But girls were vulnerable to corruption at the hands of boys and men, and not just at the hands of working-class men. As the Prud'hommes said, 'The dissolution of girls, independent of the natural inclination of the two sexes, is solely the result of the corruption of men, and it is not only male workers who address themselves to the female workers'.

In this era of bourgeois Victorianism, even in France, references to sexual behaviour were veiled, but the concern with morality was primarily a concern with sexual behaviour. Children were reared in families where 'decency is almost entirely unknown' (AN $F^{12}4705$—Prud'hommes) (almost certainly a reference to adult nudity and sexual activity within the view of children), and boys and girls were allowed to go to latrines and walk home at night without adult supervision (which meant they had opportunities for sexual experimentation). Even drunkenness, which was not in and of itself considered sexual behaviour, was regarded as leading to sexual activity. Boys were allowed to drink strong liquor (which lowered inhibitions further) and to go to cabarets where they met 'debauched' or 'corrupt' men (not simply drunks or alcoholic men). The immoral behaviour of boys and men thus took two forms— drunkenness and libertinism; for girls and women, it took only one form— libertinism.

While the Rouen societies placed responsibility for the immorality of factory children on their parents, men were clearly judged to be the primary instigators of immoral activity. For boys, initiation into drunken and libertine behaviour was regarded as largely voluntary. They were permitted, not forced, to drink and to go to cabarets. For girls, initiation into immoral behaviour was involuntary. They were corrupted by men. But the corruption was easily accomplished since like boys, girls had 'natural inclinations'. Here, despite the general attempts of the manufacturers to exculpate the factories from charges of fostering immorality, it was not simply a girl's parents who were responsible for her corruption. Male workers and employers, as well as factory latrines, were the culprits.

Once corrupted, girls and women were at least as capable of immoral behaviour as boys and men were. In fact, the Société Libre criticized the women who brought young children into their homes to wind bobbins and paid them a pittance far more severely than the Prud'hommes criticized the men and boys who corrupted young girls. The problem with the *bobineuses* was not just that they exploited the labour of young children, but they 'also looked for a supplement to their already scarcely moral income' (a veiled reference to prostitution) so that 'the children who are entrusted to them return with nothing but bodies weakened by premature work and souls degraded by the example of the most extreme depravity'. Whether these and other condemnations of working-class behaviour were based on fact, hearsay, or imagination is totally unclear. What is clear is that the Société Libre judged the *bobineuses* more harshly than the Prud'hommes judged the men who corrupted factory girls, i.e., women who corrupted children were worse than men who corrupted girls.

The manufacturers' harsh judgement of women grew out of their gender conceptions, conceptions that functioned implicitly, not explicitly, in their analyses, and that were not systematically worked out. There are, for instance, no distinctions between the responsibilities of mothers and fathers. Instead, the reports refer only to parents. But distinctions were drawn between the behaviour (if not the inclinations) of boys and girls, and men and women. Girls were viewed as more moral than boys; women as more moral than men. Boys and men seduced and corrupted girls, not the reverse; and boys and men, not women, were prone to drunkenness. Filtering through these statements is some rudimentary notion that the ideal woman and the ideal man were not the same. Hence the severe criticism of the *bobineuses*. Women were more moral than men; thus the immoral woman, having fallen further than the immoral man, committed a worse crime or sin.

In 1837 the manufacturers' conception of childhood was little, if at all, changed from that of their eighteenth-century ancestors. They did not object to child labour in principle, only to assigning children to tasks that would overtax them and impair their chances of becoming healthy adults. Childhood was not a time to play, but a time to work. Indeed, the Rouen societies were willing to employ nine- or ten-year-old children to work full time in factories. They presented no arguments that children needed to be nurtured. Their only departure from general eighteenth-century thought was to argue that children should be educated, but that was so they would grow up to be literate, law-abiding citizens, not because they conceived of children as possessing qualities that were specific to them.

Neither the government questionnaire nor the Rouen societies raised any opposition to female labour. No one questioned whether factories had an impact on women's morals, or whether their hours should be shortened. No one asked who would care for young children who were not allowed to work in factories, who would see to their moral education, or who would make sure they attended school, just as no one had previously asked who would care for children under the age of five who almost never worked in factories. Women's work and childcare were not issues. In fact, the only reference to women in any of the responses to the Bureau of Manufacturers' questionnaire appears in the report of the Chamber of Commerce, which pointed out that reducing the working day across the boards would be beneficial not only to children but also to pregnant women. In general, factory work was as acceptable for women—single, married, pregnant or widowed—as it was for men.[15]

THE WOMAN WORKER BECOMES A PROBLEM

Thirty years later, when the government again sought opinions on a new protective labour law, women's work had become a prime target for reformers, and at least some Rouen manufacturers had more fully articulated conceptions of childhood and womanhood than was the case in 1837. The evolution of manufacturers' thinking reflected several developments in the preceding decades: other countries had adopted new, stricter regulations for child and female workers; social and moral reformers had begun to argue that factory work violated the laws of nature; the size of Rouen's population and factory labour force had continued to grow; and, perhaps most importantly, the removal of children under the age of eight from factories had led to the conceptualization of childcare as a new problem.[16] Each of these developments played a role in the evolution of the manufacturers' thinking about the appropriate restrictions to place on the work of children and women, and on the nature of womanhood and childhood.

During the mid-nineteenth century, other countries, most notably Britain, whose actions the French could never totally ignore, continued to revise and strengthen their protective labour laws. In 1844 Britain grouped women with adolescents (aged 13 to 18), added them to the categories of protected persons, and limited their working day to 12 hours. In 1848, the working day of women and children was further reduced to 10 hours, although the legislation was virtually destroyed by a court case in 1850, and in 1860 workers outside the textile industry began to be protected (Heywood, 1988, p. 248).

Attempts to pass further legislation in France were hampered by continuing conservative opposition to the regulation of industry and the nineteenth-century cycle of revolution and reaction. In 1847, for instance, the French Chamber of Peers followed the 1844 British example and voted to limit the working day of women (like that of adolescents) to 12 hours.[17] Before the decision could become law, however, the July Monarchy was overthrown by

---

15 Female labour was not an issue for Villermé or the Mulhouse Industrial Society, either. See Villermé, 1840; Gueneau, 1929, pp. 424–31.

16 Passage of and adherence to the 1841 law did not create the childcare problem. The problem of who would care for the children of working mothers was initially created by the building of factories. Women had previously integrated minimal childcare with work on the farm or in the putting-out industries. When textile work moved into factories, the integration of paid work with childcare became impossible in many families. Removing five- to eight-year-old children from the factory labour force simply augmented an already existing, but ill-defined, problem.

17 The legislation accepted by the Peers in 1847 would have extended the law to cover all workshops with 10 or more employees or with five or more employees in protected categories, retained eight as the minimum age for employment in these establishments and eight hours as the maximum working day for children under 12, and instituted a system of paid state Inspectors. See Heywood, 1988, pp. 247–48; Weissbach, 1989, pp. 104–05.

the revolution of 1848, and the 1841 law remained in effect. A similar fate met the 1850 reform proposal advanced by the Conseil Général de l'Agriculture, des Manufactures et du Commerce in 1851, when Louis Napoleon's *coup d'état* destroyed the Second Republic (Heywood, 1988, p. 261).

If conservative legislators and manufacturers preferred to ignore the problem of child labour, reformers and philosophers wanted to remind them of it and of the newly-discovered inappropriateness of factory work for women. Between 1860 and 1866, a variety of books and articles urged further reforms. Armand Audiganne, following in Villermé's footsteps, combined statistics with purportedly eye-witness accounts of working-class life and argued for more extensive labour legislation in 1860 (Audiganne, 1860). Romantic philosopher Jules Michelet and moral reformer Jules Simon uttered impassioned cries for the importance of family life and against the hiring of women and young children to work in factories in 1860 and 1861 (Michelet, 1860; Simon 1860; 1867; original publication date 1861). Even the feminist Julie Daubié, on the one hand, pleaded for an end to gender distinctions in pay and jobs so single women could be independent of men, and on the other, argued, in 1861, for the withdrawal of married women from the labour force so they could fulfil their maternal responsibilities (Daubié, 1866).

The writings of reformers like Audiganne, Michelet, Simon and Daubié shifted the focus of the discussion of work and morality from the effect of factory work on the physical and moral health of children to its effects on women. With this shift came a new and fundamentally contradictory conceptualization of the relationship between work and gender. Reformers came to see working women both as the victims of an economic system that relied on their labour when it should not, and as engaging in an activity that violated the natural order of things. Having conceptualized the working woman as a problem, the only way to solve the problem, to eliminate the disorder her existence signified, would be to eliminate her, to turn her into a non-working woman.[18]

The most influential writings in terms of altering the age and gender perceptions of men like the Rouen manufacturers were those of Simon, and, to a somewhat lesser extent, of Michelet (see, for instance, AN $F^{12}4719$, 1869, p. 24). Both men ignored previously meaningful distinctions between married and unmarried women, and between mothers and non-mothers, and reconceptualized womanhood as motherhood. This collapsing of womanhood into motherhood allowed them to condemn factory work for all women, regardless of whether they literally were mothers (or even married), on the basis that it would ruin their health, make it impossible for them to care for children, and lead to the destruction of the French race (AN $F^{12}4719$, 1869, pp. 21–34).[19] Far removed from the conceptual world of the 1837 manufac-

18 For more discussion of this issue, see Joan W. Scott (1988).
19 A firm believer in the frailty of women, Michelet opposed all work for them whether it was in agriculture, domestic service, needlework, or factory manufacturing.

turers who saw nothing wrong in women working in factories, Michelet turned the occupational title '*l'ouvrière*' into an appellation of dishonour, and a symbol of all that was wrong with the 'modern' world. '*L'ouvrière!*', he exclaimed, 'impious, sordid word, that no language ever had, that no era before this age of iron ever knew, that by itself counterbalances our supposed progress' (AN F^{12}4719, 1869, p. 22).

Jules Simon, signalling his agreement, quoted Michelet in the preface to his *L'Ouvrière* (the very title of this book evoked Michelet's words), and then declared that 'in our economic organization there is a terrible vice that is the cause of misery, and that it is necessary to conquer at any price'. What was the terrible vice? It was 'the suppression of family life' that resulted from the employment of women in factories. In a statement that would become (in)famous in the history of working women, he declared: 'The woman who becomes a worker is no longer a woman'.

> . . . she lives under the domination of a supervisor, in the midst of companions of doubtful morality, in perpetual contact with men, separated from her husband and children . . . No longer able to nurse her child, she abandons it to a poorly paid wetnurse. . . Three- or four-year-old children fend for themselves on the fetid streets, pursued by hunger and cold . . . [Returned from the factory] the mother lacks the strength to prepare a meal; clothing falls into tatters: *voilà*, the family that the factories have given us.

The solution, he argued, was for industry to raise men's wages and for families to learn not to squander money in immoral pursuits like drinking and attending cabarets. Then women would be able to return to their 'natural destination'— the home (Simon, 1860, pp. v–vi).[20]

In Simon's writings, the concern with morality that had centred on children in the 1830s was replaced by a concern with morality that centred on women. With this shift, he associated immorality far more closely with factory work than the Rouen manufacturers had in 1837. Instead of criticizing peripheral aspects of factory work like unsupervised work breaks, latrines, and the walk to and from work, Simon decried the organization of work. The female worker was 'dominated' by a (male) supervisor, surrounded by co-workers of 'doubtful morality', and had 'perpetual contact with men'. Such a situation was likely to have only one outcome—illicit sexual activity and prostitution which, in turn, would lead to the destruction of the family.

The latter was the crux of the matter for Simon. His concern was not simply that women would be corrupted by factory work, but that their work was destroying the family. As evidence, he cited the high infant mortality rates in factory towns like Rouen. He was convinced that women's factory labour was

---

20 That drinking and attending cabarets were more male than female pursuits was a point that Simon chose not to pursue.

responsible for infant deaths since it prevented mothers from nursing their infants 'except at night and at noon during the suspension of work when a neighbour [i.e., a good woman] brought them to [the factory]' (Simon, 1860, p. 140). Simon laid the blame for this situation on both women workers and their employers: women were to blame for seeking jobs rather than staying at home; manufacturers, for hiring them and thereby preventing them from nursing their infants.

While married women were being reconceptualized as mothers in this literature, children, at least for Simon, were becoming innocents and victims. The immoral boys who went to cabarets with men and the more virtuous but corruptible girls with 'natural inclinations' of the 1837 reports were no longer to be seen. Now all children needed the protection and moral guidance of their mothers to prevent their corruption at the hands of adults. Moreover, as gender distinctions between boys and girls disappeared, so did girls. In an aptly titled book on child labour and the working-class family, *L'Ouvrier de huit ans*, Simon described the needs of *'le fils et la mère'* (Simon, 1867). The *'fille'* who worked (*l'ouvrière de huit ans*) did not appear, even though eight-year-old girls as well as eight-year-old boys were in the labour force in the 1860s. Children had become boys just as women had become mothers.

In addition to children/boys having the special quality of innocence, Simon also conceived of them as having a special need for nurture, a conceptualization that did not appear in the 1837 debate about child labour. He thought mothers should be at home so they could exchange 'confidences, counsels, consolations, marks of tenderness' which alone would give the boy strength against 'evil and egoism' (Simon, 1867, p. 118). That girls might also benefit from their mothers' care and advice escaped his view.

The writings of Simon and the other reformers changed the terms of the debate over protective legislation. By 1867, many bourgeois viewed children as innocents who needed to be loved and nurtured, identified womanhood with motherhood, and believed that working in factories was contrary to a woman's nature. Whether mothers who did work were victims of poverty or engaging in a wilful and immoral act remained ambiguous, but in either case, reformers thought they belonged at home, not in factories. Popular as this view was, the government as a whole preferred to sidestep the issue of women's work and to focus on increasing the protection offered to children when it once again contemplated a new labour law.

'PROTECTING' WOMEN

In 1867, le Ministère de l'Agriculture, du Commerce et des Travaux Publics drew up a proposal for a new labour law that made distinctions between male and female workers; applied to all factories, workshops, workyards and mines, regardless of size or the use of power machinery; and further reduced working hours for children and adolescents. For factories, the proposal left the minimum age at eight but reduced the working day for eight- to twelve-year-olds from eight to six hours. The working day for thirteen- to sixteen-year-old children was to be reduced from 12 to 10 hours, as was that of 'girls and women under 18'. All girls and women regardless of age were to be forbidden to work underground in mines, while the minimum age for boys was to be 10. Boys aged 10 to 12 were to be allowed to work a full day underground, but only for four days a week. Night work was forbidden for all categories of children (with certain exceptions), and two hours of education per day was to be required for children aged eight to 12 (AN $F^{12}4722$, 1867a).[21]

Two major responses to the Ministry's proposals were published before local communities like Rouen began to debate the government's proposals. Reflecting the views of men like Simon, these reports emphasized women's domestic responsibilities. M. Bénard, in his report on 'Le Travail des Enfants', supported the proposed legislation, agreed implicitly with Simon and Michelet, and argued that it was unnatural for women to work outside the home (AN $F^{12}4722$, 1867b). His major concern was not with women *per se*, however, but with the effects of their employment on men's rights and women's domestic skills. For him, the virtue of limiting the working hours of women and girls was that it would prevent them 'from being employed in jobs that ought to be reserved exclusively for men' (AN $F^{12}4722$, 1867b, p. 52) while making it possible for them to fulfil their domestic responsibilities. Without such legislation, he argued, occupied from the beginning of the day until night in a workshop, married women were ignorant of all domestic work, and girls declared that they did not have the least notion of what a simple servant knew. At home, married women were slovenly and clumsy, not knowing how to sew, or how to care for their children and how to keep house, knowing nothing about regulating expenses and wasting money in extravagances (AN $F^{12}4722$, 1867b, pp. 86–87).

Complaints about the deficient domestic skills of working-class women were common in the nineteenth century, as the bourgeoisie came to value their own domestic comforts more and more highly and to regard working-class lifestyles with suspicion and fear. As Ivy Pinchbeck observed in 1930, such complaints romanticized peasant life and falsely assumed that peasant women had greater domestic skills than their working-class descendants (Pinchbeck, 1930, rpr. 1969, pp. 309–10). That this was not the case has been well documented by Pinchbeck for England and by Olwen Hufton for eighteenth-century France. As Hufton observed, 'One has only to read a description of any cottage, shack, or tenement room anywhere in France with its rough walls, enclosed fetid atmosphere, dirty floor . . ., scanty furniture . . ., ragged bedcovering in which fleas circulated undisturbed . . . to know that domestic chores preoccupied no one' (Hufton, 1975, p. 11). What mattered in the nineteenth-century debates, however, were not the facts of peasant and working-class life, but the

---

21 The proposal was received by the Conseil d'Etat on 2 December 1867.

bourgeoisie's fear that the family, and with it law and order, were deteriorating.

M. Heurtier, Conseiller d'Etat and the reporter for the Section on Agriculture, Commerce, Public Works and Fine Arts, objected to the government's proposal, not on the grounds of protecting male jobs or women's general domestic responsibilities, but on the basis of gender distinctions and women's special responsibility for children. Implicit rather than explicit in his argument is a major tenet of the nineteenth-century bourgeois reconceptualization of woman: more moral than men, women were the logical caretakers of the family and children. A law that limited the working day of girls and women under the age of 18, but not that of adult women, made no sense, he argued, if one believed that women played an important role in the 'physical, moral and religious education of the working classes', as everyone involved in this debate did (AN $F^{12}4722$, 1867c, p. 17). Heurtier was not willing to follow the logic of his argument all the way to its end, however, and, instead of arguing for the removal of mothers from the labour force and the assumption of greater financial responsibility for their families by men (i.e., the logically more consistent position adopted by Daubié), he stayed within the parameters of the government's proposal and argued simply that it was time to limit the working day of all women to 10 hours as the British already had, so women could fulfil their wifely and motherly duties (AN $F^{12}4722$, 1867c, pp. 17, 23).

THE VIEW FROM ROUEN

By 1860, the Normand cotton industry was the largest in France. One-quarter of the 800,000 inhabitants of the Seine-Inférieure and twenty-eight per cent of the population of Rouen worked for the industry in one capacity or another (Fohlen, 1967, p. 193; ADSM 6M1103). Handweavers continued to resist mechanization, but it was a losing struggle in the Seine-Inférieure as elsewhere, and by 1867, 493 children (aged eight to 16) worked in weaving factories and 5,412 children worked in spinning mills that were subject to the provisions of the 1841 law (AN $F^{12}4722$, 1867d; Fohlen, 1967, p. 198).[22] In addition to these children, many others worked in mills and factories that employed fewer than twenty workers or used hand- rather than steam- or water-powered machinery and thus were not subject even to the mild provisions of the 1841 law. Even large mills continued to employ eight- to twelve-year-old children for full days rather than for the mandated eight-hour day, and paid little or no attention to the educational provisions of the law (AM $F^{12}4722$, 1868; AN $F^{12}4724$).[23]

In addition, and of considerable concern to the Rouen manufacturers in 1867, there were the consequences of the 1841 law for childcare. In 1837, the

22 Employment figures are for the Department.
23 On the plus side, by 1867, the normal working day for adults and children had been reduced from thirteen-and-a-half to twelve hours, not by law, but by practice (Heywood, 1988, p. 253).

manufacturers failed to anticipate that the removal of young children from factory employment and the limiting of the working day for older children would create a childcare problem. The Rouen Factory Inspectors pointed out as early as 1843 that children who were released early from the mills or were barred from them altogether by age were simply 'given up to vagabondage and indolence' if their parents worked. Even when schools were available (which was rare), these children did not attend them, because there was 'no one to take them there and require them to stay' (AN $F^{12}4713$).[24] The child-labour law in attempting to solve one problem had created another.[25] By 1867 they had been wrestling with, but not solving, the problem of who would care for and discipline the non-working children of working parents for a quarter of a century (see Table 2).

Three groups in Rouen responded to the proposed legislation in 1867, but not exactly the same groups as in 1837 and not in the same format or with the same degree of detail. The Chamber of Commerce and the Conseil général de la Préfecture du Département de la Seine-Inférieure attempted to convince the government that there were flaws in their minimum-age maximum-hour proposal with long introductory discourses on the history of protective legislation, while the Société Libre d'Emulation du Commerce et de l'Industrie de la Seine-Inférieure set out to influence the government by publishing a long, literate report written by Paul Allard (AM $F^{12}4755$; AN $F^{12}4722$, 1868; AN $F^{12}4719$). The responses were simultaneously more sophisticated and less revealing of the manufacturers' views than the 1837 reports which responded directly to questions with concrete information and opinions.

On the question of child labour, the Rouen groups agreed that more protection for children and strict enforcement of the laws were necessary, but disagreed over how to increase protection without affecting the organization of work or profits. Allard accepted the government proposal for a minimum age of eight, and half days for eight- to twelve-year-olds. The Chamber of Commerce and the Conseil général wanted a higher minimum age (11 or 12) and shorter working days for all workers (the Conseil général proposed a 10-hour day; the Chamber of Commerce left it unspecified). The effect of factory work on children's morals, so central to the discussion in 1837, was not raised by the government or the respondents, nor was the question of nurture, so dear to Simon and other bourgeois reformers. The responses to the provisions for children were perfunctory (although the Conseil général returned to them

24 One of the inspectors' major points was that a law that reduced everyone's hours would be enforceable, which the current law with a shortened working day for adolescents was not, and that it should be enforced with strong penalties.

25 Vagabondage was not a new problem in 1841. Reformers like Eugène Buret and Villermé were already concerned about the large number of apparently homeless, vagrant children who roamed city streets and engaged in petty theft before the passage of the 1841 law, but the Rouen manufacturers made no reference to them in 1837, regarding them, probably, as a separate problem (see Heywood, 1988, pp. 193ff; Chevalier, 1973, pp. 116–19).

several times in the next few years, demonstrating a very real desire for a strengthened law), and the issues they raised were purely practical: children's health, their need for education and religious instruction, the importance of their wages to their families, and the organization of factory work.

By 1867, the controversial issue for the Rouen manufacturers was not children's work but women's work. The Rouen Chamber of Commerce and Conseil général de la Préfecture chose not to address the issue at all, perhaps not only because practical solutions were difficult to reach, but because following the logic of the emerging gender conceptions would interfere seriously with the manufacturers' recruitment of cheap labour. Allard, on the other hand, addressed the issue extensively in his report for the Société Libre. That Allard spoke for all the members of the Société Libre is unlikely, but his analysis of the problems of women's work and childcare constitutes an attempt by the manufacturing community to reconcile the practical problems faced by working-class families with the gender conceptions of bourgeois reformers like Simon.

Paul Allard agreed with Bénard and Heurtier that women, and not men, had important domestic responsibilities, and he agreed with Heurtier that the proposed law was fundamentally misconceived, but unlike them, he argued that the women who needed to work shorter hours were not between the ages of 16 and 18, as the government was proposing, but were women with children (AN F^{12}4719, 1869, pp. 26–32). Married women had responsibilities at home that demanded more attention and energy than a twelve-hour working day made possible. If hours were to be shortened for any women, it ought to be for them.[26] Indeed, he observed, far from protecting young women, the government's proposal would place them at greater risk, since sixteen- to eighteen-year-old girls were neither in school nor mothers, and two hours of liberty for them would be 'two hours of idleness, consequently, two hours of peril' (AN F^{12}4719, 1869, p. 30).[27]

Simultaneously the most practical and the most logical of the three major respondents to the proposed law, Allard found himself unable to solve the problem of childcare in the working class. He believed that the best way to protect children was to forbid women to work altogether. Only such a step

---

26 It was generally agreed that one outcome of limiting women to a ten-hour working day would be the reduction of men's hours as well. Whether a reformer proposed such a solution depended on how he viewed the effects of an across-the-board reduction in working hours on production. (Heurtier believed limiting the work day to 10 hours would not interfere with production because workers would be more energetic and hence more productive. Allard was not so sure and stopped short of endorsing the proposal.) In fact, it seems likely that reluctance to mandate a change that would lead to a general reduction in the working day lay behind the government's proposal to prolong the period of protected adolescence for girls rather than to limit the working day for adult women.

27 Allard's argument is an interesting reversal of Simon's and Michelet's belief in the corrupting effects of the factory.

could solve the problem created by the 1841 legislation and accomplish the desired goal—the care of young children in clean, orderly, loving (i.e., bourgeois-type) homes. He knew as well as the factory inspectors that the children of working parents did not attend schools because there was no one to 'take them there and require them to stay', and that they were left to wander the streets (AN F^{12}4713, 1843).[28] But he could not propose a total ban on female factory labour because he knew that working-class women worked out of economic necessity. As Allard put it, 'There are two sides to the problem of women's work . . . The woman must be allowed to work; she also must remain as much as possible, *femme de ménage et d'intérieur*' (AN F^{12}4719, 1869, p. 28).

In phrasing the dilemma in terms of 'the woman' rather than 'the mother', Allard reveals the extent to which his thinking had been affected by the emerging conceptualization of women as mothers. He was far from consistent in his views of womanhood, however, and he alone of all the people in this debate would also suggest that 'when the children, being grown, have left for the *atelier*, the place of the mother is also in the *atelier* beside her children and their father, and not in her empty *foyer*' (AN F^{12}4719, 1869, p. 28).

Allard's inconsistency is as revealing as his occasional collapsing of womanhood into motherhood. He had no clearly formulated gender conceptions, no clearly formulated position on the desirability of factory work for women *per se*. What he had was a clearly formulated position on the undesirability of women working in factories while they had had young children to care for, a position that has been historically overshadowed by a tendency of scholars to focus on men like Simon and Michelet who viewed factory work as bad for all women as well as for their children. Allard argued for limitations on women's hours *not* because he wanted to protect women (unlike Simon and Michelet, he did not believe that women ceased to be women when they became workers, or that they were incapable of hard physical labour), but because he wanted to improve children's lives outside the factory and to strengthen the family.

'Protecting' women was a means to an end, not an end in itself for Allard and the Rouen manufacturers. The problem they had discovered was not woman's nature or women's competition with men for jobs, or women's physical frailty or sexual vulnerability, but childcare in the working class, a problem that itself was largely a consequence of the 1841 law. Prohibiting young children but not their mothers from working in factories, had created a problem that had not existed during protoindustrialization, when virtually everyone worked at home, or even in the early years of factory building when children accompanied their parents to work. It was a problem that had not been

28 One of the inspectors' major points was that the minimum working age should be 12 and the maximum working day for everyone should be 12 hours. They thought such a law would be enforceable (which the 1841 law with a shortened working day for adolescents was not), and should be enforced with strong penalties.

anticipated by manufacturers in 1837. By 1867, however, the reports of factory inspectors and school officials, combined with growing bourgeois sentimentality about children and the family, had convinced many Rouen manufacturers that childcare was a crucial and growing social problem.

The government's proposal to reduce the working hours of adolescent girls did not address the concerns of either the manufacturers or the bourgeois reformers like Simon and Michelet. Instead, it reflected an older, but not diminished, bourgeois concern with the sexual behaviour of young factory workers. Alarmed by the rising illegitimacy rates in France,[29] and believing girls to be more moral than boys but weak in the face of temptation, the government sought to protect girls by having them leave the factory for home two hours before the boys were released. Men like Allard viewed such a plan with a jaundiced eye. In their view, freeing young children from factory work and releasing others early had created one set of disciplinary problems; freeing adolescent girls was only likely to create another.

In short, the government and the Rouen manufacturers as represented by Allard came to the question of protective legislation for women from contrary perspectives, based on overlapping but differing conceptualizations of woman's nature and children's needs. The government continued to see boys as immoral and girls as innocent by nature, as the manufacturers had in 1837, and was concerned that girls could easily fall from a state of innocence and morality into one of sexual activity and depravity, i.e. from the ranks of virgins to those of whores. Allard, the Rouen manufacturers, and Heurtier (the government's ranks were somewhat split on this issue) portrayed all children as essentially alike, and drew no distinctions between the moral character or emotional needs of boys and girls.

On the other hand, the manufacturers perceived women as differing fundamentally from men and differentiated adult gender roles accordingly. By 1867, they had begun to see women as nurturing and domestic in orientation, and hence as the natural caretakers of children and the creators of family life. Frailty was not a part of their view of woman's nature, nor did they question women's ability to work hard, but having conceptualized womanhood as motherhood (which entailed a nurturing nature as well as the physical bearing of children), and having the non-working vagabond children of Rouen constantly before their eyes, they were drawn logically into the belief that in the best of all possible worlds, women would stay at home.

---

29 The illegitimate fertility rate had risen dramatically since the middle of the eighteenth century, as it had throughout western Europe. Between 1815 and 1870, well over 3,000 babies were abandoned annually at the Hospice des Enfants Trouvés in Paris alone, with the number frequently rising to about 5,000. Eighty-five to ninety-five per cent of these children were illegitimate. And three-quarters of all abandoned children died before they reached their first birthday (see, Shorter, 1973, pp. 606–08; Fuchs, 1984, pp. 66–68, 193). The sole exception to the abandonment figures was in 1853, when only 2,380 children were abandoned at the hospice.

The government certainly did not disagree with the manufacturers' conception of women as the proper caretakers of children, but given the advantages of cheap female labour to the manufacturers, it was loath to act upon the consequences of such a conception, as its 1867 proposal indicated. Instead, it chose to emphasize the moral and physical frailty of young women and to frame the issue in terms of protecting them, rather than in terms of serving the needs of children.

When the French legislature finally passed a new labour law in 1874 (after yet another revolution), it was the view of women as needing protection, rather than the manufacturers' view of women as mothers that was codified. The politically conservative legislature of the Third Republic ignored the practical and philosophical concerns that the Rouen manufacturers and factory inspectors had voiced, and moved further in the direction of differentiating young women from young men by extending the period of restricted working hours for girls to age 21.[30] As the Rouen manufacturers had known in 1867, such a decision made little sense in terms of the needs of working-class families.[31] It was, however, an important step in the institutionalization of the conceptualization of women as weaker and more vulnerable than men.

Nowhere in these debates did anyone consult working-class women, or consider their needs or civil rights. Indeed, once the elision was made between woman and mother, the needs and rights of adult women played little part in this debate. Having assigned responsibility for their children and housekeeping to women, bourgeois reformers and legislators ignored women's rights as individuals to sell their labour without interference. Children were perceived as having a right to protection against exploitation of their labour and injury of their health and morals, and the state was perceived as having a right to protect the national interest. In contrast, women had responsibilities, not rights. Middle-class feminists like Julie Daubié and working-class Saint-Simonian women who attempted to voice their views of women's rights and needs were little heard by the male manufacturers, reformers and legislators.[32]

CONCLUSIONS

The 1837 and 1867 reports on child and female labour are not systematic formulations of the age and gender conceptions of the Rouen manufacturers and businessmen. Nevertheless, their discussions of the 'problems' of child and female labour and their proposed solutions reveal that age and gender were

---

30 Most of the text of the 19 mai 1874 law is reproduced in *Le travail et l'enfant*, pp. 23–25.
31 Had Heurtier's and Allard's and the Rouen manufacturers' counter-proposal that the working day be reduced for all women been accepted by the government, the childcare problem still would not have been solved, since many children obviously were too young to work or to be in school and needed constant attention. But at least such a solution would have been the avowed goal of the legislation.
32 For discussion of the views of Saint-Simonian women, see Moses, 1984, pp. 41–59.

beginning to determine whether one worked in a way that they never had before. In 1837 the manufacturers regarded factory work as appropriate for both men and women. Thirty years later, they were beginning to identify manhood with the performance of paid work and womanhood with mother-hood. Influenced by the need of non-working children for care and super-vision, and by the writings of bourgeois social reformers, they believed that a woman's place was in the home (at least while her children were young) where she would perform the domestic tasks of child-rearing, cooking, cleaning and sewing.

The notion that children needed protection and nurture was also a departure from the eighteenth- and early-nineteenth-century conception of children as little workers whose need for protection, not to mention nurture, was distinctly limited. Moreover, as manufacturers began to conceive of children as having distinct needs, they moved away from their earlier conceptualization of girls as being more moral than boys and as needing protection from the sexual advances of boys and men in the workplace. While distinctions between male and female children were disappearing from their thought, they began, however, to differentiate adult male and female nature in ways that they had not in 1837, and subscribed to the view that women were the appropriate caretakers of children, not only because they bore them, but because they were more nurturing and more moral than men. Ultimately, of course, neither the Rouen manufacturing community nor the French government was willing to act upon the assumption that working-class children needed their mothers to be at home, and the problem of childcare in the working class remained unsolved in the nineteenth century.

References

Archives Départementales de la Seine-Maritime 6M1100—Statistique Sommaire, Seine-Inférieure, 1847.
ADSM 6M1103.

Archives Nationales

AN F^{12}4476 (1847), Statistique d'industrielle, Normandie, 1847.
AN F^{12}4705 (1837a), Circulaire no. 29 from the Bureau des Manufactures, Paris, 31 July 1837.
AN F^{12}4705 (1837b), Rapports, Rouen, 1837.
AN F^{12}4713 (1843), Rapport Commission d'Inspection de l'Arrondissement de Rouen, 25 August 1843.
AN F^{12}4719 (1869), M. Paul Allard, *Rapport sur le travail des enfants et des femmes dans les Manufactures: La loi de 1841 et les projets de reforme* (Rouen: Société Libre d'Emulation du Commerce et de l'Industrie de Seine-Inférieure, 1869).
AN F^{12}4722 (1867a), Projet de loi sur le Travail des enfants dans les Manufactures.
AN F^{12}4722 (1867b), Rapport Bénard: Le Travail des Enfants, 8 September 1867.
AN F^{12}4722 (1867c), Heurtier, 'Rapport'.
AN F^{12}4722 (1867d), Travail des Enfants dans les manufactures, usines ou ateliers, July 1867.

AN F¹²4722 (1868), Extrait du procès verbal des délibérations du Conseil général de la Préfecture du département de la Seine-Inférieure, 1868.
AN F¹²4724 (1869), Situation des Etablissements Industriels, au point de vue de l'observation de la loi du 22 Mars 1841, 1869.
AN F¹²4755 (1867), Rapport de la Chambre de Commerce de Rouen, 1867

Books and Articles

AUDIGANNE, A. (1860), *Les populations ouvrières et les industries de la France*, 2 vols., Paris.
BOURCART, J.-J. (1827–28), 'Proposition sur la necessité de fixer l'age et de reduire les heures de travail des ouvriers des filatures', *Bulletin de la Société industrielle de Mulhouse*, I.
BOUVIER-AJAM, M. (1969), *Histoire du travail en France depuis la Révolution*, Paris.
CHEVALIER, L. (1973), *Labouring Classes and Dangerous Classes*, Princeton.
COLEMAN, W. (1982), *Death is a Social Disease*, Madison, WI.
DAUBIÉ, J.-V. (1866), *La Femme Pauvre au XIXe Siècle*, Paris.
DUBY, G. and A. WALLON (eds.) (1975–76), *Histoire de la France* tomes II and III, Paris.
FOHLEN, C. (1967), *Le travail au XIXe siècle*, Paris.
FUCHS, R. (1984), *Abandoned Children*, Albany, New York.
GILLIS, J. R. (1981), *Youth and History*, New York.
GUENEAU, M. L. (1927), 'La législation restrictive du travail des enfants: La loi française du 22 mars 1841', *Revue d'histoire économique et sociale*, 15, 420–503.
GULLICKSON, G. L. (1986), *Spinners and Weavers of Auffay*, New York.
HALL, J. D., J. LELOUDIS, R. KORSTAD, M. MURPHY, L. A. JONES and C. B. DALY (1987), *Like A Family: The Making of a Southern Cotton Mill*, Chapel Hill, NC.
HEYWOOD, C. (1988), *Childhood in Nineteenth-Century France: Work, Health and Education among the Classes Populaires*, Cambridge.
HUFTON, O. (1975), 'Women and the Family Economy in Eighteenth-Century France', *French Historical Studies*, IX, 1–22.
HUTCHINS, B. L. and A. HARRISON (1926, rpr. 1969), *A History of Factory Legislation*, 3rd ed., New York.
LEHNING, J. (1980), *The Peasants of Marlhes*, Chapel Hill, NC.
LYNCH, K. (1988), *Family, Class, and Ideology in Early Industrial France: Social Policy and the Working-Class Family, 1825–1848*, Madison, WI.
[STEWART] McDOUGALL, M. L. (1983), 'Protecting Infants: The French Campaign for Maternity Leaves, 1890s–1913', *French Historical Studies*, XII, 79–105.
[STEWART] McDOUGALL, M. L. (1984), 'The Meaning of Reform: The Ban on Women's Night Work, 1892–1914', *Proceedings of the Tenth Annual Meeting of the Western Society for French History*, Lawrence, Kansas, 404–17.
MICHELET, J. (1860), *La Femme*, Paris.
MOSES, C. G. (1984), *French Feminism in the Nineteenth Century*, Albany, New York.
NEWMAN, E. L. (ed.) (1987), *Historical Dictionary of France from the 1815 Restoration to the Second Empire*, New York.
PINCHBECK, I. (1930, rpr. 1969), *Women Workers and the Industrial Revolution, 1750–1850*, London.
PINCHBECK, I. and M. HEWITT (1973), *Children in English Society*, vol. II, London and Toronto.
REDDY, W. (1984), *The Rise of Market Culture*, New York.
SCOTT, J. W. (1988), ' "L'ouvrière! Mot impie, sordide . . ." Women Workers in the Discourse of French Political Economy, 1840–1860', In J. W. Scott (ed.), *Gender and the Politics of History*, New York.
SEGALEN, M. (1980), *Mari et Femme dans la Société Paysanne*, Paris.
SHORTER, E. (1973), 'Female Emancipation, Birth Control, and Fertility in European History', *American Historical Review*, 78, 605–40.

SIMON, J. (1860), *L'ouvrière*, Paris.

SIMON, J. (1867), *L'ouvrier de huit ans*, 3rd ed., Paris.

STEWART, M. L. (1989), *Women, Work, and the French State: Labour Protection and Social Patriarchy, 1879–1919*, Kingston.

TILLY, L. A. and J. W. Scott (1978), *Women, Work and Family*, New York.

Le travail et l'enfant au XIX siècle (1978), Paris.

VILLERMÉ, L.-R. (1840), *Tableau de l'état physique et moral des ouvriers employés dans les manufactures de coton, de laine, et de soie*, 2 vols., Paris.

WEISSBACH, L. S. (1989), *Child Labour Reform in Nineteenth-Century France: Assuring the Future Harvest*, Baton Rouge, LA.

Chapter 13

FAMILY AND ECONOMY:
SOME COMPARATIVE PERSPECTIVES[*]

STANLEY L. ENGERMAN

I

These essays, dealing with the history of the European peasant family and economy, are organized around a theoretical construct (or term) that did not exist twenty-five years ago—protoindustrialization. As with all such protean terms, there is some imprecision in its use and uncertainty as to its precise meaning, but clearly there is a core idea that has come to influence heavily the literature on the European peasant. The first time I came across the term was in 1970, when I was co-organizer of the dissertation session for the Economic History Association. Out of 24 submissions, we were to select eight for presentation at the annual meeting. One of the submissions, fortunately chosen, was by Franklin Mendels, whose University of Wisconsin thesis, entitled 'Industrialization and Population Pressure in Eighteenth-Century Flanders', was thus presented at the September meeting, with a brief summary published in the March 1971 issue of the *Journal of Economic History*—one year before his first long article, 'Protoindustrialization: The First Phase of the Industrialization Process', was published. I should like to be able to say that in my comments at the meeting I was able to see exactly how influential this concept, and Mendel's work, were to become over the next two decades, and how it, with the work of other scholars, would help to reshape the study of modern European history— and not just European, of course, but also American, Asian, and African, as well—in part via its insights, in part also in the reaction to the claims of over-statement and over-generalization. Needless to say I lacked such prescience, as Mendels would remind me, in good spirits, when we periodically met in subsequent years, and it is truly sad that we will be missing the opportunity to hear his stimulating discussions and to benefit from his important insights.

II

Looking over these papers, I did begin to puzzle over the combined impact of the work on protoindustrialization and the peasant family and economy in

[*] For useful comments on earlier versions of this paper I should like to thank Michael Edelstein and Kenneth Sokoloff. Parts of this essay have appeared in my 'Expanding Protoindustrialization', *Journal of Family History*, **17**, No. 2, pp. 241–51, and are reprinted with the permission of the JAI Press, Inc.

recent years, and why it has been so influential in reshaping our views of the past. There has been, of course, the immense outpouring of new empirical information, of all varieties, from numerous and diverse sources. Yet there are many instances where such new information, while essential in filling in gaps in the literature, does not generate a new overarching view. What I will suggest is that by its linking together of changes in economic, demographic, and social factors, and by its focusing on the nature of choices to be made, important social, demographic, and economic changes can be better understood. And, for these reasons, the analytics of the study of Europe have had their counterparts in the study of individuals and societies in other parts of the world, where similar developments in the historiography have emerged.

I will not spend time in defining what I mean here by protoindustrialization: whether it is to be regarded as a formal theory of the stages of industrial development (and thus a return in spirit, if not precise concepts, to an earlier English and Germanic literature) or, as some prefer, as an insight into a key part of the economic and social process, suggesting a useful approach and the major variables to look at. Since many scholars have used the concept, and for many years, and have applied it to many areas over many centuries, it is difficult to set any one precise definition that all would agree on—as the current set of papers indicates. But I would defend the concept against the charge that it has all been said before (no doubt that is true of each particular aspect) and that it is all well-known and should be familiar. While this argument may be correct, to me the importance of the new constructs used to examine the peasantry is that they quite self-consciously and explicitly link together a number of different and separable aspects of the social process (e.g., family and economy) in a way that helps to provide a better understanding of the overall process than seemed to have been generally the case before.

First, there has been the changing view of the demographic process and the awareness of options open to individuals and families to regulate the number of offspring and, at times, the number and composition of survivors. Attention to marriage patterns—the changing age at marriage and its relation to the age of possible childbearing, seen in comparison with the ages of marriage in other societies—has indicated the magnitudes and variations in the shortfall from a Malthusian maximum fertility regime. These demographic patterns have been linked to economic variables, seen particularly in the importance of the so-called subsistence level of income—or at least the socially-determined target level of income, which influences individual choices in regard to marriage, migration, and work input.

Second, there has been a significant shift in attitudes as to the causes of economic growth in the past three decades, reflecting a disenchantment, among all political persuasions, with the pace of economic change in the underdeveloped world after the Second World War. There has been a turn away from what can be most simply described as the Marx-Rostow view of economic development, with its attention to large-scale industrialization, urbanization, and heavy capital investment. The unsuccessful attempts to leap directly into large-scale industrialization have led to more attention being given, in economic planning today as well as in interpreting the historical past, to the developments within the agricultural sector and to a more prolonged and less sharp transition from agriculture to industry, with a less distinct difference between rural and urban areas. The role of seasonal, part-time, and small-scale rural industry has similarly attracted attention as a step forward in economic development, permitting more effective, and, at times, rather essential, use of family labour in agricultural areas.

The existence of these alternatives has pointed to a great degree of flexibility in economic and social organization, degrees of flexibility which are now seen to have existed not only in peasant societies, but also even in various forms of unfree labour systems, including slavery and serfdom. Such flexibility is seen in choices influencing the labour supply—where there were not only choices as to occupation and industry, but also where migration to urban areas, other countries (whether free or under contract), or other rural areas was possible—and in setting the demands for consumer goods—choices possible once individuals and families were above the (however-defined) subsistence level. We can note one further aspect of the demand for consumer goods and the needs of subsistence which was emphasized in the contemporary literature, and now again in some of the recent discussions of economic growth—the link between desire for goods and the creation of a labour force. The early-day mercantilists sounded like many of our present-day cultural critics in discussing the link between consumer demand and labour input, but with a rather different set of political and economic goals in mind.

Third, there have been changes in the interests of historians that can be described as, in some broad sense, political. While there are no papers here focusing on political protest movements and political conflicts, there is a sense in which these essays are distinctly political in providing a study of the past. That is seen most clearly in the extent of choice described as available to the peasants within society, choices under constraint and limitations, but choices made from below, not above. This focus, of course, indicates a certain flexibility of the political system and of limits faced also by the rulers, for whatever reason (whether their desires or their cost calculations). This attention to non-elite decisions has become a critical aspect of the recent reinterpretation of the historical past.

III

Before getting into some specific issues and comparisons with some non-European societies, let me provide a skeleton-sketch which I have found useful in approaching economic and demographic issues—a taxonomy of options to be taken, of limits upon their operation, and a linking of courses taken with ensuing consequences. In some views, an economic approach sees the world as, described narrowly, supply and demand, but the parameters are actually, more generally, choices and constraints. The constraints can be from: (1) nature—the basic Malthusian proposition; (2) political power—e.g., other individuals; and (3) markets—or transactions among groups, which set the relative costs and returns from goods and returns to individuals as workers and/or providers of capital. These constraints are not independent; for example, reliance on the market can offset the constraints imposed by nature, and political power can impose restrictions upon the operation of market constraints.

Choices are perhaps simpler to describe, though, as is clear from these papers, harder to analyse and predict. There are three key options I want to focus on here—obviously more exist, and are described in the papers, and will be noted later. Individuals may choose between more goods for themselves, more children, and more leisure. The choices for more goods and for more children are reflected in the need for more labour input. These choices have some socio-economic basis, but underlying them are, as Lehning points out, significant cultural determinants. The simple choice between goods and leisure has as an implication the fact that the desire for increased leisure can mean that measured output is below potential output, and thus that the relevant growth of economic production is understated. Since the value of leisure can be measured, as my legal and medical friends remind me, by the possible income earned during the time away from production, this can have substantial implications for the distinction between measured output and economic welfare. Increased leisure can take several forms—fewer hours per day, fewer days per year, fewer years worked per lifetime (either by delaying entry into the labour force or by earlier departure)—even, as some accuse academics of, more on-the-job leisure. Perhaps that last item is better considered, and it is an important consideration here, as more desired working conditions and/or lessened work intensity—critical considerations in accounting for the rise of slavery and other forms of unfree labour; or, also relevant, more desired living conditions, as seen in the importance of non-pecuniary components in the choice made between working on rural farms or in urban factories. (Parenthetically, at low levels of income there might be a different relationship between more goods and less leisure, with increased food necessary for more energy to be able to work longer—what could be called productive consumption. This, however, does not appear to have been essential in the cases discussed here.)

The choice of whether or not to have more children is, of course, a variant of goods *vs.* leisure, since the need to provide subsistence of children means more labour force participation when the child is young, presumably hopefully offset when the children age, become productive, are nice to their parents, and then permit parents either to retire earlier or else to consume at a higher standard than they otherwise would. The choice to increase the number of children does, however, have important impacts on the measured per capita income. Before discussing the link between economy and demography, I would like to say a bit more about the nature of this decision to have children and its rationality on purely economic grounds, since that is an argument frequently made, both historically and for the present day.

In a study of United States slavery, for a slave society characterized by an exceptionally high rate of natural increase, Robert Fogel and I calculated the costs of raising a child and the income to be possibly obtained from the productive teenager and adult once he entered the labour force.[1] Strikingly, given that presumably the amount allowed for consumption to the slave as child and adult would be expected to be lower than for a free person and that the slave would be forced into the labour force at a relatively younger age, the age at which the discounted value of rearing costs equalled the discounted value of incomes was in the late twenties. This suggests, for free societies, either that raising children for returns in old-age was not the best of investments for parents, or else it is saying something more about the concerns of family, lineage, and the emotional value of offspring that we can now explore by other approaches.

As expected, many of these papers deal with aspects of the relationship between demography and economics. Several patterns become clear—fertility rates were variable and generally less than the biological maximum; control of fertility within marriage was limited until the nineteenth century; and, most importantly for the issues at hand, variation in the marriage age (and related changes in the frequency of marriage) and in the nature of the family system were crucial determinants of variation in the magnitude of fertility, as was the existence of systems of either partible or impartible inheritance. These patterns held with regard to both cyclical changes and to the longer-term variation found when the structure of industry and its location changed (as in the villages of England discussed by David Levine),[2] or when there were variations in the degree of land ownership in rural areas, as described by Schlumbohm.

Fertility is thus seen to be a function of the level of income—income, perhaps related to the level of physical subsistence, or more plausibly, in relation to the socially-determined subsistence level acceptable. The income level also influences population by its impact on migration. In his first writings on protoindustry in Flanders, Mendels argued that there was overpopulation in agriculturally backward areas, and thus the introduction of protoindustry permitted a higher level of income to be achieved and the population to be maintained (since loss of population via migration or starvation was now precluded).

The link between fertility, inheritance systems and size of landholdings is

---

1 Fogel and Engerman (1974, pp. 73–77, 153–55). Adjustments for plausibly different levels of infant and adult mortality at this time would not dramatically alter the conclusion, nor would it vary sharply when the calculations are restricted to survivors.

2 See, for example, Levine (1977).

often noted, but let me raise one further issue here for historical interpretation which arises in many different societies. In evaluating the extent of inequality in different societies there is often a neglected generational aspect, reflected in the problem of defining the appropriate unit of measurement. If two different families with equal size holdings have, voluntarily, different numbers of children, the holdings per adult in the next generation would differ by size, and, if the same patterns hold over time, substantial inequality in the latest generation would result due to accumulated differences in preferences for children in the past. (The same point would also hold for the choice of leisure in contrast with more goods, particularly capital goods.) Simon Kuznets, the Nobel Prize winning economist for his innovations in measuring national income, has shown the frequent divergences in income equality when measured per family or by per capita per family, and adding in the lineage's households will further complicate this analysis. Clearly such differences in fertility may not always reflect voluntary choices, but to the extent that such possibilities for choice existed, the generational complications in measuring and evaluating inequality over time do persist.

A host of variables influencing marriage strategies besides just income are described: among others, inheritance systems, availability of alternative sources of labour, and opportunities for migration, and as described by Fauve-Chamoux, the possibility of stem *vs.* nuclear family patterns. To the extent that these are childbearing strategies as well, they have long-term consequences for the supply of labour on the farm. Several of the papers point to important aspects of short-term variation in the labour supply, indicating that while the so-called family farm may have had the family as a nucleus, it often included some hired labour, on a seasonal or annual basis. Mitterauer and Ortmayr point to important ecological differences in Austria, the nature of the main crops and livestock dictating the choice between attracting short-term, seasonal labour and annual or more permanent workers, who became more integrated into the family unit. In addition, it is argued that the nature of the crops will not only influence the nature and amount of the total labour supply, but also the relative roles of the genders, and, more generally, the specific nature of labour institutions in different societies. It is no accident, for example, that in the New World sugar and rice were grown only by slave labour and wheat primarily by free family farms. Free labourers did not like to work in a gang system, under which sugar was efficiently grown. There were enough slaves (and slave traders) in New England to indicate that to argue for moral revulsion to explain the limited amount of slavery there is doubtful; clearly the benefits from that region's crops, unlike the crops in the south and the Caribbean, did not provide a sufficient return to justify large-scale slave importation.

These indications of the short- and long-term flexibility of the peasant farm, and the adjustments in response to economic and demographic pressures, point to some interesting issues in the understanding of the peasantry, issues which have arisen in, of all places, the study of eighteenth- and nineteenth-century New England. Many of us had been raised on the proposition that, in the United States, it was the northern farmers who were capitalists and the southern planters who were non- (anti-, a-, or pre-) capitalists. I would argue, with perhaps some disagreement, that the southern planters now seem, as slave-owners elsewhere, less non-capitalist than before (certainly, at the least, very commercially-minded in reacting to changing economic conditions), while others now argue that New England farmers were so non-capitalist as to be peasant-like.[3] There we supposedly find the stereotyped peasant of twenty years ago who is removed from the market sector as best he (and she) can, interested mainly in the persistence of an older culture and earlier way of life. This argument raises some interesting issues about what is meant by persistence of attitudes and behaviour in the face of changing environmental conditions and constraints, and their consistency with the reliance on a basic market-oriented mentality to seek what some might regard as traditional values. This issue is suggested also by Pfister's comment that at times protoindustry dissolves traditional society, but at others it stabilizes the patterns of a traditional society. At an individual family level it suggests that there may be new means undertaken to meet the desired old ends—of family heritage, security, and independence. It may be that the best way to achieve these old ends is quite different when the opportunities presented vary with new circumstances, and these new circumstances may reflect the impact of market penetration. Thus behavioural changes can occur for reasons other than simply changes in the ways of viewing the older ways of life.

IV

These essays provide excellent demonstrations of how the concept of proto-industrialization has been expanded in substance, as well as applied more widely in time and place. When the term came to prominence about two decades ago, it was applied primarily to small geographic areas in various parts of Europe in the period just prior to the development of industrialization, and used to explain the rise of household labour in producing textiles and other goods for sale in local and/or foreign markets. The demographic implications were rather clear: as an alternative source of income, protoindustrialization permitted higher levels of family income and, thus, via higher fertility and lower mortality, increased population growth. The essays in this volume do not ignore this pattern of production and population change. But what they have done is to use the possibility of protoindustrialization as a basis for analysing a whole set of broad choices open to agricultural families. One of the choices made was protoindustrialization, but that is not the only response that was made, and these studies are concerned with examining the conditions under

---

3 For converging arguments presenting more subtle variants in accord with the traditional view of northern society, however, see Clark (1990) and Rothenberg (1993).

which the different choices were made. The broad range of applicability of this model is seen in the essays included, which range from Swabia in the period from the fifteenth to the seventeenth century, Zurich from the sixteenth to the eighteenth century, north-west Germany from the seventeenth to the nineteenth century, Austria in the eighteenth and nineteenth centuries, to France in the second half of the nineteenth century. And these include areas of what might be generally considered to be 'free labour', as well as, in the cases discussed by Rudolph and by Plakans, forms of serf labour. And, of course, many others have examined protoindustrialization in other lands throughout the world and for many other times. But, given that these essays all deal with some specific questions that raise further concerns to be considered, and that their findings are indicative of the diversity of responses and the variations over time and place, no major substantive generalizations on the course of European history appear; none, perhaps, except to demonstrate the variety of preferences, constraints, and outcomes possible in response to changing economic and demographic forces.

The basic insight in the earlier discussions of protoindustrialization was the relation between the economy, family structure, and demographic behaviour. The nature and size of the peasant family depended upon the pattern of production, including the influence of the seasonal nature of labour requirements and the returns to be obtained from all production. Protoindustrialization also served as a reminder that peasants in agricultural areas did not just produce agricultural goods, since some produced industrial goods in the household. And while adult male labour was predominant in agricultural work, the production of goods in the household provided greater opportunities for women and children to add to household income. None of this, by itself, was of course new or previously unknown to historians, but in linking these economic and social factors, and by focusing on the nature of individual and family choice, a broader range of historical analysis emerged.

The present essays are of great interest in their pointing to the great diversity of patterns in Europe, even within rather small geographic areas, rather than any one simple path from agriculture to protoindustry plus agriculture. The studies deal with the choices open to peasant families and are concerned with what economic patterns were selected and how the choices changed over time. Choice is, of course, not unconstrained. The constraints discussed include those posed by nature, including topography and climate, which influence the particular crops, the crop technology with which they can be grown, and the patterns of production over the year. Market forces play a large role, as do various social rules and laws regarding inheritance, land ownership patterns, and various other institutions and institutional arrangements. And, while little discussed in these articles, clearly political forces and power relations can constrain behaviour. These constraints, together, will influence, but not dictate, the peasants' choices. The peasants were seeking certain goals—or rather faced trade-offs among different goals—and these aims interacted with the constraints in determining their behaviour. There was a need for a certain level of subsistence income (however established), and often a desire for more income above that level. Some leisure or time away from work was needed for physiological reasons, and again, more than that was often desired, but it came at the expense of income and consumption. And if the number of children was perhaps controllable via variations in marital patterns and other means, then this too was a factor requiring choice and decision-making. Various other utility-providing factors do feature in the discussions—desires to maintain individual and family locations, to have desired working conditions, to keep older cultural values—all 'good things', but attained only at some cost in foregone incomes.

Choices are made from a wide set of possibilities, determining what and how much of various crops are to be grown; what time, and by whom, to spend on protoindustrial activity; when should the entire family migrate to another area; at what age should various household members leave home and work elsewhere, and how far away; how large should the household be; what should be its structure, and who should be permitted to become household members; should the family be permitted to expand, etc.—the number of choices are rather large, seemingly unlimited in number. The essays deal with the range of choices listed here (and some others), demonstrating the broad range of behaviour observed in the different parts of Europe over several centuries. There was a basic similarity in the need to choose and in the factors affecting choices, even when quite different choices were actually made in different times and places. What ties the essays together is that the authors make the peasants' choices understandable on the basis of certain key variables of interest. These variables influence the choices made, and as they change (or become different), the choices made changed. Thus, the protoindustrial model is used to argue for the common aspects that help explain diverse behaviour.

In explaining this behaviour, there is no need to artificially separate cultural and economic factors, and treat them as mutually exclusive. Cultural forces influence the economic goals, as well as the nature of the responsiveness to changes in basic market forces. These forces and the responses to them can and do differ over time and between locations. And economic factors influence patterns of cultural behaviour, if not belief, by determining what options are accessible at any time by affecting the range of influences upon belief and behaviour; for example, the amounts of schooling and education, and also by influencing the forms of trading and the diverse types of contacts with other societies.

The analysis of choices under constraint is, of course, a long familiar historical procedure, although, as politico-historical fashions vary, more or less importance may be allocated to this. These essays are written emphasizing a range of choice which seems quite plausible at the time. There is another feature of all these essays that, however, has been given considerably less attention in recent years by historians, and the authors' arguments for their central importance in historical understanding are quite well-presented. The constraints imposed by the natural environment—climate, soil type, topography—will influence the relative desirability of crop *vs*. livestock production as well as the benefits of producing different crops. The choices among alternative agricultural outputs will determine the work time necessary from different family members and the seasonal pattern of this work. These, in turn, will influence the opportunity to perform other forms of work, including protoindustry.

The economically key aspect of protoindustry (and its older relatives, cottage industry and the putting-out system) has been the linking of forms of industrial production, most frequently textile production, into households in the rural agricultural sectors, to supplement the incomes earned from agricultural production. In some cases the supplement is costless in that the cost of labour-time for the additional output of industrial goods is zero, while in other cases, the protoindustrial income is at substantial cost in foregone agricultural income. (And costs would also arise depending on the extent to which leisure was considered voluntary or involuntary.) This protoindustrial labour could be seasonal, since there were periods of lowered labour demand and the crop year had distinct seasonal variations. The labour for protoindustry could also be age- and gender-selective, using children and females whose agricultural inputs tended to be regarded as less productive than those of adult males. The extent of protoindustry will be limited, on the one hand, by the productivity of the agricultural sector and, on the other, by the capability and availability of the output of the 'pure' industrial sector. The more productive agriculture and the more productive modern industry, the less important would be the protoindustrial economy and the greater the economic specialization within the economy.

Furthermore, the differing optimum sizes of farms for different crops will influence the desired size of households, as clearly seen worldwide in the distinction between those crops generally grown with slave labour and those with free labour. Household size varies with the desire to have, and then to maintain, children resident, and adjustments can be made by hiring non-family members, be it for short-term or long-term periods, depending upon the specific nature of the crops grown. The study of the optimum-size household is of interest, not only for its economic characteristics, but also as a means to see the different forms of social arrangements that emerge in the attempt to achieve that size and, also, as an indication of the possible need for migration to solve long-term economic problems.

With this sense of the importance of nature in influencing peasant choices, based on the preferences of the peasant unit, other important elements have been pointed to in these essays. Some features, being based on political, social, and legal arrangements, may be the outcome of previous decisions made in society rather than truly external forces. Nevertheless, to those choosing at any time, the presence of past decisions affects the range of options, increasing it in some cases, reducing it in others. Thus the existence of rights to use existing common land provides some possibility for incomes above those obtained from the peasants' own private holdings, so that the seizing of the commons is a frequently-described cause of social instability throughout Europe. The set of acceptable inheritance patterns, themselves often reflecting the nature of the agricultural regime, will influence fertility and household patterns. And while conventions regarding age and frequency of marriage have been widespread, setting some narrower range in which fertility will vary, there is some variation, cyclical as well as secular, in the strict observation of such conventions, permitting birth rates to change over time. Nevertheless, these changes are within relatively narrow bands, so that a western European marriage pattern with relatively late age of marriage and a lower frequency of never-married relative to the patterns seen elsewhere, is clearly found in the areas studied here.

While the study of protoindustrialization emerged somewhat separately from the relatively simultaneous interest in women's history, there has been some significant dovetailing of concerns. Protoindustrialization studies have paid great attention to the gender division of labour, and its variation over the life-cycle, within the household and within agriculture. The relative availability of female labour for protoindustrial purposes has served to highlight the direct economic contributions of women, while the attention to housework and the freeing of other household members for market-oriented work has become a central part of household and family studies, as has the interest in such demographic issues as age of marriage. With this interest in women's productive and reproductive roles has come increased attention to the role of children. The economic study of children now begins at an early age—when did they start work? what did they do? at what age did they leave home? These are among the questions given more attention than when the role of children in protoindustrialization was first examined, and represents a shift from earlier discussions focusing more on formal education (about which little is said here). Even the study of adult males now raises some different questions, with the awareness that decisions made within the household, influencing all its members, should be examined allowing some (at least indirect) influence concerning what is to be chosen to others than the male head of household.

There are numerous other issues raised in these essays that remain central to the analysis of historical change, such as the differing fortunes of workers on large and on small farms (important to the analysis of Paas), and the changing nature of land fragmentation with political changes and inheritance practices. And responses include, in addition to protoindustrialization, migration to urban areas, international migration, class strife and local unrest, choices between using family labour while hiring labour on very short-term contracts and hiring labour on a long-term contractual basis, as well as differences in the magnitude of, and the ages of, children leaving home.

The broad implication of all of this is that there was continued individual, family, and community adjustment to changing circumstances, within some conventional social rules, quite different from earlier views of a rather unchanging peasantry. While there were great diversities in behaviour, many fit into patterns that can be explained, at least in part, by ecological, economic, and cultural factors.

V

Given the attention in these essays and in the literature to the many aspects of protoindustry, I want here to make only some brief comments. First, as a basis of occupational comparison over time, the distinction between agricultural and non-agricultural workers is clearly not as sharp as our familiar occupational distribution data would suggest. Better allocations by specific labour-time in different functions would be useful to understand the changing labour linkages in these two sectors of the economy, and provide more understanding of the process of social and economic change. This problem of split occupations, over the course of the year, we now see, is general to many problems in economic history, everywhere. Agricultural locations are not just for agricultural outputs.

Second, the existence and persistence of age and gender differences in occupational structures and in relative incomes remains an important puzzle, both in their own right and also, as Gullickson indicates, as a guide to past (and present) gender politics. To some extent there may be a difference between then and now, because of the earlier greater importance of agricultural production where physical strength *may* have been more important in determining the value of the output produced by individuals, and this relative differential might vary with the nature and requirements of different crops.

In a comparative study of industrialization in the antebellum northern and southern United States, Claudia Goldin and Kenneth Sokoloff (1982; 1984) brought together data concerning productivity in specific crops that suggest that whereas males and females were relatively equally productive in cotton production, the harvesting of which took several months to complete, there were apparently sharp differences observed between the genders in the growing and harvesting of wheat. Thus, they argue, the south had a relatively more productive agricultural use for females (and children) than did the north, leaving women and children to form the basis of an industrial (and proto-industrial) labour force in the northern states.

There is, moreover, something to be learned about gender perceptions from an examination of certain aspects of the rise and expansion of slave societies. There were earlier arguments attributing the 60–40 male-female ratio in slaves shipped in the transatlantic slave trade to differential labour in field work in sugar and other plantation crops, but these arguments have been displaced since it is now clear that relatively more females than males worked in the fields (Eltis and Engerman, 1992). In cotton, sugar and rice production, there was a distinct occupational division of labour on the plantation, with males being predominantly the carpenters, blacksmiths, coopers, and other artisan-type workers, and females more frequently cooks, seamstresses, and related textile workers in what in other conditions might be called protoindustry. In an attempt to see exactly how male-female differences were perceived by slave-owners, data on the prices of slaves in a number of different societies have been collected (see Moreno Fraginals et al., 1983). In field labour it turns out that adult women were generally valued at at least 80 to 90 per cent the value of men. (Interestingly, in their early teens, girls were worth more than boys.) Curiously, the few cases in which females were valued more than males were in urban locations. Clearly there is more to be said on these comparisons, since the value of slave children influenced the value of the slave females (though that is generally found to be less than twenty per cent of the total value of a female—a point to consider when referring to the dual function of production and reproduction—Fogel and Engerman, 1974, pp. 75–77, 80–82). The persistence of these differentials by gender, in circumstances in which the attitude to sex roles and to sex power relations would be expected to be quite different than within white society, poses some questions for the examination of gender differentials in free agricultural societies.

There is another recent United States study that bears on this question of gender status, related to the study of the patterns of wealth brought into marriage and of inheritance patterns. William Newell (1986) has studied a collection of wills for Butler county in antebellum Ohio, to see how the treatment of sons and daughters varied over time, and to determine if gender-differentials in inheritance were narrowing. That they apparently were, at a time when relative female wages were apparently low, may seem conflicting if one seeks a simple answer to questions of female status, but does suggest the varied dimensions to the problem of evaluating changing gender status over time.

Third, the focus on rural industry as an income supplement to peasants and on the production of industrial goods in rural villages, raises the questions of where the demand for the commodities produced came from and what the peasants did with any incomes earned above the subsistence level. Sella points to the variety of occupations in the villages of northern Italy around the start of the seventeenth century, the extent to which much of the output was sold in immediately surrounding areas and not continent-wide markets, and the degree to which peasant demand contributed to the development of these small-scale industries. Clearly these were not peasants who were self-sufficient if that is taken to mean the absence of any purchases from other producers or sales to other consumers. While providing most of their own food and some of their clothing, there was a need to enter the market to satisfy their needs and to spend their incomes from wages and sales. While, as noted, perhaps not quite peasants, as late as 1830, in the United States it is estimated that over eighty per cent of the demand for clothing purchases and possibly three-quarters of the overall demand for consumer purchases originated from outside urban

areas (Brady, 1972, p. 62). More concentration on the consumer and investment demand from the rural sector, where most of the population still lived,
and more attention to the demand generated from the agricultural sector serve
as a useful corrective to the urban-based economic growth theories that still
frequently dominate the literature. And, as a reminder of the importance of
the small units of demand that Sella points to, as late as 1860 the demand for
household stoves absorbed more of the output of the modernizing U.S. iron
industry than did the demands generated for iron rails, while in 1849, the
overall production of nails was twice that of rails (North, 1961, p. 164; Fogel,
1964, p. 135).

The nature of the protoindustrial link between agriculture and household
production also serves as a reminder of the importance of nature and climatic
factors in the basically agricultural economy, and, more particularly, the
importance of seasonality in economic life.[4] The actual number of days, and
hours per day, that are required by most agricultural production leaves
considerable potential labour time available for other alternatives—including,
of course, leisure and other seemingly non-economically productive activities.
There remain problems in the evaluation of the choice for leisure and/or non-
agricultural production, and also the determination of the degree of labour
intensity. These are suggested by a detailed reconstruction of labour time in
agricultural production, using standard measures of labour requirements for
crops, undertaken by Robert Gallman for the antebellum United States. He
can account for only about one-half of total possible labour hours, and this is
somewhat more than a similar analysis restricted to the antebellum south, on
the basis of which Forrest McDonald and Grady McWhiney (1980) argue for a
'leisurely', but wealthy, southern economy.[5] Of interest also is the finding by
Gallman that variations in crop-mix alone, over the course of the first half of
the nineteenth century, could account for an over twenty-five per cent increase
in labour time requirements, with presumably offsetting changes in leisure
time, in non-agricultural production, or agricultural productivity, to allow for
this change.

Attention has also been given to the prospects for seasonal (in contrast with
permanent) migrations, whether to more urbanized areas or to other agricultural regions. To the extent that there were seasonal rural-urban migration
flows, the complexities in using the basic occupational data, mentioned earlier,
recur. Dual occupations could exist with migration, not just within the same
household. In either case it would mean that the availability of agricultural
incomes meant labour was available to other sectors at lower cost than might
otherwise have been the case. Even in regions where agriculture was
prosperous, seasonal protoindustrial employment may have been an alterna-

4 For a discussion of these issues, see Engerman and Goldin (1994).
5 See, also, Olson (1992) for a discussion of hours of agricultural labour in the nineteenth-century
   United States.

tive preferred to leisure, providing more income to the farmer at relatively low cost—a cost below that if labour had to be reallocated during periods of peak seasonal demand. The importance of seasonal work is something not only characteristic of agricultural areas and apparently due only to strictly climatic factors. In an early 1930s work of statistical analysis, Simon Kuznets (1933) pointed out the seasonal variations in many modern industries, suggesting that we may find it useful to rethink our definitions of full employment and of the preferred allocation of labour time over the course of the year.

The discussion of regional protoindustrialization has also led to some further questions about the nature of relative regional and national growth paths and the possibility of leap-frogging as opposed to smooth transitions in the process of economic growth—the latter a problem of some more general interest in explaining the past few centuries of worldwide economic growth. Although there are exceptions, and some questions, the more prosperous agricultural regions were presumably less frequently protoindustrial, and the more heavily protoindustrial regions tended to become more industrial—and thus the leaders in the next stage of economic development. It may be, however, that low wages can lead to an early expansion of factory employment, but also that overpopulation and low wages may also lead to a perceived lack of need to seek or adopt the new technology necessary to raise productivity and profitability to higher levels. It is of interest how much of the past centuries of writing on economic policy and economic history are split between arguments that growth comes through having things easy and that growth comes through having things difficult—and it is of interest also how difficult the historical resolution of that puzzle still remains.

Finally, it might be noted that the recent literature has helped to provide a better sense of migration patterns and their meaning. The relative importance of shorter-distance migration, and the ability to maintain social and economic contacts with the family and lineage of origin, provides a greater degree of flexibility for family reproductive strategies. Presumably migration patterns were influenced by the location of other family members and kin, so that the extent to which migration has been disruptive is now seen as not as dramatic as earlier believed, making the extent of mobility found in many societies perhaps more easily understood. Surely, if recent work on trans-oceanic migration to the United States indicates a rather lessened severance of family and cultural ties with the country of origin than some read into the image of 'The Uprooted', migration within these European societies seems a more understandable response to economic and demographic conditions.

VI

This is perhaps a useful thrust on which to end, noting why we historians, no matter what our methods and what our areas and periods, still have basic interests in common. That is because our works, as in those on peasant economy and protoindustry, reveal the rather remarkable range of human diversity and human choices in reaction to changing circumstances. When dramatic changes are most expected, we often find the most continuity; and the largest changes may appear at the most unexpected time. Clearly the search for answers here suggests that no matter how much more we learn, there are still pleasant surprises ahead.

References

BRADY, D. (1972), 'Consumption and the Style of Life', In L. E. Davis, R. A. Easterlin and W. N. Parker (eds.), *American Economic Growth: An Economist's History of the United States*, New York, 61–89.

CLARK, C. (1990), *The Roots of Rural Capitalism: Western Massachusetts, 1780–1860*, Ithaca.

ELTIS, D. and S. L. ENGERMAN (1992), 'Was the Slave Trade Dominated by Men?', *Journal of Interdisciplinary History*, **23**, 237–57.

ENGERMAN, S. and C. GOLDIN (1994), 'Seasonality in Nineteenth-Century Labour Markets', In T. Weiss and D. Schaefer (eds.), *Economic Development in Historical Perspective*, Stanford, 99–126.

FOGEL, R. W. (1964), *Railroads and American Economic Growth: Essays in Econometric History*, Baltimore.

FOGEL, R. W. and S. L. ENGERMAN (1974), *Time on the Cross: The Economics of American Negro Slavery*, Boston.

GALLMAN, R. E. (1975), 'The Agricultural Sector and the Pace of Economic Growth: U.S. Experience in the Nineteenth Century', In D. C. Klingaman and R. K. Vedder (eds.), *Essays in Nineteenth Century Economic History*, Athens, Ohio, 35–76.

GOLDIN, C. and K. SOKOLOFF (1982), 'Women, Children, and Industrialization in the Early Republic: Evidence from the Manufacturing Censuses', *Journal of Economic History*, **42**, 741–74.

GOLDIN, C. and K. SOKOLOFF (1984), 'The Relative Productivity Hypothesis of Industrialization: The American Case, 1820 to 1850', *Quarterly Journal of Economics*, **99**, 461–87.

KUZNETS, S. (1933), *Seasonal Variations in Industry and Trade*, New York.

LEVINE, D. (1977), *Family Formation in an Age of Nascent Capitalism*, New York.

McDONALD, F. and G. McWHINEY (1980), 'The South from Self-Sufficiency to Peonage: An Interpretation', *American Historical Review*, **85**, 1095–118.

MORENO FRAGINALS, M., H. S. KLEIN and S. L. ENGERMAN (1983), 'The Level and Structure of Slave Prices on Cuban Plantations in the Mid-Nineteenth Century: Some Comparative Perspectives,' *American Historical Review*, **88**, 1201–18.

NEWELL, W. H. (1986), 'Inheritance on the Maturing Frontier: Butler County, Ohio, 1803–1865', In S. L. Engerman and R. E. Gallman (eds.), *Long-Term Factors in American Economic Growth*, Chicago, 261–303.

NORTH, D. C. (1961), *The Economic Growth of the United States, 1790–1860*, Englewood Cliffs.

OLSON, J. (1992), 'Clock Time versus Real Time: A Comparison of the Lengths of the Northern and Southern Agricultural Work Years', In R. W. Fogel and S. L. Engerman (eds.), *Without Consent or Contract: The Rise and Fall of American Slavery, Markets and Production*, Technical Papers, Volume I, New York, 216–40.

ROTHENBERG, W. B. (1992), *From Market-Places to a Market Economy: The Transformation of Rural Massachusetts, 1750–1850*, Chicago.

INDEX

Abel, Wilhelm 146, 148, 151
Africa 64
agricultural labourers 11, 20, 147
agricultural revolution 54, 55, 56, 91
agriculture 10, 12, 15, 16, 20, 30, 43, 55, 57,
    72–80 *passim,* 94, 115–19, 121, 124, 126,
    129, 131, 132, 135, 137, 140–42, 151, 158,
    163, 175, 188, 191, 196, 206, 220, 235, 240–
    46 *passim;* commercial 15; intensive 57,
    119; pastoral 55; seasonality in 17;
    structure of 137; subsistence 16, 166
alcoholic men 217
Alpine 2, 9, 26, 36, 38, 45, 49–62, 97, 117,
    122, 125
Alps 26, 30, 50, 54–56, 58, 60, 61, 105
America 64, 94, 106, 107, 189, 193, 194, 198,
    203, 209; *see also* United States
animals *see* livestock
anthropologists 1, 6, 28, 29, 88, 202
anthropology 28
apprentices 40, 41, 132
Argentina 107
aristocratic 86, 87, 89, 106, 107
army 209
Ashton, T.S. 149
Asia 64
Augsburg 146, 148, 150–51
Austria 2, 9, 11, 20, 21, 26, 28, 30, 44–45, 50,
    52, 53, 56, 60, 61, 75, 87, 210, 238, 240
Austrian 12, 21, 28, 29, 38, 40, 45, 49–62,
    123
Austro-Hungarian Monarchy 61

Baltic 165–84
Baronnies 87–110 *passim*
Basque 86, 88, 90, 100
Basques 107
bastardy 99, 100
Bavaria 53, 210
Bavarian 146, 147
Belgium 16, 53, 125, 126
Berkner, Lutz 65–67, 71, 75, 87–89
birth control *see* contraception and family
    limitation
birth order 99
birth rate 57, 64, 243
Black Forest 126
boarders *see* lodgers
Bohemia 19

boys 62, 89, 97, 131, 207, 212, 216, 217, 222,
    228, 230, 245; behaviour of 215, 216, 218;
    work of 215, 223
Braudel, Fernand 45, 156
Braun, Rudolf 6, 10, 13, 14, 15, 114, 121,
    124, 128, 131, 133, 137, 202
Britain 209, 213, 219
British 15, 209, 210, 212, 213, 219, 224
brothers 21, 57, 58, 89, 90, 175, 199, 201
building trade 41, 54
Burgenland 26, 45, 51, 54

cadets/cadettes 89, 94–110 *passim*
Cambridge Group for the History of
    Population and Social Structure 11, 87,
    109
Capital 19, 118, 119, 123, 126, 128, 140, 236;
    circulating 116–18, 120, 134; costs 134;
    deconcentration of 106; goods 238; human
    126; inputs 118, 124, 130, 140, 141;
    investment 235; marginal product of 119,
    140; market 142; merchant 19, 194;
    production functions for 138, 139;
    productivity schedules 118, 119; profits
    135; rent 117, 136, 138; social 136
Caribbean 238
Carinthia 45, 49, 50, 52, 53, 60
Catholicism 60, 61
cattle 9, 26, 30, 36–38, 40, 44, 50, 53–56, 58,
    105, 121, 129, 136, 142, 147, 157, 168–69
Caux 17; *see also* Pays de Caux
celibacy 61, 87, 96, 97, 100
census 11, 28, 37, 50, 54, 72, 73, 75, 77, 81,
    82, 93, 96, 108, 109, 168, 195, 199–201
cereal 53–56, 72
Chayanov, A. V. 139, 165, 179
childcare 71, 218, 219, 224–30
children 4, 7, 9, 10, 15, 20, 37, 38, 40, 41, 44,
    45, 49, 50, 54, 59, 60, 64, 66, 69, 75–78,
    86–90 *passim,* 93, 94, 97, 102, 103, 106–09,
    123, 124, 132, 134, 135, 160, 170, 174–80
    passim, 194, 197, 198, 201, 206–30 *passim,*
    236–44 *passim;* adult 38, 76, 78, 89, 177,
    179; as consumer goods 65; as old-age
    insurance 77, 237; born out of wedlock 21;
    care of 212, 218, 219, 220, 223; cost of
    raising 237; disinherited 198, 202; earnings
    of 213–15, 226; employment of 209, 214;
    factory 211, 215, 217; foster 58; grown-up

41, 123; health of 21, 211, 220, 226;
illegitimate 49, 58–60; labour of 66, 207,
229; married 78, 79; mean number per
marriage 194, 196, 197; morals of 216;
noble 206; non-inheriting 146, 147; number
of 65, 236, 241; of working age 142;
peasant 59, 199; slave 245; surviving 99,
198; unmarried 74; urban 211; vagabond
228; vagrant 225; value of 45; welfare of
211; work of 206–10, 219, 223, 226; work
roles of 131–32; working capacity of 132;
working-class 230; working day of 219,
223–25; working hours of 222; young 208,
211–20 passim, 225, 227, 228
class 1, 3, 20, 129, 135, 139, 142, 188–203,
206; cottager 55; feudal 19; formation 4,
20; landless 106, 135, 199, 201, 202; lower
38, 40, 44, 123, 129–31, 137, 141, 142;
middle 151, 207, 213, 229; peasant 59, 223;
propertyless 188–94; rural lower 55, 56, 59,
61, 124, 142; rural middle 119, 123; strife
243; working 160, 209–30 passim
cloth 120, 121, 127, 132, 150, 151, 157, 161,
162
clothing 15, 154, 158, 160, 221, 245
coal 18, 67, 126, 127
Coal, John 11
comparative advantage 15
complex families 38, 46, 77–79, 87, 109, 110,
132, 139, 175; see also household, complex
conception, pre-marital 100
contraception 64, 100, 101, 105, 196
cottage industry 9, 13–17, 19, 20, 70, 76, 114,
115, 117, 120, 123, 124, 133, 134, 138, 146,
147, 150, 151, 162, 193, 194, 202, 206, 209,
242
cottager 11, 29, 37, 38, 40, 44, 55, 139, 147,
150
cotton 18, 30, 67, 72, 73, 77, 79, 121, 123,
125, 127–32, 150, 162, 208–10, 213, 224,
244
craftsmen 30, 36, 38, 40, 41, 54, 151, 156,
158–61, 163, 212
craftwork 91, 103
cultural 1, 2, 12, 13, 56, 92, 105, 137, 142;
anthropologists 29; anthropology 28;
attitudes 21; background 106; behaviour
241; change 102, 104, 105; critics 235;
customs 11; determinants 236; expectations
18; factors 21, 22, 60, 80, 241, 244; forces
241; identity 92; level 104, 106; model 80,
81, 110; mutation 87; revolution 94; ties
247; values 181, 241
culture 57, 86, 107, 137, 167, 239; French
107; occitan 110; peasant 2, 154, 165, 166;
popular 137; poverty 57; Pyrenean 104–05
customs 10, 11, 62, 88–90, 96, 98, 105, 110,
175, 180, 182, 197
Czap, Peter 179–80, 184

dairy 53, 136
Daubié, Julie 220, 224, 229
Davies, Kingsley 65
day-labourers 36–40, 44, 54, 147, 155, 158–61
De Vries, Jan 154
death 81, 89, 90, 108, 125, 146, 175, 177, 183,
184, 197, 198, 222
demesne 138, 171, 172, 174
demographers 1–3, 6, 9, 13, 14, 65, 86, 91
demographic transition 64–66
demography 45, 86, 138, 154, 236, 237; see
also population
domestic industry 29, 30, 40, 43, 44
domestic service 104–08 passim, 123, 230
dowry 89, 90, 106, 198

Easterlin, Robert 65
emigration 91, 96–98, 105–10 passim, 146,
189, 194, 198
Engerman, Stanley L. 4, 233–48
England 18, 122, 130, 132, 149, 151, 155, 156,
160, 223, 237
English Factory Act 209
Esparros 90–109 passim
ethnographers 88
European marriage pattern 86, 195, 243
expenses 160, 161, 223
extended 9, 12, 21, 38, 65, 66, 77–79, 109,
123, 132, 139, 200

famille-souche 86, 88
family cycle 133, 136, 142, 179
family formation 4, 65, 66, 77, 79, 91, 96,
196; access to 106; changes in 64; social
differentials in 194–97
family forms 17, 26–46
family life cycle 2, 3, 10–12, 14, 20, 58, 59
family limitation 67, 71, 79, 87, 101
family reconstitution 20, 93, 96, 100, 108,
109, 195, 200, 201
family size 64, 78, 103, 108, 115, 117, 122,
159
family structure 1, 2, 4, 12, 14, 20, 21, 29, 36,
37, 54, 58, 66, 80, 109, 110, 240; complex
132; economic influences on 7–11; impact
of outside world 3; influence of marriage
pattern 2, 56–59; peasant 9; rural 53; rural
lower-class 59; simple 179; farmhands 37–
41 passim, 43, 46, 53, 58, 59, 168, 172,
175–81 passim
Fauve-Chamoux, Antoinette 2–3, 20, 86–113,
188, 238
female 98, 99, 106, 168, 170, 173, 179, 184,
195, 199–201, 221, 242–45; adult 200; age
at marriage 184, 194; behaviour 206;
children 230; divorced 82; earning ability
213; employees 208; factory labour 227;
farmhands 53, 177; heir 89–90, 96; industry
131; labour 137, 173, 179, 218, 219, 229,

243; literacy 81, 83; peasants 10;
proportions married 82; school attendance
81; servants 49, 53, 195, 199; slaves 245;
status 245; successor 90; wages 245;
widowed 82; work 41, 43; workers 217,
219, 221, 222; *see also* women
feminists 220, 229
fertility 9, 13, 45, 69, 80, 100–02, 106, 125,
126, 128, 140, 234, 237–39, 243; behaviour
103; control 68, 73, 80, 87, 100, 101, 194,
237, conjugal 102; decline 67, 184;
differential 102; illegitimate 70, 82, 228;
limitation of 65, 80; limited 66; marital 13,
65, 67, 71, 79, 81–83, 100; natural 71; of
land 117; overall 65, 67, 69, 71, 73, 74, 79,
82, legitimate 101–02; rate 124–27, 137,
141, 228, 237; regulation 86; restricted
marital 66, 69; restrictions 102; social
differentials in 194–97; uncontrolled 66, 67,
71, 73; within marriage 69, 71, 73, 79, 184
Finland 52
Flanders 13, 121, 127, 233, 237
Fogel, Robert 237, 245, 246
forest 92, 103
forestry 53–55
fragmentation of landholding 73
France 2, 3, 17, 18, 20, 54, 66, 67, 70, 72, 75,
86–89, 97, 101, 104–06, 120, 121, 188, 206,
207, 210, 211, 217, 219, 223, 224, 228, 240
French 2, 64–83, 86–89, 100, 101, 105–07,
114, 131, 147, 202, 206–30
French Civil Code 89, 93
Friesland 154

Gallman, Robert 246
Gaunt, David 9, 10
gender 3, 17, 99, 129, 130, 139, 141, 206–08,
215–29 *passim*, 242–45; division of labour
1, 11, 12, 43, 243; relations 20; roles 12,18,
20, 43, 44, 129, 138, 228, 238
German 11, 20, 88, 89, 147, 188–203
Germany 41, 54, 120, 126, 146, 147, 151, 188,
202, 203, 240
girls 43, 60, 89, 98, 100, 109, 131, 207–30
passim, 245; adolescent 228; behaviour of
215–18; factory 218; health of 217; literacy
of 105; servant 49; work of 215; working
day of 223, 224; working hours of 223, 228,
229
Goldin, Claudia 244
Göttingen 20
grain 9, 26, 30, 37, 38, 40, 122, 126, 127, 147–
48, 152, 157, 168
Greek 88, 202
Gullickson, Gay 4, 16–18, 114, 117, 121, 125,
127, 128, 130, 131, 160, 206–32, 244
Gutmann, Myron 13, 16, 114, 126, 127, 130,
139, 165

Hagen, William 4, 165
Hajnal, John 13, 50, 59, 86, 91, 184
handicrafts 3, 40, 41, 92, 114, 115, 162, 163
Hareven, Tamara 6, 12, 165
heir 45, 69, 72, 86–110 *passim*, 196–98
heiress 89, 90, 96–102 *passim*
herbs 36
Heuerlinge 135, 193–203 *passim*
holdings 10, 12, 36, 45, 53, 55, 72, 78, 135,
147, 168, 174, 188–202, 237–38, 243
horses 37, 156, 157, 167–69, 193, 200
household 1–5, 6–22, 28, 37, 40, 41, 49, 53,
54, 57–60, 65, 73–82 *passim*, 87, 93, 108,
109, 114–42, 158, 173, 193–95, 199, 202,
203, 238, 240, 241, 243, 246; adults per 67–
71, 73, 82; agricultural 76, 242; as locus of
decision-making 64, 65; behaviour 22, 67,
73, 75; change 79; complex 11, 68, 70, 73,
75–79, 87, 110, 175; complexity 123, 141;
composition 7, 9, 12, 17, 18, 28, 109, 115,
122, 199; composition strategies 10, 11–22;
economics 65; economy 114–42;
establishment 54, 98; extended 65, 66, 68,
77–79, 123, 132; farming 134, 142;
formation 71, 75, 91, 95, 106, 107, 124,
125, 136; forms 11, 21; fragmentation 77;
'good' 107; heads 20, 72–78, 89, 90, 92, 97,
117, 120, 123, 125, 126, 132, 136, 141, 158,
195, 200, 201, 243; income 116, 117, 134,
240; industry 20; investment capacity 119;
joint 65, 68, 75, 91; labour 115–20, 123,
128, 129, 132, 134, 135, 138, 140, 239;
labour force 117, 120, 127, 134; land-poor
123, 130; landless 120–21, 126, 135, 191,
193, 199, 201; life 76; life strategies of 7;
lower-class 131, 137, 141, 142; marital units
per 68–71, 73, 82; mean size 107; multi-
generational 78, 86; multiple 78; new 95,
96, 125, 126, 137; non-family 78, 79;
nuclear 65–79 *passim*; of tenant farmers
160; of widows 43; organization 68;
patterns 243; peasant 115, 123, 154, 156,
157, 159, 200; production 246; production
of 115; proletarian 137; propertied 200;
propertyless 192, 199, 200, 203;
protoindustrial 16, 17, 114–42; residency
rules 71; residential 65; rural 117, 138, 155,
242; sibling 57; simple 91; size 9–12, 17,
107, 115, 116, 122, 123, 128, 132, 141, 199,
200, 241, 242; stem 68, 69; structure 6, 7,
9, 13, 14, 37, 65–81, 123, 124, 132, 141,
241, of peasant 2, 64–83; system 65, 71,
75–79
Huston, R. 16, 18
Hufton, Olwen 76, 131, 206, 223
Hungary 170, 173
Hutterites 82

illegitimacy 49–50, 57–60, 64, 81, 82, 99–100, 228
immigration 108, 146, 194
income 65, 72, 75, 116, 123, 124, 134–37, 142, 148, 150, 151, 159–61, 173, 196, 213, 218, 234–47 *passim*; agricultural 75, 242, 246; cash 142; copyhold 152; distribution 123; elasticity 148; family 65, 115, 125, 239; farm 148; from cottage industry 15; from protoindustry 15; household 116, 117, 134, 240; in old age 136; national 238; non-agrarian 38; of tenant farmers 160, 161; peasant 152, 154, 159, 161, 162; protoindustrial 125, 126, 137, 141, 142, 242; rent 117; rural 114, 125; sources of 30, 57, 131, 193, 239; subsistence 234, 241; supplemental 17; wage 159
industrial revolution 3, 15
infants 43, 184, 222; *see also* mortality, infant
inheritance 10, 11, 78, 86–110, 124, 126, 141, 146, 195, 198, 199, 237, 238, 243, 245; egalitarian 110; family 96; impartible 12, 20, 45, 53, 54, 57, 58, 60, 65, 87, 191, 194–97, 202, 237; land 57–60, 86; laws 3, 11, 12, 240; non-egalitarian 3, 94; partible 12, 17, 45, 53–60 *passim*, 65, 87, 146, 237; patterns 1, 3, 11, 12, 20, 21, 45, 53–54, 147, 152, 243, 245; regime 108; rules of 36, 45; rural patterns 45; strategies 12–13; transmission of property by 44
inheriting 89, 90, 98, 146, 147
Inwohner 37; *see also* lodgers
Ireland 52, 61
iron 18, 26, 30, 40, 67, 126, 150, 163, 221, 246
Italian 11
Italy l3, 10, 11, 154–63, 245

Jewish 13, 88
Jones, E.L. 14, 15, 117
journeymen 40, 41, 132, 159, 161
July Monarchy 210, 211, 219
juridical 197

Kaufsystem 130, 194; *see also* putting-out system
Kerridge, Eric 151
Kin 66, 75, 77–79, 90, 134, 172, 175–79, 200–03, 247
King Gregory 148, 160
Kinship 38, 46, 65, 88, 200, 201
Kriedte, Peter 20, 114, 124, 127, 128, 133, 137–39, 188, 194, 202
Kula, Witold 19, 165
Kuznets, Simon 238, 247

labour 4, 10, 28, 40, 41, 45, 66, 75, 76, 78, 115, 116, 118, 128, 133, 135, 163, 166–82, 193, 199, 200, 203, 211, 212, 220, 235–47

passim; agricultural 54, 55, 75, 105, 115–18, 121, 125, 128, 134, 139–42, 173; allocation 3, 114–24, 128, 138, 169; cheap 226, 229; child 41, 66, 137, 206–19 *passim*, 222, 225, 229; contracts 134; corvée 166–68, 172–82; day 55; demand 17, 18, 37–38, 150, 172, 206, 242; distribution 117; division of 16, 17, 28, 43, 53, 130, 132, 138, 173, 244, by age 12, by gender, 1, 11, 12, 43, 243, family 11, sexual 206, 213, social 202; exchange of 55, 135; factory 211, 221, 227; family 11, 12, 54, 55, 115, 118, 122, 133, 138, 139, 146–52, 235, 243; female 137, 173, 179, 218, 219, 229, 243; field 244, 245; forms 41; free 1, 240, 242; hired 12, 175, 238, 243, seasonal 10, 11; household 115–20, 123, 128, 129, 132, 134, 135, 138, 140, 239; industrial 127; institutions 238; law 219, 222, 229; legislation 220; live-in 10; male 240; marginal product of 116–18, 124, 136, 140, 141, agricultural 118, 140, 141, protoindustrial 117; marginal unit of 122; market 3, 115, 116, 122, 134, 146, 151, 152, 180; needs 38, 79, 80; obligations 40, 166, 169, 175–81 *passim*; opportunities 17; organization 36–41, 44; permanent 11; physical 227; production functions for 138, 139; productivity 119, 122, 123, 126, 129, 131, 134–36, 142, protoindustrial 116–21, 123, 125, 128, 140–42, 242; relationships 37, 41; rent 123–26, 136, 141, 168, 184; reproduction costs 118, 137; requirements 2, 9, 10, 65, 116, 133, 138, 166, 172, 179, 240, 246; rural 122; seasonal 9, 10, 11, 238, 240, 242; serf 240; servant 54; short-term 134; skilled 151; slave 238, 242; supply 115, 116, 136, 137, 142, 146, 151, 152, 235, 238; surplus 123, 174, 178; system 166, 235; temporal 134; unfree 1, 4, 235, 236; urban 18, 125; wage 55, 77, 80, 106, 122, 138; women's 17, 58, 207, 221, 229
labour force 9, 11, 38, 41, 67, 72, 119, 140, 168–69, 171, 172, 175–80 *passim*, 220, 222, 224, 235–37; captive 165; continuous 38; demand 37, 38; factory 219; family 10, 44, 75, 122, 131, 134, 135; household 117, 120, 127, 134; in iron mining 40; of the poor 120; protoindustrial 244; size 18; textile 208; urban 17; weaving 208
land tenure 72, 78, 79
landless 21, 57, 59, 106, 120–21, 126, 130, 134, 135, 140, 180, 191–203 *passim*
landlessness 17
Languedoc 122
Laslett, Peter 6, 11, 57, 87, 91, 99, 100, 109, 110, 160
Latin America 64
law 11, 89, 107, 207–29 *passim*; British 209; child labour 207, 210–12, 225; childcare

224; common 197; inheritance 3, 11, 12, 240; labour 219, 222, 229; local 10, 11; national 11; peasant 168; regional 11; Roman 88

Le Play, Frederic 7, 64–66, 70, 86, 88–90, 95, 106, 109–10

Le Roy Ladurie, Emmanuel 86, 88

Leboutte, René 16, 114, 126, 127, 139, 165

legal 45, 89, 99, 105, 146, 147, 156, 181, 198, 236, 242

Lehning, James R. 2, 64–85, 114, 120, 123, 127, 132, 206, 236

Leicestershire 128

Levine, David 13, 19, 20, 114, 117, 123, 124, 127, 128, 130, 131, 165, 237

life course 12, 21

life cycle 2, 10, 12, 56, 59, 115, 124, 132, 135–38, 142, 179, 243

linen 15, 30, 118–21, 123, 125, 127, 132, 135, 155, 157, 163, 193–96, 202, 210

liquor 217

literacy 80, 81, 83, 104, 105

livestock 37, 40, 55–56, 72, 103, 121, 122, 136, 147, 150, 152, 168–68, 174, 193, 238, 242

Livland 3, 166, 168, 181

lodgers 11, 37, 40, 44, 54, 55, 68, 108, 132, 134, 142, 201

Löfgren, Orvar 28, 29

Loire 66–68, 71, 72, 80, 81

Lombardy 155, 157–63

London 128

lords 191–93, 202

Lorimer, Frank 65

Lyon 66, 67, 72, 82

Malthus, Thomas 13, 64, 110

Malthusian 9, 10, 86, 88, 101, 234, 236

markets 1, 3, 15, 16, 36, 53, 56, 105, 118, 120, 138, 140, 142, 148, 154, 165, 166, 180, 194, 236, 239, 243, 245; capital 142; continent-wide 245; distant 15, 16; domestic 3; economy 155, 156; foreign 239; handicraft 92; housing 44; inter-regional 115; international 115, 163; local 16, 151, 239; marriage 198; property 44; proximity of 18; real estate 136; relations 41, 167; small 115; supra-regional 40; taxes 151; town 157, 158; transactions 155; urban 17

market development 80

market factors 19

market forces 124, 146, 152, 240, 241

market integration 53–55

marriage 61, 62, 66, 69, 71, 75, 77–79, 89, 90, 97, 99, 101–03, 108, 126, 128, 136, 151, 172, 175, 177, 183, 195–201 passim, 234, 238, 245; access to 86; acts 81; age at 2, 9, 11, 13–15, 44, 50, 52, 54, 55, 60, 97–101,

106, 125–28, 184, 194–96, 234, 237, 243, first 139; arranged 99; as rite of passage 60; 'beggar' 64; certificate 83, 104; duration 101; earlier 64, 98, 106, 198; early 13, 51, 65, 97, 196; fertility within 69, 71, 73. 79, 184, control of 68, 73, 80, 194, 237; first 98, 197, 198; frequency 127, 237, 243; frequent 65, 66, 73, 80; ideology 38; late 49–62, 97, 108; later 98; local 99; market 198; multiple 68; non-conformist 96, 99; number of children per 194; patterns 2, 7, 49–62, 67, 139, 234; possibilities 56, 106, 109; rate 124–27, 141; restricted 60, 65, 66, 71, 73, 79; selection 98; social 100; universal 51, 194

marriageable age 10, 97

Marx, Karl 6, 15, 19, 234

Massachusetts 210

medicine 36

Medick, Hans 20, 29, 43, 44, 114, 115, 117, 120, 123, 127, 130, 137–39, 165

Mediterranean 107, 115, 122

Mendels, Franklin 3, 6, 9, 13–16, 18, 66, 71, 72, 88, 106, 114, 116, 121, 122, 124, 126, 127, 132, 134, 165, 188, 233, 237

merchants 19, 67, 72, 115, 151, 161, 194, 206, 212; international 156; linen 30; textile 209; urban 17, 18, 114, 130; wholesale 158

Michelet, Jules 220–21, 223, 226–28

migration 12, 146, 183, 234–38 passim, 242, 243, 246, 247; downward 38; in- 73; international 243; out- 73, 74; permanent 246; rate 83, 87; rural-urban 246; seasonal 246; to North America 194; to the city 151; to villages 151

Milan 155, 158–63 passim

military 62, 92, 104, 106, 211

mining 10, 26, 30, 36, 38, 40, 41, 44, 56, 127, 150

Mitterauer, Michael 2, 9–10, 20, 26–48, 52, 59, 60, 123, 135, 165, 238

morality 4, 13, 64, 66, 80, 106, 172, 182, 209–12, 216–30 passim, 239

Moravia 19

mortality 13, 73, 74, 77, 125–27, 141, 239; adult 198, 237; as controller of growth 86; child 13, 197; infant 13, 197, 221–22, 237; rates 21, 106, 125, 126

Moslem 13

New England 238, 239

Newell, William 245

nobility 11, 19

noble 146, 206

non-conformism 95, 110

non-conformist 96–106

Normandy 121

Notestein, Frank 64

nuclear 3, 11, 21, 64–79 *passim*, 87, 91, 123, 238
nuptiality 9, 13, 16, 67, 69, 71, 80, 86

occitan 86–88, 92, 93, 105, 106, 110
Ohio 245
Ortmayr, Norbert 2, 20, 36, 37, 40, 44, 49–63, 238

Paas, Martha White 3, 10, 18, 146–53, 243
Pallot, Judith 17
patriarchy 20, 44
patrilineal 46
Pays de Caux 121, 125–31 *passim*, 209
peddling 30, 36, 41
pedlars 36, 41, 130, 156–58, 161
Pinchbeck, Ivy 209, 223
Pfister, Ulrich 3, 12, 13, 16, 18, 55, 114–45, 239
Plakans, Andrejs 3, 4, 165–87, 240
Poland 10, 12, 19
population 13, 28, 30, 61, 68, 74, 76, 82, 87, 91–93, 95, 104, 107, 123, 125, 130, 135, 146, 158, 170, 173, 175, 178, 180, 183, 184, 195, 237, 246; ageing of 98, 110; behaviour 64; boom 106; census 81; change 239; decline 79, 99; density 53; depression 93, 102; fall in 94; farmstead 171, 172, 176, 179; German 11; growth 9, 13–15, 17, 54–59 *passim*, 64, 87, 94, 95, 125, 126, 188–94, 199, 239; increase 87, 147; Italian 11; landless 201; local 29, 198; movement 106; of Rouen 219, 224; of working age 160; pattern 126; pressure 87, 91, 93, 99, 101, 107, 146–48, 233; protoindustrial 128, 139; rural 29, 55, 71, 101, 158, 160; size 124
potatoes 55–57, 91, 125
power 1, 13, 21, 124, 151, 167, 180–82; aristocratic 107; balance 37, in marriage 43; earning 44; economic 4; labour 9; of big estates 107; peasant 107; political 4, 19, 236; relationships 12, 14, 20, 240, 245
prices 13, 14, 18, 115, 116, 125–28 *passim*, 141, 147–52, 161, 213, 245
primogeniture 89, 92, 99, 146
productivity 56, 117–24 *passim*, 126, 129, 131, 134–36, 140, 142, 173, 175, 242, 244–47 *passim*
proletarian 105–07, 137, 202
proletarianization 20, 77, 105–07
proletariat 20, 106, 121
proportion married 13, 71, 81–83
proportion never married 51–55 *passim*, 60
Protestantism 60
protoindustrial 3, 12, 13, 17–20, 116, 119, 188–203, 241, 243, 246; activities 117, 118, 126, 127, 129, 133, 136–38, 140–42, 241; areas 40, 115, 136; business cycles 127; communities 124; economy 242;

employment 123, 124, 131, 137, 246; expansion 139; family 29, 41; family economy 43, 44; family labour 138; growth 114; household 16, 17, 114, 115, 119, 123, 138, 141; household economy 114–42; income 125, 126, 128, 137, 141, 142, 242; labour 116–21, 123, 125, 128, 140–42, 242; labour force 244; lower classes 123, 131, 137, 142; populations 128, 139; prices 127; process 17, 18; producers 115; production 117, 118, 120, 124, 132, 142, 154; productivity 131; regions 45, 50, 122, 194, 202, 247; sector 72, 118, 119, 121, 123–25, 127, 130, 132, 134, 138–41; stage of industry 15; systems 128; tasks 117; textile manufacturing 129; theory 114, 138, 140; trades 130, 132; village 73–77, 130; weavers 45; work 115, 116, 125, 134, 135; work-unit 43; workers 120; workforce 131; zones 40
protoindustrialization 3, 4, 9, 13–19 *passim*, 29, 43, 44, 57, 114, 115, 132, 137, 139, 141, 152, 165, 188, 202, 227, 233, 234, 239, 240, 243; demographic corollaries of 115, 124–28, 138; effect on peasant family 1; in agriculture 121; regional 247
protoindustry 15, 17, 18, 20, 43, 70, 92, 117, 121, 123, 126, 131, 135, 137, 138, 142, 237–47 *passim*; effects on the household 16, 20; rural 125; Russian 135
Prussia 210
putting-out system 16, 19, 40, 44, 121, 147, 208, 242; *see also Kaufsystem*
Pyrenean 87–93, 101, 104–06, 109, 110
Pyrenees 91, 93, 97, 105–07

Ransel, David 13, 21
remarriage 37, 108
rent 44, 72, 78, 79, 116–18, 121–26, 134, 136, 138, 140, 141, 147, 150, 151, 154, 167, 168, 173–75, 184, 191–93, 200, 203
Rhine 30
Rhineland 151
Rhône 67, 72
rice 238, 244
Riehl, Wilhelm 7, 88
Riga 167, 168, 173–75
Roanne 67, 73, 77, 82
Roman 88, 89, 92, 146
Rostow, W.W. 234
Rouen 101, 160, 206–30
Rudolph, Richard L. 1–5, 6–25, 135, 165, 240
Russia 10, 13, 21, 170, 180, 183, 184
Russian orthodox 13

Saint-Etienne 66, 67, 82
Saint-Hilaire 72–80
Saint-Simonian 229
salt 26, 43, 156
Salzburg 50, 54, 56, 60, 61

Saxony 87, 150
Schlumbohm, Jürgen 4, 10, 119, 120, 127, 135, 188–205, 237
Scott, James C. 182
Scott, Joan W. 17, 165, 206, 220
seasonal 9, 37, 125, 133–35, 194, 199, 202, 242; demand 247; employment 135, 246; labour 9–11, 238, 240, 242; migration 246; rural industry 235; unemployment 17; work 54, 105, 242, 247
seasons 16, 54, 115, 116, 133–37, 142, 194, 196, 199
Sella, Domenico 3, 154–64, 245, 246
Senior, William Nassau 64
serfdom 138, 139, 165–68, 172, 180–82, 184, 235
serfs 3, 4, 19, 165–84, 240
servants 20, 21, 38, 40, 49, 50, 53–55, 59, 60, 68, 75–78, 87, 90, 108, 109, 122, 124, 131–35 passim, 142, 195, 199–200, 223
sex 38, 114, 115, 128–33, 138, 159, 172–78 passim, 183, 195, 199, 201, 206, 216, 217, 245
Shanin, Theodor 10, 165
siblings 20, 21, 38, 44, 57, 58, 71, 75, 198, 201, 202
Sieder, Richard 20
silk 67, 72, 79, 120, 121, 126, 130, 132, 135, 157, 160, 162, 163, 210
Simon, Jules 65, 220–23, 225–28, 232
sisters 57, 58, 89, 90
slavery 235–39
slaves 3, 4, 19, 193, 237–39, 242, 244, 245
Slovenia 36
Snell, K.D.M. 16, 18
Sokoloff, Kenneth 233, 244
Sombart, Werner 6
South America 94, 107
Spain 105, 106
Spanish 86, 100, 155
spinners 125, 126, 130, 132
spinning 30, 43, 67, 117–19, 121, 123, 125, 128–31, 136, 194, 207–09, 213, 215, 224
steel 67
stem family 3, 21, 65, 68–69, 75, 86–110, 238
Stewart, Mary Lynn 207
Styria 26, 50, 53–55
Sugar 238, 244
Swabia 3, 146–52
Swiss 13, 125–27
Switzerland 30, 36, 53, 54, 97, 120–22, 125–27, 130, 157

Tatar 13
taxes 72, 81, 82, 91–93, 96, 128, 150, 151, 154, 160, 161, 163, 168, 191, 192
technology 10, 128, 240, 247
Temin, Peter 166, 167
tenant farmers 155, 158–61

textiles 12, 13, 15, 18, 30, 40, 43, 44, 56, 70, 73, 82, 92, 103, 114, 120, 125, 128–31, 150, 162, 193, 194, 207–10, 213, 219, 239, 242, 245
Thirsk, Joan 14, 15, 122, 155
Tilly, Charles 106
Tilly, Louise 17, 165
timber 31, 32
tools 15, 40, 116–18, 123, 154, 156, 158, 163
transmission 3, 44, 45, 86–91 passim, 94, 96, 99, 105, 107
Tugan–Baranovskii, M.I. 19
Tyrol 30, 36, 41, 45, 50–61 passim, 89

Ulster 121
United States 237, 239, 244–47
urbanization 2, 64, 80, 87, 211, 235

Verrières 72–74, 77–80
Verviers 125, 130
Viazzo, Per Paolo 28, 38, 45, 100
Vienna 26, 28
Viniculture 26, 29, 30, 37, 38, 43–45
Virgin Mary, cult of 61–62

Wall, Richard 11, 12, 87, 109, 124, 131, 132, 138
weavers 40, 41, 45, 120, 123, 126, 128, 130, 132, 150, 151, 156, 163, 208, 224
weaving 30, 43, 67, 72, 76, 79, 117, 119–21, 125–27, 130, 132, 135, 136, 147, 150–51, 193, 207–08, 224
Weber, Max 6
West Riding 121, 132
Wetherell, Charles 3, 4, 165–87
widowers 82, 198
widowhood 37
widows 43, 82, 131, 168, 177, 180, 198
Williamson, Jeffrey 15
wine 33, 34, 43, 45, 119, 121
Wolf, Eric 11, 53
women 4, 13, 17, 20, 21, 43, 71, 78, 98, 101–05 passim, 125, 129–32, 135, 141, 160, 172, 173, 175, 184, 194–96, 198, 200, 206–30, 240, 243; able-bodied 172; adult 169, 224, 226, 229, 245; age at marriage 52, 99, 101, 103, 196, first 194; as heads of household 20; attending school 83; attitudes towards reproduction 103; domestic responsibilities of 223, 224, 226; earnings of 131; employment of 209, 212, 221, 223; labour of 17, 58, 207, 221, 229; life cycles of 132; lower-class 130; married 83, 219–226 passim; noble 206; of working age 160; peasant 223; pregnant 219; respect towards 106; rights of 107, 229; status of 20, 131; sub-fertility of 101; unmarried 68, 71, 220; wages of 160; work of 17, 43, 160, 206, 207, 218–24, 226, 227; workers 206–30;

working-class 227, 229; working day of
    219, 223, 224, 229; working hours of 223,
    226, 227; young 213, 226, 229
wood 30, 41, 55, 92, 191
woodcutters 40, 41, 55
woodcutting 30, 38, 41
woodland 26, 121, 191
wool 120, 121, 125, 126, 130, 163

woollen 121, 157, 162, 163, 210
Worobec, Christine 10, 20
Wrigley, E.A. 13, 194, 197

Yorkshire 121, 132
Young, Arthur 121

Zurich 10, 120–37 *passim*, 240